THE IRON SEA

THE
IRON SEA

HOW THE ALLIES
HUNTED AND DESTROYED
HITLER'S WARSHIPS

SIMON READ

hachette
BOOKS
New York

Hachette Books
Hachette Book Group
1290 Avenue of the Americas
New York, NY 10104
HachetteBooks.com
Twitter.com/HachetteBooks
Instagram.com/HachetteBooks

First Edition: November 2020

Published by Hachette Books, an imprint of Perseus Books, LLC, a subsidiary of Hachette Book Group, Inc. The Hachette Books name and logo is a trademark of the Hachette Book Group.

The Hachette Speakers Bureau provides a wide range of authors for speaking events. To find out more, go to www.hachettespeakersbureau.com or call (866) 376-6591.

The publisher is not responsible for websites (or their content) that are not owned by the publisher.

Print book interior design by Trish Wilkinson.

Library of Congress Cataloging-in-Publication Data

Names: Read, Simon, 1974– author.
Title: The iron sea : how the Allies hunted and destroyed Hitler's warships / Simon
    Read. Other titles: How the Allies hunted and destroyed Hitler's warships
Description: First edition. | New York : Hachette Books, [2020] | Includes
    bibliographical references and index.
Identifiers: LCCN 2020019934 | ISBN 9780306921711 (hardcover) | ISBN
    9780306921704 (ebook)
Subjects: LCSH: World War, 1939–1945—Campaigns—Atlantic Ocean. | World
    War, 1939–1945—Naval operations. | World War, 1939-1945—Aerial operations.
Classification: LCC D770 .R43 2020 | DDC 940.54/293—dc23

LC record available at https://lccn.loc.gov/2020019934

ISBNs: 978-0-306-92171-1 (hardcover); 978-0-306-92170-4 (ebook)

Printed in the United States of America

LSC-C

10 9 8 7 6 5 4 3 2 1

This one's for Sarah and Benny.
With love.

AUTHOR'S NOTE

Two of the German warships in this book, the *Scharnhorst* and *Gneisenau*, are—depending on the source—alternatively referred to as battle-cruisers or battleships, the primary difference being that cruisers sacrificed armor for speed and maneuverability. To keep things simple, I refer to both vessels as battleships.

CONTENTS

Prologue: The Killing Seas   1

1   In Search of Prey   11

2   Cataclysm   24

3   The Hunted   51

4   Avenged   70

5   Cerberus   85

6   Chariot   112

7   Dogs of War   131

8   Lethal Passage   150

9   Arctic Fire   164

10   Target: *Tirpitz*   172

11   X-Craft   192

12   "Hell on Earth"   208

13   Return to *Tirpitz*   227

Epilogue: The Sea Is a Mass Grave   245

Acknowledgments   251

Notes   253

Bibliography   301

Index   311

No Captain can do very wrong if he places his Ship alongside that of the Enemy.

—Memo from Vice Admiral Horatio Nelson to his captains, written on board HMS *Victory* on October 9, 1805, twelve days before the Battle of Trafalgar

PROLOGUE

***

THE KILLING SEAS

The bombers flew through pitch-black skies.

The British crews stared into darkness as a blacked-out Germany passed beneath them. All appeared quiet in the predawn hours of April 6, 1940. For the crews in the twin-engined Wellingtons and Hampdens, the night's operation was an exercise in futility: dropping propaganda leaflets urging the German people to surrender. String secured the leaflets, printed by the Ministry of Information, in heavy bundles of 1,500. A crewmember would cut the binding over the target area and shove the bundles down the aircraft's flarechute. Caught in the bomber's slipstream, the leaflets would scatter into the night and litter the towns below.[1]

The gunners in their turrets maintained their lonely vigil, while the navigators studied their charts and relayed coordinates to the pilots. All appeared routine until a curious site presented itself against the obsidian void below. The yellow glare of numerous headlights, making up what appeared to be a large motor convoy, could be seen moving rapidly between the port cities of Hamburg and Lübeck. Over Kiel, the crews saw "great activity among shipping under the glare of brilliant arc lamps."[2]

The crews returned to their bases as dawn began to break and made their reports. "The Germans," the Air Ministry subsequently noted, "made no pretense of concealment. When all is on the hazard they rarely do, believing that speed is more important than secrecy." A

Royal Air Force (RAF) reconnaissance flight dispatched later that afternoon to investigate photographed the German battleships *Scharnhorst* and *Gneisenau* anchored off Wilhelmshaven.[3]

Two of the Royal Navy's most wanted, each ship—steeled in Krupp armor—displaced 32,000 tons and bristled with nine 11-inch guns set in triple turrets, two forward and one aft. Secondary armaments included fourteen 4.1-inch and sixteen 1.5-inch antiaircraft guns, and twelve 5.9-inch guns. With a top speed each of 31 knots, they were faster than any British ship. First Lord of the Admiralty Winston Churchill, well aware of this fact, deemed them "targets of supreme consequence."[4]

The previous November, the two ships had slaughtered the British patrol vessel *Rawalpindi*, sending the 16,000-ton ship and 238 members of her crew—including the captain—to the icy depths between Norway and Iceland. They retreated in the aftermath to the German port of Kiel and spent the winter frozen to their moorings.

That winter proved a savage one. A contagion of ice and snow swept across Europe, as temperatures plunged to their lowest in nearly a century. Six inches of snow fell on Rome, the city's heaviest snowfall in recorded history. The mercury in Spain and France dropped below freezing. An eight-mile stretch of the river Thames in London froze over. Ice choked the Danube, used by Germany to import shipments of Baltic oil, metal, and grains to feed its hungry war machine. "News of the appearance of ice in the stream," reported the *New York Times*, "was greeted with joy by Allied diplomats."[5]

Further north, where the Finns waged their fierce defense against the invading Red Army, there was little cause for jubilation. "The cold numbs the brain in this Arctic hell," noted one war correspondent. "Snow sweeps over the darkened wastes, the winds howl and the temperature is 30 degrees below zero. Here the Russians and Finns are battling in blinding snowstorms for possessions of ice-covered forests." At the scene of one battle, the corpses, it was reported, were "all frozen in fighting attitudes. . . . Their bodies were like statues of men throwing all their muscles and strength into some work, but their faces recorded something between bewilderment and horror."[6]

For the men on board *Scharnhorst* and *Gneisenau*, the blistering season was "a time of boredom"—a mundane, frigid existence of waiting. When conditions allowed, they ventured into the North Sea for training exercises—but nothing more. Granted leave, the men could "walk ashore over the frozen surface of the anchorage."[7] It offered no reprieve from the overwhelming sense that the war, somewhere beyond the ice, was passing them by.

Then slowly, the days lengthened; the temperature gradually warmed and, at long last, released the ships from their frozen captivity. Now anchored in Wilhelmshaven, they lay in wait for orders to commence their next lethal run. They didn't have to wait long. On April 7, the day after being photographed by RAF reconnaissance, the two battleships put to sea as part of the German invasion of Norway.[8]

＊ ＊ ＊

Iron-ore mined in Sweden passed through Norway on its way to Germany. Merchant ships from the Reich carried the precious metal from the Norwegian port of Narvik. Churchill, having long wanted to choke Germany's supply chain, urged the War Cabinet to allow the Royal Navy to mine Norwegian waters. The War Cabinet gave its approval on April 3. Royal Navy ships mined the approaches to Narvik five days later. Landings by British and French troops were to follow at Narvik, Trondheim, Bergen, and Stavanger—but the Germans moved first.[9]

Now, on that bright April morning, as *Scharnhorst* and *Gneisenau* powered their way north from Wilhelmshaven, crews with No. 107 Squadron at RAF Wattisham in southeast England "stood by for striking duties." At 10:45 a.m., the squadron received coordinates of the ships' latest sighting and orders to immediately attack. At 11:30 a.m., twelve Blenheim bombers led by Wing Commander Basil Embry took off in two formations of six to intercept the German warships.[10]

The bombers flew in a cloudless sky with visibility stretching out thirty miles. The North Sea passed beneath them gray and endless in all directions. As the two formations closed in on their targets, the weather began to deteriorate. The sky darkened and gathering clouds cut visibility down to five miles.[11] Embry and his men nevertheless had no problem spotting their quarry off the coast of Denmark.[12]

From their cockpits and gun turrets they could clearly see "seventeen ships of the German navy, including *Gneisenau* and *Scharnhorst*," their white, foaming wakes scarring the surface of the sea. It was, noted Embry, "a very grand sight."[13] The bombers wheeled in the sky and positioned the pale sun behind them, attacking out of its cold glare in groups of three from 6,000 feet.[14]

The first wave, achieving surprise, thundered over the ships and dropped twelve 250-pound armor-piercing bombs, hitting nothing but water. As the second and third waves swooped in, the enemy fleet came to life in a violent spectacle of muzzle flashes and smoke. Flak and pom-pom fire forced the bombers to break formation.[15] "When they shot at me," wrote one pilot, "it was like lightning flashing in daylight all around me."[16] The aircraft dropped their payloads, which fell harmlessly into the churning sea. The bombers turned for home and left the *Scharnhorst*, *Gneisenau*, and the rest of the fleet to carry on its way.[17]

✳ ✳ ✳

Attacks from the sea and air in the days and weeks that followed failed to sink or inflict damage on the two battleships, which came at great cost to the Royal Navy. At 4:45 p.m. on June 8, a lookout on *Scharnhorst* spotted what appeared to be a tendril of smoke twenty-eight miles off the starboard bow.[18]

The crews on both German ships, now sailing without escorts, ran to battle stations. At 5:10 p.m., *Scharnhorst*'s chief gunnery officer phoned the bridge from the foretop to report sighting a "thick funnel, and mast with turret. Probably also [a] flight deck." For the German fleet commander, Vice Admiral Wilhelm Marschall, an aircraft carrier was a target worthy of his ships' stature—unlike the outgunned *Rawalpindi*. The target took on a greater luster when the gunnery officer eyed the masts of two escorting destroyers.[19]

Across the gray stretch of sea, Captain Guy D'Oyly-Hughes on board the 22,500-ton carrier HMS *Glorious* received word of the approaching German hunters. Accompanied by the destroyers *Acasta* and *Ardent*, the *Glorious* had on deck and in her hangar more than fifty fighters and torpedo bombers. Launching them would require the ship to "turn into wind" and place her on a collision course with her pursuers. Seeing no other alternative but to attempt an escape, Captain D'Oyly-Hughes ordered *Glorious* to full speed. *Scharnhorst* and *Gneisenau* gave chase.[20]

Hunter and hunted soon closed within striking distance. At 5:32 p.m., from a range of 28,000 yards, *Scharnhorst* opened fire. It took fifty-two seconds for the shells to fly their violent arc toward the target and fall short.[21] Angle and trajectory corrected, the guns roared again and found their mark. The carrier's bridge disappeared in a ball of flame. One salvo punched a hole through the flight deck; another pierced the engine room. From the deck of *Scharnhorst*, "the glow of fire was to be seen in the *Glorious*."[22]

The carrier was a flaming pyre within minutes but somehow remained afloat. The distant roar of explosions as aircraft succumbed to the flames drifted across the water like muted thunder. The carrier began to list. Through his range finder on the bridge of *Scharnhorst*, Marschall watched burning Hurricanes and Gladiators slide off the carrier's punctured, sloping deck and fall into the sea. "Slowly," noted one German sailor, "*Glorious* began to turn on her side. Pouring out flames and smoke, she drifted with the wind. A moment later, she sank."[23]

While the *Ardent* fell victim to enemy fire early in the engagement, the *Acasta* proved a stubborn adversary. Her guns booming, she sought temporary cover in a smoke screen. On board, the captain passed a message to all battle stations: "You may think we are running away from the enemy. We are not. Our chummy ship [*Ardent*] has sunk, the *Glorious* is sinking. The least we can do is make a show. Good luck."[24]

Acasta emerged from the thick haze, turned to starboard, and fired two torpedoes from her port side. The crew roared its approval as the ominous wakes bubbled up and away from the ship. "I'll never forget that cheer that went up," remembered Leading Seaman Cyril Carter, who manned the aft torpedo tubes. "On the port bow of one of the ships [*Scharnhorst*] a yellow flash and a great column of smoke and water shot up from her."[25]

The torpedoes slammed into *Scharnhorst* "just below the after triple gun turret." A column of flame leapt from beneath the three massive guns and knocked them out of action. The torpedo ripped "a great hole" in her side, flooding her lower compartments in a nightmare of water and oil from a ruptured fuel tank. Forty-eight men died in the carnage.[26]

Scharnhorst hammered away with her secondary armaments even as she began to list. Hopelessly outgunned, *Acasta* once more disappeared behind her smoke screen. She altered course, broke cover, and emerged into a crucible of fire. "The enemy let us have it," Carter wrote. A shell ripped through the destroyer's engine room. The fiery blast threw Carter from his control seat and killed the crew working the aft torpedo tubes. Carter lost consciousness but soon came to and discovered the ship had stopped and was listing sharply to port. He got to his feet and staggered back to his battle station, fighting against the deck's precipitous incline.[27]

Through smoke and haze, he saw the blurred outlines of *Scharnhorst* and *Gneisenau*. "I fired the remaining torpedoes," he later wrote. "No one told me to. I guess I was raving mad." The battleships unleashed another volley of steel and fire. An explosion rocked the destroyer with such force Carter believed the ship momentarily left the water. It was then the captain gave the order to abandon ship.[28]

The men on *Scharnhorst* could not help but admire the tenacity of *Acasta*'s crew. "The [*Acasta*] did not give up. Our guns silenced her forward guns, but the aft guns continued firing," remembered one German sailor. "More salvoes from our guns, and the enemy was at length silenced. The destroyer was in flames and slowly began to sink. Steam arose, probably through the boilers bursting. Then the waves closed over these brave opponents, too."[29]

Of *Acasta*'s 138-man crew, only Leading Seaman Carter survived; the rest went down with the ship or died in the water and lifeboats of exposure. "I will always remember the surgeon lieutenant," Carter later wrote, "his first ship, his first action. Before I jumped over the side, I saw him still attending to the wounded, a hopeless task, and when I was in the water, I saw the captain leaning over the bridge, take a cigarette from a case and light it. We shouted to him to come on our raft, he waved 'Good-bye and good luck'—the end of a gallant man."[30]

A frigid wind soon carried away the smoke and noise of battle, leaving behind the ceaseless waves and the floating detritus of shattered men and ships. The blood toll proved high, with 1,474 officers and men of the Royal Navy and 41 men of the Royal Air Force lost to enemy fire and the sea. The Germans pulled six survivors from *Glorious* out of the water.[31] Three days later, a Norwegian steamer found another 39 men—nearly frozen to death—clinging to rafts and floats.[32]

Scharnhorst, her starboard propeller ripped from her hull and with 2,500 tons of water in her bowels, made her way to Trondheim for temporary repairs before braving the open sea back to Germany.[33] To focus British attention elsewhere, *Gneisenau* ran a diversionary sortie toward Iceland. The Royal Navy, fearing the battleship was attempting to break into the North Atlantic, took the bait. On the night of June 20, the submarine HMS *Clyde* located the German vessel.[34]

Scanning the moonlit waters from the bridge of *Gneisenau*, Captain Harald Netzbrand saw "a torpedo track on starboard beam approaching from astern at about 300m." Two additional tracks sliced the water just ahead of the ship. "Hard to port!" Netzbrand yelled, but it was too late. The torpedo ripped a hole in *Gneisenau*'s starboard side "slightly abaft bow anchor."[35] Water stormed her lower decks; black oil bled from her wound into the sea. The ship was hurt—but not mortally—and managed to limp back to the safety of Trondheim. From there, she soon joined *Scharnhorst* for repair work in Kiel.

＊ ＊ ＊

Damage suffered in the Norway campaign kept the two ships out of action for six months. Grand Admiral Erich Raeder, a hard man to please, dismissed the sinking of *Glorious* as "target practice, so hardly to be termed a momentous victory." It was, he argued, hardly worth the wounds inflicted on his ships. He relieved Marschall as fleet commander and replaced him with Vice Admiral Günther Lütjens.[36]

A man of fierce reputation and supremely confident in his abilities, Lütjens saw no reason to explain his decisions. He expected nothing but total loyalty from those beneath him and offered the same to those he served. He followed orders whether he agreed with them or not—a trait that would prove his undoing. In late January 1941, he returned the *Scharnhorst* and *Gneisenau* to sea.

Lütjens's orders were clear. He was not to engage enemy battleships. His sole purpose was to sink convoys and drain Britain's lifeblood. The two ships broke into the North Atlantic on what would prove to be their bloodiest run. In the two months that followed, they sank or captured more than 115,000 tons of Allied shipping. On March 15 and 16 alone, they sank thirteen ships and captured another three.[37]

"This mortal danger to our lifelines," noted Churchill, "gnawed at my bowels."[38] Each successful conquest put Lütjens and his men under more pressure, as the Royal Navy scoured the waves for its tormentors.

The ships retreated to the French port of Brest on March 22. Raeder, "radiant with joy," congratulated Lütjens on a job well done. In their wakes, the *Scharnhorst* and *Gneisenau* had left a cold, wind-swept sea of unmarked graves. Even docked in Brest, the ships posed a major threat to Britain's lifeline to the United States and the Allied war effort. The Royal Navy may have been the most powerful maritime force on earth, but Britain's struggle for survival in the North Atlantic had stretched its resources thin.

The threat against merchant shipping, Churchill noted, "compelled the employment on convoy duty of nearly every available British capital ship. At one period the Commander-in-Chief of the Home Fleet had only one battleship in hand."[39] While the situation benefited Germany, her surface fleet was nevertheless miniscule by comparison. She had the 14,000-ton heavy cruiser *Admiral Hipper*, and her sister ships the *Prinz Eugen* and *Blücher*. Her two pocket-battleships—the 12,000-ton *Lützow* (formerly the *Deutschland*) and the *Admiral Scheer*—were merely heavy cruisers equipped with large-caliber guns.[40] A third ship in this class, the *Graf Spee*, was lost to the British in December 1939.

The *Scharnhorst* and *Gneisenau*, ordered by Hitler in June 1934, were the only two modern capital ships in the Nazi arsenal at the outbreak of war. Each represented a "brazen and fraudulent violation" of the Treaty of Versailles, which limited German warships to a maximum displacement of 10,000 tons. In 1935, London and Berlin signed off on the Anglo-German Naval Agreement, which allowed Germany to build warships displacing up to 35,000 tons.[41] The nearly completed sister ships *Bismarck* and *Tirpitz* would violate the agreement in spectacular fashion with a displacement of 42,500 tons. Once at sea, wrote Churchill, they would "be the strongest vessels afloat in the world."[42]

Together, these four ships—*Scharnhorst*, *Gneisenau*, *Bismarck*, and *Tirpitz*—posed a mortal threat to Britain's survival, killers ready to sever the nation's vital arteries to its empire and the United States. Convoys were Britain's lifeblood, helping sustain its heavily rationed population and its war machine with food, equipment, and raw materials. Likewise, convoys sailing from Britain supplied Allied armies fighting overseas and, eventually, the Russian war effort—but the Atlantic would prove to be the crucible of the Royal Navy's epic struggle to secure the waves.

The German ships and the imposing threat of their running rampant across Britain's sea-lanes plagued Churchill from afar. "The Battle of the Atlantic was the dominating factor all through the war," he later wrote. "Never for one moment could we forget that everything happening elsewhere, on land, at sea or in the air depended ultimately on its outcome, and amid all other cares we viewed its changing fortunes day by day with hope or apprehension."[43]

That Britain is an island proved a blessing and a curse. It saved the nation from Hitler's blitzkrieg in the desperate summer of 1940 but left it vulnerable in other ways. A minimum of 23 million tons of supplies a year had to be shipped across the Atlantic to keep Britain fighting.[44]

With Western Europe under the Nazi heel, German aircraft operating from France and the Low Countries could easily bomb and strafe convoys in the Channel destined for Britain's southern and eastern seaports. Hitler's surface ships, U-boats, and the long-range Focke-Wulf Fw 200 savaged her western approaches.[45] Every precious ton delivered to a British port was a hard-won victory. The convoys crossed the ocean at a sluggish pace, forced to go no faster than their slowest ship. The savagery of the sea, the freezing conditions, and the psychological strain of attacks from above and below the waves put the merchant sailors, in the words of one, through "sheer unmitigated hell."[46]

Britain's survival and ultimate victory meant supremacy in the Atlantic. It was not merely to ensure the vital delivery of food and materials of war—but the safe transport of Allied armies across the waves. "When we think of the great struggles of those years," notes one historian, "our minds generally turn to the Blitz, El Alamein, Anzio, Arnhem, Moscow, Leningrad, Stalingrad, Berlin . . . those battles could not have been fought, let alone won, without the Allied victory in the Atlantic."[47]

Victory in the Atlantic was not merely dependent on destroying the U-boat menace or the threat from long-range German air patrols, it also meant smashing Hitler's surface fleet and consigning its capital ships to the ocean floor. Britain's lifelines remained in stark peril as long as *Scharnhorst*, *Gneisenau*, *Bismarck*, and *Tirpitz* remained afloat.

Their destruction would become Churchill's obsession.

CHAPTER 1

* * *

IN SEARCH OF PREY

Beneath an early morning sky the color of dark slate, Pilot Officer Gordon Green trudged across the sodden grass of the airfield to his waiting Spitfire. Clad in a wool-lined leather jacket and boots, a parachute pack strapped to his chest, he pulled himself up onto the fighter's wing and opened the cockpit canopy. The date was March 28, 1941, the airbase RAF St. Eval in Cornwall.[1]

Green, a pilot with the Royal Air Force's Photographic Reconnaissance Unit, lowered himself into the cockpit and buckled the harness over his legs and shoulders. He pulled on his helmet and plugged its radio cable and oxygen tube into their respective sockets. Reaching forward, he turned the master switch to ON. "Contact!" he yelled in warning to the ground crew. He pressed the starter button and pushed in the priming pump handle. The Merlin engine roared and brought the instrument panel to life, its many needles dancing in their gauges. He checked fuel and oxygen, magneto drop, revs, boost, break pressure, oil, and air readings. Satisfied all was well, Green flashed a thumbs-up to his crew and signaled "Chocks Away."

The morning's target was the French port of Brest. Reconnaissance flights out of St. Eval covered Western France and "the full length of the Franco-Spanish frontier."[2] It was a hazardous and solitary undertaking—"the ideal job," in the words of one reconnaissance pilot, "for a loner."[3]

Green knew full well the dangers that lay in wait over Brest. The port's antiaircraft fire could be devastatingly accurate, having—on one occasion—knocked a reconnaissance flight from the sky at 30,000 feet.[4] A continuous patrol of Bf 109s in the vicinity of Ushant, an island off the Brittany coast at the southwestern end of the English Channel, intensified the peril. Green personally knew five pilots lost over the target, but had little time to dwell on such matters as he guided the Spitfire across the grass.[5]

He glanced at the windsock above the control tower and turned the fighter's nose into the damp wind. With final clearance for takeoff, he released the break lever, opened the throttle, and gently pushed the control column forward. The machine gathered momentum, the power of its engine creeping up Green's arms, the pressure against his body intensifying as the plane left the ground. Through the canopy, as the Spitfire climbed higher, Green watched the lanes and rooftops of Cornwall recede and merge into a larger patchwork of fields and villages.

He shot over England's southwest coast in turbulent skies and crossed the Channel in ever-thickening cloud. In the wings of his fighter were two cameras, each one equipped with a 20-inch-focal-length lens. Visibility dwindled to nearly nothing as he approached the French coast, yet he still checked the small mirrors on either side of the canopy to ensure he left no vapor trail in his wake.[6] Beneath him, the English Channel churned cold and unforgiving.

Reconnaissance pilots had to wait three hours past daybreak for "first photographic light," when the sun burned away shadow and haze, for optimal conditions. Such outings necessitated maximum vigilance and a high threshold for discomfort. The freezing temperatures at high altitude could drop as low as -50 C and bleed through the pilot's thick leather jacket, gloves, and boots. The cold was but one concern. "Perhaps the most important survival requirement on photo reconnaissance operations throughout the war," recalled one pilot, "was the ability to keep a really effective lookout for all enemy aircraft."[7]

Photographing a target was an art unto itself and required the pilot to know—almost by instinct—where the cameras were aimed. "One flew alone to the general area of the target," Green remembered, "and then tipped the aircraft on its side to check one was properly lined up."[8] Such maneuvering could prove a challenge even in mild weather, let alone gray and turbulent skies. Green, staring out of the cockpit at the rolling bank of cumulus beneath him, saw through the overcast a sudden flash of color. The clouds had parted, if only briefly.

He banked the Spitfire through the break and swooped over his objective at 30,000 feet. He braved a second pass, the antiaircraft batteries below stabbing the air with white spearheads of flame.[9] Green pressed a button on the yoke. The shutters of both cameras opened and closed in rapid-fire succession. Not until analysts developed and examined the film could one judge the accuracy of the images.[10] Satisfied, Green aimed his fighter out to sea with the port's guns thumping the sky in his wake.

Ground crew, upon Green's landing back in England, dismounted the cameras and retrieved the film. It was sent to RAF Medmenham more than 250 miles away in Buckinghamshire for immediate development and analysis. The pictures revealed, in grainy black and white, the *Scharnhorst* and *Gneisenau* sitting in dry dock.

The British could not ignore such a glaring threat. The ships could launch easily from Brest into the Atlantic and wreak bloody havoc, sending Allied merchant ships and supplies into the frigid depths. Indeed, the Germans believed possession of the French port gave them "a unique strategic advantage."[11] Ready to join the *Scharnhorst* and *Gneisenau* was the heavy cruiser *Prinz Eugen* with her primary armaments of 8-inch guns mounted in four twin turrets. While the *Tirpitz* was not yet ready for action, the *Bismarck* would soon be done with her sea trials in the Baltic. These surface ships, coupled with the U-boat menace, would—in the words of Grand Admiral Raeder—"strike the British supply system a mortal blow."[12]

"Besides the constant struggle with the U-boats," Churchill wrote of this time, "surface raiders had already cost us over three-quarters of a million tons of shipping."[13] The presence of *Scharnhorst* and *Gneisenau* in Brest caused the prime minister great consternation, as no one knew when they might once more go on the hunt. Tracking the ships down would necessitate diverting convoys "from their danger zones" and placing a greater burden on British naval resources. The navy, also charged with operations in the Mediterranean, already felt the heavy strain of trying "to fulfill too many responsibilities with too few ships" without having to embark on a search-and-destroy mission across the vastness of the Atlantic Ocean.[14]

"All the advantages," noted one Royal Navy officer, "lay with the enemy, both through their reluctance to fight and through their superior speed which enabled them to escape when challenged."[15]

The ships could not be allowed to leave Brest.

✳ ✳ ✳

An assessment by the Air Ministry in 1941 detailed the risks of bombing operations over Brest:

> The difficulties of an attack on Brest are not always realized. The Germans have done their utmost since it fell into their hands to make it immune from air attack. In this they have not succeeded, but an assault upon it by bomber aircraft is a hazardous operation. Brest is protected by a very heavy concentration of AA guns, by a balloon barrage and by a formidable array of searchlights. There are also patrols of fighters on the watch to intercept our bombers. . . . It is not uncommon for a pilot to report that his aircraft has been held in a cone of searchlights for more than five minutes while he was over the target.[16]

In the fading twilight of March 30, two days after Gordon Green's flight, a convoy of army trucks delivered small teams of German soldiers to the outskirts of Brest. Numbering no more than three men, each team had in its possession a large, metallic canister. The drop-off locations formed a wide semicircle around the town from Saint-Anne in the west to Saint-Marc in the east.[17]

The soldiers, wearing gas masks, moved quickly. Each team positioned its canister upright and opened it by twisting a valve. A steaming liquid oozed from the top and forced the soldiers back. It dripped down the sides and puddled on the ground, scorching the earth in a twenty-yard radius of each canister. Chemistry quickly worked its strange magic on the liquid content. Thick smoke began seeping from the top of the canisters like steam from a witch's cauldron. In the harbor, from Basins No. 1 and No. 2, thirty fishing boats with fuming canisters on their decks fanned out across the water. The heavy, swirling miasma soon enveloped Brest, leaving a thick, yellow stain on the streets.[18]

"In 20 minutes the smoke screen is completely effective," notes a subsequent report by British intelligence. "The gas produced appears to be slightly heavier than air, for visibility at ground level is reduced to a few yards, whereas the tops of buildings can sometimes be distinguished. Only an extremely strong wind could render the screen ineffective."[19]

That night, 109 bombers left England for the French port. They took off from airfields in East Anglia, Lincolnshire, and Kent. Above dark, silent villages and thatched roofs, the night sky rumbled with mechanized thunder. As the bombers crossed the Channel beneath a sliver of moon, air gunners—sitting in cramped and freezing turrets—test-fired their .303 Browning machine guns. Red-and-green tracer shells fell like fiery rain into the surf below.

The French coast soon loomed ahead: a black outline beneath columns of white and blue light. The bombers passed through the groping luminescence. Black starbursts of flak seemed to hang motionless in the air. In the skies above the port, searchlights burned the night away. Bombardiers peered through their sites into the heavy man-made fog below and dropped their payloads. One-by-one, the aircraft—released of their burden—turned for home. All crews touched down safely without having inflicted the slightest damage on their cloud-shrouded targets.[20]

They returned five nights later, on April 4. In Brest's Continental Hotel, tuxedo-clad waiters had just commenced serving the evening's meal under elegant candelabra. Officers from the *Scharnhorst* and *Gneisenau*, clad in their naval finery, conversed over the rims of cocktail glasses between mouthfuls of food.[21]

The civility of dinner and drinks continued, even as the drone of approaching bombers grew louder and the port's guns began thundering into the night. In the darkness above, as aircraft weaved amongst the searchlights, their undercarriages opened to reveal rows of 500-pound armor-piercing bombs, which now began to fall. One nearly scored a direct hit when it fell between *Gneisenau* and the side of her dry dock. Sparks flew as it scraped steel and concrete on the way down and landed in twelve feet of water without detonating.[22]

If the ships escaped severe damage, the same could not be said for the Continental Hotel. At least one bomb hit the building. Shattered glass and masonry blew across the dining room and killed several officers enjoying their last meal.[23]

Even before the noise of the retreating bombers had completely faded away, the *Gneisenau*'s captain, Otto Fein, was debating how to handle the unexploded bomb lying alongside his ship. The initial plan called for a crane to lift the bomb out of the dry dock, but Fein worried it might result in detonation. The safest course of action, Fein decided, was to move his ship. A bomb disposal unit could then defuse the explosive. Filling the dry dock with enough water to allow *Gneisenau* to maneuver out of it took several hours, and it was not until noon on April 5 that she took up her new position alongside a mooring buoy in the inner harbor.[24]

That same day, a reconnaissance Spitfire on a fortuitous flight over Brest photographed the exposed warship. The pictures showed the *Gneisenau* berthed along a wall on the north shore of the harbor and protected by "a stone mole bending round it from the west."[25] Her sister ship, *Scharnhorst*, remained in dry dock.

*　＊　＊　＊*

Rain fell dark and cold in the early morning hours of Sunday, April 6, turning the airfield at RAF St. Eval to sludge. Six Bristol Beauforts—a twin-engine torpedo bomber—of No. 22 Squadron slowly sank into the muck.[26]

Orders had reached Wing Commander Francis Braithwaite the night before, urging an attack on the exposed *Gneisenau* at first light. Under normal circumstances, any operation would have been canceled due to the weather—but the risk of *Gneisenau* returning to dry dock meant normal considerations did not apply.

Braithwaite, resigned to the matter's urgency, devised a plan of attack. He would dispatch his six bombers in two separate waves. The first wave of three would bomb from 500 feet any torpedo nets protecting the ship; the second wave would then swoop in at sea level and torpedo the target. Survival depended on surprise. The crews tasked with dropping the torpedoes would take off first and assume a holding pattern outside the harbor until the bombing aircraft had wrought their assigned havoc.[27]

The three pilots selected for the torpedo run were Flying Officer J. Hyde—a recent recipient of the Distinguished Flying Cross, twenty-three-year-old Flying Officer Kenneth Campbell, and Pilot Officer A. W. Camp. This would be Campbell's twentieth operation.[28]

In the predawn gloom, two of the six bombers got stuck in the mud. The remaining four took off between four thirty and five fifteen with only one bomber in the first-attack wave—piloted by Flight Sergeant Henry Menary—making it into the sky. Hyde and Campbell reached their rendezvous point outside the harbor just prior to sunrise. Camp, thwarted by the filthy weather, flew miles off course. Menary, likewise, got lost. He dropped his bombs on an enemy convoy spotted near Île de Batz, an island off the Brittany coast, and turned for home. Hyde and Campbell, unaware of the situation, continued circling outside the harbor. Through mist and rain, the first olive moments of daylight began to pale the sky in the east. As Hyde continued his holding pattern, he saw Campbell's plane dive sharply toward the port.[29]

Campbell's Beaufort thundered into the harbor at sea level, rocketing below mast-height past the antiaircraft gunships. Flak exploded over the water, lacerating the dark-gray surface. Through the hot-metal mist, Campbell could see *Gneisenau* anchored alongside the harbor's north quay. Beyond the harbor, the ground—studded with guns—rose sharply toward the sky.[30]

The water passed beneath Campbell's bomber in a blur as the warship's cannons boomed their malevolent welcome. He maintained a steady heading despite the ferocity of fire and the shockwaves buffeting his aircraft. His plane, holding steady just above the water, skimmed the top of the mole (a stone breakwater), while on the deck of *Gneisenau*, men ran to and from battle stations. The ship loomed ever larger in the aircraft's Perspex windshield.

Campbell dropped the torpedo at 500 yards. It sliced the water and cut a frothy wake in a straight line toward the target. He pulled back on the control column and banked away from the ship. As his aircraft climbed above *Gneisenau*, the guns on the hills beyond the harbor blistered the sky above the port with fire. The plane faltered in its trajectory and, trailing smoke, smashed into the raised ground, killing its four-man crew.[31]

Almost simultaneously, the torpedo from Campbell's plane slammed into *Gneisenau*'s stern on the starboard side, sending flame and water deck-high. The blast ripped open her hull below the waterline and damaged the starboard propeller and shaft.[32]

Hyde, still in his holding pattern outside the target area, banked his aircraft and flew for England.[33] Sergeant Camp, having eventually found his way in bad weather, arrived over the target in the wake of Hyde's departure. Unaware of Campbell's attack minutes prior, he aimed his bomber at the harbor and charged headlong into a tempest of steel and fire. It was now full daylight. Camp brought his bomber down "to a few feet above the water" and aimed for the mole protecting *Gneisenau*. "I passed three flak ships and nearly reached the mole itself," Camp reported. "By then I was being fired at from batteries all round the harbor."[34]

The blasts rocked the plane; the stench of cordite filled the cockpit. "Continuous streams of fire seemed to be coming from every direction," Camp said. "It was by far the worst flak I have ever encountered." Staring straight ahead, he saw the *Gneisenau*, her guns throwing shells into the sea and sky, when out of nowhere a protective smoke screen consumed her from one end to the other. Having lost visual contact with the target, Camp pulled up, pointed his plane for safer skies, and "climbed into cloud."[35]

Gneisenau took on a pronounced list. Crews worked frantically to stem the violent rush of water flooding two turbine compartments and the well of her aft triple-gun turret. The following day, tugs pulled the crippled vessel back into dry dock. Engineers, after inspecting the ship, offered a bleak assessment. Campbell's torpedo had knocked the starboard propeller out of action. Repairs would take an estimated six months.[36] *Gneisenau's* ordeal, however, proved far from over.

The bombers returned on the night of April 10. Two bombs slammed into the ship's dockside. Flame, shrapnel, and broken masonry lacerated the upper deck. Three more bombs ripped through her superstructure, the explosions twisting metal and incinerating men. Before the final bomb fell, fifty of *Gneisenau's* crew were dead and another ninety injured. The majority of casualties proved to be young midshipmen posted to the ship to complete their training. The *Scharnhorst* survived the attack unscathed.[37]

For his valiant efforts and sacrifice, Campbell received a posthumous Victoria Cross. It was, noted Wing Commander Braithwaite, "the most courageous of all the attacks" on the German ships in Brest.[38]

✳ ✳ ✳

Despite the apparent results, the RAF's efforts against *Scharnhorst* and *Gneisenau* did little to impress the man whose opinion mattered most. On April 17, Churchill sent a strongly worded memorandum to his chief of the Air Staff, Sir Charles Portal. "It must be recognized that the inability of Bomber Command to hit the enemy cruisers in Brest constitutes a very definite failure of this arm," he wrote. "The German battle-cruisers are two of the most important vessels in the war, as we have nothing that can both catch and kill them."[39]

While Churchill remained unimpressed, the attacks alarmed German naval commanders. In Berlin on Saturday, April 26, Fleet Commander Günther Lütjens met with Grand Admiral Erich Raeder to receive his briefing for Operation Rheinübung, a sortie into the North Atlantic against Allied shipping by the new battleship *Bismarck* and her heavy cruiser consort, the *Prinz Eugen*. The initial plan called for *Gneisenau* to participate, but the damage she had suffered rendered that all but impossible.[40] Lütjens, wary of striking out with half his attack force damaged and pinned down in Brest, voiced his reservations. The point of Operation Rheinübung was to obliterate Britain's lifelines and knock her out of the war—something the *Bismarck* and *Prinz Eugen* alone could not accomplish. "There is a powerful case," Lütjens argued, "for waiting at least until *Scharnhorst* has been prepared—if not until the crew of the *Tirpitz* have finished their training."[41]

Raeder sympathized with his lieutenant's point of view, but stressed time was of the essence. "*Scharnhorst* and *Gneisenau* were under constant British air attacks in their exposed French berths," Raeder wrote after the war, "and there was no telling when they would be in fighting shape again. And if the undertaking was postponed until *Tirpitz* was ready for sea, it would mean at least a half-year's inactivity."[42]

Hitler, ready to send his armies east into Russia, needed Britain dead in the water. And there remained one other concern. "The probable entry of the United States into the war is drawing closer and closer," Raeder said, "and this will greatly worsen the situation at sea for us."[43] Lütjens's orders were clear. The primary target for Operation Rheinübung was merchant shipping. The *Bismarck* would engage warships escorting Allied convoys long enough for the *Prinz Eugen* to send the cargo ships to a watery grave. Lütjens was to preserve *Bismarck's* "combat capacity as much as possible" and not expose her to "excessive risk."[44]

Lütjens accepted his fate. He knew, in a one-on-one confrontation, *Bismarck* would overwhelm the Royal Navy's best—but the British would not rely on a solitary vessel to hunt and destroy the German leviathan. They would throw at her whatever they could. Lütjens rightly believed Operation Rheinübung to be a suicide mission. Before leaving the Admiralty, he stopped by a friend's office. "I'd like to make my farewells; I'll never come back," he said. "Given the superiority of the British, survival is improbable."[45]

The days passed in a frenzy of preparation. Men and supplies flooded the Polish port of Gotenhafen on the Baltic coast, where *Bismarck* lay at anchor. Cranes loaded food, fuel, and ammunition around the clock. Still some "2,000 tons short of her stowage capacity," *Bismarck*, by early May, was prepped for three months at sea.[46]

On May 5, Hitler arrived at the port to inspect *Bismarck* and *Tirpitz*. He looked, according to one witness, "somewhat pale" as he and his entourage reviewed *Bismarck's* crew on the upper deck. Accompanied by Lütjens and Raeder, he said little. He appeared most interested when lectured on the ship's considerable firepower but asked no questions.[47] Following his inspection, he retired to Lütjens's cabin, where the Fleet Commander assured Hitler of *Bismarck*'s superiority in all aspects of naval warfare. When Hitler remarked the British enjoyed a strong advantage in numbers, Lütjens—hiding his own concerns—said no enemy ship could survive *Bismarck*'s "hitting and staying power."[48]

Hitler, so effusive in other matters when it came to Germany's military might, remained subdued. Merchant-raiding seemed a waste of time for a ship of *Bismarck*'s caliber. Losing one of his capital warships on such a venture would do little for his—or his navy's—prestige. But what other options did he have? He could not hope to rival the Royal Navy's supremacy. Meaningful conquest for Hitler lay on the land, not the seas. He listened to Lütjens without making further comment.[49]

When Lütjens finished his short dissertation, the men made their way to the wardroom for lunch. Hitler dined on pea soup while the others ate sausages. Food seemed to reinvigorate the Führer, who, over his meal, said he believed the United States would stay out of the war. Raeder joked the Americans would bide their time and join the conflict only when it was over. Hitler found little humor in the comment.[50]

Hitler concluded his four-hour visit with an address to the *Bismarck*'s crew. As he spoke, the Führer's standard, hoisted above the bridge, flapped in the cold breeze blowing off the sea.[51] "You are the pride of the Navy," he declared, "and in your skill, your courage, and your determination lies the key to victory. I know that you will do what I and every German expect you to do, and, therefore, final victory is with you." Raeder, standing alongside Hitler, added his own postscript: "We shall defeat the Englishmen wherever we find them."[52]

* * *

At two o'clock in the morning of Monday, May 19, *Bismarck* and *Prinz Eugen* put to sea. "The crew," noted one sailor, "was in the state of tense anticipation that comes when a long period of preparation is finally over and the action of which it was designed is about to begin. Their faith in their captain and their ship was boundless, even though they knew nothing about the operation on which they were embarking."[53]

The air of mystery did not linger long. At noon, Admiral Lütjens's voice came over the loudspeaker. "The day that we have longed for so eagerly has at last arrived," he said, "the moment when we can lead our proud ship towards the enemy." He explained their mission was the "imperiling of England's existence" and the sinking of British merchant shipping in the Atlantic. "I know it is, has been, and will remain the crew's sincerest wish to participate successfully in Germany's final victory," he said. "I give you the hunter's toast: 'good hunting and a good bag!'"[54]

Two minesweepers and the destroyers *Friedrich Eckoldt* and *Hans Lody* joined *Bismarck* and *Prinz Eugen* on their westerly voyage beneath a battleship-gray sky. The flotilla navigated a German minefield on the afternoon of May 20 without major incident; the minesweepers' guns detonated three drifting mines that got too close.[55] *Bismarck* and her escort continued at seventeen knots on a zigzagging course toward Norway, the coast of which came into view against the flaming backdrop of a setting sun. "The outlines of the beautiful, austere landscape, with the black silhouettes of its mountains raised against the red glow of the sky," noted *Bismarck* gunnery officer Burkhard von Müllenheim-Rechberg, "enabled me to forget for a moment all about the war."[56]

On Wednesday morning, May 21, *Bismarck* entered Grimstadfjord, south of Bergen, and dropped anchor some 700 yards offshore. German freighters took up position on either side of her to protect against submarine attack. Her escort sailed to a bay farther north for refueling.[57]

A pair of Bf 109 fighters circled above in the crystalline skies. "We simply waited for the day to pass," recalled Müllenheim-Rechberg. "The sun shone continuously and many members of the German occupation forces in Norway, understandably eager to see the new *Bismarck*, came out to visit us."[58]

One visitor went unnoticed. Flying at 26,000 feet in an "unheated, unarmed, and unpressurized" long-range Spitfire, twenty-year-old Pilot Officer Michael "Babe" Suckling soared over Grimstadfjord. He had taken off that morning from RAF Wick in Caithness, Scotland, tasked with photographing Norway's maze of fjords and inlets. The reconnaissance flight had revealed nothing of interest—until now. What he saw appeared to be a "huge" battleship surrounded by supply vessels. Aware *Bismarck* had sailed from her Baltic port days prior, he triggered his cameras and photographed the distant scene below.[59]

He landed late that afternoon in Scotland and was ordered to fly the film at once to RAF Coastal Command headquarters in Northwood, just outside London. He scrambled back into his Spitfire and took off into the darkening sky. With daylight rapidly fading—and his Spitfire running low on fuel—he landed in a field near his home in Nottinghamshire and ran to the house of a nearby friend, who drove him the rest of the way to London. They reached the city near dawn and delivered the film.[60] The developed images revealed "a Bismarck-class battleship and an Admiral Hipper-class cruiser in the vicinity of Bergen."[61]

Word immediately went out to the British Fleet. The German hunters had been found.

CHAPTER 2

* * *

CATACLYSM

The loudspeaker system on HMS *Hood* crackled to life with the voice of Commander William Cross—the ship's executive officer—on the morning of Thursday, May 22. The men, eating their breakfast on the mess deck, glanced up from their food. RAF reconnaissance, Cross said, had photographed the battleship *Bismarck* and an unidentified cruiser refueling in Korsfjord near Bergen, Norway. A breakout into the Atlantic seemed imminent. The *Hood*—accompanied by the newly minted battleship HMS *Prince of Wales* and six destroyers—was proceeding to an area north of Iceland to run interception.[1]

"The announcement did not cause a stir," remembered Ted Briggs, then an eighteen-year-old signalman. "We had heard it all before and nothing had happened. We were fairly confident it would not happen this time, and if it did, the *Hood* was capable of handling any 'jumped-up German pocket battleship.'"[2]

The pride of the Royal Navy, the "Mighty *Hood*" imposed upon her crew a sense of near invincibility. The 42,000-ton battle cruiser with her eight 15-inch guns could once boast of being the largest warship afloat—but technology and ship design had passed her by in the twenty-three years she'd been traversing the world's oceans. Age had done nothing to diminish her looks, however, and she remained a stunning ship with a distinct silhouette of sleek lines. "I'd never seen anything quite so powerful and beautiful," remembered Briggs. "'Beautiful' for a battleship sounds an awful word, but there's no other way to describe her. She was unique . . . she was recognized throughout the world, and her graceful lines had a lot to do with it."[3]

Even the men on the 35,000-ton *Prince of Wales*, with her ten 14-inch guns, took comfort in *Hood*'s presence. "We were the new boy," remembered one of *Prince of Wales*'s crew, "but we felt perfectly confident that there was the mighty *Hood*."[4] For sailor Richard Osborne, stationed on *Prince of Wales* and long mesmerized by the sea, it was all something of a dream. When his time and duties allowed, he stood at the railing and gazed across the water at *Hood*. "I used to watch her, fascinated, for hours on end," he recalled. "The sea creamed over her bow and around down her sides. . . . She had a high center amidships, where the water seemed to roll along. I was quite fascinated watching this and listening to the sea."[5]

The squadron—under the command of Vice Admiral Lancelot Holland—had put to sea the night before from Scapa Flow, the British Fleet's home base in the Scottish Orkney Islands. The vice admiral was a man of quiet demeanor and a source of fascination to the young Briggs. The fifty-three-year-old Holland rarely raised his voice or showed any outward emotion. His subdued nature lent him an air of mystery. How, Briggs wondered, had a man of such meek nature advanced up the Royal Navy ranks?[6]

Although a gunnery specialist who had "invented gadgets to improve anti-aircraft control in warships," Holland had minimal combat experience. He had led a strike force of five destroyers the previous November against the Italian fleet in the Mediterranean, but the skirmish ultimately proved minor with neither side inflicting any losses. Now, Holland stared through the rain-streaked windows of *Hood*'s compass platform. Beside him stood the ship's captain, Ralph Kerr.[7]

The ships pushed on, cresting the dark waves, unaware their prey was on the move. A signal arrived at 10:30 p.m. from Admiral Sir John Tovey, commander in chief of the British Home Fleet. Briggs brought the message from the wireless office to the compass platform and passed it to *Hood*'s signal officer, who scanned it quietly before reading its content aloud: "*Bismarck* and consort sailed. Proceed to cover area south-west of Iceland."[8]

Fear and excitement tied an uneasy knot in Briggs's stomach. Maybe this whole exercise wasn't a false alarm after all. "Perhaps," he wondered, "this is the big one."[9] He glanced at his fellow crewmembers and saw them "yawning nervously and trying to appear unconcerned."[10]

✳ ✳ ✳

Admiral Frederic Wake-Walker's 1st Cruiser Squadron—comprised of HMS *Suffolk* and flagship HMS *Norfolk*—patrolled the Denmark Strait, a 300-mile long channel separating Iceland to the east and Greenland to the west. Its dark and wild waters stretched south from the Greenland Sea and overflowed into the North Atlantic, making it a likely route for German warships intent on breaking into the North Atlantic. "By this time," remembered Lieutenant D. N. Paton on the *Suffolk*, "the crew had become accustomed to working under conditions of great hardship. Heavy seas, piercing winds, blinding sleet, and freezing spray all made a nightmare of long hours on watch."[11]

Throughout the day and early evening of Friday, May 23, the men suffered through their duties. On lookout, Able Seaman Newall scanned the snow-blurred distance for signs of the enemy. At 7:22 p.m., he saw through his binoculars a ship emerge from a snow squall seven miles to starboard. "Ship bearing green-one-four-oh degrees!" he cried. He glanced once more through his binoculars and saw another ship appear. "Two ships bearing green-one-four-oh degrees!"[12]

The immensity of *Bismarck* was apparent even at a distance. "This," noted Paton, "was the culminating moment of all those weary months of training and waiting."[13] The chase was on. As her crew moved to action stations, *Suffolk* made a sharp change of course to shadow her quarry. A cold, white mist enveloped the ship, her straining engines rattling the heavy cruiser from bow to stern. The trembling needle in the ship's pitometer log clung desperately to 30 knots. The wireless operator immediately sent a report to the Admiralty: "One battleship, one cruiser in site at 20 [degrees]. Range seven nautical miles, course 240 [degrees]."[14]

At that same moment, *Bismarck*'s radar picked up something in the swirling mist off her port bow. Her alarm gave voice to the situation's urgency and echoed deep into her bowels. In the aft fire control station, Müllenheim-Rechberg stared through his director—used to track a target's bearing and range—and saw nothing but a heavy veil hanging over the water. The moments ticked by as he searched for a ghost in the fog. *Bismarck*'s guns, ready to fire, lacked a target—but still the shadow remained on her radar, gradually growing fainter.[15] "As the contact moved out of sight," wrote Müllenheim-Rechberg, "the shadowy outline of a massive superstructure and three stacks was discernible for a few seconds." He recognized it at once as a British cruiser.[16]

On board *Suffolk*, its "doors, hatches, and ventilation valves" closed in preparation for battle, the men kept a weary eye on their prey.[17] "Every moment," remembered Paton, "we expected *Bismarck* to open fire." Patrolling roughly fifteen miles to the south, *Norfolk*—having received *Suffolk*'s signal—turned to join the chase. Captain A. J. L. Phillips moved his ship through thick fog with a plan to maneuver astern of *Bismarck* and *Prinz Eugen*. When *Norfolk* broke cover at 8:20 p.m., Phillips—much to his horror—discovered the two German warships six miles off his port bow, well within range of *Bismarck*'s guns. "Hard astarboard!" he ordered.[18] *Norfolk* began to turn with her smoke screen rolling gray and heavy across the sea.

Bismarck's alarm bells sounded once more. "Enemy in sight to port," Captain Ernst Lindemann declared over the ship's speaker system. "Our ship accepts battle."[19] Müllenheim-Rechberg again peered through his director and saw *Norfolk*'s three smokestacks partially obscured by fog. *Bismarck*'s guns flashed and roared before the British ship could fully disappear.[20]

The 15-inch shells blew apart the surface of the sea; angry, frothing columns of water, as explosive as any fiery detonation, soared 150 feet into the sky. The shots landed on either side of *Norfolk* and peppered her deck with smoldering, twisted shell fragments.[21] And then *Norfolk* was gone, swallowed by her smoke screen.

Müllenheim-Rechberg scanned the distance and saw her reappear shortly thereafter alongside *Suffolk*, astern of *Bismarck*—two distant and constant shadows. The violent concussion of *Bismarck*'s guns knocked out her forward radar, prompting Lütjens to order *Prinz Eugen* into the lead position.[22] It was a move that would have lasting consequences.

The game of cat and mouse dragged on through the Arctic night, which never achieved full darkness. Daylight lingered like a weak bulb shining through a black veil. It was disorienting and seemed to violate the well-established laws of time. For Paton, standing at the *Suffolk*'s plotting table, the minutes and hours ticked away a strange and endless twilight.

"Bully beef and hot cocoa were brought round from the galley," Paton wrote. In the rolling sea, some men spilled their drinks. Paton would never shake the image of the "hot, sticky liquid spilling over the deck," a grotesque memory that forever turned him off the stuff.[23] Commander L. E. Porter would later remember *Suffolk*'s crew as having "lived and eaten at odd moments at the guns. An odd doze snatched during lulls served for sleep. Some slept on their feet."[24]

✳ ✳ ✳

Hood **and** *Prince* of *Wales* steamed through the pale Arctic night three hundred miles to the south. The weather had turned filthy for May. Razor-sharp winds and snow flurries lashed the British squadron as it cut through a heaving sea.

Ted Briggs, in *Hood*'s wireless office, felt his neck "prickle with excitement" when—at 8:32 p.m.—a message arrived from the *Norfolk*: "One battleship, one cruiser in sight."[25] It not only confirmed the enemy's presence in the Denmark Strait, but also their intention to break into the North Atlantic. *Prince of Wales* and *Hood* surged forward, crashing up and down on the waves, and began to leave their destroyer escort behind.

Shortly before 9:00 p.m., Holland signaled the destroyers: "Regret if you cannot keep up this speed. I will have to press on without you."[26] On the destroyer HMS *Electra*, the men braced themselves against the drastic pitching and rolling. "Sheets of spray shot up and over the ship like heavy rain," noted the ship's commanding officer, Lieutenant

Commander T. J. Cain. "Our sisters, the rest of the destroyers, were often quite invisible beneath the water they displaced, and the battle-wagons rose and fell with the sound of thunder as they pressed majestically on."[27]

Hood and *Prince of Wales* pushed through the wind and flurries with "blackish, purple smoke" billowing from their stacks.[28] There was, at present, little for Ted Briggs to do other than wait. At 10:00 p.m., Commander Cross addressed *Hood*'s crew. "We expect to intercept at 0200 tomorrow morning," he said. "We will go to action stations at midnight. In the meantime, prepare yourselves—and, above all, change into clean underwear."[29]

Wearing clean underclothes minimized the risk of infection in the event of an injury. Nervous tension rippled through the ranks. "There was fear, yes," Briggs recalled. "As far as I was personally concerned, I was frightened. But my main fear was a fear of showing fear. It wasn't a fear of death; it was fear of being maimed and not being able to do anything about it."[30]

"The night before we met the *Bismarck*," remembered Richard Osborne, on *Prince of Wales*, "we left our turret and went below. We had a bath and put on clean underclothes, in case of wounds and so on."[31] The sixteen-year-old, having yet to see any real action, had no clear concept of war. His mind couldn't comprehend the horrors it inflicted on men. "My impression of wounds in those days, before the action," he said, "was that one got a slight nick on the shoulder, got up, and said 'I'm okay.'"[32] He would soon learn otherwise.

Bathing and changing duties complete, a long, uncomfortable night was spent at action stations as *Prince of Wales* followed *Hood* to her fateful reckoning. The men shivered at their posts as the ships carried on their lonely hunt. The knowledge of imminent combat only lengthened the dark and desperate hours.

For Briggs, "action stations" meant the compass platform, where he would assist the flag lieutenant and respond to any messages relayed over the voice-pipes. It was dark when he entered, lit only by the lights of the binnacle and plotting table.[33] In the pallid glow, he could see the squadron's gunnery officer on the starboard wing, looking out to sea. William Dundas, the eighteen-year-old midshipman of the watch, stood by the phones and voice-pipes on the port side of the platform. "It was," Briggs remembered, "very, very calm."[34]

Admiral Holland—dressed in a greatcoat that seemed to emphasize his slender build—sat ramrod straight in the captain's chair at the front of the platform with Captain Ralph Kerr standing close behind. The two men were the only officers present not wearing steel helmets or bundled in thick duffel coats. Holland wore a pair of binoculars around his neck and drummed a nervous cadence on them with his fingers.[35] Briggs knew he would experience the coming battle from a unique vantage point. "I was in a position," he said, "to see everything that was going on and to hear everything that was going on."[36]

On *Hood*'s upper deck, stationed at a four-inch antiaircraft gun on the port side and exposed to the elements, Able Seaman Robert Tilburn struggled against the blistering cold. He stood at his action station wrapped in "long johns, vest, sweater, overalls, trousers, overcoat, duffel coat, oil skin, anti-flash gear, tin hat, gasmask, and gloves"—basically, "anything to keep warm."[37] The freezing temperatures, bitter as they were, did little to numb the tensions on deck. "I was scared," Tilburn said. "Anyone who's not scared is an idiot, but we were still going to win in the end. . . . Everybody was reasonably scared of the unexpected."[38]

Back on the compass platform, Briggs watched the drama unfold as if watching actors on a stage.[39] "Hoist battle ensigns," Holland ordered at 12:15 a.m.[40] The battle ensign—twenty-four feet in length and twelve feet wide—unfurled from *Hood*'s mainmast; its bright red cross with the Union Jack in the upper left quadrant was a living, writhing thing in the Arctic wind. It flapped high above the deck, a glaring exclamation point emphasizing the approaching danger. "But," noted Briggs, "it was an anticlimax." Thirteen minutes later, a message arrived from the *Suffolk*: "Enemy hidden in snowstorm."[41]

Murmurs of quiet consternation rippled through the compass platform. Holland got up and studied the charts on the plotting table. Under the cover of inclement weather, *Bismarck* would most likely alter her course—probably turning south. Heading north would put her on a direct collision with *Suffolk* and *Norfolk*, while the Greenland icepack ruled out an escape to the west. Holland ordered a change of course to the north and a reduction of speed to 25 knots. If he did not establish contact with *Bismarck* by 2:10 a.m., he would swing *Hood* back around.[42]

Briggs, fascinated, watched Holland bear the heavy burden of command. Tension had creased the admiral's brow. "Apart from the muttered comments of officers around me," remembered Briggs, "the compass platform became a strangely somnolent citadel."[43]

Hood and *Prince of Wales* sliced through the ocean swell, seesawing up and down on their new course. Holland kept his gaze out to sea, staring through windows frosted with snow and glistening with sea spray. The night offered bad seas and miserable weather, but no sign of *Bismarck* or her consort. Afraid of bypassing the enemy ships, Holland ordered *Hood* and *Prince of Wales* to turn south and then southeast.[44] He ordered his destroyer escort, languishing some distance behind, to continue the "search towards the north."[45]

On board HMS *Electra*, Lieutenant Commander Cain didn't hold out much hope for success. "We were convinced by now that the Germans were well away," he wrote. "It seemed that the enemy, thanks to such accidents as the size of the sea, the unpredictability of the climate, and Britain's chronic shortage of cruisers, was always to have the last laugh. The prospect was depressing."[46]

✳ ✳ ✳

The German crews, like their British counterparts, were not immune to doubt and apprehension. *Suffolk* and *Norfolk* had proven to be "annoying hangers-on," in the words of one *Bismarck* crewmember.[47] From his post, and throughout the long evening, Müllenheim-Rechberg could often see *Suffolk*'s mast outlined on the pale horizon.[48] *Norfolk*, shadowing on *Bismarck*'s port quarter to prevent the enemy's escape to the south, sought frequent cover in rolling banks of fog.[49]

Hunter and hunted passed through rain and snow, the Arctic winds whipping the length of the decks, chilling men to the bone, infiltrating the bridges and platforms, and adding its own misery to the affair. "There were ice-floes and mirage effects," notes one naval dispatch, "which occasionally deceived the *Suffolk* into thinking the enemy had closed to very short range."[50] The two British cruisers, although no physical match for *Bismarck* and *Prinz Eugen*, symbolized a larger threat. What other ships had the British frantically summoned to join the chase?[51]

At 10 p.m., as *Bismarck* passed through a dark and heavy rain, Lütjens decided to rid himself of his tormentors. He ordered *Bismarck* to make a 180-degree turn and attack *Suffolk*. Completing the maneuver, he had discovered the cruiser—perhaps wise to his cunning—to be nowhere in sight. He turned *Bismarck* back around and was soon once again being pursued.[52]

Lütjens's luck had temporarily changed for the better when, shortly before midnight, a blinding snowstorm passed over the ships. "Visibility," noted Müllenheim-Rechberg, "shrank to a nautical mile."[53] It was at this moment *Hood*, having just raised her battle ensign, received the signal from *Suffolk* that contact with the enemy ships had been lost.

✳ ✳ ✳

The men on *Hood*'s compass platform wrestled with a high-strain compost of exhaustion and anticipation. They drank cups of hot cocoa and gazed across the endless sea, tumultuous and empty.

Nearly three hours had passed since *Suffolk*'s and *Norfolk*'s last contact with the German ships. Dawn broke at 2 a.m. This far north, the first gray light of day already revealed an ominous sky choked with black clouds. Waves broke against the ship and showered the deck and guns in a frigid spray of needles. "Even a film of this morning," Briggs later wrote, "would not have brought out a brighter hue."[54]

A signal arrived from *Suffolk* at 2:47 a.m. saying she had reestablished contact with *Bismarck* and the still unidentified cruiser.[55] The news went out to the crew via loudspeaker as the ship altered course to intercept the enemy. "The *Hood* began to shudder more as speed was raised to 28½ knots," wrote Briggs, "the maximum she could obtain from her engines after months of over-use."[56] He stayed at the back of the compass platform, a silent observer to the unfolding drama.

Hood made radar contact with *Bismarck* thirty miles off her starboard bow at about three o'clock on the morning of Saturday, May 24.

The German ship appeared to be making for the Atlantic at 29 knots. Staring into the heavy mist beyond the compass platform, Holland decided to maintain a parallel course to *Bismarck* until the weather and visibility improved.[57]

Hood continued to shudder and tremble as her aging engines strained to keep pace. "There was a mixture of excitement and tension and apprehension—but mainly excitement," remembered Briggs. "This was something we'd been waiting for and something we'd been wanting. There wasn't a man onboard [*Hood*] who had any doubts about her capabilities. She was the epitome of British sea power; she was the mightiest ship afloat, and we were proud of it."[58] The excitement Briggs felt morphed into fear when, at 5 a.m., Holland ordered, "Prepare for instant action."[59]

Apprehension, likewise, permeated the *Prince of Wales*. The ship's chaplain said "a few words of prayer"[60] over the loudspeaker: "Preserve us from the dangers of the sea and from the violence of the enemy, that we may return in safety to enjoy the blessing of the land and the fruit of our labors."[61] It seemed to Osborne a rather impersonal way of delivering an invocation. From his gun turret on the catapult deck, he could see the Royal Navy battle ensign fluttering on the forward mainmast and the traditional white ensign blowing on the after mainmast. "It was like playing 'Land of Hope and Glory,'" he said. "You get chills going up and down your spine when you see that white ensign . . . seeing that go up is quite remarkable."[62]

At 5:35 a.m., a lookout on *Hood*'s spotting top made visual contact with their targets and relayed the news to the compass platform via voice-pipe. Holland turned around in his chair. "Alter course, please," he said. "Forty degrees to starboard in succession. And Chief Yeoman, take a signal for wireless transmission: 'Enemy in sight. Am engaging.'"[63]

Captain Kerr ordered the pilot to immediately pass a report to London: "Emergency to Admiralty and C-in-C, Home Fleet. From BC1— one battleship and one heavy cruiser, bearing 330, distance 17 miles. My position 63-20 north, 31-50 west. My course 240. Speed 28 knots."[64]

Two minutes later, at 5:37 a.m., the flag signal "Blue pendant four" appeared on *Hood*'s yardarm and waved violently in the sharp wind.

Both *Hood* and *Prince of Wales* turned 40 degrees to starboard and stormed headlong into battle, their angle of approach meaning only their forward guns could be brought to bear.[65]

The men on *Bismarck* first caught a glimpse of *Hood* and *Prince of Wales* at 5:45 a.m. on the pale horizon. They appeared first as thin plumes of smoke on *Bismarck's* port beam. Gradually, solid shapes took form beneath the hazy columns. Müllenheim-Rechberg peered through his director and watched the British ships materialize against the cold glare of day.[66] They appeared to be charging *Bismarck* bow-on in a suicide move. "Whatever the British tactic was," Müllenheim-Rechberg noted, "the exciting reality was that the ships were getting nearer and nearer to us."[67]

On *Hood's* compass platform, Ted Briggs continued watching everything with a strange sense of detachment. He found it hard to accept the reality unfolding in front of him. Everyone went about their duties with a surreal calmness; no one raised their voice. Admiral Holland remained seated in the captain's chair at the front of the platform, with Captain Kerr standing close behind him.[68]

With *Bismarck* and *Prinz Eugen* appearing no larger than two small specks on the murky horizon, Holland hoped to reduce the distance between his ships and the enemy as quickly as possible. *Hood's* lack of heavy deck armor allowed for more speed but rendered her vulnerable to plunging fire at long ranges.[69] Fighting at closer range meant enemy shells would have a more horizontal trajectory, as opposed to dropping onto the ship from above. *Hood's* maximum effective gun range was twelve miles, but Holland hoped to close the distance to eight.[70]

The admiral's initial plan called for *Hood* and *Prince of Wales* to attack *Bismarck*, while *Norfolk* and *Suffolk* set their guns on *Prinz Eugen*. An order to maintain radio silence, however, lest the British squadron risk betraying its presence, meant *Norfolk* and *Suffolk* never received these orders.[71]

"Things happened," remembered Briggs, "with bewildering rapidity."[72] *Hood* and *Prince of Wales* charged forward with their destroyer escort some fifty miles astern.[73] Through the sea-streaked windows of the compass platform, Briggs could see the guns in the two forward turrets lift toward the charcoal sky. The sound of the fire gong traveled the length of the ship.[74]

On the *Prince of Wales*, Petty Officer John Gaynor watched *Bismarck* grow larger in his binoculars. "As we got near her, she seemed to be entirely unawares," he said. "She looked an awful, frightening thing—and I thought, 'My goodness, if she turns on us, we're going to have some trouble here.'"[75]

Gaynor glanced down at his range finder and saw the distance between the British and German ships shrinking at an alarming rate: 20,000 yards . . . 19,000 . . . 18,000. Why get so close, he wondered, when the guns on *Prince of Wales* could easily throw a shell more than 24,000 yards. "If it had been me—and being a coward—I would have laid off at the range of [our] 14-inch guns and walloped him from there. But, no, we were going to do it the good-old-fashioned Drake-and-Nelson way." The distance now closed to 15,000 yards. "My goodness," he thought, "in a minute we'll be getting out our cutlasses."[76]

Admiral Holland, through his helmsman, ordered the gunnery officers on *Hood* and *Prince of Wales* to aim for the enemy ship on the left, which he believed to be the *Bismarck*. The order given, Holland commenced hostilities. "Open fire," he said. The command passed through the chief yeoman, who bellowed up to the flag deck, "Flag 5, hoist."[77] The time was 5:52 a.m.

"The warning gong replied before *Hood*'s first salvo belched out in an ear-splitting roar, leaving behind a cloud of brown cordite smoke, which swept the compass platform," Briggs wrote. "Seconds later a duller boom came from our starboard quarter as the *Prince of Wales* unleashed her first fourteen-inch salvo."[78]

Still staring through his director on *Bismarck*, Müllenheim-Rechberg saw "flashes like lightning" erupt from the approaching enemy ships.[79] The shots, although well grouped, fell short and landed in a massive eruption of water. Müllenheim-Rechberg waited for the order to return fire and the violent reply of *Bismarck*'s guns—but no such order came. The tension in the after station took on a palpable, physical quality. It weighed upon the men and lengthened time. Seconds seemed like minutes, and minutes like hours.[80]

Bismarck continued on her collision course. Every conquered yard of thrashing sea brought her closer, it would seem, to destruction. The enemy ships, coming into sharper focus, now more fully revealed themselves against the morning light. Müllenheim-Rechberg heard second gunnery officer Helmut Albrecht yell, "The *Hood*—it's the *Hood!*"[81] "There she was," he wrote, "the famous warship . . . that had been the 'terror' of so many of our war games."[82]

The lookout on *Hood*'s spotting top watched the plumes of water from her shells crash into the sea. Heavy gray-and-white clouds of spray and foam cleared to reveal a grave error. *Hood* had fired not on *Bismarck* but on the *Prinz Eugen*, mistaking the ship in the lead as the primary target. It was an easy mistake to make, as both German ships had the same silhouette: four turrets and one funnel.[83] He sent a desperate message to the compass platform: "We're shooting at the wrong ship. *Bismarck* is on the right, not the left."[84]

Holland, in the captain's chair, showed no outward sign of concern and simply ordered the guns onto the correct target. "Within the next two minutes *Hood*'s foremost turrets managed to ram in six salvoes each at the *Bismarck*," Briggs wrote. "I counted each time, expecting to see a hit registered."[85]

But it was *Prince of Wales* that found her mark and hit the German leviathan three times. One shell passed right through the ship without exploding, entering on the port side above the waterline, ripping through her innards, and blowing a five-foot hole in her starboard side before vanishing into the sea. Another shot ruptured her fuel tanks and exploded against her torpedo bulkhead. The third shell shattered one of *Bismarck*'s lifeboats, plastering a nearby gun crew with wooden splinters before bouncing off the ship and splashing into the water. *Bismarck*'s crew escaped the pummeling without casualties.[86]

The men on board *Bismarck* wondered, even as their ship shuddered under enemy fire, why Lütjens refused to respond in kind. They didn't know the admiral had been ordered not to engage British warships.[87] The whistling shriek of each enemy shell only fueled their desperation. "As the shells passed over our heads," remembered one sailor, "they literally whipped the noise through my body. A noise that cannot be described."[88] On the bridge, Captain Lindemann bristled with impatience. "I will not let my ship be shot out from under my ass," he said, as *Hood*'s distant guns flashed in anger.[89] His voice echoed from the ship's intercom. "Permission to fire!"[90]

Briggs saw flames leap from *Bismarck*'s 15-inch guns. Excitement and anticipation had temporarily overcome all other emotion, but now "deep, clammy, numbing fear returned."[91] The shells, as they hurtled toward *Hood*, sounded "very much like an express train going through a tunnel. It was a terrifying noise."[92] It was a sentiment echoed by many. Gaynor, on board *Prince of Wales*, likened it to hearing a train approaching as you're standing on a station platform. "There's nothing like waiting for a bomb or a shell when it's coming your way," he said. "The sound of an express train. That's the sound of a 15-inch shell approaching you, with all the noise and rattle."[93]

A shell from *Bismarck* slammed into *Hood* and threw the men on the compass platform off their feet. The sound was deafening, not unlike the tolling of a massive bell that rattled the skull. Briggs hauled himself upright and struggled to gain his equilibrium. Gunnery officer Commander Edward Gregson ventured onto the starboard wing of the platform and gazed down the length of the ship. He returned a minute later to inform Holland the shell had struck the base of the mainmast and set the ship alight. The situation played out with all the quality of a nightmare. "It just seemed as if this wasn't happening," Briggs later recalled.[94]

Beyond the relative safety of the compass platform, Briggs could hear the cries of men as the fire took hold. The shell had ignited an ammunition store full of antiaircraft rounds. The men on deck flattened themselves and took cover as rounds began to detonate. The explosions, noted Bob Tilburn, sounded "rather like a big Chinese Cracker."[95]

Heavy thunder rumbled once more across the water. A shell from *Prinz Eugen* cut a vicious arc through the sky and smashed into *Hood*'s foretop, dropping human body parts to the deck below. In the compass platform, Captain Kerr saw a man fall past the window. He turned to Midshipman William Dundas and asked him to see who it was. Dundas glanced outside and grimaced at the gory mess. "I don't know, sir," he said. "It's a lieutenant, but I can't see who it is. He has no hands . . . and he has no face."[96]

Two minutes had passed since *Bismarck*'s guns opened fire. To Briggs, it felt more like two hours. The screams of the dying and maimed pierced the compass platform's dark interior; still, Holland maintained his unruffled façade. He had by now closed the distance between *Hood* and *Bismarck* to eight and a half miles. Satisfied, he ordered a 20-degree turn to port to bring the after turrets into action. The corresponding flag went up the yardarm to signal *Prince of Wales*. The ships began their turn.[97]

Somewhere in the overcast void above, *Bismarck*'s fatal salvo hurtled toward its target. Captain John Leach on *Prince of Wales* believed it to be the "third or fourth salvo" from *Bismarck* that struck *Hood* and sent a jagged cloud of debris into the sky. "There was a very fierce upward rush of flame the shape of a funnel," Leach noted, "rather a thin funnel. Almost immediately, the ship was enveloped in smoke from one end to the other."[98]

On board *Bismarck*, the navigator's assistant witnessed the kill shot through the eyepiece of the forward conning tower. The smoke of guns and exploding columns of water at first blocked *Hood* from view— then she appeared. Although nearly 20,000 yards away, she seemed almost close enough to touch. *Bismarck*'s guns thundered once more. The navigator's assistant kept his eyes glued on the enemy ship, as *Bismarck*'s shells screamed along their fatal trajectory. "What we saw moments later," he recalled, "could not have been conjured up by even the wildest imagination."[99]

One moment, *Hood* filled the viewfinder; the next, she appeared to split in two—seemingly cut in half by a molten column of flame. Parts of the ship blew skyward like confetti and fell twisted and smoking into the sea. The navigator's assistant closed his eyes against the blinding flash of fire, but forced himself to look once more. "It was like being in a hurricane," he remembered. "Every nerve in my body felt the pressure of the explosions. If I have one wish, it is that my children may be spared such an experience."[100]

Müllenheim-Rechberg—now gazing at the horizon through his director for any sign of the *Suffolk* and *Norfolk*—heard someone shout, "She's blowing up!"[101] He turned the director in *Hood*'s direction, almost disbelieving the news. A thick, swirling column of black smoke marked the spot where the cruiser had been only minutes ago. Through the haze, he caught a glimpse of her bow sticking out of the water—a scene that almost defied reality. Even in her death throes, *Hood* managed a final salvo from one of her forward turrets. The shot appeared through Müllenheim-Rechberg's director as "a flash of orange" against the eddying backdrop of smoke. "I felt great respect for those men over there," Müllenheim-Rechberg wrote.[102]

The *Bismarck*'s war diary notes an "extraordinarily violent detonation on the *Hood*" and places the time of her destruction at "0601 hours and 20 seconds."[103]

A powerful flash distracted gunnery officer Colin McMullen, eyeing the enemy ships through his binoculars from the spotting top on *Prince of Wales*. "The whole of the inside of our spotting top; it was like there was a sudden sunset," he recalled. "This was when [the] great ship, which we were following, blew up."[104] The psychological impact was immediate. "It didn't help matters," he said. "One moment we were full of confidence astern of the 'Mighty *Hood*.' The next moment, we were a new, untried ship . . . facing the *Bismarck* and the *Prinz Eugen*."[105]

On *Hood*'s compass platform, Briggs—knocked once again to the floor—heard no explosion but saw a massive curtain of flame whip around the front of the ship.[106] Even as he pulled himself to his feet, he could feel *Hood* listing slowly to starboard. She had gone no more than 10 degrees when—to his great relief—she began to right herself. The voice of the quartermaster, however, signaled more trouble: "The steering's gone, sir."[107]

Captain Kerr, a blank slate of emotion, ordered a change to emergency steering. Holland, having climbed back into his chair, gazed through binoculars across the sloshing field of battle at *Bismarck*.[108] For Tilburn, on the upper deck, the experience proved drastically different. "There was a terrific explosion," he remembered, "and then there was dead silence. I'd never heard anything like this before—I didn't know if I'd been deafened."[109]

Tilburn was taking cover behind the blast shield of an antiaircraft gun when the fatal shell struck the ammunition stores to the after turrets. Hot and ragged steel debris fell across the deck. Bodies, some dismembered, did likewise. The bloody remains of some poor soul torn asunder landed on the back of Tilburn's legs.[110]

Tilburn proved lucky; the three men taking cover alongside him were not so fortunate. One simply disappeared in the blast and another was killed outright. The third, Tilburn recalled, "had his side cut open. It looked like a butcher had got to him. All his innards were coming out."[111] Tilburn felt his stomach turn and thought, with dreadful certainty, he was going to throw up. He staggered to the side of the ship, bent over the railing, and noticed the water appeared closer than normal.[112]

The relief Briggs felt as *Hood* righted herself proved fleeting. No sooner had she leveled out than she began listing heavily to port. The horizon, through the windows of the platform's foreport, assumed an increasingly steep angle.[113] With *Hood* now listing at 45 degrees it became apparent to everyone she wasn't coming back. "There was no order to abandon ship," Briggs later wrote, "nor was a word uttered. It was just not required. The *Hood* was finished, and no one needed to be told that."[114]

Briggs, fighting the precarious slant of the floor, made his way to the platform's starboard door. The navigating officer stepped aside and let Briggs through. As he looked over his shoulder one last time, Briggs "saw Holland slumped on his chair in total dejection."[115] Kerr stood beside him, struggling to remain upright as the ship continued to list. Both men, adhering to naval tradition, would slip with *Hood* beneath the waves. Briggs groped the ladder leading to the next bridge down—the admiral's bridge—and got no more than halfway before the frigid sea began crashing about his legs.[116]

Robert Tilburn, his nausea quickly forgotten, had moved forward to the boat deck and lowered himself onto the ship's forecastle with the freezing gray water drawing closer. Knowing he would soon be submerged, he stripped from his body anything he feared might weigh him down. He threw off his tin helmet and tossed away his gas mask. He pulled off his overcoat just as the water reached him and dragged him into the sea. He felt wrapped in a blanket of ice and struggled against the waves, unable to draw a proper breath. The problem, he realized, was his leather belt. It was fastened too tight and restricting his breathing as he swam.[117]

Tilburn groped for the knife he wore around his waist on a lanyard and sawed through the belt.[118] "Then," he recalled, "I looked around and saw the ship was rolling over on top of me."[119] He turned and pulled himself through the water with all the strength his shocked and tired body could muster. It wasn't enough.

Ted Briggs could feel the water pulling him away from the ship. Although he escaped the compass platform with at least two other men, he saw not another living soul around him—not even a body. He discarded his gas mask and tin helmet—as Tilburn had done—before the water swallowed him "with a roar."[120] The deck head to the compass platform was directly above him and threatened to push him deeper as it sank. "I kicked out away from it as fast as I could," he recalled. "At the same time, I felt myself being dragged down."[121]

He fought against the downward pull of the sea as it flooded the sinking ship, filling *Hood*'s empty spaces and claiming her crew. His lungs throbbed, desperate to draw breath. The sea discarded Briggs's efforts and held him tight; above him the pale-lit surface slipped further away. Everything was pressure and noise. It rumbled in his ears and squeezed his chest. He opened his mouth in desperate reflex to breathe and let the bitter saltwater in. His tongue recoiled to the back of his throat. His body had nothing left to give and surrendered to the depths.[122]

"I just couldn't do anymore," he later said, "and I felt quite a feeling of peace."[123] Death, when it came, would be a blessed release. He floated in the cold abyss and waited for the end—but to no avail. "Suddenly," Briggs recalled, "I seemed to shoot to the surface."[124] He broke the surface and sucked in great gulps of air to feed his starving lungs. Each desperate breath bolstered his flagging will to survive despite the glaring horror nearby. No more than 200 feet away, he saw *Hood*'s bow sticking straight out of the water, her forward turret sinking fast.

"It was the most frightening aspect of my ordeal," Briggs later wrote, "and a vision which was to recur terrifyingly in nightmares for the next forty years."[125]

Fearful the sinking ship would again pull him under, he turned to swim away. The water around him had turned to a thick sludge, as oil seeped from the shattered battle cruiser and spread across the surface in a slick some four-inches thick. He slogged through the sticky mess and fought his way to a nearby raft he saw floating on the black-coated waves. Freezing and covered in oil, he braved another look over his shoulder. "When I turned again," Briggs remembered, "she had gone and there was a fire on the water where her bows had been."[126]

Tilburn continued his own desperate struggle on the port side of the ship. The wireless aerials of the shattered masthead hit the water and wrapped around one of Tilburn's boots. As the ship went under, she pulled the ensnared Tilburn with her. Still grasping his knife in one hand, he began hacking away at the boot. He sawed and sliced, his movements hampered by the water, until the boot slipped off his foot. "I shot to the surface like a cork out of a bottle," he said. "And she was just there, with her bows out of the water."[127]

Vertical to the sea like some massive gray tombstone, she loitered for a moment before slipping beneath the waves.[128] The world's mightiest warship—the pride of the Royal Navy—was gone. Only six minutes had passed from the moment *Hood* opened fire to *Bismarck*'s fatal salvo. It took a mere three minutes for her to sink.[129]

Not far away, Briggs clung to his raft despite the throbbing pins-and-needles in his hands and arms. He kicked his legs, his heart thrashing against his ribs, and moved away from a burning patch of oil. The heavy rumble of guns still rolled across the water as *Bismarck* and *Prinz Eugen* turned their collective might against *Prince of Wales*. He watched the lone British ship—straddled by shell-bursts—turn to make a fighting escape with her guns roaring in desperate response.[130]

Would she get away or suffer the same fate as *Hood*? A ship fighting for its survival would not stop to retrieve survivors. On board, her crew grappled with the horror of *Hood*'s demise. "There were all sorts of cries—a lot of them," remembered Ordinary Seaman Harold Checketts. "The word went round so quickly. '*Hood*'s been hit and is down!'

It was all so quick—and the shock, of course, was terrible."[131] Richard Osborne, having been so enraptured by *Hood*'s majestic lines, couldn't grasp the fact she was gone. "It was just unbelievable that *Hood* was there one minute," he said, "and then just wasn't there."[132]

As *Hood* rolled over in her final agony, *Prince of Wales* turned hard to starboard to avoid colliding with the wreckage, but she did not escape unharmed. Two shells struck her aft below the waterline and flooded her bowels with 600 tons of water.[133] Another shell from *Bismarck* drilled thirteen feet into her hull below the waterline before the anti-torpedo bulkhead stopped its trajectory. Other shots knocked out her forward fire control station and aircraft crane.[134]

One shell from *Prinz Eugen* screamed across *Prince of Wales*'s deck and pierced the chamber beneath the aft 5.25-inch gun turret. It ricocheted around the chamber with an apocalyptic racket, sparking and clanging off metal; it scorched the air near one sailor's head and burned off all his hair, "leaving behind fresh, pink skin," but failed to explode.[135] A petty officer and able seaman undertook the rather delicate operation of removing the unwanted ordnance from the ship. They hoisted the shell through an upper hatch onto the deck with a deliberation that was almost painful and lowered it into the sea.[136]

A 15-inch shell from *Bismarck* delivered the most devastating blow. It punched through one side of *Prince of Wales*'s superstructure like a battering ram and exploded as it passed out the other. One crewman on the bridge described a noise not unlike a "violently onrushing cyclone."[137] It blew apart the compass platform, killing everyone except Captain Leach and the yeoman of signals.[138]

Leading Seaman Sam Wood was climbing a ladder from the armored wheelhouse to the bridge at the moment of impact. Although he heard no explosion, he felt "enveloped in a pocket of searing heat."[139] The blast threw him into the air. The shockwave seemed to carry him for an eternity, over scenes of carnage, before slamming him into the deck "amidst a shambles of torn steel fixtures, collapsed searchlights, and human bodies."[140] The sweet, sickening smell of cooking flesh brought him to his senses. "Gradually, my brain cleared and the red fog lifted from my eyes," Wood recalled. "Everything was enveloped in dark gray smoke."[141]

In the compass platform, Leach found himself surrounded by smoldering wreckage and shattered corpses. A splattered mess with a cap floating on top of it appeared to be all that was left of two midshipmen.[142] Leach made his way down to the admiral's bridge and assessed the situation. Although not mortally wounded, *Prince of Wales* was injured and hopelessly outgunned. Her untested armaments had proved faulty in combat, with only three of her ten 14-inch guns sometimes able to fire.[143]

Leach knew facing *Bismarck* and *Prinz Eugen* alone would prove a futile exercise. "Prior to the disaster of the *Hood* I felt confident that, together, we could deal adequately with *Bismarck* and her consort," Leach wrote in his after-action report. "The sinking of the *Hood* obviously changed the immediate situation . . . I did not consider it sound tactics to continue single-handed the engagement with two German ships, both of whom might be expected to be at the peak of their efficiency."[144] Having no desire to risk his men and ship on a losing proposition, he ordered a withdrawal.[145]

"The noise," remembered Richard Osborne, as the ship retreated, "one could almost feel it; the noise of the ship under full power. Those big intakes sucking in air, the exhaust going—all contributing to the immense power of a ship like *Prince of Wales*."[146] Osborne was called away from his turret and summoned to the bridge to help clean up the gore and wreckage. "I was very keen in those days," he said. "I went in expecting to see people, and the first thing I saw was the wood paneling with just little bits of flesh spattered all around. I turned around and came out quite unseeing."[147]

He had never grappled with such trauma. Not sure what to do or how to cope, he turned to a crewmember next to him and asked for a cigarette and light. In his daze, Osborne noticed the person offering him the smoke "had gold braid all the way up his arm."[148] He half expected to be ordered back into the bridge and start scrubbing. Instead, the young sailor was kindly left to his cigarette and thoughts. As he pulled the smoke into his lungs—coughing and sputtering, but gradually mastering the technique—he pondered the horror unfolding around him. "It was a very big shock to me," he recalled years later. "It made me appreciate that war was no fun. I don't think I ever got over that."[149]

✳ ✳ ✳

Lütjens and Lindemann now faced a decision: pursue *Prince of Wales* and finish her off or put in somewhere for repairs. With more than 2,000 tons of water in her foredeck, *Bismarck* listed 9 degrees to port and was bleeding oil. The tips of her starboard propeller blades glistened above the oil-slick surface of the sea, a result of her overburdened bow sagging in the water.[150]

In her present state, *Bismarck*'s top speed was capped at 28 knots, per Lütjens orders. She had lost her advantage over the Royal Navy's fastest ships. Oil followed in *Bismarck*'s wake like the bloody trail of a fleeing killer. The loss of fuel meant a smaller radius of operations.[151]

Lindemann, dismissive of such concerns, argued for sinking *Prince of Wales*. Lütjens rejected the idea. The British would undoubtedly be out for blood. Returning to Germany was not a pleasant option, for the enemy might anticipate such a move. He opted instead to make for the French port of Saint-Nazaire on the Brittany coast, some 1,700 miles away and the only North Atlantic port with a dry dock big enough to accommodate a ship of *Bismarck*'s size.[152]

The *Prinz Eugen* could still wreak havoc on Allied shipping while *Bismarck* made a temporary detour for repairs.

✳ ✳ ✳

Tilburn paddled in the water with the chill bleeding into his bones. He could see nothing but debris and a thick patch of oil—burning in some areas—spreading across the surface. The thought of swimming through the slime and getting it in his mouth and eyes and hair and all over his skin repulsed him, but he cast aside his revulsion when, after an hour, he saw two solitary figures some distance off floating on life rafts. He swam his way through the muck, came across his own float, and pulled his upper body onto it.[153]

All three men, having now noticed one another, began to wave frantically to each other. They kicked and splashed in the water, desperate
to draw their rafts close. Soon Able Seaman Robert Tilburn, Signalman
Ted Briggs, and Midshipman William Dundas—who escaped *Hood*
through a hole he kicked in a starboard window on the bridge—were
together, holding tight onto one another's rafts.[154]

In the distance, Briggs could see the funnel tops of either *Suffolk* or
Norfolk fading beyond the horizon. The three men were completely
alone in the open sea with a fresh mass grave beneath them. They were
the only survivors out of *Hood*'s 1,421-man crew. Even in their current
state of shock, they realized the magnitude of the loss. "There was nobody in the water," Tilburn recalled years later. "There was nobody
alive and nobody dead. There was nobody—except we three."[155] The
trio floated on the oil-slicked waves and waited for deliverance.

Despite the dire nature of their circumstance, both Briggs and Tilburn found time to focus on a particular annoyance. While both remained half submerged in the water, Dundas sat comfortably upright
on his float. "For some odd reason," Briggs later wrote, "it infuriated
me that he was perched comfortably and perfectly balanced."[156] Both
men tried to sit on their floats, but failed. "Every time you pushed
down on [the float]," Tilburn said, "the thing would fall over on top of
your face."[157] The more the two men tried without success, the more
their frustration morphed into anger. Briggs felt on the verge of tears
before he finally gave up.[158]

The sound of an approaching plane drew their collective gaze to
the sky. A Sunderland emerged from the clouds and passed over the
scene. "We splashed the water and shouted," said Briggs, "but obviously they couldn't see us. It was impossible."[159] The men watched in
despair as the flying boat vanished once more on its mystery course.
Adrift, the freezing conditions became almost too much for the men
to bear.

Tilburn, as a young man, enjoyed reading adventure stories set
in northern Canada and Alaska, where men—overcome by hostile
climates—succumbed to hypothermia. Tilburn recalled reading that
"in the snow, if you get very, very cold, you tend to go to sleep and die

in your sleep." It now struck Tilburn as a pleasant alternative. "I tried to go to sleep," he said, "thinking that if I'm going to die, it'll be a nice, easy, quiet way out."[160]

Briggs—also overcome with cold—felt consciousness slipping away, despite Dundas's efforts to maintain morale "through his cheerfulness."[161] He led the three men in sing-alongs but could only do so much. Briggs, deciding "what will be, will be," began to let himself doze off.[162]

✳ ✳ ✳

At ten past six, Yeoman George Tingle on HMS *Electra* appeared on the bridge. He stood in stunned silence, his face a pale mask of shock, perhaps wanting to speak but not able to muster the words. The man's muted presence began to grate the nerves of Lieutenant Commander Cain.

"Any further news?" Cain snapped.[163] The last message from *Hood*, received at six o'clock, had said she was engaging the enemy. The ten minutes between then and now may well have been hours, so desperate was *Electra*'s crew for additional word. The news of battle had riled the men with both excitement and envy. Could *Hood* "keep the party going" until *Electra* arrived?[164] Indeed, Tingle had delivered the message with "feverish enthusiasm"[165]—so much so, Cain felt the need to "pour cold water from a great height"[166] on the crew's joviality. It proved an impossible task; the anticipation was infectious. "I myself am carried away by it all," he later wrote. "It's impossible not to be."[167] But now Cain saw nothing joyful in Tingle's manner.

"From *Prince of Wales*," the yeoman said, his voice thick and unsteady in his throat. "Sir . . . *HOOD* SUNK!"

"You can keep your sense of humor to yourself," Cain roared, rebelling against the news.

The yeoman blinked tears from his eyes. "My God, sir, but it's true," he said. "It's just come through. I have told the Captain."[168]

Word of *Hood*'s destruction "flashed around the ship like wildfire."[169] "Blankets, medical supplies, hot beverages, and rum were got ready," remembered Able Seaman Jack Taylor. "Scrambling nets were flung over the ship's side, trailing into the water. Men were lining the side ready with handlines, eyes straining into the greyness ahead."[170]

The *Electra* pushed forward through high seas, passed through a rolling bank of mist, and soon emerged on the other side into a sea choked with wreckage. Shirts and boots drifted atop the waves, alongside hammocks, tattered books, crumpled photographs, unfinished letters, hats, and other items that once made up the lives of more than one thousand men. Taylor looked across the water—a graveyard without tombstones—in stunned silence. He and his shipmates had expected to find hundreds of men afloat in the water, clinging to rafts and debris. Instead, they saw none. "Good Lord," said a nearby sailor. "She's gone with all hands."[171]

The men surveyed the scene in awed silence. "Where were the boats, the rafts, the floats?" thought Cain. "And the men? Where were the men?" It was, he noted, "a revelation of horror."[172] A lookout on *Electra* noticed thrashing in the water. Three survivors. "But there must be more of them. There can't only be three of them!" a crewmember cried. "Where the hell are all the others?"[173]

It was Dundas who first saw the *Electra* appear in the distance. "What's that?" he asked, his voice piqued by an urgency that drew Briggs and Tilburn from their hypothermic daze. "I looked around and saw one of our destroyers tearing into the wreckage," Tilburn said, ". . . a marvelous site!"[174] Briggs, lifting his head, felt life surge back into his stiff and frigid body when he recognized the ship's pendant number: H27. "*Electra! Electra!*" he screamed and began beating the water. The other two men followed suit.[175]

The destroyer's deck buzzed in a frenzy of activity as the ship pulled alongside the survivors. Taylor and several other men climbed over the side and worked their way down the scrambling nets until the sea slapped against their knees. "We hung onto the net, our arms outstretched, as the first man floated alongside," Taylor said. "Quickly, we grabbed him and lifted him onto the net."[176]

Men on the deck above reached down, grabbed the sodden, shivering bundle, and carefully pulled him up. "They grabbed hold of us and just hoisted us onboard like a sack of potatoes," Tilburn remembered.[177]

Briggs was surprised his fingers could even grasp the net. "Don't let go of it!" a sailor told him. "You bet your bloody life I won't!" Briggs replied.[178]

"We were just stone cold," Tilburn said. He watched, with not a little envy, as Dundas stood up from his float and appeared—at least to Tilburn's tired eyes—completely dry from the waist down. "How he didn't get wet, I have no idea," Tilburn mused years later.[179] The three men were helped down to the forward mess and had the ragged remains of their clothes cut away. They were scrubbed with warm swabs of cotton to remove some of the oil and get blood flowing once more to their extremities. Someone passed them hot cups of tea. "I think that tea was half rum and half tea," Tilburn said, "which warmed us tremendously."[180]

Briggs swallowed the strong brew and felt his stomach—full of oil and seawater—lurch in immediate revolt. Thick sludge pushed its way up from his gut. "I'd swallowed a lot of oil," he recalled. "[The tea] brought most of it up."[181] Medics carried Briggs and Tilburn to the sickbay, where—as warmth and sensation returned—Briggs's muscles seized in a violent cramp. "That was the most agonizing side of it," Briggs recalled.[182] But exhaustion overcame the pain, and he soon drifted off to sleep.

As Briggs slept, *Electra* passed slowly through *Hood*'s debris. Her crew scanned the waters for signs of anyone, living or dead. One item floating on the waves, "a desk drawer full of ratings' documents," caught Cain's attention.[183] Such a thing would generally be stored in the lower decks. The fact it made it to the surface, Cain wrote, meant it "must have been blown straight from the bowels of the ship by the force of the explosion."[184] The scant remains of *Hood* rode the gray sea. "We searched for a long time among what remained of this once proud ship," Taylor recalled, "but there was no one. Not even a body."[185]

Electra turned away from the scene after several hours of searching and set a course for Reykjavik. The short journey proved to be a solemn one. "We were invited to the seaman's mess, and there we had sipper after sipper of rum to make us forget," Briggs wrote. "If we had drunk everything which was offered, it would have been more lethal than the sea that nearly claimed us."[186]

Electra reached Reykjavik on the evening of May 24. Briggs, Tilburn, and Dundas disembarked and climbed into a waiting ambulance. They spent the night at a local hospital, where their only orders were to take a hot bath, get to bed, and not talk to anyone. As Tilburn walked to his room, he passed a soldier. "Hey, sailor," the soldier said, "I just heard on the radio that HMS *Hood* has been sunk."[187] It was all Tilburn could do to restrain himself.

Two days later, they boarded a troop ship bound for Britain and arrived home on Wednesday, May 28. The men still wrestled with the question of their survival. Why them and no one else? "That is a question . . . I have thought about time and time again," Tilburn said some forty years after the tragedy. "I can only say I have no idea whatsoever."[188]

CHAPTER 3

*** * ***

THE HUNTED

Winston Churchill traveled up from London on Friday, May 23, 1941, to Chequers, the prime minister's official retreat in the Buckinghamshire countryside. His guests for the weekend included President Roosevelt's personal representative to Britain, Averell Harriman. The excursion offered no respite from the strains of war. Allied resistance against the Germans on Crete was fast approaching collapse, while on the high seas *Hood* and *Prince of Wales* were expected—sometime in the early morning hours—to engage *Bismarck* and *Prinz Eugen*. The prime minister and his guests stayed up through most of the night hoping to hear some news before retiring to their beds at three in the morning. Four hours later, Churchill awoke to the awful news.[1]

To the British, *Hood* was not merely a warship but a national treasure, a monument to the nation's naval might and a goodwill ambassador on the seas. For two decades, through her speed, power, and the grace of her design, she had reigned as "the queen battleship of the world."[2]

"She . . . was one of our most cherished naval possessions," Churchill later wrote. "Her loss was a bitter grief."[3] He left his bedroom and padded down the hall to Harriman's room. Harriman stirred in bed to find the prime minister standing in his doorway wearing "a yellow sweater, covering a short nightshirt, his pink legs exposed." Churchill shook his head and almost seemed to be speaking to himself. "Hell of a battle," he said. "The *Hood* is sunk. Hell of a battle."[4]

Churchill spent that weekend in a grim mood. Naval charts set up in the Hawtrey Room at Chequers kept the fixated prime minister constantly abreast of *Bismarck*'s movements. "Time and again," noted Churchill's bodyguard, "sighting reports were followed by signals that the shadowing cruisers had lost the *Bismarck* once more."[5] Upon his return to London, he followed the pursuit at sea in the Map Room at No. 10 Downing Street. "Under these brilliant lights shining on all the maps around the room where the plotting continued hour by hour," recorded Captain Richard Pim, who oversaw the Map Room, "phases of the great sea battle were recorded."[6]

Colored pins on a map, however, could hardly convey the story of vengeance playing out in the North Atlantic.

❋ ❋ ❋

At the time of *Hood*'s demise, the *Norfolk* and *Suffolk* were some fifteen miles away. Admiral Wake-Walker observed the confrontation from *Norfolk*'s bridge and witnessed the fatal hit. A pink glow appeared to radiate from *Hood* beneath a cloud of black smoke. "It quickly developed and lengthened until the whole amidship part of the ship appeared to be on fire," he wrote. "It then died down slightly and almost immediately, at 0559, *Hood* blew up."[7]

Clouds of black smoke spun and swirled above *Bismarck* as her guns spit flame and inflicted their carnage. He watched *Prince of Wales* retreat behind her smoke screen with plumes of water erupting in her wake. "I ordered *Prince of Wales* to remain in company and to follow me at her best speed," Wake-Walker wrote in his official report.[8] In her damaged state, and with 400 tons of water in her lower compartments, the battleship could muster no more than 27 knots. As *Prince of Wales* joined *Norfolk* and *Suffolk*, the *Bismarck* and *Prinz Eugen* fled on a southwesterly course toward the Atlantic with the three British ships giving chase.[9]

Word of *Hood*'s destruction reached Commander of the Home Fleet Sir John Tovey on his flagship, the 42,000-ton HMS *King George V*. The signal from Wake-Walker was blunt: "*Hood* has blown up."[10] Tovey had put to sea the night of May 22 from Scapa Flow with the aircraft carrier HMS *Victorious*, a destroyer screen, and four cruisers. He was still some 300 miles away to the southeast when *Hood* sunk. The Admiralty ordered Wake-Walker to "continue to shadow BISMARCK, even if you run out of fuel, in order that the Commander in Chief may catch up in time."[11]

Wake-Walker had no intention of letting the German ships slip away, but he worried the damaged *Prince of Wales* might prove easy prey should *Bismarck* make another stand. The Admiralty, harboring similar concerns, asked him his "intentions as to PRINCE OF WALES re-engaging." He responded: "She should not re-engage until the other heavy ships are in contact . . . doubtful she has speed to force action."[12]

The weather, with visibility varying at times between two and seventeen miles, favored the hunted. The two German ships made frequent and drastic changes in course, sailing through mist and rain-squalls. As conditions worsened, Wake-Walker ordered *Prince of Wales* to close within one mile of the *Norfolk*. *Prince of Wales*, the admiral noted, "was still engaged in washing down her bridge in an attempt to remove the remains of the men killed there."[13] By 11 a.m., a gray, wet curtain had all but obscured the *Bismarck* and *Prinz Eugen* from view, rendering them blurred and distant outlines. Within an hour, they had vanished into a heavy drizzle.[14]

The men on *Bismarck* had grown accustomed to their constant British shadow. They knew full well the dire nature of their circumstance, but—buoyed by their victory—believed the day would be theirs. "Morale on board did not suffer," noted Müllenheim-Rechberg. "The crew was optimistic, or seemed to be."[15] Oil bled from the back of the ship, trailed across the waves, and stretched away to the horizon. Damage-control teams worked feverishly to repair what they could.[16]

His ships veiled in fog, Lütjens pondered his next move. He wanted to separate from *Prinz Eugen* to allow the cruiser to refuel and commence raiding operations against enemy convoys. At 2:20 p.m., *Bismarck*'s semaphore lamp flashed through the murk and relayed the plan to her consort. In the next rainsquall, *Bismarck* would break away to the west. *Prinz Eugen* would maintain her southerly heading for three hours after *Bismarck*'s departure before setting a course for two German auxiliary vessels—*Belchen* or *Lothringen*—south of Greenland to refuel. She would then proceed with Operation Rheinübung and storm the North Atlantic shipping lanes. The two ships would detach when *Bismarck* flashed the code word "HOOD."[17]

Twenty-two minutes after signaling *Prinz Eugen*, Lütjens radioed Rear Admiral Karl Dönitz, commander of Germany's submarine fleet: "Boats in the west assemble in quadrant AJ 68. Tomorrow at dawn, *Bismarck* intends to draw the stalking heavy cruisers, coming from the north, through quadrant AJ 68."[18] Translation: Lütjens wanted whatever U-boats might be available in the area to form a line from "the southern tip of Greenland" and lie in wait for his British pursuers.[19]

Bismarck and *Prinz Eugen* steamed through worsening seas. The world around them grew increasingly opaque as the weather closed in. At 3:40 p.m., Lütjens got what he wanted. The sky, as dark and inhospitable as the sea, opened up. Through the rain, Captain Helmuth Brinkmann on the *Prinz Eugen* saw *Bismarck*'s semaphore lamp flash "HOOD."[20] The battleship's great bulk veered quickly to starboard and vanished into the storm—but the weather refused to cooperate. The rain began to thin almost immediately and thwart *Bismarck*'s cover. Lütjens abandoned his maneuver and rejoined *Prinz Eugen* nineteen minutes later.[21] The ships pressed on through the "roughening waste of water" and "dark, sinister waves."[22]

At 5:22 p.m., *Bismarck* received a radio message from German Navy Group West, warning her the British aircraft carrier *Ark Royal*, the heavy cruiser *Dorsetshire*, the light cruiser *Sheffield*, and the aging battleship *Renown* had set sail from Gibraltar.[23] This was Force H under the command of Vice Admiral Sir James Somerville. The Royal Navy was throwing every available ship into the hunt.

As reinforcements steamed from the south and the east, Admiral Wake-Walker continued his tireless tracking, although he still had no visual contact with the two enemy ships. He nevertheless took precautions and ordered *Prince of Wales* to take the lead, "as, in this visibility, we were likely to meet the enemy inside gun range."[24]

He had no overwhelming desire to engage the enemy with only a damaged battleship and two cruisers—but he must have feared the possibility of losing his prey before Tovey's force arrived on the scene. Communicating with *Prince of Wales* via semaphore lamp,

Wake-Walker relayed his intentions: "I intend to get nearly astern of the enemy," he signaled. "After we get within range, I want to try and draw the enemy to the eastward towards [Tovey]."[25]

Bismarck and *Prinz Eugen* steamed through another rainsquall at 6:14 p.m. Once again, *Bismarck*'s semaphore lamp flashed "HOOD."[26] Lieutenant Commander Fritz-Otto Busch on *Prinz Eugen* watched *Bismarck* break off to the west, her numerous gun barrels "menacingly erect on every side like drawn swords."[27] The *Prinz Eugen*'s gunnery commander watched the rain and mist devour the battleship until she vanished from view. "There goes our big brother," he said. "We are going to miss him very, very much."[28]

✳ ✳ ✳

The shadowing *Suffolk*, tracking *Bismarck* on radar, was sixteen miles off the battleship's starboard quarter when her radar screen conveyed the altered nature of the chase. Instead of moving away from *Suffolk*, *Bismarck* was now drawing closer. The distance rapidly dropped to ten miles. *Suffolk* changed course to close ranks with *Norfolk* some twelve miles away.[29]

Bismarck, at that moment, emerged a glistening monster from her shroud of filthy weather. Her guns flashed huge bursts of white flame. "For half a very slow minute we waited," wrote Commander L. E. Porter, "and then short of us the huge fountains of water leapt into the air. Again and again she fired, the salvos jumping nearer and nearer."[30]

The noise and spectacle of *Bismarck*'s guns cut through the gray murk, painting—in the words of one sailor—"the sea, clouds, and rain squalls a dark red." On board *Prinz Eugen*, the second gunnery officer noted "the brown powder smoke that follows makes the scene even more melancholy. . . . In the fire of his after turrets, we see clearly again the outline of the mighty ship . . . which look[s] like one, sturdy building."[31]

Bismarck's fire straddled *Suffolk* and buffeted her with shell splinters as she fell back behind a smoke screen. "The noise was deafening," remembered Lieutenant D. N. Paton. "Great fountains of water rose into the air nearby. From the comparative safety of the plotting table, exploding shells sounded like extra loud machinegun fire."[32]

Lieutenant Commander C. T. Collett waited for the inevitable impact; every burst of flame from *Bismarck*'s guns foreshadowed imminent destruction. "The urge to get behind something was terrific," he later wrote. The screaming approach of German shells prompted Collett to duck behind *Suffolk*'s gun director, which offered only the scantest protection. He envied those sailors with immediate tasks to perform. "People who had something to do and to occupy their minds were lucky because they probably did not realize our imminent danger," he wrote. "Or, if they did, they couldn't just drop it and hide."[33]

Suffolk's 8-inch guns returned a pointless fire, as she cut a desperate zigzag through the swell. The rapid turn of events caught Admiral Wake-Walker by surprise. "Instead of finding myself astern of the enemy," he reported, "I was actually on his port quarter."[34]

At 6:47 p.m., *Prince of Wales* turned toward *Bismarck* and opened fire "at extreme range." Her second salvo straddled the German ship. *Norfolk* altered course thirty degrees to starboard and brought her guns to bear. *Suffolk* continued firing. Her shots, falling short and splashing harmlessly into the sea, prompted a terse signal from Wake-Walker: "Do not waste ammunition."[35]

Again, the blunt-force roar of *Prince of Wales*'s guns rolled across the waves. *Bismarck* turned away from *Suffolk* and responded in kind, but her salvos were punctuated by long intervals. Sitting in *Bismarck*'s foretop at the main fire control center, first gunnery officer Lieutenant Commander Adalbert Schneider struggled against the sun reflecting off the smoke and water.[36]

Both sides lobbed several more salvos at one another, inflicting neither damage nor casualties, until 6:56 p.m. when Wake-Walker ordered *Prince of Wales* to cease firing. He did not want *Bismarck* to flee in the opposite direction of Tovey on *King George V*.[37]

At 3:09 p.m., Tovey had ordered the aircraft carrier HMS *Victorious*—accompanied by the cruisers *Aurora*, *Galatea*, *Kenya*, and *Hermione*—to steam ahead. The squadron was to close within 100 miles of *Bismarck*, allowing the carrier to throw her torpedo bombers at the enemy.[38]

Victorious, having been commissioned just ten days prior, had on board only nine Swordfish torpedo bombers and six Fulmar fighters.[39]

With its lumbering speed of 137 mph, the Swordfish—a biplane introduced in 1936—was already antiquated by the outbreak of war. The voice of Captain Henry C. Bovell came over the carrier's speaker system and informed the Swordfish crews of Fleet Air Arm Squadron 825 they would soon take off with torpedoes, attack and sink the *Bismarck*, return to the carrier to rearm, and then take off once more to attack the *Prinz Eugen*. "That seemed optimistic, to say the least," remembered telegraphist/air gunner Donald Bunce. "To prepare for the operation, the men went down to the Nafi (mess), dined on huge bars of chocolate, and filled our water bottles with lime juice."[40]

War, of course, does not abide by plans. *Bismarck*'s engagement with *Prince of Wales* had pushed her further west. This meant *Victorious* remained 120 miles shy of her target.[41] Violent seas prevented the carrier from getting any closer. It was only one of several concerns nagging at Bovell. The men tasked with attacking *Bismarck* from the air were ill prepared for such an endeavor. The pilots of No. 825 Squadron had minimal experience taking-off and landing on a carrier, with several having only done it for their first time the week before.[42] The weather, cloudy and wet, did little to enhance their prospects. To better the odds, Bovell decided "nothing less than the whole of 825 Squadron could be expected to produce any result in a torpedo attack." Antisurface vessel (ASV) radar would assist the pilots in their search.[43]

Pilot Officer Patrick Jackson had last seen *Hood* from the deck of *Victorious* several days prior. The carrier had been returning from exercises at sea when she passed *Hood* and *Prince of Wales* on their outward—and fateful—journey. "It was a beautiful evening, the sun was going down in broken clouds," he would later recall, "and coming towards us at full speed was a wonderful sight: the *Hood* and *Prince of Wales*. The *Hood* I shall always remember. She was wet and glistening gray, the waves on her bow breaking on each side as they went past at high speed."[44]

Now, waiting for the order to climb into his plane and take off for some unknown fate, Jackson felt besieged by nerves. "I must admit," he later said, "there were butterflies in my stomach. The prelude to our Air Strike was horrible, sitting and waiting your turn to get into the ring. You feel, 'God, I'd get out of this if I could.'" He wondered if he would live to see his birthday, which was the following day—May 25.[45]

The nine Swordfish left the carrier's wind- and rain-swept deck at 10:10 p.m. The planes rattled violently as they climbed through a colorless void of wind, clouds, and rain. At 11:30 p.m., the squadron established radar contact with *Bismarck* and altered course to the south.[46] As the weather worsened, the contact weakened until *Bismarck* vanished once more. The squadron dropped beneath the overcast and located the *Norfolk*, which relayed a bearing to the *Bismarck* some twelve nautical miles off her starboard bow.[47] The Swordfish climbed once more above the rain-swollen clouds. "We got another return on our ASV," said Donald Bunce. "We went down and, to our surprise, it was a U.S. Coast Guard cutter [the *Modoc*] between us and *Bismarck*."[48]

The *Modoc*'s crew had no clue of the drama unfolding around them. The ship—out of Wilmington, North Carolina, and assigned to the waters around Greenland—was searching for survivors of a recently attacked convoy. "The search proved fruitless," wrote Vice Admiral T. R. Sargent and Captain B. M. Chiswell, "as we were continually buffeted by heavy North Atlantic seas and snow squalls, reducing visibility to zero and life on *Modoc*'s forecastle head to about the same."[49]

Conditions had slightly improved by Saturday, May 24. The men not on watch that afternoon had gathered in the mess for a movie. The *Modoc* plied the waves in its pointless search for wreckage and survivors. The day passed as an exercise in tedium until the onset of evening when "a huge gray shape" emerged from the gloom "on the starboard horizon."[50]

The *Modoc*'s quartermaster of the watch turned on the ship's signal lamp and flashed the mystery vessel "AAs," the international signal for "identify yourself."[51] The great shadowy bulk in the distance failed to respond. An attempt to contact her by radio and ask if she'd seen any debris in the vicinity met only with silence. "She just crossed our bow," Sargent and Chiswell wrote, "and passed down our port side two miles off."[52]

The men on *Modoc* had no idea the mystery vessel was the *Bismarck*, the world's largest battleship. They watched it continue on its ghostly course and recede into the cold distance. As the men watched it fade from view, they heard a distant drone approaching in the gloom above. "Hey," one sailor said, peering into the sky. "That's an airplane!" A speck revealed itself through the haze and drew closer. The crewman did a double-take. "My God! That's a landplane!"[53]

The aircraft's surprise appearance triggered the *Modoc*'s general alarm, rousing those on watch to battle stations. Men rushed to close doors and hatches; a horizontal and vertical American flag flew up the mainmast to signal the *Modoc*'s neutrality. The men rushed to the ship's 5-inch guns mounted fore and aft. Six more planes appeared in short order. "It didn't take long," wrote Sargent and Chiswell. "Suddenly, seven British Swordfish torpedo planes were using us as a point of departure, flying low over our masthead, wagling [sic] tips, and heading for that distant gray shadow."[54]

Roughly three miles away, the *Bismarck*'s crew watched in surprised admiration as the antiquated biplanes approached. Each Swordfish, powered by a 645 HP Bristol Pegasus engine, moved so slowly they appeared to hang motionless between the clouds and sea.[55]

Bismarck's antiaircraft and 15-inch guns roared to life. Tracer rounds cut a blazing path between the approaching planes. Smoldering shells fell into the sea and sent up massive plumes of water that threatened to knock the approaching Swordfish from the sky. "Daringly they flew through our fire," noted one German sailor, "nearer to the fire-spitting mountain of the *Bismarck*, always nearer and still nearer. . . . Incredible how the pilots pressed their attack with suicidal courage, as if they did not expect ever again to see a carrier."[56]

The *Modoc*'s crew, safely removed from the battle, gathered on the deck and watched the spectacle play out. "A Fourth of July display like nothing ever before seen soon embellished the evening twilight!" Sargent and Chiswell wrote. "Those of us not accustomed to warlike intentions were enjoying the show when a couple of brilliant flashes and tremendous explosions brought us back to reality."[57]

Across that stretch of sea and sky, the Swordfish swooped down on their target. "I remember looking across at the other two flights and a burst of gunfire exploded at the same height," recalled Donald Bunce. "I looked through this burst at the other aircraft. That's how accurate it was—and, to me, that seemed to be the indication that we should go down."[58]

The planes began their dive through cloud, tormented by wind and the concussion of *Bismarck*'s fire. Pilot Officer Jackson guided his Swordfish through black bursts of shrapnel. The controls shook violently in his hands, the wind screamed in his ears, the smell of cordite stung his nose. Below, the *Bismarck* grew larger. As he focused on his target and fought to keep the tortured biplane on course, he felt an urgent tapping on his shoulder. It was his observer, Lieutenant "Dapper" Berrill. "Oh Lord," Jackson thought, "someone in the back's been hurt—or something's happened because there had just been a nasty, great crump."[59] Jackson glanced over his shoulder. "What's the matter, Dapper?" he yelled. Dapper tapped his watch. "Happy Birthday!" he shouted. Jackson glanced at his watch and saw it was 12:01 a.m.[60]

The first subflight of three—led by Lieutenant Commander Eugene Esmonde—closed in. Esmonde planned to lead his formation around the *Bismarck* and attack from the starboard side with the setting sun behind them. The intensity of *Bismarck*'s fire, however, laid the plan to waste. With his aircraft damaged on its approach, Esmonde dropped his torpedo while his Swordfish remained airworthy.[61] The other two planes in his subflight followed suit, but not one found their mark.

The *Bismarck*, moving at 27 knots, zigzagged between the frothing torpedo trails. "This was almost an impossible task," wrote Müllenheim-Rechberg. "Some of the planes were only 2 meters above the water and did not release their torpedoes until they closed to 400 or 500 meters."[62]

One after the other, the Swordfish dropped their torpedoes. "Everything came at us," Bunce recalled. "Tracers of all types were flying past." The moment the torpedo hit the sea, Bunce's pilot swung the Swordfish around, providing Bunce a perfect—if terrifying—view of *Bismarck* and "every shell that was fired and every tracer that came towards me."[63]

Petty Officer Les Sayer, a telegraphist/air gunner, watched the *Bismarck* grow ever larger behind its shield of ceaseless fire. Shells continued to throw massive spouts of water 100 feet into the air. The Swordfish weaved between the violent, foaming columns, the frigid spray lacerating the plane and its crew. One eruption of water caught the underside of Sayer's Swordfish and stripped away its fabric skin. Sayer looked down, startled to see open air, churning waves, and the plane's torpedo between his feet.[64] The pilot of Sayer's plane, Lieutenant Commander Philip "Percy" Gick, unhappy with his angle of attack, decided to circle around for another pass—much to Sayer's dismay. "God," he thought, "we've been through all that and now we're going to have to do it all again."[65]

Gick attacked on the ship's starboard side with the setting sun burning a pallid gold behind him. He closed within 500 yards of the target, released the torpedo, and turned the battered Swordfish around to make his escape.[66] The plane skimmed the crest of the waves and then slowly gained altitude. As he kept his eyes on the *Bismarck*, its guns still throwing flame and steel, Sayer saw the ship's hull erupt in an explosion of water. The torpedo, he realized, had found its mark and struck amidships at the waterline.[67]

On board the *Bismarck*, the detonation and force of impact was heard and felt above the roar and concussion of the guns. Nuts and bolts blown loose in the engine room sparked and ricocheted off machinery, sending men ducking for cover. The explosion's shockwave rumbled through the lower decks and hurled sailors off their feet. Petty Officer Kurt Kirchberg flew with lethal force into "something hard" and became *Bismarck*'s first fatality.[68] The ship, for one horrifying moment, felt as though it was tipping to starboard before quickly righting itself. "Look here," shouted one sailor, "only the dear God can sink our ship!"[69]

The American Coast Guard crew on the *Modoc*, still glued to the proceedings, soon found themselves in a precarious situation. "Sail-ho!" the *Modoc*'s lookout cried. "On the starboard bow! Holy Jesus Cristo—lots of sails ho!"[70] The men turned to see the source of the lookout's excitement and were staggered by what appeared to be "the entire [British] Home Fleet . . . about equidistant from us as we were from the *Bismarck*." The men decided now was the ideal time to be somewhere else, and orders were given accordingly. "The engineers moved," wrote Sargent and Chiswell, "the vessel moved, and soon we were getting the hell out of there."[71]

The Swordfish—some trailing the tattered remnants of their fabric skins—groped their way through the encroaching darkness back to the fleet. As if by some miracle, not a single biplane had been lost in the action, yet they still faced the challenge of locating the *Victorious*. The fact the carrier's homing beacon was currently inoperable did little to help the situation.[72]

The men, exposed to the elements, flew through a whipsaw wind and lashing rains. "The weather," Pilot Officer Patrick Jackson said, in typical British understatement, "was very, very unpleasant."[73] The sea beneath them vanished into twilight and the horizon receded into darkness; the ships had disappeared in the fading light. "It's getting really cold back here," Sayer told Gick as the men peered through the rain for any sign of the fleet.[74]

By 1:55 a.m., the planes were an hour past due "and uncomfortably close to the end of their endurance."[75] They had overflown the carrier in the darkness. On board *Victorious*, Captain Henry Bovell ordered the ship's searchlights on and aimed vertically into the thick clouds—a daring move that risked exposing the ships to possible U-boats. Almost immediately, the task force's senior commander—Rear Admiral Alban Curteis on HMS *Galatea*—signaled *Victorious* to kill her lights. Bovell "acknowledged this instruction by using his brightest signal lamp" in hopes of guiding the Swordfish home.[76]

Cold and weary, their planes reduced to shreds, all Swordfish crews eventually landed safely.

✳ ✳ ✳

Bismarck **escaped the** Swordfish attack without major damage, but not without injury. Her violent maneuvering and the concussion of her guns weakened the watertight matting used to seal her damaged bow after the confrontation with *Hood*. The sea invaded once again. "The result," noted Müllenheim-Rechberg, "was that we were still more deeply down by the bow."[77] The damage caused by her evasive action proved more extensive than that caused by the torpedo hit, which was dismissed as "inconsequential."[78]

Lindemann ordered the ship's speed reduced to 16 knots to allow for repairs and turned his attention once more to reaching the safety of Saint-Nazaire.[79] It was now the early morning hours of Sunday, May 25—Gunther Lütjens's fifty-second birthday. Shortly before 12:30 a.m., a radio telegram arrived from Grand Admiral Raeder:

Heartiest Birthday Wishes! In view of your recent great armed feat, may you be granted many much more successes [as you enter] a new year of your life![80]

At 1:16 a.m., *Prince of Wales* and *Norfolk* reestablished faint visual contact with *Bismarck* on the port bow at a distance of eight miles. The British ships turned to port and brought their guns to bear. Admiral Wake-Walker ordered the *Prince of Wales* to engage. The battleship fired two salvos; *Bismarck* responded in kind before vanishing behind a cloud of funnel smoke.[81] Wounded and alone, she fled into the Arctic night with "four battleships, two battle cruisers, two aircraft carriers, three heavy cruisers, ten light cruisers, and twenty-one destroyers" in pursuit.[82]

✳ ✳ ✳

The giant swells of the North Atlantic thrashed hunter and hunted alike; rain fell hard and cold. "To step out onto the open deck," noted one sailor on *Prince of Wales*, "was like walking through a waterfall . . . it was a miserable night, fit only for howling banshees."[83]

On *Norfolk*'s bridge, Wake-Walker felt ill at ease. "I was in some doubt as to the best dispositions during the night," he later reported. He didn't fully trust the radar on the damaged *Prince of Wales*, and *Norfolk*'s older radar would lose contact with *Bismarck* should the German ship turn and position herself for a head-to-head confrontation. His best option was to order *Suffolk* "to act independently and keep touch with the enemy" while continually reporting *Bismarck*'s course and speed. Eleven miles of mountainous seas separated the two ships.[84]

With *Suffolk* leading the way, the *Norfolk* following behind in close support, and the *Prince of Wales* astern, the ships sailed in wide zigzags—steaming ten minutes to port and then ten minutes to starboard—to avoid U-boats. During the turn to port, *Bismarck* would temporarily fall off *Suffolk*'s radar but reappear when the British cruiser began its starboard turn.[85]

The monotonous vanishing-and-reappearing act continued until 3:06 in the morning when, as expected, *Suffolk* lost contact as she turned on the outward leg of her zigzag. Captain Robert Ellis, running on a compost of high tension, coffee, and pills from the ship's doctor after thirty hours on duty, stared from the bridge into the stormy night. He expected to see *Bismarck* reappear on his ship's radar at 3:30—but when the appointed moment arrived, the radar remained eerily silent. The *Bismarck* had vanished.[86]

Whether Lütjens pulled off a brilliant tactical move or simply got lucky is not known for sure. At three o'clock, temporarily released from the grip of *Suffolk*'s radar, Lütjens turned the *Bismarck* in a massive circle and increased his speed to 27 knots. The ship veered to the west, ultimately cutting behind the *Suffolk*, *Norfolk*, and *Prince of Wales*, before setting a course across the open Atlantic waters to France.[87]

The news of *Bismarck*'s disappearance proved a bitter blow—particularly for *Suffolk*'s crew, who had effectively served as the "eyes" of the British Fleet since the drama began. "By this time, the ship's company had been at action stations for 32 hours," wrote Lieutenant Paton on *Suffolk*. "We tried to snatch an hour's rest in turn if opportunity allowed."[88]

The British dispersed in search of their prey as the first glimmer of daybreak revealed itself on the horizon. Wake-Walker, examining his plotting table, believed "the enemy had made a large turn to starboard at about 0310 . . . I ordered *Suffolk* to search to the westward on this assumption."[89] The *Norfolk* would search on a course slightly to the north of the *Suffolk*, while the *Prince of Wales* would join the *King George V* to assist Admiral Tovey.[90]

The Home Fleet's commander in chief believed *Bismarck* had only two available options: flee to a port or make for an oil tanker to refuel at sea. If Lütjens planned to rendezvous with a tanker, he would most likely—Tovey theorized—order *Bismarck* northwest to the Davis Strait in the Labrador Sea, midway between Greenland and Baffin Island, "which offered an excellent hiding place for an oiler."[91] If *Bismarck*'s objective was a port, she would most likely be making for the North Sea or steaming on a southeasterly course for Brest, the Strait of Gibraltar, or the Atlantic port of Dakar in West Africa. "I had insufficient forces to search all the possible courses of the enemy," Tovey reported. "I therefore decided to cover the possibility that they were joining a tanker—a course more menacing to our interests than a run for home."[92]

Tovey spread his forces out. He dispatched *Victorious* and her four cruisers to search northwest of *Bismarck*'s last known position. The battleship *Rodney*—past her prime and in need of an overhaul—fired up her tired engines and steamed with three destroyers on a course to intercept *Bismarck* in the event she was bound for Brest. Although Tovey's combing of the seas proved futile, he did catch a faint scent of his prey at ten thirty that morning when he received a signal from the Admiralty.[93]

Hearing stations along the coasts of Britain, Iceland, and Gibraltar had picked up radio signals "that appeared to come from the same ship which had transmitted several signals soon after the torpedo-bomber attack of the night before."[94] The location of the "radio fingerprints,"[95] when plotted, placed the ship—assumed to be *Bismarck*—on a heading for the North Sea, probably attempting a return to Germany or Norway. "I broadcast this position of the enemy and instructed all Home Fleet forces to search accordingly," Tovey wrote. "The course of *King George V* was altered . . . to make for the Iceland-Faeroes gap."[96]

At noon on Sunday, May 25, Lütjens addressed the *Bismarck*'s crew over the ship's loudspeaker:

Soldiers of the battleship *Bismarck*! You have covered yourselves with glory! The sinking of the battle cruiser *Hood* has not only military, but also psychological value, for she was the pride of England. Henceforth, the enemy will try to concentrate his forces and bring them into action against us. I therefore released the *Prinz Eugen* at noon yesterday so that she could conduct commerce warfare on her own. She has managed to evade the enemy. We, on the other hand, because of the hits we have received, have been ordered to proceed to a French port. On our way there, the enemy will gather and give us battle. The German people are with you, and we will fight until our German gun barrels glow red-hot and the last shell has left the barrels. For us seamen, the question now is victory or death![97]

The words, with their undercurrent of defeat, rippled like a dark wave through the crew. Most of the sailors on board were young men assigned to *Bismarck* right out of training. They'd been at sea for no more than six weeks. The more seasoned men took pity on their younger colleagues. "We warrant and petty officers," said machinist Wilhelm Schmidt, "trusting in what fighting power we had left and in timely intervention by our long-range bombers, did everything we could to revive and sustain the men's morale."[98]

✳ ✳ ✳

While the *Bismarck* continued her solitary and desperate voyage, a twenty-year-old codebreaker named Jane Hughes arrived at Hut 6 on the sprawling grounds of the Bletchley Park estate another world away in Milton Keynes, Buckinghamshire.[99]

Fifty miles northwest of London, Bletchley Park is an ugly red-and-white slab of a mansion. Sir Hugh Sinclair, the head of MI6, purchased the house and fifty-eight acres of surrounding land in May 1938 to house Britain's code-breaking operations, formally known as the Government Code and Cypher School. It was here mathematician Alan Turing would lead the successful effort to crack the German "Enigma" code—and it was here Jane Hughes worked in Hut 6 as part of an all-female team tasked with intercepting and translating messages from the Luftwaffe and German army.[100]

Despite the important work done inside it, Hut 6 left a lot to be desired. "It was just horrid; there were very leaky windows," Jane later recalled, "so it was very cold with just a frightful old stove in the middle of the room that let out lots of fumes but not much heat, and just one electric bulb hanging on a string, which was quite inadequate. We were always working against time, there was always a crisis, a lot of stress, and a lot of excitement."[101]

Hughes did not set out in life to work for British intelligence. She dreamed of being a ballet dancer and attended the Royal Ballet School. Her dancing career fizzled before it even began when the school's principal told her she was too tall. Depressed, she sought solace overseas and moved to Zurich to study German before eventually returning to England.[102] In February 1940, the nineteen-year-old Hughes received a letter from a friend working at Bletchley Park. "Well, Jane," the letter read, "I'm at Bletchley and it's perfectly frightful. We're so overworked, so desperately busy. You must come and join us."[103] She took her friend up on the offer, was subsequently hired, and told her parents she now worked for the Foreign Office.[104]

Jane had only been at work for an hour on the afternoon of May 25, translating and typing out an intercepted message from Luftwaffe headquarters, when a reference to the *Bismarck* seized her attention. The signal in question was to a Luftwaffe general who had inquired as to the well-being of his son serving on the battleship. The response informed the general that *Bismarck* was heading to the French port of Brest. Jane alerted her superiors, who passed the communiqué up the military chain of command. It quickly reached the appropriate people at the Admiralty.[105]

The "radio fingerprints" intercepted from *Bismarck* were plotted once again in the Admiralty's operations room. Seven hours after Tovey had set a northerly course in pursuit of *Bismarck*, he received word from the Admiralty he was heading in the wrong direction. "As more information came in, it became apparent," Tovey noted in his official report, "that the enemy was making for a French port and had a start of about 100 miles; course was adjusted accordingly."[106]

✳ ✳ ✳

The PBY Catalina seaplane—a workhorse used for long-range patrol, rescue, and convoy escort operations—took off from Lough Erne in Northern Ireland at 3:25 on the morning of Monday, May 26, and climbed into a predawn sky thick with cloud. Rain splattered the windshield; strong winds from the northwest rattled the lumbering aircraft as it fought the elements for speed and height. The plane climbed to 3,000 feet, breaking through the cloud cover before turning for Ireland's west coast. At 4:30 a.m., the Catalina passed over Eagle Island—a small, uninhabited pile of rock off the northwest coast of Ireland—and headed out to sea.[107]

It took nearly seven hours for Ensign Leonard Smith, an American flyer, and RAF Pilot Officer Dennis Briggs to reach their assigned search area. Smith reported that the trip "was uneventful other than several course changes which were necessitated by weather conditions."[108] They arrived in their designated sector at ten o'clock to slightly improved weather conditions. Visibility beneath the clouds at 800 feet was eight to ten miles. The sea, charcoal gray, the wind whipping its surface white, stretched vast and empty beneath them. Smith started his search pattern and banked the great plane through a light mist.[109]

At 10:10 a.m., he spotted a ship eight miles off the Catalina's port side. The weather made it impossible to identify the vessel at such a distance. Smith pulled the plane's nose skyward and aimed for the clouds, keeping the mystery ship to port. He hoped to remain concealed in his approach, get close enough to make a positive identification, and then shadow the ship. As the plane climbed in a gentle starboard turn, Briggs left his station at the controls and moved to the wireless in the back to prepare a contact report. Smith guided the plane through the heavy cumulus and climbed to 2,000 feet before breaking cover.[110]

"I didn't do a very good job of driving the airplane," he later recalled, "so we came right out over that silly ship. I could have spit on it, and I thought, 'My God, what have we done?'"[111] The Catalina emerged from cloud "into a terrific anti-aircraft barrage [on] our starboard quarter."[112] Flak appeared like ugly blemishes against the clouds. Below, the *Bismarck* appeared as an angry, living thing, a violent white wake stretching out behind it like a tail, as the ship veered

90 degrees off its course.[113] One member of the crew came forward from the back to inform Smith "we were full of holes."[114]

Smith, not wasting time, dropped the Catalina's four depth charges lest a well-placed shot send them all up in a ball of flame. He pushed the throttle wide open, pulled hard on the yoke, and climbed in a series of sickening S turns.[115] Having transmitted his contact report, Briggs returned to the cockpit and strapped himself into his seat. No sooner had he done so, a piece of flak blew a two-inch hole directly beneath the plane's control panel, missed him by a matter of inches, and passed through the roof.[116]

The Catalina left the firestorm behind. Smith performed several sharp turns and tested the engines to ensure the plane remained airworthy. Convinced damage was negligible, he turned the Catalina around and attempted to locate *Bismarck* once more and shadow her—but all he saw below was empty sea.[117] It hardly mattered, for Briggs had already transmitted her location: "One battleship bearing 240 degrees five miles, course 150 degrees, my position 49 degrees 33' North, 21 degrees 47' West. Time of origin 10.30/26."[118]

The *Bismarck* had been found. The job done, Smith set a course for home.

CHAPTER 4

* * *

AVENGED

News of *Bismarck's* discovery reached the British fleet at 10:54 a.m. on Monday, May 26.[1] What ships remained in the hunting party were now steaming toward France. *Prince of Wales* had been forced to abandon the chase, as had *Victorious*, her four-destroyer escort, and the *Suffolk* to refuel in Iceland's Hvalfjord. *King George V* had 1,200 tons of fuel remaining—roughly 32 percent of her full capacity—and *Rodney* had enough to see her through until eight the following morning.[2]

With the loss of *Hood* and the *Prince of Wales* currently out of the fight, "*King George V* was the only effective capital ship remaining" in action.[3] The 4th Destroyer Flotilla—HMS *Sikh*, HMS *Zulu*, HMS *Maori*, the Polish destroyer *Piorun*, and the flagship HMS *Cossack*—steamed fast toward the chase, having been pulled from convoy duty.[4] Its commander, the aggressive Captain Philip Vian, gained notoriety in 1940 when he pursued the German tanker *Altmark* into neutral Norwegian waters and sent a raiding party on board to rescue 300 captured British merchant seamen.[5]

Bismarck was roughly 130 miles south of Tovey when he received the signal she'd been found. Admiral Somerville, commander of Force H—with the carrier *Ark Royal*, the battle cruiser *Renown*, the light cruiser *Sheffield*, and the heavy cruiser *Dorsetshire*—was forty miles northeast of the fleeing battleship. Tovey realized he had little chance of closing the distance without *Bismarck* reducing speed or somehow being thrown off course. "The only hope," he wrote, "lay in torpedo attacks by the aircraft of *Ark Royal*."[6]

Seas "known to be rising and falling 56 feet" presently battered the *Ark Royal*.[7] The carrier's deck, buffeted by a 35-mile-per-hour wind, shot upward on each foaming crest before crashing in a deep dive between the mountainous waves. The violent conditions strained the skills of the Swordfish crews returning from that morning's reconnaissance flight. As one plane made its approach, the deck came up beneath it and shattered the plane's undercarriage. The crew fortunately escaped without injury.[8] The planes, having flown in the general area where the Catalina crew spotted *Bismarck*, had also found the ship, now less than 800 miles from the French coast.[9]

Somerville, a popular commander known for his love of dirty jokes, hoped his force of antiquated biplanes might finish the job. "With any luck," he broadcast in a message to his crews, "we may be able to finish her before the Home Fleet arrives."[10] From his flagship the *Renown*, he ordered the light cruiser *Sheffield* south via signal lamp at 1:15 p.m. to shadow *Bismarck*. Captain Loben Maund, on the *Ark Royal*, did not receive word of the order. It would prove nearly calamitous.[11]

In the carrier's hangars, the fifteen Swordfish assigned to the noon reconnaissance flight "had been armed with torpedoes to meet any sudden demands for a striking force."[12] The miserable weather, however, delayed their takeoff. Not until 2:50 p.m. did the biplanes struggle down the deck against the elements. "The take offs were awesome in the extreme," recalled Sub-Lieutenant Charles Friend, an observer. "The aircraft, as their throttles were opened, instead of charging forward on a level deck were at one moment breasting a slippery slope and the next plunging downhill towards the huge seas ahead and below."[13]

One by one, fighting the wind and rain, the Swordfish—led by Commander J. A. Stewart-Moore—gained air. From *Ark Royal*'s bridge, Maund watched the planes disappear into the gray, swirling sky. "Weather was particularly bad in the vicinity of the target," notes the official report, "and reliance was placed in [a radar set] carried in one of the aircraft." At 3:50 p.m., the radar-equipped Swordfish located a ship "20 miles from the expected position of the enemy."[14]

Stewart-Moore—an observer in the lead aircraft—peered into the iron-colored void. A break in the clouds soon revealed the mist-blurred glimpse of a warship. As far as he knew, there were no British ships in the area—none were mentioned in that afternoon's briefing aboard *Ark Royal*. The planes dropped through the clouds and swarmed the ship. Its guns, much to Stewart-Moore's puzzlement, did not open fire. Something seemed off. "It's the *Sheffield*!" Stewart-Moore's pilot, Lieutenant Hugh de Graaff Hunter, yelled and pulled hard on the plane's yoke.[15]

On *Sheffield*'s bridge, Captain C. A. A. Larcom ordered engines full ahead. Only three of the twelve aircraft realized their mistake; the other nine released their torpedoes. Larcom deftly maneuvered the cruiser between the bubbling trails in the water. "It was certainly a frightening affair," recalled the *Sheffield*'s pilot, Charles Fenwick. "The last straw came when one of our own Swordfish, having dropped its torpedo, flew across our bow and sprayed us with its rear gun."[16]

The *Sheffield*'s guns remained mercifully silent through the ordeal, though Larcom paced the bridge "purple with rage."[17] The Swordfish, their crews humiliated, returned to *Ark Royal*. Stewart-Moore, in his report, gave voice to his frustration. "It was a perfect attack," he wrote. "Right height, right range, right cloud cover, right speed, and the wrong fucking ship."[18]

The planes refueled without delay and were armed with torpedoes "set to run at 22 feet."[19] Beyond the cavernous confines of *Ark Royal*'s hangar, the dull-colored day began its slow surrender to night. To the south, on the *Sheffield*, Sub-Lieutenant Paul McLaughlan—the officer of the watch—surveyed the darkening horizon. At 5:40 p.m., he spotted through his binoculars the *Bismarck* ten miles off the starboard bow. Sub-Lieutenant Colin Ross received word at his battle station in *Sheffield*'s forward turret. "We were all ready to loose off," he later wrote, "but we didn't fire as we could have no effect at that range and, anyway, we were only required to shadow." Ross turned to his turret captain. "Every ship in the navy must be plotting us on their charts now," he said. "If we lose him, we'll never be able to lift our heads again."[20]

The weather had improved little by the time the fifteen Swordfish on *Ark Royal* were once more ready for action. Strong winds continued to assault the deck as the carrier heaved in forty-four-foot waves.[21] "The wind hit you like a hammer, threatening to knock you down," remembered one pilot. "The deck crews were really struggling with the aircraft; spray was coming over the side and the waves were breaking over the front of the flight deck."[22] The beleaguered aircraft—now led by Lieutenant Commander Tim Coode—took to the skies at 7:10 p.m. with the waves grasping at each plane's undercarriage. They arranged themselves in the ever-darkening tumult above *Ark Royal* into six subflights and set off on their hunt.[23]

The planes struggled through a punishing wind before locating the *Sheffield*. The ship's signal lamp, flashing into the murk, relayed the *Bismarck*'s location on a bearing of "110 degrees, 12 miles" to the south.[24] The planes turned accordingly and began their run toward the enemy. "We started our climb to get some height for our attacking dive," remembered Lieutenant Edmund "Splash" Carver, the observer in Coode's plane. "In doing so, we entered much denser cloud and, as a result, [the] sub-flights became separated."[25]

The men carried on undaunted. It was not long before Coode believed he was well positioned to attack *Bismarck* from astern. With the three planes of his subflight—and one that had become separated from its group—Coode dropped below the cloud. The cold, gray miasma gave way to a view of churning sea. The aircraft emerged from their cover, not astern of the target, but four miles in front of the ship and fighting against a strong headwind. "We came out of the cloud base at about 700 feet," remembered Carver. "Immediately, all the AA weapons opened up. It was a very impressive, and frightening, volume of glowing billiard balls flashing past."[26]

✵ ✵ ✵

The alarm on *Bismarck* voiced its warning at 8:30 p.m. The ship, in the words of one crewman, "became a spitting mountain of fire."[27] Her guns stabbed the sky with flame and metal as Coode—and the others who had descended below the clouds—once more sought cover to find a better angle of attack.

Other Swordfish soon approached on her starboard beam, or swooped around her stern to target her port side. Some braved the tempest in twos and threes; others did so individually. Bismarck's guns thundered without respite, the noise a merciless head-pounding assault. Many of her gun crews had been on duty since she left the safety of Norwegian waters and now struggled against a relentless exhaustion. One gun-layer, a Bismarck survivor reported, overcome by the noise and the ceaseless hours of tension, lost his mind at his post.[28]

Lieutenant Commander John Moffat followed Coode on his second attack run, but the thick cloud made it impossible for the planes to maintain formation and the two became separated. Two explosions battered Moffat's Swordfish as he dove through the heavy overcast. For one horrifying moment, he feared his plane might tumble from the sky, but it held steady as the sea materialized beneath him. Bismarck lay roughly two miles away on Moffat's starboard beam.[29]

"Even at this distance," he wrote, "the brute seemed enormous to me—this was a huge ship." He aimed his Swordfish for Bismarck's bow, his eyes glued to the massive tongues of flame leaping from the ship's guns.[30] He could hear the cannonade over the screaming wind and the noise of his plane's Pegasus engine. "It was utter confusion," wrote Moffat. "I felt that every gun on the ship was aiming at me. . . . I do not know how I managed to keep flying into it: every instinct was screaming at me to duck, turn away, do anything—an impulse that it was hard to fight off."[31]

The airspace in front of the plane appeared awash in burning color as countless tracer rounds blazed a furious path against the evening sky and sea. The controls shaking in his hand, Moffat brought the Swordfish down to fifty feet above the waves and held her steady. The Bismarck grew ever larger, its guns louder, and the fiery bursts propelling the shells into the air more vibrant. All he craved was to hear his observer give the go-ahead to drop the bloody torpedo. Finally, Moffat heard the blessed words yelled in his ear: "Let her go, Jock!"[32]

He did as instructed and turned the Swordfish around, keeping low to the sea to avoid *Bismarck*'s big guns. As the ship—its shells still splashing into the water—receded behind him, Moffat pulled the Swordfish back into the clouds and set a course for the *Ark Royal*.[33]

Lieutenant Commander Ken Pattison and Lieutenant "Feather" Godfrey-Faussett, having lost sight of their subflight in a snow squall, dove through cloud with ice on their wings, the wind a cold razor's edge against their faces. Their planes broke cover at 900 feet, the sea a foaming cataract beneath them, and aimed for *Bismarck*. Antiaircraft fire peeled away the canvas skin of the planes and pummeled the waves.[34]

Pattison and Godfrey-Faussett held steady on their course, their Swordfish being picked apart around them—but the violent weather favored the attackers. A strong northwesterly wind, building over the course of the day, had whipped the sea into a frenzy, rocking the *Bismarck* and thwarting the accuracy of her fire. Her guns hurled shells into the water to detonate the torpedoes slicing toward her. The warship heaved violently one way and then another to avoid the on-slaught of bubbling trails in the water. At his position in the aft fire control tower, Müllenheim-Rechberg watched the rudder indicator swing back and forth. It never stopped moving.[35]

Pattison and Godfrey-Faussett dropped their planes to 90 feet above the sea, their fuselages peppered with holes and trailing shredded can-vas. Nine hundred yards from *Bismarck*, they released their torpedoes and turned to make their escape.[36]

Seaman Corporal Georg Herzog, from his station at a portside anti-aircraft gun, watched the two torpedoes approach *Bismarck*'s stern. "I felt a severe shock in the ship," he later recalled. "I also saw a high col-umn of water off the astern portside."[37] Müllenheim-Rechberg heard the explosion at the back of the ship and shot a frightful glance at the rudder indicator. It was stuck at "left 12 degrees."[38]

He stared at it for what seemed an eternity, hoping to see it move. It didn't. As if to accompany his surge of despair, a message crack-led through the ship: "Rudder machinery inoperable. Rudder is jammed to starboard."[39] *Bismarck* was stuck turning in a wide circle.

At 10:40 p.m., Lütjens signaled German naval headquarters: "Ship un-maneuverable. We will fight until the last shot is expended. Long live the Führer."[40]

✳ ✳ ✳

The battered Swordfish turned for *Ark Royal* at 9:25 p.m. *Sheffield* had lost sight of *Bismarck* during the air assault and used radar to track her movements. At 9:30 p.m., the two ships reestablished visual contact at 18,000 yards. *Bismarck* responded with six salvos from her 15-inch guns.[41]

"The first salvo," remembered one sailor on *Sheffield*, "burst near the ship, which gave a vicious whipping movement."[42] The men on deck dropped to the ground as massive columns of water blew skyward. The noise was deafening. "An enormous black curtain rose in front of me," wrote one able seaman, "and never before or after have I heard a sound of more terrifying quality."[43]

Metal splinters from *Bismarck*'s shells scarred the bridge, sparked off guns, and cut through fourteen men—three of whom would ultimately die from their wounds. And no sooner had the engagement began, it ended without *Sheffield* firing a single shot, as *Bismarck*—her steering damaged—turned away.[44]

✳ ✳ ✳

Admiral Sir John Tovey on the *King George V*, having recently been joined by the battleship *Rodney* and her escort of three destroyers, was still 100 miles north of *Bismarck*. He had reduced his speed to 22 knots to conserve what limited fuel he had left. Unless things changed, he would have to surrender the chase at midnight and return home for refueling.[45]

The *Rodney* would have to do likewise by eight the following morning. Tovey still hoped the torpedo bombers would slow *Bismarck* down and allow him to stay in the game. Beyond the salt-and-rain-streaked windows of the bridge, Tovey watched night gather above the leaden sea.[46]

The mood on the bridge remained morose until 9:36 p.m., when a signal arrived from the *Sheffield* saying *Bismarck* was not holding a steady course and that her steering appeared to be damaged. "Hope," notes the Royal Navy's official battle summary, "shone out anew."[47] Tovey set a course to intercept *Bismarck* from the east, hoping to use the oncoming night to his advantage—but the weather continued to deteriorate. "I therefore decided to withdraw," he later noted, "and engage [the enemy] from the westward at dawn."[48]

✳ ✳ ✳

"For about an hour and a half after the air attack," wrote Müllenheim-Rechberg, "the battle zone around the *Bismarck* was deserted. Then, somewhere before 2300 we saw destroyers."[49]

The ships in question belonged to Commander Vian's 4th Destroyer Flotilla. The Polish destroyer *Piorun* closed to 13,500 yards and opened fire. *Bismarck* responded in her own thunderous way, sending up plumes of water twenty yards off *Piorun*'s port and starboard sides. Aggressive in spirit but hopelessly outgunned, the Polish ship retreated behind a smoke screen. The brief engagement underscored Vian's dilemma: should he shadow *Bismarck* or attempt to sink her in the night with torpedoes?[50]

Tovey made the ultimate decision and ordered Vian's force to keep track of *Bismarck* until daybreak. Vian, however, would do his utmost to ensure a long and torturous night for the German crew.[51]

Between 1:22 and 1:46 that morning, the destroyers *Cossack*, *Zulu*, and *Maori* attacked multiple times with torpedoes, but the rough seas and *Bismarck*'s erratic course frustrated any chance of accuracy. The grim reality of their situation had by now become an inescapable fact for *Bismarck*'s crew. "We would have totally illogical flashes of hope," remembered Müllenheim-Rechberg, "that despite everything we were going to escape. . . . But the destroyers always came back, and the noise of our guns brought us back to the immutable present."[52]

British star shells flared with grating frequency above the ship and burned away its nocturnal cover, turning the sea to mercury. The night seemed to stretch on forever; the thought of daybreak delivered no comfort. "The minutes crept past," wrote Müllenheim-Rechberg. "It didn't seem to want to pass, this sinister night of waiting, and waiting for nothing but the end."[53]

Not even a predawn message from Hitler could rouse the crew's despondent spirits. "I thank you in the name of the entire German nation," the message read. "To the crew of the battleship *Bismarck*! All of Germany stands by you. Whatever can still be set in motion will be done. Your devotion to duty will inspire our nation in the fight for its existence."[54]

The morning of Tuesday, May 27, dawned cold and gray. Tovey, realizing the enemy remained "a formidable opponent . . . still capable of heavy and accurate fire," opted to wait until full light before closing in for the kill.[55] Admiral Wake-Walker, approaching from the north on *Norfolk*, caught sight of her—"a dark grey blot of a large ship"—first at 7:53 a.m.[56]

He initially mistook the ship for *Rodney* and was prepping to send her a signal when he realized the vessel's true identity. He promptly ordered *Norfolk* to turn away and reported the sighting to Tovey. "We could have fired at *Bismarck*," Wake-Walker later wrote, "but I felt it unwise to irritate her unnecessarily before she had someone else to distract her attention."[57] At 8:15 a.m., *Norfolk*'s lookout spotted the destroyers *Mashona* and *Tartar* five miles away and approaching as they emerged from the rain, followed three minutes later by the *Rodney* and *King George V*.[58]

Tovey finally laid eyes on his ultimate prize at 8:43 a.m. He hoped the sight of *Rodney* and *King George V*, steaming headlong into battle, "would shake the nerves of [*Bismarck*'s] range-takers and control officers, who had already had four anxious days and nights." Tovey hoped to quickly close the distance between himself and the enemy "to a range at which rapid hitting could be ensured."[59]

On the *Bismarck*, alarms bellowing, men readied themselves for battle, knowing full well their destruction was at hand.[60]

From *Bismarck*'s foretop, first gunnery officer Lieutenant Commander Adalbert Schneider ordered the main and secondary batteries aimed at *Rodney*—but the British ship commenced hostilities. *Rodney*'s 16-inch guns opened fire at 8:47 a.m. from 25,000 yards, followed one minute later by *King George V*. Their shells sent columns of water 150 feet into the air as *Bismarck* turned to starboard and returned fire with her forward turret.[61]

Her first two salvos fell short, but her third and fourth straddled *Rodney* with only 20 yards to spare. "Her fire was accurate at the start," wrote Tovey, "though it soon began to fall off. In view of the damage she had suffered and the strain of the past few days, this was hardly a matter of surprise. She made continual alterations of course, but it is doubtful whether these were deliberate."[62]

Smoke hung thick and heavy above the waves, obscuring visibility, but the guns on both sides roared and flamed unabated. With the two British battleships attacking on *Bismarck*'s port side, *Norfolk*—approaching from the starboard bow—joined the fray five minutes in. The *Dorsetshire* opened fire at 9:04 a.m.[63] The range between *Bismarck*, *Rodney*, and *King George V* had by now decreased amidst the cacophony and smoke to 11,500 yards. Shell after shell hammered *Bismarck*, thrashing her upper deck into a tangle of burning, snarled metal, and blowing holes in her two yards wide.[64]

"By 0930," noted Tovey, "*Bismarck* was on fire and virtually out of control. But she was still going about the same speed; her guns were still firing—and her secondary armament had now come into action."[65]

Bismarck was a burning charnel house. Her guns failed to inflict any significant damage on her attackers. British shells pierced her upper deck and detonated in the ship's bowels, rendering her lower decks a nightmare of gore and wreckage. A direct hit blew to pieces 200 men trapped in the canteen. Crews trapped in two magazines drowned when the chambers had to be flooded to extinguish fires threatening ammunition stores.[66] Everywhere was blood-soaked carnage. The British guns continued to inflict their dreadful punishment. The air "was dense with smoke, fumes, and the gases generated by bursting shells."[67]

Steam pipes ruptured and scalded the flesh off men; paint bubbled and blistered on the bulkheads. The screaming of the wounded and dying drew little sympathy from those fighting for survival. One crewman would later recall having to slog his way through "mountains of flesh and bone."[68] Conditions on the smoke-choked, blood-slicked deck proved to be no better. The gaping holes left by shells posed as lethal a hazard as the incoming enemy fire.[69]

Beyond the screams and flames, across a relatively short stretch of sea, *Rodney* and *King George V* closed to 3,300 yards "to increase the rate of hitting."[70] *Bismarck*, her guns finally silent, presented a fiery nightmare by 10:15 a.m. and was listing badly with her mainmast completely gone and her superstructure ablaze. "Men could be seen jumping overboard," wrote Tovey, "preferring death by drowning in the stormy sea to the appalling effects of our fire."[71]

At 10:24 a.m., the *Dorsetshire* launched two torpedoes into *Bismarck*'s starboard side. She steamed around the tortured, flaming wreck and fired another into the ship's port side to deliver the final and fatal blow.[72]

Otto Peters, a stoker on *Bismarck*, emerged from the lower decks as the ship suffered her ordeal. "I looked around and the devastation was awful," he said. "Everything had been shot away and masses and masses of dead comrades lay around."[73] As jumping into the wind-swept sea offered little chance of survival, Peters decided to remain on board and try his luck. It didn't last long. A dark wave swept over the now half-submerged ship and threw him into the water. His life vest brought him up to the surface. Some part of his mind registered the frigid temperatures, but the adrenaline coursing through his body numbed him to the cold.[74]

"I was thinking about my girlfriend in Hamburg," he later said, "and how I had to stay alive to see her again." Peters, unlike other men in the water, was lucky to not be surrounded by oil. The men called to one another as they struggled to stay afloat, saying whoever survived should contact the loved ones of those who didn't. "I was near one guy I knew well who wasn't saved," Peters said, "and afterwards I wrote a letter to his parents."[75]

Johannes Zimmermann, also a stoker, was in one of the boiler rooms when the British shells began to land. He made his way to the upper deck and discovered a scene of horror. "The sight of it was terrible," he said. "Blood and pieces of comrades. You couldn't tell what came from one man and what came from the other."[76]

The ship rolled over as he tried to comprehend the hellscape around him. The deck tipped at a perilous angle and threw Zimmermann off his feet. He slid toward the sea, unable to stop his descent. He hit the water and was tossed about like a piece of flotsam. He saw other men flailing around him as waves crashed over them. He struggled to stay afloat and fought to move his arms and legs in the thick, oily water, his mouth bitter with its taste.[77]

He was still close enough to *Bismarck* to reach out and grab her upper deck, but his oil-coated hand couldn't get a firm grip on anything. He tried repeatedly to climb out of the sea, only to keep sliding back down. The only thing to do now was swim away from the wreckage. "I was swimming alongside a friend of mine who was a neighbor from home," he later recalled. "We had gone to the same school. He died in that water."[78]

Müllenheim-Rechberg waited until the British stopped firing before he left his station and made his way to *Bismarck*'s deck. "The destruction round about was frightful," he wrote. "Everything up to the bridge bulwarks had been erased. Stumps indicated the columns on which nautical apparatus had once rested."[79] He congregated with other men near a shattered turret on the ship's starboard side and watched as the water edged closer up the hull. It was time to jump.[80]

He pulled on his life jacket, saluted the ship's flag, and plunged overboard. He hit the water and swam as hard as he could to escape the ship's pull.[81] He soon found himself floating alongside another sailor from his action station. "Careful, careful," the man said, "don't get too close to me. I've lost a foot." Müllenheim-Rechberg tried to reassure his stricken comrade all would be well once the British pulled them from the water, but it was too late. The man, bleeding and frozen, surrendered himself to the sea.[82]

Leading Stoker Bruno Rzonca passed several crewmen sitting on a bench as he made his way up to the deck. Why, he asked, were they not moving? "There is no ship coming," one replied. "The water is too cold; the waves are too high. We are going down with the ship."[83] Time, Rzonca knew, was too precious to convince them otherwise and kept going. He worked his way through the cramped, narrow bowels

of the ship and made his way up. He stopped to try and help one sailor
with both heels blown off, but the injured man insisted on being left
alone. When Rzonca finally made it deck side, he recoiled at the abat-
toir before him: shattered bodies and severed limbs everywhere, and
the deck a sticky crimson mess.[84]

He ran for cover behind a 6-inch gun turret, its base thick with
twisted corpses. The ship began to list violently to port. Rzonca, on
the starboard side, fought against the deck's steepening angle before
deciding it was time to sink or swim. "I took off my heavy leather suit
and jumped into the water," he recalled. "I thought this should be the
end. I was only 23 years old and starting my life; I was engaged, and
there was no chance to save myself."[85]

He plummeted fifty feet into the sea, the freezing impact knocking the air from his lungs. He forced himself to move and kicked
away from the sinking ship, putting about 100 feet of violent sea between himself and *Bismarck* before he dared look back. She was now
almost completely on her port side. He watched two men fling themselves off the ship's side. They failed, on launch, to push themselves
out far enough and hit the hull on the way down before slamming
into the ship's stabilizer. Their limp bodies dropped into the waves
and disappeared. Rzonca, having seen enough, turned once more to
swim.[86]

An hour passed before the *Dorsetshire* appeared in the valleys between the rolling swell with her rescue lines dragging in the water.
The nets and ropes hanging down her side were slick with oil and hard
to grasp. The ship's drastic up-and-down movement on the waves did
nothing to make things easier. Müllenheim-Rechberg grabbed a rope
and hauled himself up but lost his grip and tumbled back into the sea.
He tried again, grasping tight with tired hands, and saw two British
sailors staring down at him from the deck above. "Please," he said,
"pull me on board."[87] They hauled him from the water, his muscles
screaming as he held tight to the lifeline. And then he felt solid ground
beneath his feet. He stood on the deck of the British ship, a prisoner of
war in a uniform reduced to oily rags.[88]

Rzonca pulled himself through the freezing water in a ceaseless
fight against waves that towered feet above him. He could see nothing

but gray sea and men floundering in the deep. The sounds of battle still raged about him. "That was," he would later say with great under-statement, "the worst part of my life."[89] Certain he was all but dead, he began to pray. As if in answer, a ship with a British flag fluttering from its mainmast appeared in the near distance. He turned to a man strug-gling next to him and pointed to their possible salvation. The sailor, despite his desperate circumstance, was incredulous. "I don't want to do anything with the British," he said through a mouthful of saltwater. "They want to shoot." It was the last Rzonca saw of him.[90]

From *Dorsetshire*'s bridge, Captain B. C. S. Martin could see hun-dreds of men floundering in the waves. "I then steamed to where the men in the water were thickest and stopped," Martin wrote. "Every available officer and man in *Dorsetshire* was employed throwing life-lines with bowlines, trailing grass hawsers with rafts and buoys at-tached, over the side and hauling survivors inboard."[91]

Half-drowned men clawed at the ship's glistening sides before let-ting go and sinking from view. "The survivors were in many cases unable to help themselves," Martin wrote, "a large number of them dying when close alongside the ship."[92] Chief Electrical Artificer John Wheeler, having left his station to witness *Bismarck*'s final moments, was stunned by the "mass of bobbing heads" in the "raging sea."[93]

Rzonca made a desperate grab for one of the ropes and clung to it for dear life. His muscles flaring, his fingers numb with cold, he pulled himself up the rope until he felt hands grab at his clothing and pull him on deck. They removed the tattered remains of his uniform and wrapped him in a blanket before taking him downstairs and plying him with whiskey. "I had swallowed some of the oil in the water," Rzonca said. "The whiskey was better."[94]

Fighting to keep his head above water, Otto Peters watched *Bis-marck* in her final death throes. Flames writhed and reached outward from her sides as she rolled over and slipped beneath the surface. The time was 10:37 a.m.[95] He now saw the *Dorsetshire* moving slowly through the swell. "I thought," Peters confessed, "I was going to be killed."[96] Several attempts to climb the side of the ship failed, until a wave pushed him into the outstretched arms of British sailors. He would spend the rest of the war in a POW camp.[97]

Likewise, Johannes Zimmermann was eventually pulled aboard the *Dorsetshire*. A British sailor offered him a large bottle of gin to help calm the nerves. Zimmermann pulled deeply from the bottle and felt his gut twist in immediate protest. "All my insides came out," he remembered, "all salty water—everything. Since then, I've never touched gin."[98]

Martin stood on the port wing of the bridge and directed the rescue operation. Eighty survivors had been hauled aboard when he received word from the compass platform of a "suspicious smoky discharge"[99] two miles away on the starboard beam. Fearing it might be a submarine, Martin later wrote, "I was reluctantly compelled to leave some hundreds of the enemy personnel to their fate."[100]

With its engines at full power, *Dorsetshire* fled the scene. Wheeler stood at the railing and grieved for the men being left behind. "What a dreadful sight it was to see all the remaining survivors left to their fate and to hear their screams," he later recalled. "Eleven months later, I spent 30 hours in the water in the Indian Ocean after the *Dorsetshire* was sunk by Japanese aircraft. I still recall what those sailors, enemy or not, must have felt."[101]

Of the 2,131 men on the *Bismarck*, only 115 survived. The Royal Navy had successfully avenged *Hood*, a ship that never really stood a chance against the likes of *Bismarck*. In the end, it was the commander in chief of the British Fleet who provided *Bismarck* and her men with a fitting epitaph. "The *Bismarck* put up a most gallant fight against impossible odds worthy of the old days of the Imperial German Navy," Tovey wrote, "and she went down with her colors still flying."[102]

Her power and destructive potential immense, *Bismarck*'s reign of terror proved short-lived. She nevertheless inflicted a deep and bloody wound on the British psyche. In avenging the *Hood*'s death, the Royal Navy eliminated Germany's greatest threat on the waves and gave Churchill's beleaguered island a significant and symbolic victory against Hitler's war machine.

CHAPTER 5

* * *

CERBERUS

At the beginning of June, the *Prinz Eugen*—her engines in need of an overhaul—joined the *Scharnhorst* and *Gneisenau* in Brest. Heavy camouflage netting obscured the ships by day; a thick smoke screen settled over their berths at night. It did little to deter the RAF. So often were the ships attacked, their crews christened the beleaguered trio the "Brest Bomb Target Flotilla."[1]

A nighttime ritual played out with grating regularity. "The sirens howled their warning over the rooftops of the harbor town," remembered Lieutenant Commander Fritz-Otto Busch, who served on *Prinz Eugen*, "while alarm bells and gongs sounded in the coastal A.A. batteries all round. On board the three ships, the aircraft alarm bell sent out its familiar nerve-racking shriek."[2] Beams of blue and white light canvassed the sky for the machines overhead. The detonation of bombs and the crashing of antiaircraft batteries overpowered everything; noise and fire was all there was until the bombers, relieved of their high explosives and incendiaries, turned for home. By July 10, 1941, the RAF had bombed the French port sixty-nine times.[3]

On the night of July 1, one of the fifty-two attacking aircraft—a twin-engined Wellington—crashed in a fiery tangle alongside the *Prinz Eugen*. An armor-piercing bomb, believed to be from the downed aircraft, struck the warship on her port side and wiped out "the switch room, amplifier compartment, compass department, and gunnery transmitting station." It killed fifty-one of her crew and wounded another thirty-two.[4] The extensive damage would keep *Prinz Eugen* out of action for the remainder of the year.

The Germans, although they occupied the port, relied on French manpower out of necessity to keep it running. A French naval lieutenant named Jean Philippon worked in the dockyard, maintaining its gardens—a task he picked for himself as it did nothing to actively help the enemy. The job gave him free access to roam anywhere, which, in turn, enabled him to observe German activity in the dock. "Philippon's sensitive ears," notes one account, "absorbed a good deal of information."[5]

The intelligence Philippon mentally cataloged could not help the French situation, but it might prove useful to the British—and therein lay a matter of personal conflict. He harbored little affection for Britain. His animosity was born the previous July when the Royal Navy attacked the French fleet in the Algerian port of Oran. The raid seriously damaged the battle cruiser *Dunkerque*, the battleship *Provence*, and several destroyers. The 26,000-ton battleship *Bretagne*, suffering grievous wounds, rolled over and sank with a heavy loss of life. Nearly 1,300 French sailors died in the attack—an action of last resort ordered by Churchill to keep French warships out of German hands. An ardent Francophile, Churchill later described the action as a "hateful decision, the most unnatural and painful in which I have ever been concerned."[6]

Yet as much as Philippon hated the British, he hated the Germans more—so when a family friend, and member of the French Resistance, convinced Philippon to become an agent for British Naval Intelligence, he agreed to do so and quickly proved his worth.[7]

In early July, he informed London that a large order of supplies had been placed for *Scharnhorst* with a delivery date set for July 20. The British Admiralty knew this meant *Scharnhorst* was preparing to put to sea. On July 21, the battleship slipped unnoticed out of Brest and traveled to La Pallice, a seaport in the town of La Rochelle on the Bay of Biscay to the south. Powered by her refurbished engines, she cut easily through the water at 30 knots and safely made the 240-mile journey. The Germans placed an old tanker in the *Scharnhorst*'s vacated anchorage at Brest and concealed it with camouflage netting.[8]

The ploy hardly had time to work. An RAF reconnaissance Spitfire photographed *Scharnhorst* at La Pallice on July 23.[9]

Fearing the ship was preparing to wreak havoc once more in the North Atlantic, the RAF threw six Stirling bombers from No. 7 Squadron at her that evening. Six Messerschmitts tormented the raiders over the target area and knocked one, billowing smoke and flame, into the sea. One Stirling, however, managed to score a direct hit.[10]

The next day, Thursday, July 24, the RAF went all out. The bombers appeared in brilliant relief against a clear afternoon sky. One hundred aircraft—including three American-built Flying Fortresses in RAF colors—swept over Brest.[11] The Fortresses commenced the attack shortly after two o'clock and bombed from 30,000 feet. "The black bursts [of flak]," noted one Fortress pilot, "looked from a distance like a huge flock of starlings."[12] Their 1,100-pound payloads, slamming into the dock, harbor, and quaysides, buffeted the *Prinz Eugen* in "plumes of water, concrete, and flame."[13]

Furious antiaircraft fire and a swarm of enemy fighters, which seemed to materialize out of nowhere, bled the attacking formations that followed. Far beneath the vapor trails left by the Fortresses, eighteen Hampdens and seventy-nine Wellingtons collided with Messerschmitts in a savage tangle, yet crews still managed to drop their bombs. Explosions trampled across the port as the aerial battle raged for more than an hour. In the twisting, diving tumult, two Hampdens and ten Wellingtons went down. Although crews would report hitting *Gneisenau* six times, the claims could not be substantiated.[14]

Over La Pallice, fifteen Halifaxes from Nos. 35 and 76 Squadrons waged their own desperate struggle against the *Scharnhorst*. "On approach to target area," notes an operations report, "a very heavy barrage of AA fire was immediately put up, and some thirty enemy fighters were observed, some in the air, others taking off from aerodromes in and about La Rochelle." The weather was "excellent, brilliant sunshine and no cloud, with perfect visibility."[15] Perfect hunting weather.

The Halifaxes attacked in echelons but the murderous fire from the ground and the strafing fighters unglued the bomber formations and left individual aircraft easy prey. "The sky turned black with all the smoke from the bursting shells," wrote Sergeant Ernie Constable, a wireless operator on Halifax L9512 TL-U, "and the acrid smell of cordite filled the interiors of the aircraft. The enemy fighters, paying little heed to their own flak, made repeated attacks. The gunners in the Halifaxes fought back fiercely as the fighters came in."[16] One bomber went "down in a slow spiral with smoke coming from one or two of its engines."[17]

Every crew succeeded in dropping their bombs, but "shell bursts, evasive action, and damage permitted no reasonable sighting." The German fighters continued to wreak bloody havoc. "Sgt. Bolton, the first operator of the leader's aircraft, was killed and the second pilot injured," notes a No. 35 Squadron combat summary. "Pilot Officer Stone, tail gunner of another aircraft, was killed by cannon fire which went on to rake the aircraft and injure both beam gunners. Another wireless operator was wounded, seriously, and another tail gunner slightly wounded."[18]

The pilot of Constable's Halifax, Flight Sergeant Stanley Greaves, asked his crew if they wouldn't mind another pass at *Scharnhorst* after the bombardier managed to release only half the plane's payload. The crew voiced its unanimous approval. The plane thundered over the target and dropped its remaining bombs. It was the only plane "seen to obtain a direct hit," according to a squadron report. "This aircraft did not return to base."[19]

Seven Bf 109s pounced on the Halifax as it made its second run. "Gilly" Gillbanks, the rear gunner, had no shortage of targets and sent two Messerschmitts spinning away. Cannon fire raked the length of the aircraft, injuring both beam gunners in the legs and Gillbanks in the face. Enemy fire blew through the cockpit, puncturing metal and shattering the Perspex windows, the shards burying themselves in Sergeant Greaves's face. The second pilot took a round in the ankle.[20]

"By this time three engines were on fire and the fuselage looked like a colander," Constable wrote. "It was a miracle that anyone survived the ceaseless onslaught." Despite his injuries, Greaves wrestled the controls to keep the aircraft level and ordered everyone to bail out. Greaves dropped last through the escape hatch and plummeted into the sky just as the plane vaporized in a ball of flame. The Germans rounded up the downed crew. After receiving medical treatment, they were dispatched to POW camps and spent the rest of the war in captivity. Greaves would later be awarded the Distinguished Flying Medal for his actions that day.[21]

Five of the fifteen Halifaxes never made it home; the surviving ten suffered varying degrees of damage. Eight of those ten aircraft "returned to their bases with twenty-one dead or wounded men on-board."[22] It was not in vain. The *Scharnhorst* took five direct hits. Three armor-piercing bombs "passed straight through the ship, leaving small holes in the bottom only." Two bombs detonated and flooded her bowels with up to 7,000 tons of water.[23]

His ship having sunk three feet, Captain Kurt-Caesar Hoffmann decided it best to move *Scharnhorst* back to the more heavily fortified harbor at Brest. The ship steamed from La Pallice at seven o'clock that evening and made 20 knots back to her previous anchorage. Although still seaworthy, she was hardly fit for operations. The damage inflicted would take at least four months to repair.[24]

But even Brest, bristling with all its defenses, remained a favorite RAF target. Between August 1 and December 31, British bombers "dropped nearly 1,200 tons of high explosives" on the port.[25]

✳ ✳ ✳

The new year, 1942, brought with it no signs of relief from the RAF. On the night of January 6, a bomb fell between *Gneisenau*'s starboard side and the dock, peeling away her outer plating and causing extensive flooding.[26]

Six days later at Hitler's Wolf's Lair, Vice Admiral Otto Ciliax presented a plan to break the ships out of Brest. It was Hitler who originally proposed moving the *Scharnhorst*, *Gneisenau*, and *Prinz Eugen* eastward up the English Channel and back to Germany. He charged Ciliax, now fleet commander following Günther Lütjens's demise on the *Bismarck*, to work out the details. The air and naval staffs had invested much effort in planning for what one officer morbidly called "the burial of our ships at sea."[27]

Grand Admiral Erich Raeder, likewise, believed disaster to be the most likely outcome. "If the enemy were even reasonably alert and prepared," he later wrote, "I did not see how the dash could proceed." Hitler threatened to decommission the ships and dismantle their guns if Raeder proved a hindrance.[28] He compared the ships' predicament "with that of a patient having cancer, who was doomed unless he submitted to an operation," according to one meeting account. "An operation, on the other hand, even though it might prove to be a drastic one, would offer at least some hope that the patient's life might be spared." Navigating the *Scharnhorst*, *Gneisenau*, and *Prinz Eugen* through the Royal Navy's home waters and bringing them back to Germany would be such an operation.[29]

The ships, Ciliax explained, would leave Brest under the cover of night to avoid detection. This would mean navigating the narrow Strait of Dover in daylight hours and passing within twenty miles of southern England's coastal defenses. The ships would avoid convoy traffic along the French coastline and stick to waters "of sufficient depth to maintain a high speed."[30]

Occupied ports along the route would remain on high alert in the event any ship needed emergency repairs. Two fighter squadrons operating out of Le Touquet and an airfield in Amsterdam would provide continuous air cover from sunrise to sunset. Reserve units in Haamstede (the Netherlands), Octeville (France), and Coxyde and Sint-Truiden (Belgium) would be ready to fly with short warning. The ships would sail from Brest escorted by six destroyers and would rendezvous with the 2nd, 3rd, and 5th Torpedo Boat Flotillas on the outward journey. Three flotillas of E-boats—essentially, fast and heavily armed attack craft—would join the squadron off the French coast at Cape Griz Nez. Minesweepers would clear the route to be traveled several days ahead of time and sweep as much of it as possible once again on the actual night.[31]

The Germans christened the operation "Cerberus" after the multi-headed hound of hell in Greek mythology charged with guarding the gates to Hades and preventing the dead from escaping.

✳ ✳ ✳

The British, not ignorant to the possibility of a German breakout, had devised a counterplan the previous year. Codenamed "Fuller," the scheme—on paper—lacked significant firepower, relying on motor torpedo boats, destroyers, and antiquated aircraft. The Royal Navy, having lost the cruiser *Repulse* and the battleship *Prince of Wales* to Japanese air attack in the Pacific three days after Pearl Harbor, refused to commit any capital ships to the operation lest the Luftwaffe send them to the bottom of the English Channel.[32]

On February 2, 1942, the British Admiralty issued a rather prescient appreciation titled "Possible Departure of the Brest Ships." In it, naval intelligence anticipated a daring blitz up the Channel should the ships breakout, noting the "Germans must be anxious to get them away to safe harbor." The British believed the enemy—knowing the Royal Navy would not send its capital ships to intervene—would rely on a destroyer escort and "20 fighters constantly overhead" to safeguard the desperate passage.[33]

Indeed, activity in the English Channel that first week of February gave hint to some pending scheme. "A marked increase in minesweeping," states a Royal Navy report, "was noted along both the coastal and outer routes. On the night of February 8/9 several German destroyers passed down the Channel."[34]

Vice Admiral Bertram Ramsay—flag officer in charge, Dover, and architect of the Dunkirk evacuation—planned to attack the fleeing ships in the Dover Strait, the narrowest stretch of Channel and well within range of British coastal batteries. Should the German ships survive, British destroyers would be lying in wait thirty miles to the northeast with fighter and bomber support from the RAF. Starting February 3, all forces were placed on nightly standby to be ready at a moment's notice.[35]

* * *

All was feverish activity in the bomb-cratered port of Brest. Ciliax scheduled the breakout for the night of February 11, "four days before the new moon."[36] Acts of deception failed to hide the frenzied preparations. London received reports of crews loading the ships with sun

helmets, khaki uniforms, and barrels of oil with "For Use in the Trop-
ics" stenciled on the side.[37]

On Wednesday, February 4, his flag now flying above *Scharnhorst*,
Ciliax issued the battle order for Cerberus. He declared the operation
to be "a bold and unheard of" undertaking—one that would find its
rightful place in the battle-hardened history of the German navy. Ultimate success would depend on a strict adherence to orders; there
would be "no margin for interpretation."[38]

Although he believed the Royal Navy would keep its heavy ships
out of the fray lest they risk serious damage, he anticipated attacks
from the air and light naval forces. Mines would pose a considerable
hazard. The storm would ultimately break when they ran the Strait of
Dover with its coastal batteries and close proximity to England's southern airfields. Victory would not be measured in British ships sunk or
planes shot down. Making it through the Channel, Ciliax stressed, was
the only task that mattered. He ordered his captains to "seek combat"
only as a last resort.[39]

On the evening of February 11, Ciliax met with his senior commanders on board *Scharnhorst* for a final council of war. The ships—with
Scharnhorst in the lead, followed by *Gneisenau* and *Prinz Eugen*—would
depart at 7:30 p.m. They would make haste at 25 knots and, if all went
according to plan, pass through the Strait of Dover at 11:30 the following morning.[40] Ciliax wished his men luck and dismissed them.
They walked through the man-made vapor that canvassed the port
after sunset and returned to their ships to await the go-signal from
Scharnhorst. From each vessel, one could hear "the roaring noise of
boiler-room fans" and the urgent bark of last-minute orders.[41]

All was ready by zero hour, 7:30 p.m., when the air-raid sirens began to howl. Fifteen British flares floated down from the darkness,
their light a ghostly spectacle through the thick, yellow gauze of artifi-
cial fog. And then the bombs began to fall. For more than an hour, Brest
trembled under the onslaught. The ships, defined in silhouette against
a backdrop of flame, remained "blacked-out, silent" in their berths.[42]

The bombing eventually ceased and the antiaircraft guns fell silent. At 9:14 p.m., with the all-clear sounding, the ships came to life.

Within thirty minutes, they had cleared the antisubmarine netting at the mouth of the harbor and were heading to sea at 17 knots, escorted by six destroyers and three motor torpedo boats (MTBs).[43]

The ships made good time despite starting two hours late. Steaming at 27 knots, they reached Ushant—a French island at the southwestern edge of the English Channel—a mere seventy-two minutes behind schedule and began their arduous passage up the Channel without interference.[44] At four o'clock that morning, the escorting destroyers and MTBs "formed a circular submarine and AA screen" around the vessels.[45]

The ink-black sky began its slow fade to gray. The approaching dawn sent the crews to their battle stations. Weary eyes scanned the distance in dreadful anticipation of the RAF and Royal Navy—but all remained clear and silent. At 7:45 a.m., sixteen German fighters roared over the squadron, firing recognition flares and "dipping their wings in salute."[46]

The naval squadron, with its covering fighters swarming like hornets overhead, pushed deeper into enemy waters. It was soon joined by another ten MTBs and a flotilla of E-boats. At 10:25 a.m., the ships reached a stretch of water in the Pas-de-Calais off Berck-sur-Mer, which only hours before had been littered with mines. On *Scharnhorst*'s bridge, Captain Hoffmann reduced speed to 10 knots.[47]

Minesweepers had worked the ominous stretch eight times over the previous hours and cleared "a gap 400 yards wide through what was thought to be the middle." Ciliax studied the overcast gloom, the empty stretch of sea, and questioned his luck. Was it possible to have been at sea for nearly fourteen hours—four hours in broad daylight—and have made it this far without being detected? Why question good fortune? [48]

Ciliax would take whatever luck providence supplied. It took twenty-two jaw-clenched minutes to navigate the passage, after which *Scharnhorst*, *Gneisenau*, and *Prinz Eugen* resumed their urgent course at 27 knots. And still there remained no sign of the enemy.[49]

✳ ✳ ✳

Two Spitfires piloted by Group Captain Victor Beamish and Wing Commander R. F. Boyd took off from Kenley outside London at 10:10 a.m. They climbed through snow beneath a stormy sky, crossed the coast, and dropped to sea level for better visibility. The sea passed beneath them, a violent blur of gray, frothing waves.[50]

As the French coast took shape on the horizon, Beamish and Boyd spotted two Bf 109s above them at 1,500 feet. "We chased them at full throttle," Beamish later reported, "but did not gain much on them— they were going very fast." In their pursuit, Beamish and Boyd stumbled across a stunning sight, framed by a break in the clouds. "We were about five miles off the French coast near Le Touquet," Beamish said. "I saw two ships roughly in line astern, surrounded by around twelve destroyers, circled again by an outer ring of E-boats."[51]

The two pilots turned for home with a fiery storm of red and green tracer shells rocketing skyward from the guns below and enemy fighters dropping like birds of prey on them from above. They made for cloud cover, escaping injury and damage, and returned to base at 11:09 a.m. They scrambled out of their fighters and made their breathless reports. The news made its way to Fighter Command Headquarters, the Admiralty War Room in London, and then Admiral Ramsay in Dover. The ships would be passing through the Strait of Dover in less than an hour. "Their sudden appearance," notes a Royal Navy report, "came as an unpleasant surprise."[52]

Ramsay had, in fact, received word from another RAF reconnaissance flight shortly before Beamish's report of "25 to 30 vessels, made up of small destroyers or sloops" in the Channel. But, believing it to be a convoy, he took no action. Now, urgent orders went out from Dover putting MTBs to sea and alerting destroyers to fast-approaching prey.[53]

Shortly after noon, the batteries along England's southern coast received word of the situation. Officers crowded every observation post, field glasses glued to their eyes, as they strained to glimpse the enemy ships through the mist.[54] *Scharnhorst, Gneisenau,* and *Prinz Eugen* had by now entered the Strait. Ciliax, "knowing full well that his career was irrevocably tied to the success or failure of the operation," turned to his yeoman of signals. "Tell the port side screens to make smoke," he said, his voice betraying not a hint of concern. "A decent smoke-screen should give the English something to think about."[55]

The British let Ciliax know what they were thinking at 12:18 p.m. The Mark X 9.2-inch guns of the South Foreland Battery on the Kent coast opened fire. The thunderclap of the cannonade rolled across the water, the flash of the guns a bright, temporary scar on the dark shape of the English coastline.[56] The shells cut a silent, distant path across the sky; their screaming only became audible to the German crews as they hurdled ever closer to the ships. They landed in a massive eruption of water more than a mile to port. For the next seventeen minutes, the battery fired one salvo after another and hit nothing but sea.[57]

Elsewhere on the water, five MTBs led by Lieutenant Commander Edward Pumphrey sped from Dover at 36 knots and charged into the fray. At 12:10 p.m., only fifteen minutes after leaving the safety of their berths, the MTB crews spotted the distant billowing of the German smoke screen. It clung to the water "in two distinct patches on the starboard bow." Against the swirling backdrop, Pumphrey could see "ten or twelve" E-boats heading northeast in "two divisions half a mile apart."[58]

Pumphrey altered course to intercept the enemy. The MTBs pushed hard across the water, their hulls thumping through the swell with bone-jarring force. Both sides opened fire at a thousand yards. Behind the E-boats, a massive shape dispersed the smoke. "The enemy main forces came gradually into view behind the smoke screen," Pumphrey reported. "They were about 4,000 yards beyond the E-boats." Pumphrey sent a signal back to base at 12:23 p.m., "which at long last confirmed the presence of all three heavy ships."[59]

Wanting to pull ahead of the E-boats and make a wide turn into the *Scharnhorst*, *Gneisenau*, and *Prinz Eugen*, Pumphrey—in MTB 221—opened his engines full throttle. The boat surged forward, her bow lifting, and her engines giving voice to the strain. Enemy fire straddled the MTBs as they raced against the German ships. Pumphrey braced himself against the hammering of the sea and alternately cast his gaze from the empty Channel ahead of him to the E-boats approaching from behind. Try as he might to coax more out of her, his MTB had nothing left to give. The other boats in his flotilla kept up the desperate pace. Further back, the three big German warships thundered up the Channel at 23 knots.[60]

As MTB 221 slammed through another wave, one of her three engines stuttered and died.[61] No way could Pumphrey pull far enough ahead to execute his plan of attack. With his reputation for calm under pressure and "knowing when the risks outweighed the gain," he swung his boat around, intent to smash his way through the E-boat's defensive line.[62] "I considered the prospect of success for this maneuver," he later noted, "to be extremely slight."[63]

The dead engine, although quickly revived, gave out again as Pumphrey lined himself up for the charge. His speed dropped to a sluggish 15 knots. Enemy fighters plunged from thick cloud and flayed the sea with cannon fire. Pumphrey "ordered the other boats to continue the attack."[64]

The four MTBs peeled away and aimed for the German ships. MTBs 219 and 48 sped across a windswept expanse of waves that battered men and boats alike. Eighteen-year-old R. J. Mitchell sat at his radio below deck on MTB 48. There was little for him to do; the violent motion of the sea had rendered his radio inoperable. He informed the skipper, Sub-Lieutenant Mark Arnold-Forster, who shrugged such a minor concern aside. "Come up on top," Arnold-Forster said, "and grab a rifle or something." Mitchell did as ordered. "What a sight met my eyes," he said. "A rough, choppy day, grey and scudding clouds, bouncing about on five-to-six-feet-high waves. Not much to a ship—but to us, heavy weather."[65]

His attention seized on "two filthy great battleships and a heavy cruiser with around eight destroyers" in the near-distance.[66] The MTBs closed the range to roughly 4,000 yards before firing their torpedoes "through [a] gap between the two divisions of E-boats." The torpedoes missed.[67]

Lieutenant Hilary Gamble, commanding MTB 45, aimed for the gap between the two E-boat divisions. The flash from their machine-gun muzzles looked like flickering lights in the gray haze. The heaving sea jumped and boiled with enemy rounds, as Gamble fought to maintain a steady trajectory and get close to the *Prinz Eugen*. He gave the order to fire torpedoes, but one misfired. As the crew scrambled to reload the tubes, a gray curtain of smoke drew across the water and smothered the heavy ships. It came via the destroyer *Friedrich Ihn*, which veered out to port from behind the three main German vessels and barreled down on Gamble's tiny craft. Gamble swung his MTB around to meet the oncoming threat "but was again frustrated by a misfire."[68]

Enemy fire chewed away at the MTB. Gamble opened up his engines and turned sharply on a northwest heading for home with the *Friedrich Ihn* devouring his wake in close pursuit. Two British motor gun boats (MGBs) now stormed into the chaos, the clatter of their Browning machine guns a frantic cadence above the heavy thunder of naval artillery.[69] They maneuvered between the destroyer and Gamble's MTB, and laid down their own smoke screen. "The destroyer's fire," noted the gunboat commander, "especially when it was concentrated on the MGBs at about 1,000-yards range, was unpleasantly accurate."[70]

As the destroyer and gunboats waged their running battle through smoke and pounding sea, MTB 44—hampered by engine trouble— maneuvered astern of the enemy flotilla and fired her torpedoes at *Prinz Eugen*. The German ship continued on its way, unscathed, cutting through a sea that looked like liquid metal beneath the dark sky. MTB 44 turned and sped away to join the torpedo boats now heading for home, while another desperate struggle played out overhead.[71]

✳ ✳ ✳

At 12:25 p.m., six Swordfish torpedo bombers from Fleet Air Arm Squadron 825 took off from their airfield at RAF Manston in the northeast of Kent. In the leading aircraft was Lieutenant Commander Eugene Esmonde, who had successfully spearheaded the squadron's attack against *Bismarck*. "Certainly, to most of us who were 21, 22," recalled Pilot Officer Pat Kingsmill, "[Esmonde] seemed a very old man. He was about 32."[72]

Admiral Ramsay, aware that ordering Swordfish to attack *Scharnhorst* and her consorts was a suicidal endeavor, had placed the final decision that morning in Esmonde's hands. The German ships, steaming through the Channel, were less than forty miles from the squadron's airfield.[73] "I think that must have been a very difficult decision for him," Kingsmill said, "because he was a very brave man—and to have dropped out at that stage would have been much more difficult than to go ahead with the attack."[74]

As the Swordfish crews went about their final preparations, Wing Commander Tom Gleave, the station commander, made the rounds and wished them luck. "Although [Esmonde's] mouth twitched automatically into the semblance of a grin and his arm lifted in a vague salute, he barely recognized me," Gleave said. "He knew what he was going into. But it was his duty. His face was tense and white. It was the face of a man already dead. It shocked me as nothing has ever done since."[75]

Gleave stood in falling snow at the end of the runway and saluted each aircraft as it lifted into the gray-white sky.[76] The planes set a course for Ramsgate, a seaside town on England's southeast coast, where they planned to rendezvous with five squadrons of Spitfires before heading into the maelstrom over the Channel. "We waited in Ramsgate for about five minutes for the RAF escort to arrive," Kingsmill said. "In fact, only one squadron arrived at about half-past twelve. Esmonde decided it was time to take off on our attack."[77] And so with only ten Spitfires to provide cover, the Swordfish—grouped in three subflights—flew out to sea.[78]* German fighters swarmed them within minutes.

"I remember looking forward and seeing a destroyer," said telegraphist/air gunner Donald Bunce. "The next thing I know, Focke-Wulf 190s were on our tail. They seemed to circle us constantly. No sooner had one left us, there was another one in its place. All that went through my mind was that a .303 [machine gun] wasn't going to be a match for any cannon they had." Bunce laid down a heavy fire, as the

---

*In his post-operational report (AIR 20/3061/033), Ramsay wrote: "That the plan to escort the Swordfish miscarried must be counted as a major tragedy, as it practically gave no hope of success or of survival to the Swordfish who had to face a sky full of enemy fighters, as well as very heavy flak from the destroyer screen and the capital ships themselves."

enemy "[came] at us from all sides." The Focke-Wulfs, struggling not to rocket past the lumbering biplanes, attacked with their flaps up and wheels down. "I could actually see the pilots out of the corner of my eye as they turned away," Bunce said.[79]

The first subflight, despite being ravaged, pushed forward. On the port bow, the three big warships "could be dimly made out through the smoke and fume."[80] Esmonde led the charge over the E-boat and destroyer screen, his plane all but disintegrating around him with most of its lower port side having been completely shot away.[81]

Esmonde maintained control of Swordfish W5984 even as enemy fire reduced it to tatters—and then, it finally had enough. "I was following Esmonde about 150 yards behind him," said Kingsmill, "and then I saw his aircraft rear up in the air."[82] Esmonde's Swordfish plunged into the sea 3,000 yards from the capital ships and killed all on board.[83]

Kingsmill also found himself in trouble, his Swordfish a flaming projectile of fluttering rags. "I took evasive action to port," Kingsmill said. "I came round in a very wide circle and started the attack again. I don't think I got near enough to the ships, but by that time I'd been personally hit three times. The aircraft had obviously been very badly damaged. A couple of cylinders on top of the engine had been shot away, and a certain amount of the wings were ribbons."[84]

Kingsmill dropped his torpedo less than 3,000 yards from what he believed to be the *Prinz Eugen* but missed.[85] On the *Scharnhorst*, Captain Kurt-Caesar Hoffmann watched—in admiration and disbelief—as the Swordfish suffered their terrible plight. "Poor fellows," he exclaimed. "They are so very low. It is nothing but suicide for them to fly against these big ships."[86]

Kingsmill turned his burning plane, Swordfish W5907, in a last-ditch effort for home. Bunce, Kingsmill's air gunner, took stock of the damage. "The fabric was peppered with three-cornered tears, as you would tear a coat on barbed wire," he later recalled. "There was no fabric at all on the tail plane on the port side. I turned to sit down—and to one side of my seat, and partly underneath it, there was a big hole."[87]

The radio in front of Bunce's seat had been shot through. Oil, thick and black, splattered the port side of the plane as it bled from the shot-up engine. The dinghy on the upper port main plane had been shot away, leaving nothing but a gaping hole. Kingsmill, working feverishly at the controls, struggled to maintain altitude. Realizing they were destined for the sea, he banked the plane toward what he believed to be three British MTBs. "They turned out to be E-boats," Bunce said, "and it was then that I emptied my last bullets into them."[88]

Bunce turned around to check on Sub-Lieutenant "Mac" Samples, the observer, who raised a blood-covered hand from his right side. As Bunce leaned forward to inspect Samples's wound, the plane's emergency flares detonated and threw brilliant streaks of light off the plane's port side.[89] The Swordfish could take no more. "We very gently entered the sea," Kingsmill remembered. "The aircraft settled beautifully on the water."[90]

The three men scrambled from the sinking plane and watched it sink. They were only in the water for several minutes before an MTB appeared alongside them. The men were pulled on board and stripped out of their wet clothes. "Someone handed me a cup of rum," Bunce said, "and I was left with my thoughts." The boat returned them safely to England, where a waiting ambulance transferred the men to hospital—not that Bunce needed medical attention. He escaped the ordeal unscathed.[91]

Kingsmill and his crew proved to be the lucky ones from Squadron 825 that day. Sub-Lieutenant Brian Rose, flying Swordfish W5983 and "severely wounded in the back" by shrapnel, dropped his torpedo from a range of 2,000 yards.[92] He watched it cut a path toward one of the German warships. Satisfied the torpedo was "running well," he turned his stricken plane—with its ruptured fuel tank and sputtering engine—away but crashed into the Channel. The observer, Sub-Lieutenant Edgar Lee, pulled Rose from the cockpit. The two men climbed into the Swordfish's emergency dinghy. Air gunner A. L. Johnson, his lifeless body slumped over his guns, went down with the plane.[93]

Four of the nine men who flew in the first subflight were killed, another three injured.[94] The second subflight of three Swordfish was last seen "taking violent evasive action" over the E-boat and destroyer

screen at roughly the same time Kingsmill was carrying out his torpedo run. "None of them," notes a postoperation report, "was seen
again."[95]

Not a single torpedo, despite the abysmal blood toll, found its mark.
The Germans, nevertheless, found much to admire in the British effort.
"Such bravery was devoted and incredible," noted *Scharnhorst*'s navigation officer, Commander Helmuth Giessler. "One was privileged to
witness it."[96]

The German ships forged on beneath darkening clouds and a thickening mist. Ahead of them, the Channel widened into the North Sea.
The attack by torpedo boats and Swordfish, Ciliax noted, had almost
come as a relief. "The tension onboard the ships," he wrote, "had risen
to its maximum because of the hours of waiting."[97] The British assault
had channeled the crews' anxiety into a desperate defense of their
ships—but now, all fell quiet again.

Then, at 2:30 p.m., a powerful blast sucker-punched the *Scharnhorst*
and brought it to a violent halt. The men on the bridge, as they pulled
themselves to their feet, knew instinctively they had struck a mine. An
inspection revealed minimal structural damage. The ship remained
in fighting shape despite "one turret of the main armament" being
knocked out of action and another two damaged, along with the "secondary armament mountings."[98] At 2:49 p.m., Ciliax ordered *Scharnhorst* on her way at 25 knots.[99]

On land, confusion reigned as the British tried to meet the German challenge. RAF Bomber Command, having been "stood down"
for the day, was not prepared for the morning order to attack. It took
three hours of frenzied activity to ready men and machines.[100] The first
bombers appeared over the ships at 2:44 p.m. and dropped their payloads from 1,000 to 2,000 feet, but heavy cloud all but camouflaged
the targets. In Bomber Command's largest daylight operation thus far,
242 bombers, dispatched in three waves, flew operations against the
ships until five o'clock that evening. Only thirty-nine succeeded in
dropping their bombs, none of which found its mark.[101]

Wellington Z1081 from No. 214 Squadron, blinded by heavy cloud,
failed to locate the ships. As its crew searched in vain for the targets,
the plane began to ice up. "The port engine packed up," remembered

Sergeant Robin Murray, the wireless operator and forward air gunner. "After about twenty minutes, part of the propeller broke away, came through the side of the aircraft, and damaged the hydraulics." At the controls, Wing Commander R. D. B. McFadden struggled to keep the stricken bomber airborne, but the damage proved catastrophic and sent the Wellington into the Channel shortly before 5 p.m.[102]

The force of impact caved in the nose turret, where Murray sat braced behind his guns. An explosion of icy water and shattered Perspex blew him backward out of the turret, into a bulkhead, and knocked him unconscious. He came to underwater and clawed his way through the rear cabin and into the cockpit, where he escaped the sinking plane. His stomach convulsing from all the seawater he had swallowed, he joined four of his crewmates in a dinghy floating just off the wing.[103]

Two crewmembers, Sergeant George Taylor and Flight Lieutenant Patrick Hughes, were nowhere to be seen. The men in the dinghy paddled around the plane looking for them; one even lowered himself into the water to search the submerged part of the wreckage, but it soon became apparent the two men had been lost forever. The five survivors, soaking wet, huddled together and struggled to keep warm as waves sloshed into the raft. All they saw through the mist and drizzle was empty sea. One crewman had possessed the foresight to load the dinghy with rations but forgot to bring a tin opener. "All we had," said Murray, "was Horlicks malted milk tablets."[104]

Night soon settled over the water, and the men forced themselves to stay awake. The belief they would be rescued come daybreak helped maintain their spirits—but the following day brought with it only a fleeting glimpse of deliverance. A ship revealed itself in the distance, too far off to be identified as British or German, but that hardly mattered. The men fired an emergency flare into the overcast but failed to get the ship's attention. "We tried to set off another, but it wouldn't work," Murray said. "It was damp. None of the flares worked at all after that."[105]

At four o'clock that afternoon, air gunner Martin Stephens succumbed to hypothermia. The four remaining men survived the bitter night only to lose McFadden at daybreak. Delirium consumed his final hours, as he believed he was driving in his car. "It was very strange," Murray said, "because people just went into a coma. They just sort of lost themselves." The cold claimed one man after another. One moment they'd be conversing, the next their voice would start to fade and they'd simply drift away. All attempts to rouse them failed. Murray couldn't help but notice it seemed a peaceful way to go.[106]

By the third morning, Murray was the only one still alive. He kept his fallen crew in the raft, resting his frostbitten feet on their bodies to keep his lower extremities out of the water. "It sounds terrible," he said, "but by this time they were beyond help." At eleven o'clock that morning, he spotted land—what turned out to be Holland—and a gun battery sitting high atop a cliff. He grabbed a ration tin and angled its lid to reflect the sun, hoping to get the battery's attention. It did the trick.[107]

A German patrol boat with a red cross on it soon pulled up alongside the dinghy. The crew helped Murray aboard, tied a rope to the raft, and returned to the harbor at Vlissingen. Members of the German crew helped Murray down the boat's ramp onto the quayside and to a waiting ambulance. "I'll never forget that moment," Murray said. "There were five or six German sailors there, and they all came to attention and saluted me."[108]

Murray received medical attention for his frostbite and spent the next two years in a POW camp before being repatriated. The Germans buried his four dead crewmates with full military honors in the Northern Cemetery at Vlissingen.[109]

Murray's Wellington was one of fifteen bombers lost that day; flak and enemy fighters damaged another twenty. Seventeen out of 398 British fighters that flew cover operations failed to return.[110] Below the clouds, flying barely 100 feet above the waves, Beaufort torpedo bombers of Coastal Command closed in on the German vessels. The decks of each ship glimmered with flame as the heavy naval guns tossed shells into the sea and threw up foaming walls of water. "The shells were so close," remembered Beaufort air gunner Maurice Mayne. "Huge splashes were coming up all over the aircraft."[111]

The bomber staggered like a punch-drunk fighter as one heavy column of water after another crashed down upon it. The crew dropped their torpedo and wasted no time speeding for home. "I got a view of the ship," said Mayne, "and could see the shells coming over." He watched, from his turret, the torpedo's trail leave its white scar on the sea. Mayne thought they had scored a hit—but it was never registered as such.[112]

Navigator Arthur Beach braced himself as his Beaufort lined up with one of the big ships. The plane shuddered around him with each blast of the German guns. It came as an intense relief to hear the torpedo was away and feel the plane scramble for the clouds. "We'd been flying back for about ten minutes," Beach said, "when the gunner came on and said we're being pursued by a fighter. I said, 'Are you sure?' He said, "Yes, I'm sure. It's so bloody fast."" The gunner kept an eye on the dark shape growing ever larger through the Perspex of his turret. "It's an Me 110," he informed the crew. "We're in trouble," Beach thought. The lumbering Beaufort made easy prey. "He's gaining on us," the gunner said, disrupting the uneasy silence.

Beach peered through the window near his navigation table and saw two lines of British destroyers in the near distance. He told the pilot to aim for the ships. The pilot did as instructed and passed over with the Me 110 still some distance back. "I flashed the first destroyer 'EA Astern'—Enemy Aircraft Astern," said Beach, "and he just flashed me back, 'OK.'" The Beaufort crew heard a low bang behind them as the destroyer's guns knocked the Messerschmitt into the sea. "That was a tremendous thing," Beach said, "I thanked the Navy like mad, because we couldn't have done anything about it. We went on and we landed, and that's the first time I've been really happy about the Navy."[113]

Sixteen out of twenty-eight Beauforts found the German ships in the afternoon filth, and thirteen dropped their torpedoes—but not one scored a hit. Three Beauforts failed to return.[114]

The *Scharnhorst*, *Prinz Eugen*, and *Gneisenau* steamed ever closer to home waters. "The sea had now become very rough," wrote one sailor. "Breakers thundered over the bows, and in the *Prinz Eugen* the anti-aircraft guns positioned on the forecastle had to be moved."[115] The weather, continuing to close in around the ships, soon reduced visibility to four miles.[116]

✳ ✳ ✳

Roughly twenty miles west of the Hook of Holland, Captain Charles Pizey—commander of the 21st Destroyer Flotilla—stood on the bridge of HMS *Campbell* and peered through binoculars into a gray void of sea and sky. The world appeared without color. In addition to *Campbell*, Pizey had four destroyers under his command: *Vivacious*, and—from the 16th Destroyer Flotilla—*Mackay, Worcester,* and *Whitshed.* A fifth, the *Walpole,* had returned to harbor earlier in the day after her "main bearings commenced to run."[117] Not one of the destroyers currently being tossed about in gale-force winds was less than twenty years old.[118]

Pizey checked his watch and noted the time: 3:17 p.m. A signal from the Admiralty had arrived minutes before ordering him to the southwest in search of the enemy. No sooner had the signal been placed in Pizey's hands, "two large echoes bearing 140 degrees 9½ miles" appeared on *Campbell's* radar—followed two minutes later by a third.[119] The enemy had come to him.

Pizey knew his destroyers would hardly be a match for the German armada, but he hoped the limited visibility would play in his favor. Splitting his force in two—*Campbell, Vivacious,* and *Worcester* comprising the first division, *Mackay* and *Whitshed* the second—he moved fast to close the distance between himself and the Germans. By 3:42 p.m., Pizey could see the flash of antiaircraft guns and the fiery blur of tracer rounds arching up from the enemy ships.[120]

The sky was a chaotic jumble of British and German airplanes. "Low down were large numbers of Bf 109s and an occasional Beaufort," notes one report. "Higher up were Hampdens, Dorniers, and Me 110s, while still higher a few Halifaxes were to be seen. Junker [*sic*] 88s, Heinkel IIIs, Spitfires, Wellingtons, Whirlwinds, and Manchesters were all represented."[121]

The scene presented one of complete pandemonium. Many of the German planes mistook the British destroyers for German ships and fired their recognition flares—"four red balls in the shape of a diamond"—in greeting. A number of British planes mistook the Royal Navy vessels as those of the Kriegsmarine and acted accordingly.[122] A Hampden swooped over the *Mackay* and dropped its payload, the bombs bursting on either side of the ship. "Check, check, check. Do not open fire," the *Mackay*'s gunnery officer yelled. "That aircraft is friendly, although it has a funny way of showing it."[123]

Roughly four miles ahead, Pizey saw the *Gneisenau* and *Prinz Eugen*—one in front of the other—take shape with their destroyer screen following on the port bow. The British ships began zigzagging violently through the water and opened fire with their 4.7-inch guns. Shells from both sides exploded in the waves. "Shells of all calibers," noted one British report, "fell very close."[124]

Pizey's ships continued to close the distance with their 3-inch and 12-inch guns hammering away at the strafing German fighters. *Gneisenau* and *Prinz Eugen* maintained a relentless fire. "It seemed incredible," noted Pizey, "that we were not hit . . . a German destroyer came out of the mist to deliver a torpedo attack against *Vivacious*, which passed down her side about 15 yards away."[125]

Having now closed to 3,500 yards, Pizey knew his luck could not hold. "Ships were being well straddled and we were closing fast," he reported. "At 3,300 yards I saw a large shell, which failed to explode or ricochet, dive under the ship like a porpoise, and I felt this was the time to turn and fire torpedoes."[126]

Vivacious—on Pizey's starboard quarter—turned with *Campbell*, both firing their torpedoes before retiring. Unaware, Lieutenant Commander Ernest Coates on board the *Worcester* drew closer to the enemy "under an even heavier and more concentrated fire."[127] At 2,400 yards she fired her torpedoes but not before taking direct hits in her two boiler rooms and coming to a dead stop. She floated with her port side "exposed to the close-range fire of both battle cruisers for about ten minutes."[128]

Shells smashed her deck, battered her bridge, and scattered bodies. The blast from one salvo "blew a group of freshly wounded sailors overboard," prompting First Lieutenant J. W. L. Winterbottom to leap into the sea and pull each man, one by one, back to the ship.[129] Four salvos, one after the other, pummeled *Worcester*, obliterating men, twisting metal, and reducing her still-firing guns to ruins. Coates, not sure how much more his ship could take, gave the order to "Prepare to abandon ship!" Some men only heard "Abandon ship!" in the chaos and gathered the wounded, put them in life floats, and cast them off.[130]

"I watched our heavy guns score direct hits on the English destroyer and it seemed to me that she heeled so far over under the impact that she nearly capsized," wrote Captain Otto Fein on the *Gneisenau*. "I ordered our guns to cease fire, as there seemed to be no point wasting shells on a ship already sinking. No destroyer, or any ship of that size, could be hit that heavily and survive."[131]

The German ships steamed on. Lookouts on *Campbell* and *Vivacious* alerted Pizey to *Worcester*'s ordeal two miles away. "She was lying stopped," Pizey wrote, "badly on fire forward and amidships, with smoke and steam pouring from the funnels, rafts and floats adrift clear of her, and men in the water."[132] The two ships raced to her rescue. Efforts to pull the men from the water were "rendered specially arduous by the rough weather, and the helplessness of the men, wounded, cold and exhausted."[133]

German fighters plunged from low cloud and strafed all three ships. "The confusion in the air was amazing," reported Pizey. "During these operations we were beaten up and bombed by both the enemy and our own aircraft."[134] A torpedo attack by three Beauforts at 4:15 p.m. forced Pizey to order *Campbell* full-speed astern—even with rafts of wounded men at her sides—to avoid a calamity. In the tumult, the crews of *Campbell* and *Vivacious* hauled forty-six men, including nineteen wounded and four dead, from the water. One hundred men, out of *Worcester*'s 130-man crew, were either killed or wounded.[135]

As *Worcester* burned, Pizey's second division—the *Mackay* and *Whitshed*—moved in on *Prinz Eugen*, the German crew failing to recognize the British destroyers as enemy ships. The *Mackay* fired her torpedoes at 4,000 yards. The moment they left the tubes, the *Prinz Eugen* swerved to starboard to avoid an air attack. "The mixture of aircraft in our vicinity," noted Captain John Wright on the *Mackay*, "was extraordinary."[136] The *Whitshed* fired her torpedoes from 3,000 yards and missed before joining the *Mackay* for the voyage home.[137]

The *Campbell* and *Vivacious* also steamed for English shores—as did the smoldering *Worcester*, which "had managed to raise sufficient steam to move slowly ahead" at 6.5 knots. Her battered engines and boilers could only stand so much strain, and she was soon reduced to 3.5 knots as the sea worsened. Not until the following dawn did she reach her harbor at Harwich.[138]

Gneisenau and *Prinz Eugen* pushed on with the *Scharnhorst* still lagging somewhat behind. The arrival of dusk forced planes from both sides to peel away and return to their airfields.[139] Full dark soon descended with the sea all but disappearing. No starlight or moonlight made it beyond the clouds. "With nightfall," pondered a Royal Navy report, "Admiral Ciliax must have felt well satisfied with the day's work as he entered on the last lap of the race for home."[140]

The ships moved along the north coast of Holland, each passing mile breathing life into the reality of home—a reality that floundered for the *Gneisenau* crew north of Vlieland at 7:55 p.m. A column of flame and water shot up the ship's starboard side, briefly turning night into day, and tearing a hole at the waterline. She came to a stop with one engine dead on impact.[141]

The mine-inflicted wound near the stern proved minor. Repair teams staunched the flooding with a collision mat, and the ship was on the move thirty minutes later at 25 knots.[142] The *Scharnhorst*, groping through the darkness, struck a second mine in the same vicinity at 9:34 p.m. The blast knocked out her engines. She began to drift as a thousand tons of water flooded her compartments. Engineering teams worked frantically and soon had her center and starboard engines working again. She resumed her slow crawl home, like the wounded warrior she was, at 12 knots.[143]

The *Gneisenau* and *Prinz Eugen* reached the Elbe, "covered with drift-ice," at 7 a.m. on Friday, February 13.[144] "A great cheer welled up" from *Gneisenau*'s crew as the pale light of a winter sun welcomed them home.[145] The two ships entered the Kaiser Wilhelm Canal and dropped anchor in the north chamber. The *Scharnhorst* staggered into Wilhelmshaven several hours later at 10 a.m. Ciliax signaled Berlin: "It is my duty to inform you that Operation *Cerberus* has been successfully completed."[146]

Hitler was jubilant, relieved to have his ships back home and no longer vulnerable to British attacks. Grand Admiral Raeder viewed the operation through a more complex lens. "Tactically," he wrote, "the dash up the Channel was a great success. Strategically, it was an outright retreat."[147] In bringing the ships back to Germany, the Kriegsmarine had surrendered much of its offensive power and removed a major threat to Atlantic shipping.[148]

Raeder's assessment aside, Ciliax was not wrong when he wrote in his final report: "Now that the three ships have put into German estuaries, the operation 'Cerberus' is ended. With it closes one day of the war at sea, a day which will probably go down as one of the most daring in the naval history of this war."[149]

✳ ✳ ✳

In London, a grim silence settled over the Admiralty War Room when it became apparent the German ships were home free. It fell to Admiral Sir Dudley Pound, the First Sea Lord, to inform Churchill. He placed the call to No. 10 Downing Street at 1 a.m. on February 13. The prime minister barked a harsh greeting down the line. "I'm afraid, sir," Pound said, "I must report that the enemy battle cruisers should by now have reached the safety of their home waters." The phone call proved mercifully short. Churchill, upon hearing the news, simply uttered one word, "Why?" and slammed the receiver down.[150]

It was a question that echoed across Britain come daybreak. A nation whose prestige was built on the might of her navy had failed miserably in her own home waters. The national outrage and condemnation was near universal. Newspapers decried the humiliation in banner headlines and scathing commentary. "Vice-Admiral Ciliax has succeeded," lamented *The Times*. "With trifling losses he has sailed a hostile fleet from an Atlantic harbor, up the English Channel, and through the straits of Dover to safe anchorage in a North Sea port. Nothing more mortifying to the pride of sea-power has happened in home waters since the seventeenth century."[151]

The Germans reveled in their accomplishment. "The dying British nation," extolled a Nazi radio broadcast, "no longer possesses the power or authority to prevent strangers from moving flowers from her own garden."[152] Churchill tried to soothe the national wound in the House of Commons, correctly portraying the German ships' abandonment of Brest as beneficial to the war at sea:

> The threat to our convoy routes has been removed, and the enemy has been driven to leave this advantageous position. Whatever smart of disappointment or annoyance may remain in our hearts that the final forfeit was not exacted, there is no doubt that the naval position in the Atlantic, so far from being worsened, is definitely eased.[153]

Churchill's eloquence on this occasion carried little sway with the public. So severe was the British humiliation, so resounding was the shock, it briefly impacted war production. Workers toiling on factory floors and the assembly lines neglected their labor to pass resolutions blasting the government's handling of the war.[154] "It is certainly not strange," Churchill conceded in his memoirs, "that the public confidence in the Administration and its conduct of the war should have quavered."[155]

In the public eye, the Germans reigned supreme in the Channel. The national outcry became so deafening that it forced Churchill, one week after the episode, to convene a judicial inquiry into what happened. The three-man investigative board, comprised of a high-court judge, the inspector-general of the RAF, and a Royal Navy admiral, found multiple shortcomings in the British response over the course of their fifteen-day review. Key to British countermeasures was the belief the "enemy ships would seek to pass the Narrows at Dover under cover of darkness." The fact their breakout caught the British by surprise was blamed on inadequate night patrols and the failure to maintain "a strong morning reconnaissance" of the Channel.[156]

Although the Royal Navy and RAF made every effort to coordinate their plans, both services erred. Bomber Command was not given enough advanced warning of the enemy's presence in the Dover Strait, while the Air Ministry failed to alert the Admiralty that bomber crews were on stand-down that morning. There were other misfires, too, including Fighter Command's failure to provide cover for the Swordfish biplanes on their suicidal mission. On top of all that, the "enemy's oc-cupation of the Continental seaboard from Norway to Spain" rendered the use of British capital ships "impractical" and therefore hampered the Royal Navy's response. Even if the British had learned sooner of the dash up the Channel, the forces deployed to stop the German ships were insufficient to do anything about it.[157]

The board of inquiry, despite such findings, had no intention of being harshly critical in its conclusions. British morale had to be taken into consideration. "The circumstances of war," notes one account, "dictated that the nation's arms could not be seen by the public to be incompetent."[158] Indeed, the official report issued by the board was gentle in its overall assessment. "The board," it states in conclusion, "would like to say how much they are impressed by the countless acts of gallantry which have come to their notice, and the evident determi-nation of all our forces to press home their attacks."[159]

The decision was nonetheless made to classify the report and not publish it until 1946.[160] In America, the public and government also questioned how such a thing could happen. Churchill cabled Roos-evelt and stressed once more the strategic benefit of having the en-emy ships back in German waters. "From [Brest] they threatened all our eastbound convoys enforcing a constant two-battleship convoy," Churchill wrote. "Our bomber effort can now be concentrated on Germany."[161]

Roosevelt agreed. "When I speak on the radio next Monday eve-ning," he cabled Churchill, "I shall say a few words to those people who treat the episode in the Channel as a defeat. I am more and more convinced that the location of all German ships in German waters makes our North Atlantic naval problem more simple."[162]

But if the world perceived the Channel Dash as an international embarrassment, the British would quickly redeem themselves with an action heretofore unequaled in daring.

CHAPTER 6

*** * * ***

CHARIOT

On January 27, 1942, Winston Churchill sent a memorandum to the First Sea Lord:

> Is it really necessary to describe the *Tirpitz* as the *Admiral von Tirpitz* in every signal? This must cause a considerable waste of time for signalmen, cipher staff, and typists. Surely *Tirpitz* is good enough for the beast.[1]

The beast plagued the prime minister. While *Bismarck* rusted in the frigid depths of the North Atlantic, her sister ship sat unscathed in Fættenfjord, Norway—sent there by Hitler in mid-January to dissuade any Allied action against occupied Norway and to threaten the flow of supplies between Britain and the Soviet Union. Her war had thus far been a quiet one, comprised of sea drills and training exercises.

Although her armaments, including eight 15-inch guns and twelve 5.9-inch guns, had yet to fire a shot in anger, she cast a long shadow over the Allied war at sea. The very threat of *Tirpitz* leaving the safety of her anchorage to savage Arctic convoys or plow into the Atlantic and crush Britain's lifeline with the United States forced the Royal Navy to keep four capital ships at the ready to hunt her down should the need arise. Churchill deemed her "destruction or even crippling . . . the greatest event at sea at the present time. No other target is comparable to it."[2]

It's hard to imagine one ship exerting such terror, but Britain's survival—dependent on convoys—was a precarious thing. *Bismarck*'s victory over *Hood*, though avenged, underscored the danger of Germany's surface fleet. Hitler's three remaining capital ships—*Tirpitz*, *Scharnhorst*, and *Gneisenau*—along with the heavy cruiser *Prinz Eugen* "possessed a psychological hold on British decision-makers in 1941 and 1942 far in excess of their puny numbers." The fact "a quarter of Britain's merchant fleet" lay on the ocean floor by the end of 1941 only added to the psychological stress.[3]

*** *** ***

The French town of Saint-Nazaire and its port sit on the north bank of the river Loire, six miles up from where the river—churning gray and green—spills into the North Atlantic.[4] A working dockyard town, home to some 50,000 people, Saint-Nazaire lacked the luxurious amenities of more opulent destinations along the Biscay seaboard. "No fashionable hotels here earn multiple stars in the traveller's guidebook," notes one account. "No smart shops tempt the wealthy client."[5] That hardly mattered to the Germans. Its port housed not only "every kind of facility for the maintenance, arming, provisioning, and repair of U-boats,"[6] but the massive Normandie dry dock—the very dock *Bismarck* may have been trying to reach when she met her fate.[7]

Built in 1932 to accommodate the 80,000-ton luxury liner SS *Normandie*—then the largest passenger ship afloat—the dock stretched the length of three football fields and was 164 feet wide and 52 feet deep. It was the only dock on the Atlantic coast capable of holding a leviathan the size of *Bismarck* or *Tirpitz*.[8]

The mere possibility of *Tirpitz* breaking into the Atlantic was a nightmare scenario the British were desperate to prevent. As with the doomed *Bismarck*, stopping *Tirpitz* would require a powerful fleet of capital ships and aircraft. With Britain fighting multiple fronts on land and sea, "the availability of these weapons in the vast wastes of the North Atlantic was limited."[9]

Churchill's insistence that something be done about *Tirpitz* fell on Combined Operations Headquarters, established in 1940 to conduct amphibious operations against German-occupied Europe. The Commandos, a force of handpicked and specially trained troops from the army and Royal Marines, formed the spear-point for such attacks.[10]

To be a Commando was to be trained in all "portable weapons . . . from the rifle and the tommy gun to the three-inch mortar and the anti-tank rifle." The training in the Scottish Highlands—subjecting men to live fire, merciless weather, and unforgiving terrain—pushed minds and bodies to the limit. Men learned to kill with their bare hands and be independent in their thinking. In the maelstrom of battle, they didn't wait for orders. "They must do the sensible, obvious thing," noted one report, "just because it is the sensible, obvious thing."[11]

In February 1942, Combined Operations Headquarters conceived a daring plan to rid *Tirpitz* of its Atlantic safe harbor. Christened Operation Chariot, the scheme, boiled down to its bare essence, was brutal in its simplicity. A destroyer, loaded with time-delayed explosives, would venture up the Loire estuary and ram the Normandie dock's outer caisson. Eighty Commandos on board would storm ashore and destroy various port facilities and related German defenses. Twelve motor launches—each carrying fifteen Commandos—would accompany the destroyer on its fatal voyage. The launches would throw their raiding parties at the port's Old Entrance and Old Mole pier to inflict carnage on the U-boat pen, destroy gun emplacements, blow up a power station, and secure the Old Mole as the point of withdrawal back to England.[12]

The plan assumed there would be survivors to make the journey home. It was a suicide mission—but the only viable option if the British wanted to render the Normandie dock unusable. Attacks by the RAF might cause some damage to the facility, but to destroy the dock would require a level of precision not yet attainable through bombing. Naval bombardment was out of the question, and an airborne assault would eliminate any element of surprise. Hopelessly outgunned, the Chariot attack force would number 611 men, including 166 raiding Commandos, 345 sailors, 91 demolition experts, 3 liaison officers, 2 war correspondents, and a 4-man medical team.[13]

The Joint Chiefs of Staff approved the plan on March 3. Thirty-four-year-old Commander Robert Ryder was placed in charge of the operation's naval forces. A man of vast experience, his past adventures included three years in the submarine service, an Arctic expedition, and spending four days at sea clinging to a piece of wreckage after a U-boat torpedoed a ship under his command.[14]

Lieutenant Colonel Charles Newman, thirty-eight, would lead the Commandos into battle. Good-humored and kind, Newman—a former amateur boxer—reminded one of his subordinates of a "benign elephant . . . due to the downward curve of his prominent broken nose."[15] The sacrificial destroyer selected for the operation was the HMS *Campbeltown*, formerly the USS *Buchanan*. Twenty-four depth charges—loaded into steel drums, encased in cement, and weighing a combined total of more than four tons—would be secured near *Campbeltown*'s forward fuel tanks and rigged with an eight-hour delay fuse.[16] Lieutenant Commander Stephen Halden Beattie, thirty-three, would captain the ship on her final voyage.[17]

The twelve motor launches (MLs) accompanying *Campbeltown* each measured 112 feet long and just under 20 feet wide with a top speed of 20 knots. Their armaments included two .303 Lewis machine guns and two Oerlikon 20mm guns, but their mahogany construction would offer scant protection for their ten-man crews and Commando forces.[18] The headquarters ship—commanded by Lieutenant Dunstan Curtis—would be Motor Gun Boat (MGB) 314, with machine guns amidships and two-pound guns fore and aft. Motor Torpedo Boat (MTB) 74, four torpedo motor launches, and the escorting destroyers HMS *Atherstone* and *Tynedale* completed the flotilla.[19]

Even before reaching the target, defended by some 6,000 Germans, the Chariot armada would have to run a gauntlet of searchlights and coastal batteries along the Loire. The town and dockyards also bristled with heavy artillery; the Germans had put much effort into bolstering the existing French defenses. "It was, indeed," writes one historian, "the most strongly fortified German base along the whole of the western seaboard of Europe, except Brest."[20]

From Brest in the north to Bordeaux in the south, France's conquered seaports provided U-boats "direct access to the Atlantic."[21] By the end of 1941, the Germans had transformed them into impregnable citadels of concrete bunkers, pillboxes, and antiaircraft batteries. By March 1942, they had built nine massive U-boat pens at Saint-Nazaire with plans to construct five more. These concrete monstrosities, still standing today, proved immune to the heaviest of air attacks. The British considered Saint-Nazaire a target of strategic consequence not only because of its massive dry dock, but also its U-boat facilities.

Getting to Saint-Nazaire presented its own challenge. From the harbor at Falmouth on the south coast of England—the operation's designated point of departure—the distance to the target was 263 miles, an estimated two-nights' travel time, across U-boat-infested waters. The Chariot task force would be at the mercy of the elements; rough seas could easily overwhelm the motor launches, while clear skies left them vulnerable to air attack. Operating beyond the range of British fighter cover, the small armada would be on its own.[22]

The Charioteers faced a challenge wholly disproportionate to their numbers. They would charge into battle with "no artillery . . . or heavy mortars, and no air-to-ground support." Armed with light machine guns, rifles, assorted blades, grenades, and Colt .45s, the men were not equipped for heavy combat or a prolonged engagement.[23] Of course, there was no guarantee they'd even reach the target. Mudflats and shoals dominated the six-mile approach to the harbor from the mouth of the Loire River. The British would have to navigate these natural barriers in darkness under the watchful eye of the coastal batteries along both shores, including two 240mm railway guns.[24] Luck would be just as vital as speed and surprise.

Through mid-March, the ships and men assigned to Operation Chariot arrived in Falmouth. The ships rocked idly on the harbor waters; the men—on the carrier vessel *PJC*—simply waited. Colonel Newman briefed them one morning below deck and detailed the task at hand. "He went on to explain that the raid had a high element of risk and that we could not expect any guarantee of a safe return," noted Commando Lieutenant Stuart Chant-Sempill. "If there were those who were married, or had reservations about going on the raid, now was the time to say so, with no reason of being ashamed or fear of being criticized."[25]

No one said a word; the men sat in silence, fully accepting their stark reality and the likelihood of death. "We understood well what he was trying to convey to us," Chant-Sempill later wrote. "We were expendable."[26]

✳ ✳ ✳

At two o'clock on the afternoon of March 26, the Chariot Strike Force sailed from Falmouth beneath a bright blue sky. The destroyer HMS *Atherstone*, towing MGB 314, led the way. *Tynedale* followed in her wake with *Campbeltown*, laden with explosives, not far behind. The motor launches in two columns on either side of the destroyers completed the formation. A single Hurricane circled above on a lonely vigil.[27]

A moderate breeze swept the sea from the east-northeast and stirred the haze that clung to the Channel. Behind the task force, the safety of home slipped away. Lookouts scanned the skies and water for possible enemy activity, but all appeared calm, and the ships cut through the gentle sea unhindered.[28] They passed through the first checkpoint of their outward journey, where the Channel surrendered to the rougher waters of the North Atlantic, at 7:11 p.m.[29] "My own feelings at this stage are difficult to describe," Ryder later wrote, "but the whole thing seemed faintly unreal, and under the circumstances I decided to get as much sleep as possible."[30]

The men on the boats passed the time drinking cocoa or eating sandwiches with bully beef—minced corn beef, a staple of the British Army diet.[31] "Some bought Mars bars, cigarettes, etc. from the ship's canteen until it was realized that the entire stock would go up with the ship and that no payment was necessary," remembered Lieutenant Corran Purdon on *Campbeltown*. "Others made dreadful sandwiches containing such things as Brylcreem, shaving soap, and toothpaste and offered them to unsuspecting friends."[32]

The sea remained mercifully calm—a small blessing. In the event of seasickness, the operation's official orders called for men to soothe their innards with "dry bread, ship's biscuits, potatoes cooked in jackets, and dried fruit." If one had to vomit, orders prohibited them from leaning over a ship's railing, but instead "vomit in the scuppers on the leeward side for safety."[33]

Accompanying the task force was Gordon Holman, a war correspondent for *Reuters*. He stood at the railing and watched the light slowly bleed from the sky as the sun disappeared beyond the sea. An almost impenetrable black void fell upon the ships. "The whole force," wrote Holman, "moved silently and without the slightest glimmer of light."[34] The waters soon began to glow, as though a shimmering city lay beneath the dark surface of the waves. Seaman Ralph Batteson, a gunner on ML 306, noticed countless jellyfish to be the source of illumination. "There were millions of them," he recalled. "You were cutting through them. I'd never seen so many of them, and they seemed to send this phosphorescent light up from the sea."[35]

In the dead of night, the sloshing of the sea and the sound of the engines seemed strangely amplified, but the ships made their nocturnal passage undisturbed.[36] At 2:30 a.m. on March 27, the task force lost its natural camouflage when the marine haze cleared. "Surface visibility," Ryder later noted, "was extreme when dawn broke."[37]

As the sun emerged and revealed the task force in the cold light of morning, Ryder ordered the ships to lower their white ensigns and hoist German ones. No one was allowed on deck during sunlight hours unless they wore "duffle coats and steel helmets or oilskins" to hide their military uniforms from possible reconnaissance aircraft.[38] "Although we realized that we were taking part in a most audacious operation," remembered Purdon, "most, if not all of us, had made dates for the next weekend with our fiancés, wives, or girlfriends, none of whom, of course, knew anything about the forthcoming operation."[39]

At 7 a.m., the task force—now 160 miles southwest of Saint-Nazaire—turned east toward the French coast and reduced speed to 8 knots in an effort to minimize their visibility from the air.[40] Twenty minutes later, the lookout on *Tynedale* saw an object on the "horizon to the north." Was it a trawler or the conning tower of a submarine? Ryder dispatched *Tynedale* to investigate. The destroyer veered away to intercept the unknown vessel.[41]

Tensions ran high as the possible threat of a U-boat attack suddenly seemed very real. Several minutes passed before *Tynedale* signaled back that the object was indeed a surfaced submarine. Ryder placed Beattie—on board *Campbeltown*—in charge and ordered *Atherstone* to assist *Tynedale*. As the second destroyer steamed off toward possible combat, a lookout spotted two trawlers to the starboard side of the sub. Ryder ordered *Atherstone* to change course and intercept the two trawlers, fearing the submarine might do the same thing and use the radio on board one of the trawlers to notify German coastal defenses.[42]

The *Tynedale*, now five miles from the enemy vessel, stayed on its present heading. On U-593, Captain-Lieutenant Gerd Kelbling eyed the approaching destroyer from the conning tower. Battered by depth charges during a recent foray against British convoys, the U-boat was bound for Saint-Nazaire for repairs. The submarine's hydroplanes and rudder controls had suffered extensive damage that made underwater maneuverability all but impossible.[43]

Kelbling felt some relief to see the German ensign flapping from the destroyer's mast as it closed the distance and ordered the firing of a recognition signal. The flare shot upward, bright against the early morning sky, and exploded into six silver starbursts that fanned out like a fiery "umbrella." On the *Tynedale*, now a mere 4,000 yards away, the German ensign came down and the white Royal Navy one went up in its place. This done, she opened fire with her 4-inch guns.[44]

The U-boat dived. *Tynedale* circled and dropped depth charges, the detonations below breaking the surface in a violent boil. The U-boat's conning tower appeared once more as a dark blemish against the foaming sea. The destroyer's short-range machine gun coughed and clattered. Shells ripped across the water and sparked off the sub's side before it dived once more. The *Atherstone*, meanwhile, had turned to join *Tynedale* after identifying the two trawlers as French fishing vessels. The destroyer passed over the spot the U-boat had last been seen. "Contact," Ryder noted, "was obtained with a good echo in about the correct position, but this faded out at about 1,000 yards."[45]

The destroyers continued the hunt for the better part of two hours without luck. They disengaged at 9:20 a.m. and traveled seven miles in a southwesterly direction before turning to rejoin the task force.[46] The U-boat weighed heavily on Ryder's mind. "In breaking off the hunt for this U-boat," he later wrote, "I took into account that within two hours she might surface and make an enemy report. I considered, however, that the U-boat had not sighted the MLs and that we would simply be reported as two destroyers steering southwest. I decided therefore to continue."* He took additional consolation in the low cloud cover, which would make it difficult for enemy aircraft to spot them.[47]

The ships continued on their way, a vast and empty sea presenting itself to the men on board. At 11:35 a.m., another trawler moving in from the north and flying the French tricolor disturbed the scene. Ryder ordered *Tynedale* to intercept the ship. *Tynedale*'s Commandos boarded the French vessel, rounded up the crew without incident, and moved them to the destroyer. The trawler's captain explained he and his men were merely out fishing and produced a German fishing license to prove his point. Ryder accepted the man's story but ordered that the trawler be sunk. Nothing could be left to chance.[48]

Less than half an hour later, at noon, Ryder spotted another trawler on *Atherstone*'s starboard bow. "This one I considered my bird," he wrote, "and slipped MGB 314, ordering her to take off all the crew, all the papers, charts, etc., that they could find. I then sank this trawler, which like the other, was French. The whole crew appeared friendly and professed to be keen to come to England. The captain seemed particularly friendly and quite a good sort. He stated that he had swept up some mines, some of which exploded. . . . It seemed quite clear from these two trawlers that none of them carried radio, so I did not consider it necessary to investigate any of the large number that were subsequently seen."[49]

The Germans were thus far unaware of the British approach— though it hardly meant their guard was down. The *Atherstone* received a British naval signal at 5:18 p.m., stating five torpedo boats had been reported patrolling the waters around Saint-Nazaire. Ryder knew the

---

* U-593 would, in a strange quirk of fate, torpedo HMS *Tynedale* in the Mediterranean on Dec. 12, 1943, and sent her to the bottom with 73 of her crew.

risk the boats posed to his task force but saw no reason to divert from their current heading or established plan of attack.[50]

The sky began to darken. With the French coast drawing ever closer, Ryder took no chances and signaled the motor launches: "Glass on wheelhouses most conspicuous at night. Must be covered with paint, paper, or grease on outside."[51] The fleet set a final course for the enemy shore. At 8 p.m., Ryder and Newman transferred their headquarters from *Atherstone* to what would now be the command ship, MGB 314. The ships fell into a three-column formation, with the *Campbeltown* occupying the middle lane between the motor launches. The *Atherstone* and *Tynedale* fanned out to starboard and port to guard against U-boats.[52]

At 10 p.m., Ryder spotted a signal light from the submarine HMS *Sturgeon*—serving as a navigational marker—flashing the letter "M." The arrhythmic pulse of light possessed an almost ghostly quality amidst the black sea. This was Checkpoint Z, the final rendezvous before the fateful run.[53] "We passed close enough to thank them through the loud-hailer," Ryder wrote.[54] "Good-bye and good luck," Lieutenant Commander Mervyn Wingfield responded from the sub's loudspeaker. "Good luck boys!" he said as the motor launches steamed past.[55] *Atherstone* and *Tynedale* now broke formation to commence their patrolling duties.

The Chariot Strike Force began its final approach to the Loire estuary shortly before midnight, its many wakes churning white on the dark sea. Distant antiaircraft fire could be seen blazing skyward in the northeast. "It was obvious," Ryder wrote in his postoperation report, "that considerable air activity was in progress, as gun flashes extended over a wide arc with considerable flak."[56] Ryder watched from the bridge of MGB 314 as vibrant streams of red and green tracers disappeared in the starless vault above.[57]

Blue columns of searching light weaved patterns across the sky, as British bombers circled over the Saint-Nazaire port. Low cloud cover, however, thwarted any attempt at accuracy, while freezing temperatures and severe icing forced a number of crews to abandon their attack run.[58] If the weather proved a challenge for the British airmen, it served the naval force well.

"The weather, for our purposes, was perfect," Ryder wrote. "The sky was completely overcast with low cloud; indeed, it was at times misty with a light drizzle, while the full moon above the cloud prevented the night from being too dark." Ryder marveled that luck had not yet abandoned them. "No searchlights had been used and we were obviously undetected," he later reported. "We were greatly elated by this . . . this was a moment of tense excitement for everyone. Jokes were exchanged and a note of cheerfulness prevailed."[59]

✻ ✻ ✻

The German ensign still fluttered from every mast in the Chariot convoy and had so far kept the enemy from realizing the threat heading its way. At 12:30 a.m., the ships entered the Loire River and passed the shadowy wreck of SS *Lancastria*, sunk in June 1940 while evacuating British troops and civilians from France. Her hull, jutting from the black surface, marked the final resting place of some 4,000 souls—the greatest loss of life in British maritime history. Ryder turned his eyes from the grim memorial and looked at the small fleet following in his vessel's wake. Like ghost ships in the night, the attack force slipped past the German radar station at Pointe de Chémoulin, its radio signals groping skyward for British bombers.[60]

The coastline remained dark as the strike force passed the 75mm coastal batteries of Pointe de Saint-Gildas on the river's south shore, but suspicions stirred on land.[61] The weak British air raid—having now petered out—worried Captain Karl-Conrad Mecke, commander of the 22nd Naval Flak Brigade responsible for the port's defense. The British generally dispatched multiple waves of bombers to saturate their targets with incendiaries and high explosives. This was something different.

Not wanting to leave anything to chance, Mecke alerted all Wehrmacht command posts: "The conduct of the enemy aircraft is inexplicable and indicates suspicions of parachute landings." He ordered his antiaircraft batteries to kill their searchlights and silence their guns. His men, however, remained on high alert and cast their attention out to sea.[62] Despite Mecke's warning the enemy might be up to something, an official German report states, "the possibility of a landing from the sea was hardly taken into account."[63] Such incredulity played well into British hands.

The ships continued up the Loire, headlong into what many on board knew would be a grim conclusion. On ML 307, Dr. David Paton of the Royal Army Medical Corps made his rounds. "I went forward and found two of my chaps changing their uniforms from trousers to kilts," he wrote. "They explained that as they were probably going to die they preferred to die in kilts." He looked across the black expanse of water, the only illumination being "the phosphorescence of the sea."[64]

The throbbing of the engines seemed almost deafening in the dead of night. The men kept their voices low, not wanting to add to the noise. "We wondered," remembered Private Peter Nagel on the bridge of MGB 314, "how much longer the Germans would let us continue without resistance."[65] On ML 377, Sub-Lieutenant Mark Rodier approached Sub-Lieutenant Frank Arkle. "He started talking to me about making provision for letting his mother and father have his belongings when we got back from St. Nazaire," Arkle recalled.

"What's this all about?" Arkle asked.

"I'm sure," Rodier replied, "I won't be getting out alive."[66]

The black outline of land passed silently on both sides of the river. British gunners, their palms wet against the metal of their Oerlikon cannons and Sten guns, stared into the night, waiting. Backdrop to the agonizing tension was a strange reminder of a more tranquil time and place. The scent of grass and trees—"the sweet smell of the countryside," as one sailor put it—hung over the water.[67] Breathing in the pastoral air, the illusion of a peaceful world, Lieutenant Dunstan Curtis on MGB 314 turned to his coxswain. "This is a queer do," he said. The coxswain nodded in agreement. "It will soon be a bloody sight queerer, sir!"[68]

The time was 12:45 a.m. Behind MGB 314, HMS *Campbeltown*—burdened by the five tons of concrete-encased explosives in her hull—labored up the river. The risk of the ship running aground remained Ryder's primary concern. The operation's planners had taken into consideration *Campbeltown*'s draft and timed the raid to coincide with "an unusually high spring tide."[69]

The task force was now making its way through the shallows near the Le Chatelier shoal, when a heavy vibration rippled up from the ship's bowels. She groaned and shuddered as her keel scraped a sandbank.[70] "We were wondering," remembered Lance Corporal Harold Roberts, "are we going to get stuck? Are we going to get stuck?" *Campbeltown* powered through the obstruction to the relief of all on board. "If we'd got stuck," opined Captain Robert Montgomery, "we'd have been a sitting duck."[71]

As the estuary fell away into darkness behind the Chariot force, a German patrol boat materialized up ahead. "We held our course as well as our breaths," Ryder recalled, "praying that we should go unnoticed." Alongside Ryder on the bridge, manning the machine gun, Private Peter Nagel "could see German sailors staring at us, and the tension was unbearable." With his finger on the trigger, cold and wet from the night's fine drizzle, he "waited for the order to open fire."[72] It never came. The German vessel passed without incident, its crew curious as to the unidentified convoy's destination. As the boat did not have a radio, the captain could not report what he had just seen. It was now one o'clock.[73]

From his headquarters "between Le Pointeau and Pointe de Mindin," Lieutenant Commander Lothar Burhenne—commander of Mecke's 809th Flak Battalion—scanned the water through his field glasses. The silhouettes of ships and the foam of their wakes, silver and bubbling in the faint moonlight, caught him by surprise. He placed a call to the port commander and said a fleet of unidentified vessels was currently making its way up the estuary.[74] The voice on the other end of the line dismissed Burhenne's concerns with obvious contempt. "Don't be stupid," it said. "It's not your business. You would be better employed looking at the sky instead of the river."[75]

Burhenne, not taking any chances, alerted Mecke's headquarters. Only minutes later, a lookout at Saint-Marc spotted "about seventeen vessels" steaming up the estuary. An urgent call confirmed the harbor commander was not expecting any German ships at this hour. Mecke, now confident something was amiss, signaled all stations: *Achtung Landegefahr* (Beware landing).[76]

On the Pointe de Chémoulin, Lieutenant Commander Edo Dieck-mann of the 280th Naval Artillery Battalion stepped outside and surveyed the silent waters. He had now received multiple reports of unidentified ships heading in his direction. Should it be an enemy incursion, it would have to pass through a hell-storm of fire. The bat-talion's twenty-eight 77mm, 150mm, and 170mm guns lined the estu-ary's north shore, covering a deepwater channel all ships had to pass through when entering the port. At 1:15 a.m., Dieckmann signaled his batteries: "Stand by to attack naval targets."[77]

While confusion reigned on land, the attack force steamed ever closer to its objective. At 1:20 a.m., the ships, now two miles from the port, passed the dark shape of the Les Morées light tower.[78] A search-light on the north shore to the rear of the convoy came to life and burned away the cover of night. "For a few breathless moments," re-membered Ryder, "it swept up towards the last craft in the line but was switched off without, apparently, having detected anything."[79]

Ryder's relief proved short-lived. Two minutes after the search-light went dark, both shorelines erupted in blinding white light and exposed the convoy in agonizing detail. It transformed the black water into shimmering mercury and flared off bulkheads and gun barrels. On board, men—accustomed to the dark—shielded their eyes against the dazzling brilliance. From somewhere beyond the light, two can-nons boomed warning shots into the night. Ryder turned on impulse to observe his small fleet. "It was difficult to imagine that there could be any successful deception," he wrote. "Each craft, with her silvery bow-wave, stood out clear and bright, and *Campbeltown*, rising con-spicuously over the smaller craft, could be seen by her funnel smoke to be increasing speed."[80]

Two German signal stations on shore flashed a challenge to the British ships. Ryder now relied on Leading Signalman Seymour Pike, trained in sending and receiving German Morse code. Working the Aldis lamp on MGB 314's bridge, Pike flashed the code for "wait," buying the convoy a few precious seconds. Then, on Ryder's orders, he flashed the following: "Two craft, damaged by enemy action, request permission to proceed up harbor without delay."[81]

Sporadic fire sent up silvery plumes of water. Ryder, in a desperate gambit, ordered Pike to flash the signal for "a vessel considering herself to be fired on by friendly forces."[82] The men on ML 192 could see Pike's lamp blinking its frantic message into the glaring searchlights. "We waited," noted one officer, "in breathless suspense for the response."[83]

The deception worked. The guns on shore fell silent and remained so for four minutes.[84] One-by-one the searchlights blinked out and allowed darkness to once more settle across the water. On shore, watching through his field glasses, Mecke felt increasingly ill at ease. The *Campbeltown*, despite its German ensign, did not look like a ship of the Kriegsmarine. And what reasoning lay behind the large number of smaller vessels? [85]

It was now 1:28 a.m. With the attack force a mile from its target, searchlights and guns on both shores roared and flashed to life.[86] "In a second," wrote Gordon Holman, the *Reuters* correspondent, "the whole river was covered with a fantastic criss-cross pattern of fire, marked by the varied coloured tracer shells and bullets."[87]

Ryder was more to the point. "The fight," he wrote, "was on."[88]

✳ ✳ ✳

On *Campbeltown*'s bridge, Commander Stephen Beattie turned to his yeoman of signals. "Hoist battle ensigns," he said. Above the bridge, the German colors came down. The Royal Navy battle ensign ran up the pole in the bone-white glare of a searchlight. The ship, on Beattie's orders, now sliced the water at 18 knots, its guns no longer silent.[89] The motor launches behind her followed suit with the British colors unfurling in the maelstrom. In those opening moments of hellacious fire, it seemed the assault would end before it began. "A very inferno of fire swept down on the whole convoy," noted one Commando. "It seemed almost impossible that any ship could survive the run-in."[90]

Blue-green tracers from the coastal batteries—and orange-red from the British guns—blazed across the water, its surface reflecting a fiery rainbow. It was, thought one sailor, "very pretty!"[91] Rounds sparked and ricocheted off the sides of ships; everything was noise, fire, and smoke.

"There was banging and crashing and lights and tracer," recalled Captain Robert Montgomery on board *Campbeltown*. A fusillade of fire raked the vessel's wheelhouse. The coxswain fell dead to the floor, leaving the wheel briefly unmanned. No sooner had the quartermaster stepped forward than he too was cut down. "I seemed to be next in line," wrote Montgomery, "so I grabbed the wheel but I wasn't very certain what to do with it." In the fury and excitement, Montgomery could not remember what direction to turn the wheel for starboard and port. "Luckily, at that moment," he said, "someone took [the wheel] away from me."[92]

The *Campbeltown*'s 20mm Oerlikon cannons battered both shorelines, spitting orange flame into the blazing cacophony. The ship's 12-pound gun and 3-inch mortars added to the din and carnage.[93] Up and down the line of ships, cannons and machine guns stuttered and roared. The coastal defenses responded in kind. The hungry searchlight beams, the luminescent flare of tracer rounds, and the flash of countless muzzles torched the night in a violent kaleidoscope of color.

British gunner crews, denied flesh-and-bone targets, fired just below the line of incoming tracers and directly into the searchlights. "They were one of the biggest problems, the searchlights," recalled Ralph Batteson, the gunner on ML 306. "The Germans were switching them off when we got a line of fire on them—and then as soon as we'd swing off, they'd switch back on and be just as deadly as ever."[94] The British soon caught onto the German tactic and kept their guns on point. "It was like a fireworks display and you're in the middle of it," Batteson said. "You don't want to see anything like that again. It was enough, just once."[95]

Enemy rounds hammered the *Campbeltown* from bow to stern. "The weight of fire," noted one sailor, "caught one's breath."[96] Men not engaged in some immediate and necessary task flattened themselves against the deck. Shells clanged off railings and the ship's superstructure, sparking and splintering into hot shrapnel that cut down several men.[97]

On MGB 314, Ryder marveled at the ferocity of it all. The night had become a tangible barrier—one almost impossible to pass. "It is difficult to describe the full fury of the attack from both sides," he wrote in his official report. "The air became one mass of red and green tracer travelling in all directions."[98] Gordon Holman thought the tracer shells rocketing skyward on either side of the estuary "form[ed] a strange Gothic archway of fire." The noise was thunderous, elemental, and "so filled the night that it was impossible to hear orders shouted only a yard or so from the bridges of the motor launches to the gunners on the deck below." Holman guessed the searchlights numbered in their dozens and watched as one occasionally vanished in a cloud of yellow flame and blue sparks.[99]

MGB 314, still in the lead position, approached the outer harbor. In the ambient glow of searchlights, a hazy form took shape off the boat's starboard bow. Fire and light soon revealed a superstructure and guns. It was the German guardship *Botilla Russ*.[100] A bright white flash appeared against the dark silhouette of her body as she opened fire. Her rounds missed their target and fell into the water, already boiling with bursting shells. Able Seaman William Savage, without protection or cover, manned the forward pom-pom on MGB 314. At 200 yards, he squeezed the trigger and pumped explosive rounds into the guardship's hull and the length of her deck.[101] "It was indeed," noted Ryder, "an unfortunate day for the vessel."[102]

Flame shot skyward from her battered deck and reached from her punctured body across the water, but her ordeal had only just begun. The flaming wreck caught the attention of German crews on the opposite shore, who, mistaking it for a British ship, brought their guns to bear.[103]

MGB 314 entered the port under a steady assault from nearby antiaircraft batteries. The firing, recalled one Commando, "was so intense that nobody knew exactly what was going on."[104] Behind the motor gun boat, *Campbeltown* closed in on her final objective and drew the bulk of the German punishment. One Commando, watching from the bridge of another boat, noted *Campbeltown's* "sides seemed to be alive with bursting shells."[105] Rounds punctured her hull and caused havoc in the engine and boiler rooms, ricocheting through heat and steam as men sought cover between the main engines. The Commandos on deck took cover, "lying cheek to jowl" behind welded armored plates that offered scant protection.[106]

A shell exploded somewhere above the mass of huddled bodies. The blast's concussion rolled over the prostrate forms like a violent wave, tossing men aside and showering the deck in shrapnel. Lieutenant Stuart Chant-Sempill—waiting for the storm in his skull to subside—became aware of a burning discomfort. Blood flowed from a wound in his right arm and pooled in the palm of his hand; his left leg, punctured by shrapnel, was "wet and sticky."[107] He ran his tongue across dry lips and tasted the "sweet, sickly flavor of almonds." It was, he realized, nitroglycerine from the shell-burst. He wiped blood from his face, stinging with "numerous pinpricks," and gingerly ran his hands down the length of his body. Tiny slivers of metal dotted his skin and uniform, underscoring just how close death had come.[108]

Campbeltown's guns punished the shore batteries with an unrelenting and thunderous fury. Exposed gunners on the Oerlikon platforms fell to enemy rounds, only to be replaced by others who rushed to fill the blood-stained void. Watching the gunners in action, one Commando could not help but admire "their bravery and discipline and thought what fine fellows they were."[109] Shells seemed to hammer every inch of the ship.

Riding the violent wake stretching out behind the destroyer, ML 307 ran the blazing crucible. "Searchlights by the dozen illuminated us from both sides," recalled Captain David Paton. "I couldn't see anything of the big shells that must have been falling but the air was thick with tracer shells coming from all directions rather like cricket balls. You could see them coming and jump out of the way, or jump in the air for the same reason."[110] He initially sought cover behind a depth charge but thought better of it when a piece was shot away and passed within inches of his head. He pressed himself against the deck and gazed ahead at the beleaguered *Campbeltown*.[111]

Her smokestack billowing, the destroyer charged past the wounded *Botilla Russ* and hammered her broadside with a ferocious fire, sending up new bursts of flame. Every searchlight along the shore now ensnared *Campbeltown* in its hot-white grip. The sight mesmerized

Sub-Lieutenant Richard Collinson on ML 192. "She was surrounded by shell splashes," he wrote. "Her gun flashes and the glare of shells bursting about her lit her upperworks vividly. Tracer shots ricocheted off her, sailing up into the air, in all directions."[112]

Tortured and pummeled, *Campbeltown* increased speed for her final charge. The motor launches followed in her wake, their wooden bodies chewed and mangled by the German guns. "Several of our launches were hit," recalled Peter Nagel on MGB 314, "and as they were made only of wood and filled to the brim with petrol, they exploded."[113] The river itself caught fire as burning petrol spilled into the water. "There was wreckage, smoke, tracer and exploding shells," wrote Lance Corporal Stanley Stevenson on ML 156. "I could feel and hear our ML being hit time and time again."[114]

Against a backdrop of burning motor launches, *Campbeltown* charged to her fate. Her cannons continued hammering away as her battered sides absorbed blistering punishment. In the wheelhouse, Beattie felt the ship lurch as she tore through a torpedo net and saw through the shattered windscreen the dock's massive outer caisson looming ever closer.[115] A well-placed shot hit the ship's forecastle and sent up a dazzling column of flame. Beattie and Montgomery turned away from the blinding flash, but the ship maintained her course. The two men braced for impact right before *Campbeltown* slammed into her target.[116]

Thirty-six feet of her bow crumpled like a tin can and forced her over the caisson. The noise of grinding, crunching metal and shattered masonry deafened the men in the wheelhouse. The force of impact threw them to the floor, as *Campbeltown*—her guns still firing—completed her final voyage in spectacular fashion.[117] The ship came to a sudden and violent halt, protruding some thirty-five feet into the port's dry dock. Beattie pulled himself from the floor and looked over at Montgomery, who was hauling himself up. Beattie gave a quick glance at his watch. It was 1:34 a.m. "Four minutes late!" he exclaimed in good humor.[118]

The truly desperate and savage hours now began.

CHAPTER 7

* * *

DOGS OF WAR

Rounds continued to spark and ricochet off the dead ship, its deck strewn with debris and bloody human wreckage. Major William "Bill" Copland worked his way through the upright Commandos, yelling the order to disembark: "Roderick Off! Roy Off!" The assault troops under the commands of Captain Donald Roy and Lieutenant Johnny Roderick worked their way forward, stepping over the dead and writhing injured.[1] Their footing was precarious, made more so by a massive hole in the forward deck through which a column of thick, black smoke clawed its way skyward through burning tracer shells and searchlight beams.[2]

Roderick's team, numbering fourteen men, was tasked with destroying the four searchlight and gun emplacements on the southeast corner of the Normandie dock and forming a defensive perimeter against an attack from the northeast.[3] Mindful of fallen comrades, shredded timber, and jagged metal, moving through smoke that stung the eyes and choked the lungs, the men could not easily take cover from the endless fusillade of fire.

Dressed in a kilt and armed with a Tommy gun, twenty-two-year-old Lance Corporal John "Jock" Donaldson fell mortally wounded. With no other option available to them, the men in Roderick's column stepped over the fallen Scotsman as he bled out on the deck. The men carried bamboo ladders to throw over the starboard railing and descend to the caisson but discovered at this desperate moment that most were broken. They instead employed ropes to escape *Campbeltown*'s devastated carcass and commence their assault.[4]

Corporals Arthur Frank Woodiwiss and Nicky Finch hit the ground first with enemy rounds tearing up the wooden walkway beneath their feet. In the glow of battle, both men saw a sandbagged machine-gun nest spitting flame as the rest of Roderick's men descended ropes and broken ladders.[5] As he fought through the noise and confusion to gain his bearings, Woodiwiss noticed an object cutting a high arc through the air and falling toward him. Only at the last moment did he recognize it as "a potato-masher grenade."[6]

Driven more by instinct than common sense, he fly-kicked the grenade away from himself and lunged forward before the sound of its detonation had joined the greater din of battle. He rushed the gun emplacement, his Tommy gun burning hot as he cut the German sentries down. His gun still smoking, he wrenched open the gun bunker's door and sprayed the interior, the screams of men audible over the weapon's angry clatter.[7]

In the small space, now thick with gun smoke and the stench of cordite, Woodiwiss pulled a prepared explosive from his pack and wrapped it around the gun's breech. He ran from the bunker as the breech vaporized in a ball of flame behind him.[8] Satisfied, he joined Roderick and the rest of his team. The battle fully joined, Roderick felt "relief that at last we had got going. . . . My main concern was that I hoped I would behave myself throughout the action and—not through my inadequacy—let the party down."[9]

The men hurried toward their second objective, a 37mm gun atop a concrete bunker. "There was," noted Roderick, "a hell of a lot of firing going on."[10] Several lobbed grenades rendered the gun useless; inside the bunker, a burst of machine-gun fire reduced the three-man crew to a bloody, twisted heap.

The team moved quickly from one objective to the next through a blizzard of hot rounds and flying shrapnel. "It was," remembered Roderick, "a fulltime job keeping our eyes open to all around us."[11] The team darted between Nissen huts, tossing in grenades and spraying the flimsy metal structures with machine-gun fire. At full strength, Roderick and his men numbered fourteen—but now, the storm of battle had whittled them down to fewer than ten. On this small group lay the burden of defending the eastern flank of the Chariot landing ground.[12]

* * *

While Roderick's men waged their desperate action on the east side of the dock, Captain Donald Roy and his thirteen Scotsmen—all decked out in kilts—stormed the dock's western flank.[13] Their primary target: two guns atop the pumping station.[14]

Their disembarkation from *Campbeltown* proved no less chaotic. One member of Roy's team, Private Arthur Ashcroft—thrown off-balance by a heavy load of weapons and grenades—fell through the gaping hole in the ship's deck. Although he escaped major injury, he did lose his helmet and Tommy gun.[15] Another, Lieutenant Johnny Proctor, lay in a thickening pool of blood, his leg nearly severed by a shell.[16] Roy's team scrambled over the ship's forecastle and joined the fight on solid ground.

They ran toward the pumping station. The Germans manning the two guns had little desire to fight, abandoned their posts, and fled into the night. Roy and his men tossed grenades onto the pump station's roof for good measure before climbing up to the guns and destroying the breeches.[17] Standing on the roof, looking out at the burning water and the silhouettes of ships, Sergeant Don Randall felt a strange sense of stillness. "There was an atmosphere of quite extraordinary serenity and detachment from the hurly-burly below and around," he recalled. "The crisscross streams of colored tracer not far above our heads only seemed to emphasize and bear witness to reality."[18]

His point of view differed greatly from Private Ashcroft—providing cover below and still without a helmet—who couldn't help but notice "a lot of German ships spread about the St. Nazaire basin." The guns aboard the vessels seemed to fire at no particular target but instead saturate the night with incandescent rounds, forcing Ashcroft, as he put it, to "dodge the flak."[19]

It came almost as a relief when Roy ordered his men to move on the bridge at the Old Entrance and secure an escape route from the northern dock area. The Commandos from *Campbeltown* would have to cross this bridge to reach the reembarkation area at the Old Mole for their journey back to England.[20]

Roy led his team across a heat-shimmering landscape of shadow and fire. They reached the bridge without incident and found the place deserted: no Germans and—perhaps more ominously—no sign of the demolition team tasked with rigging the bridge to blow.[21] As the sounds of battle raged about them, Roy's men took flimsy cover behind their Bren guns and began their anxious wait.

The success of the operation very much depended on Lieutenant Stuart Chant-Sempill and the four men who comprised his demolition team. Should the explosives in *Campbeltown* fail to detonate, it was imperative the impeller pumps and electrical gear controlling the water flow in and out of the dry dock be destroyed. This would leave the dock useless for at least several months.[22]

Chant-Sempill and his men moved up the gore-slicked deck. "We encountered more dead and wounded sailors and commandos where they had been caught in the murderous German fire," he recalled.[23] The concentration of bodies thickened the further forward they went. He saw his friend John Proctor lying prostrate among the dead and wounded, the remains of his shattered leg protruding from his torn and blood-spattered kilt. In obvious agony, Proctor begged for help— but there was nothing the men could do but continue moving toward the bow.[24]

The going proved tough. The shell-burst Chant-Sempill survived on *Campbeltown*'s attack run had left his arms, legs, and hands peppered with shrapnel. The same burst had left Sergeant Bill Chamberlain unable to walk without assistance, leaving two members of Chant-Sempill's team to haul Chamberlain along.[25]

Bearing the weight of "explosives, sledgehammers, axes, and incendiaries," and trying to maintain his balance, Chant-Sempill felt the deck disappear beneath his feet.[26] He looked down and saw nothing but flame and smoke as he fell through the hole in the deck. Only his rucksack spared him a fiery end when it caught on a jagged outcropping. There he dangled, staring into a burning void, until his men could pull him free.[27]

At the front of the ship, Chant-Sempill's small team struggled down the last remaining ladder and moved with all the speed they could muster toward the pump house. With German tracer shells painting fiery trails above their heads, they reached their objective—only to find the thick-steeled pump house door locked.[28]

Captain Robert Montgomery, a demolition expert who trained the Commandos prior to the operation, materialized with impeccable timing from the surrounding chaos and slapped a magnetic charge on the door.[29] He stepped aside, inviting Chant-Sempill to light the fuse. With his fingers raw and sticky with blood and his hands trembling, Chant-Sempill found it impossible to light a match. "I asked him to do it for me in case the soldiers would think I was frightened," he recalled, "which I was."[30]

Montgomery lit the fuse and stepped away. The door swung open with a violent bang and gave access to the pump house's dark interior. Chant-Sempill and his team stepped inside with the noise of the small blast still echoing between the concrete walls. They moved quickly, the beams from their torches cutting thin, white trails of light in the pitch black. At the far end of the room they came to a metal staircase that descended forty feet into darkness.[31]

Chant-Sempill cast a weary glance at Chamberlain, sweating in the pallid light, and realized the man's injuries would not allow him to navigate the zigzagging stairs. Thinking quickly, he told Chamberlain to stay put and keep guard. Chant-Sempill and the rest of his men descended into the murk. When they reached the bottom of the stairs in the damp subterranean depths, they discovered the four impeller pumps that brought water in and out of the dock.[32]

The men went to work and placed forty pounds of explosives at the base of each impeller. They blinked the sweat from their eyes and performed their task mostly in silence, startling when the sound of thunder rumbled down from above and rattled the structure in a powerful embrace. Chant-Sempill stared up into oblivion and realized the noise was Roy's men destroying the guns on the roof.[33] He turned his attention once more to the explosives, his fingers—still crusted with blood—meeting the challenge. It took roughly twenty minutes to get the charges in place and wire them to a pair of percussion igniters. He ordered Sergeants Ron Butler and Alfred King back up the stairs to carry the wounded Chamberlain to safety.[34]

With Sergeant Arthur Dockerill by his side, Chant-Sempill watched the two men ascend and disappear into darkness. An eternity seemed to pass before they heard the all-clear from above. He passed Dockerill an igniter. Remembered Chant-Sempill: "We looked at each other as I slowly counted, one—two—three—and I pulled the pin of my igniter and Dockerill did the same."[35]

The two men hurried up the stairs with only ninety seconds to go until detonation.[36] Chant-Sempill, in considerable pain, struggled with a limp. They made it to ground level and hurried for the door. He held tight with lacerated fingers to Dockerill's arm.[37] He could see the glow of fires outside, the rainbow blaze of tracers, and feel the cool rush of night air. They fled the building with moments to spare when an ear-bleeding roar escaped the bowels of the pump house, throwing up flame and twisted machinery. The structure's roof blew like a volcano top and propelled massive slabs of shattered concrete into the sky. A broad column of fire shot up and out into the night and over-powered—if just momentarily—all other sources of light. The noise of the blast swept across the entire dock and, just as quickly, retired to its devastated point of origin.[38]

Chant-Sempill and his men emerged from their cover and watched the final shattered blocks of concrete and smoldering metal hit the ground. With the explosion still echoing in their ears and rattling their bones, they returned to the pump house to inspect the damage and en-sure the completion of their task. Inside was a decimated ruin. Allow-ing himself a brief moment of relief, Chant-Sempill ordered his men to drop a few incendiary bombs for good measure before making their way to the rendezvous point for evacuation.[39]

At roughly the same time Chant-Sempill's team obliterated the pump house, another four-man demolition crew led by Lieutenant Chris Smalley broke into the nearby winding house—the closest target to the *Campbeltown*—and rigged the machinery that controlled the dock's massive caisson.[40]

As Smalley's men ran for cover, the single-story structure blew apart in a flash of red-orange flame, throwing more heat and debris into the burning night. Their job complete, and with permission to withdraw, Smalley and his men ran down to where the water lapped against the quayside—instead of the prearranged evacuation point at the Old Mole—and climbed aboard a motor launch that had just disembarked another Commando team.[41]

No sooner did the launch pull away than it sparked and splintered under savage German fire. "Rather him than me," thought Chant-Sempill, watching. "I hope they make it."[42] As rounds blistered the length of the beleaguered craft, setting it alight, Smalley ran forward to help unjam the boat's sole Oerlikon cannon only to be shot dead.[43]

While Chant-Sempill and Smalley wreaked havoc, Lieutenants Corran Purdon—only twenty years old—and Gerard Brett led two additional demolition teams in a charge against the winding house and the caisson on the north end of the dry dock. Lending support was the monocle-wearing Lieutenant Robert Burtinshaw and his small team.[44]

Machine-gun and small-arms fire chipped the concrete at their feet as they ran beneath the weight of their rucksacks, weapons, and explosives. One corporal, a man named Johnson, took a round but kept pace despite the pain.[45] There was no time to care for the injured. "It had been impressed upon us," remembered one Commando. "'You must get to your target, doesn't matter how many are killed, don't stop to help anybody, just get to that target and lay your charges.'"[46]

With lungs burning, Purdon's men reached the winding house and broke in with a sledgehammer. "We laid our made-up charges and connected them up," Purdon later wrote, noting his team was "cool as ice and as cheerful as if on holiday."[47] The plan called for Purdon to detonate his explosives after Brett and Burtinshaw had destroyed the caisson. Corporal Ron Chung ran to tell Brett all was set to go. Purdon watched Chung sprint into a glaring threadwork of searchlights, turn to silhouette, and fade from view against the heavy rattle of machine-gun fire. He soon emerged from the gauntlet, his mission accomplished, despite being shot.[48]

On the exposed roadway that crossed the top of the caisson it was smoke, noise, and chaos. Rounds to his right arm and both legs sent Brett sprawling upon his arrival. Burtinshaw, with his monocle still in place, assumed command of Brett's team and urged the men on "with his casual and jaunty air."[49]

With bullets ricocheting and clanging about, the Commandos managed to secure several eighteen-pound charges against the caisson's outer wall. Plans to place charges inside the caisson fell apart when the men discovered the timber-and-tarmac road upon which they stood covered the entry hatch.[50]

The air burned bright with incendiary shells and buzzed with small-arms fire. The deck of two tankers in the dry dock below came to life with shadowy figures, their forms taking shape in the white flash of muzzle blasts as they strafed the top of the caisson. From the Penhoet Basin on the caisson's other side, large tongues of flame lashed the night as German naval guns opened fire.[51]

The Commandos took what scant cover they could, but survival seemed unlikely. Great swaths of the roadway disappeared in hot bursts of steel; the sound of shells ringing off the caisson's ironworks pierced the skull. The men returned fire with their sidearms, shooting at targets almost impossible to discern.[52] Burtinshaw rallied men to his side and led them into the maelstrom, all the while singing "There'll Always Be an England."[53]

They charged the tanker in the dry dock and fired indiscriminately as they ran. Two men armed with Tommy guns rushed the tanker's gangway plank and swept the ship's deck with a murderous barrage. Firing from the ship fell silent, but the staccato rattle of machine guns quickly filled the void. Burtinshaw, still singing, turned and saw German soldiers approaching from behind. In a final daring act, he raised his voice in a patriotic swell and ran at them with nothing more than a pistol.[54]

✳ ✳ ✳

Not until all Commando teams had disembarked *Campbeltown* and the casualties vacated did Beattie give the order to abandon ship. Enemy rounds still punished the dead ship, ricocheting about the lower decks and battering the machinery in the engine and boiler rooms.[55]

It fell on Chief Engine Room Artificer H. Howard to oversee the scuttling operation. "No time could be wasted," he recalled, "and I had to get busy opening valves, etc., to flood the ship."[56] The lights in the ship no longer working, Howard performed his task by torchlight and the red-orange glow of fires. *Campbeltown* was by now a burning coffin, as flames devoured the lower decks and burned their way topside. Howard worked through the blistering heat and soon emerged on the deck. "On reaching the forepart of the ship I found several of my shipmates standing and these I told to follow me," Howard later wrote. "Through the flames of the forecastle we scrambled down the ladders placed by the Commandos and got on shore."[57]

Relentless machine-gun fire in the Saint-Nazaire harbor thrashed the motor launches attempting to land their assault teams at the Old Mole and Old Entrance. The wooden boats splintered and burned. Lacking any meaningful armor, they were ill equipped to withstand what one contemporary account calls "the tornado of metal."[58]

A storm of hot steel blazed from the rooftops of surrounding buildings; the colored tracer shells—bright against the night—looked to one Commando like "stitches on a piece of cloth."[59] Flames and petrol spread across the water. The barking of commands and the screams of dying men carried above the noise and drifted through the smoke. One boat after another, drawing close to their disembarkation points, suffered bow to stern as rounds ripped through men and timber.

Lieutenant Kenneth Horlock's ML 443 attempted to make its way to the Old Mole but somehow missed its mark. When Horlock and his naval beachmaster, Lieutenant Reginald Verity, tried to get their bearings, they realized a mile of water lay between themselves and their objective. "When we saw it, we both laughed," recalled Verity. "It seemed extraordinary that we had got through all that heavy fire and missed the place."[60]

ML 447—commanded by Lieutenant T. D. L. Platt—approached the Old Mole with Captain David Birney and his thirteen Commandos on board. The water in front of the launch jumped and writhed with heavy fire until the boat itself was caught in the tempest, its sides quickly reduced to smoldering ruins. Men crumpled to the deck or were blown into the water.[61]

On ML 307, Dr. David Paton wondered how anyone might survive. He was tasked with setting up a medical post. Prior to leaving England, he had penned a possible final letter to his wife. "It may be of some comfort to you to know that if I go down," he wrote, "at least I go down in an attack, and I want you to hold your head high as I am managing to do despite my forebodings."[62]

Somehow, the ML managed to pull up alongside the Mole. Paton and the other Commandos pushed their ladders up the pier's side and began to climb, not unlike medieval raiders storming a castle. Above them, German soldiers kicked the ladders away from the wall and sent men crashing to the deck or into the fiery water.[63]

Then, the enemy dropped grenades onto the launch. "We were all dancing about," remembered Paton, "kicking them into the water."[64] Behind him, Paton saw one Commando on the shoulders of another, attempting to fire a Bren gun "over the angle of the Mole." The gun's recoil sent both men sprawling.[65]

The launch's skipper tried to pull away but was blocked by another burning vessel. Paton watched a German—no more than twenty-five yards away—furiously work the aim and elevation wheels of a Bofors antiaircraft gun and attempt to bring the weapon to bear. It was then Paton noticed his Red Cross armband "shining white and fluorescent in the searchlights."[66]

He ripped the target from his arm just as the gun above him roared. The first round cut a trail above the launch and splashed down ten yards from the boat. The gun boomed a second time and sent up a frothy column of spray five yards off. Paton could do nothing but watch as the German gunner worked furiously between shots to correct his aim and trajectory. Two more times the gun bellowed into the night. The third shot disappeared into the burning void of battle—but the fourth whistled loudly and sucked the air away as it flew past Paton's head and splashed ever closer to the boat.[67]

All the while the skipper kept trying to pull the boat away. A cry for help alongside the launch diverted Paton's gaze to the water. A burning slick of petrol fast approached the launch. Between the boat and the creeping flames Paton saw a friend—Captain Birney from ML 447—thrashing in the water. He reached down in a desperate effort to pull the man on board. "We managed to lock our hands," Paton recalled, "but then the boat's propellers gave a great surge in reverse and our hands were torn apart because of the oily water."[68]

Paton could do nothing as the man drifted helplessly away. Angry at the increasing scope of disaster, he turned from the water and moved below deck to tend to casualties. As he wrapped clean dressing around one soldier's bleeding wound, the boat lurched violently and sent the doctor tumbling backward, his foot striking "the poor casualty on the head."[69]

Peering through a hole in the ship's side, Paton realized the boat was speeding away from the combat zone. "By the time I got back on deck," he recalled, "we had left the harbor and were racing for the open sea." The burden of retreat weighed heavily on the soldiers and crew. "We continued grimly with our run," Paton noted. "Now, another ML joined us, and together we made for the center of the Atlantic."[70]

Other motor launches fared no better. Lieutenant Commander William L. Stephens, a "daredevil" who "walked as if he was permanently on the deck of a ship,"[71] took a beating as he tried to navigate ML 192 alongside the Mole. Two large shells slammed the launch in quick succession. "The results," noted Stephens, "were sudden and disastrous."[72]

The force of impact threw the boat hard against the Mole. Several Commandos leapt from the vessel and hurried up the wall before the craft drifted away again. The launch presented an easy target with both engines destroyed and no functional steering. "The damage was simply frightful," Stephens recalled. "There was virtually no engine room left and some incendiaries must have hit our tanks, because we were blazing fiercely in the petrol compartment."[73]

More shells from a shore battery hastened the boat's demise. Stephens knew he and his men had no choice but to abandon ship. If ever a moment called for a drink, it was now. He pulled a hip flask from his pocket, took a deep swig, and—feeling the whiskey warm his gut—gazed across the awful seascape, at the white-hot glare of searchlights and the other burning boats. Stephens took one more drink and gave the order, sending the few survivors on ML 192 into the water.[74]

Stephens struggled against the freezing current and the creeping panic he felt at being swept away from shore. His extremities numb with cold, he mustered everything he had. He soon reached land and pulled himself halfway out of the water, too exhausted to exert any additional effort; his muscles screaming from the strain, his heart beating like a jackhammer against his ribs. He surrendered to his predicament for the briefest of moments and found he cared little about his fate—but he soon rallied. It hardly mattered. Germans quickly surrounded Stephens and his men—by now "a very bedraggled bunch . . . all dripping wet and with very little of our clothing left"—and marched them off into captivity.[75]

On Lieutenant Henry Falconar's ML 446, wireless operator Thomas O'Leary sat below deck with his tin helmet secured tightly in place. "By now," he recalled, "the bullets were going through [the boat] and out the other side." If he wanted to move anywhere, he did so on his hands and knees.[76] Not everyone took such precautions. One Commando commented how beautiful the tracer rounds looked. A moment later one "blew the back of his head out."[77]

Above O'Leary, bodies littered the launch's deck. The crews manning the machine guns on the bridge lay dead beneath the wreckage of their guns. Captain Hodgson, commander of the assault troops on board, died before the ship even reached the harbor. Falconar, despite the blood and damage, tried to approach the Mole only to give up and turn for the treacherous voyage home.[78]

The Old Mole by now presented a "terrible site," remembered Lieutenant Ronald Swayne on ML 306. Everywhere he looked he saw burning, sinking motor launches, and men struggling in the water.[79]

The Saint-Nazaire harbor more resembled a sea of fire. Swayne and the other Commandos on his launch did their best to knock out as many searchlights as they could. He fired his Bren gun until the barrel burned red-hot. "I changed the barrel and took all the skin off the inside of my hand," Swayne remembered. "But it was very good target shooting."[80]

The launch's skipper, Lieutenant Ian Henderson, tried to maneuver the vessel through the flaming detritus on his approach to the Old Mole—but it proved impossible, prompting Henderson to turn the boat around and run the gauntlet of searchlights and shore batteries out to sea.[81]

Lieutenant Tom Collier's ML 457 maneuvered past burning wreckage, through searchlights and fire, and reached its disembarkation point. It took two attempts under heavy bombardment to get the ship's Commandos ashore.[82] No sooner had he reached solid ground, Lieutenant Eric de la Torre felt a blast, a ripsaw current of heat and noise that sent flame and masonry into the sky. Falling debris knocked him flat. He clawed his way out of the rubble and struggled to get back to the motor launch before it withdrew.[83]

Collier pulled the launch away under devastating machine-gun fire and awaited the signal to retrieve the remaining men upon the completion of their mission.[84] On board was a living nightmare. "Shells were coming inside one end of the ML and coming out the other," remembered de la Torre. "There were bodies lying all around the mess deck." Of the six ships tasked with landing Commandos at the Old Mole, only Collier's succeeded.[85]

Collier gave the order to abandon ship. "It was a desperate scene," de la Torre said. "Pools of burning fuel were floating on the water, and as we tried to steer past them, shells and bullets were splashing in on either side. Motor launches were on fire. It was chaos. I thought nobody could live through it."[86]

He leapt into the water and promptly sank, weighed down by two pistols in his tunic. His inflated life preserver brought him slowly back to the surface. No sooner did he feel the cold night air on his face than shrapnel punctured his inflatable and sent him back under.[87]

He struggled against the current and the weight of his boots and clothing, and emerged near a life raft filled with casualties. Out of breath, freezing and exhausted, he somehow managed to grab hold and cling for dear life. Other men in his same predicament lost their grip and simply floated away, disappearing into the flames or the black deep below. "Through all this confusion," de la Torre said, "I could hear a voice singing 'O God, Our Help in Ages Past.'"[88]

The raft drifted toward shore, where de la Torre saw the silhouettes of waiting Germans. On dry land, an enemy officer took de la Torre's two pistols and offered, "in exchange, a souvenir ring bearing the coat of arms of St. Nazaire."[89] Other Germans huddled around the injured men and congratulated them on their courage before marching them off to a hospital for treatment. Although a prisoner, de la Torre fared better than most of the men on ML 457—including Lieutenant Tom Collier—who died on the water.[90]

✷ ✷ ✷

Efforts at the port's Old Entrance fared no better. Only fourteen Commandos out of a possible fifty made it onto terra firma, the motor launches suffering much the same fate as those assaulting the Old Mole. Through the crisscross pattern of searchlights and unyielding fire, Ryder's MGB 314 managed to land Lieutenant Colonel Charles Newman and his headquarters staff of six. The men established an operations center in what, ironically, was the German dockyard headquarters just south of the bridge currently being held by Captain Roy.[91]

In reality, Newman exercised little command over the raging land battle, as effective communications proved impossible to establish in the chaos and tumult. Gradually, worn-out members from the *Campbeltown* assault parties trickled in to give their reports. Newman, a calming presence no matter how dire the circumstances, offered each man the same warm smile and words of gratitude: "Well done, old boy. Better move along now towards the Mole."[92]

German artillery, machine-gun fire, and grenades had left barely a hundred Commandos standing—none of whom escaped injury. Bleeding and spent, they gathered in the shadows of the railway cars and warehouses outside Newman's headquarters and prepared to dash to the reembarkation point on the Mole.[93] None of them had any idea as to the massacre on the water. Soon joined by Newman and Major Bill Copland, second-in-command of the Commando force, the men moved out, keeping close to the buildings.[94]

As they neared the Mole, they caught their first glimpse of the carnage in the harbor. "We were quite cheerful," remembered Chant-

Sempill, "but suddenly became very quiet."[95] The harbor was now a sea of red and yellow flame, cluttered with burning motor launches beneath a heavy cloud of black smoke. The men stared, momentarily disbelieving the sight. Newman broke the silence. "Good heavens, Bill!" he said. "Surely, those aren't ours!"[96]

Shock quickly surrendered to a creeping sense of dread, as the men realized there was no way home. "As more of our soldiers reported in from all directions in the dock area, the situation began to look desperate," wrote Chant-Sempill. "The enemy were virtually within yards of us but had not seen or realized where we were, sheltered as we were by the railway trucks."[97]

The men, hiding in the shadows, heard "a rush of feet and shouts of 'Heil Hitler!'"[98] Newman peered into the darkness and ordered his men to hold their fire until the approaching soldiers closed within yards. "When the [firing] ceased," remembered one Commando, "I heard some moaning and nothing more."[99] As the gun smoke drifted away, Newman and Copland briefly discussed their predicament and agreed surrender was not an option. They would fight their way out of the dockyard, battle through town into the surrounding country, and attempt to make their way south to Spain.[100]

Newman grouped the men into teams of twenty and presented the daunting proposition. He did this—remembered one soldier—"quietly and coolly."[101] He appeared totally unruffled by the growing intensity of enemy fire and the clearly audible barking of German commands on the other side of the railway trucks. "Colonel Newman's indomitable spirit did so much towards dispelling any momentary misgivings and to maintain the general level of morale," remembered one Commando. "He made several 'cracks' and even found a cheery remark when a grenade landed unpleasantly close to him."[102]

The only way out of the dock area and into the town lay across a narrow lifting bridge held by enemy infantry and covered by German machine guns.[103] At 3 a.m. the men moved out, with those armed with Tommy guns leading the way.[104] They moved as quickly as their injuries allowed and kept to shadows cast by the rows of warehouses. The sound of enemy fire never relented; the cold groping fingers of searchlights remained an unnerving constant. All the while, Newman urged his men forward. "Keep going, lads! Keep going!"[105]

German rounds tore into the warehouses and churned up the cobblestones as the Commandos ducked and dashed their way toward the bridge. The thunderous clamor of heavy artillery, machine guns, and small-arms fire rolled across the dockyard. "All I had was my Colt .45 and I wished I had a bloody sub-machine gun of some kind," remembered Lieutenant Corran Purdon. "We literally fought our way from one patch of shadow to the next."[106]

Up and down the advancing lines men began to fall. The injured had to be left behind, for where could they be taken? "They were patched up as best we could," remembered Purdon, "and we just had to hope that the Germans would look after them."[107]

They soon lost the scant cover offered by the warehouses and reached the port's fire-swept lock basin with the bridge on its left-hand side. Purdon nearly found himself a casualty when he tripped over a piece of barbed wire. A bullet struck the spot where he'd been standing a second before.[108]

He came to a full-length sprawl at the feet of Chant-Sempill, who couldn't help but laugh at his friend's mishap. "I didn't laugh for very long, however," he recalled, "for almost immediately, I was hit again by a bullet, fired at us by one of the Germans retreating before our charge, and a bullet lodging in one's knee is a most painful way of stopping one's mobility."[109] When two Commandos tried picking him up, Chant-Sempill collapsed and insisted he be left behind. He would spend the next twenty months in a prison camp.[110]

"Our progress was slow because firefights were breaking out all over the place and we were heavily outnumbered," remembered Purdon. "No one wanted to get themselves killed, but neither did we want to be captured."[111]

The situation was dire. "By the time we reached the lock basin we had lost so many men that the three parties were formed into one," recalled one Commando. "We came under very heavy machinegun fire—not only from both sides of the lock, but also from a ship anchored in the basin."[112]

Newman, appearing oblivious to the maelstrom, strode among his men, "placed the Bren guns and personally directed their fire."[113] The men slowly fought their way forward and left in their wake a trail of blood. And now the iron-girded bridge glowed in the harsh embrace of searchlights.

The men approached and stopped in the shadow of a low building. Roughly 250 yards to the left of the expanse, Newman spotted some fifty Germans in white naval uniforms. He summoned two Bren-gunners from his ranks and sent them forward to cut the enemy down.[114] The noise hardly mattered, for there would be no storming the bridge by surprise. Remembered a Commando named Haines: "[Newman] called me up and told me to collect as many machine-gunners as possible. He gave us our final orders, which were to make a combined rush across the bridge."[115]

Newman studied the bridge with Germans clearly visible on the crossing and the opposite side. "We are going to cross it," he said. "Cost what it might."[116]

He gave the order—"Away we go, lads!"—and the Commandos stormed forward.[117] They charged from the shadows into the glare of searchlights, screaming and firing, with Newman and Captain Donald Roy—in his kilt—at the point of the spear. "We all went for it like dogs," said Purdon. "A hail of enemy fire erupted as we crossed the bridge, projectiles slamming . . . into its girders, bullets whining and ricocheting off them and from the cobbles."[118]

The muzzle flashes formed an impenetrable wall on the other end of the expanse. "They were putting down everything they had," one Commando later recalled.[119] Sparks from rounds clanging off the overhead girders showered the men in a fiery downpour. The hail of fire sent men sprawling, but some carried on despite their wounds. Purdon, his shoulders grazed by bullets and punctured by shrapnel, had nearly crossed the bridge when a grenade went off by his feet and threw him into the air. He landed hard but forced himself up and kept moving, his trouser leg soaked in blood.[120]

The men had reached the far side with Newman still roaring his encouragement. Newman, noted one of his men, "infused into [us] the desire and the determination to carry the attack back into the enemy's ranks until the last round had been expended."[121]

A German pillbox now stood between Newman's rapidly shrinking force and the narrow, winding streets of the town. Major Bill Copland—bleeding from shrapnel wounds—charged the concrete nest, jammed his machine gun through the slot, and emptied his magazine into the cramped enclosure. Survival remained the only strategy. A German motorcycle with a machine-gun-mounted sidecar emerged from a nearby street. A barrage of blistering fire turned it quickly into a smoldering heap of man and machinery.[122]

The iron-fist punch of a mortar blast threw one Commando, Lance Corporal Jimmy Brown, to the ground. The force of impact knocked him out. "When I came to, I saw the rest of the party disappearing up one of the side streets," Brown recalled. "I managed to make my way to a shed, where I found cover and was captured the next day."[123]

For the Commandos Brown saw disappearing down the street, a desperate game of cat and mouse ensued. The survivors split up and spread through the town. A dozen or so men followed Newman. "We . . . fought our way on," noted Lance Sergeant E. Douglas. "Some more Germans called on us to surrender, but the colonel's answer was to carry on firing."[124]

The men slogged their way through the claustrophobic warren of streets, firing into windows, taking cover in doorways, every spent shell casing further diminishing their chance of escape. "[Newman] led us through back streets, gardens, over walls, and through houses," remembered Sergeant D. R. Steele. "When small parties of the enemy were encountered, his prompt orders and action enabled us to maintain the upper hand."[125]

But the sound of motorized transport and the yelling of German commands signaled the turning tide, as reinforcements—including "one or more infantry companies [and] half a company of machine-gunners"—flooded the town.[126] The field of battle began to constrict as the Germans applied pressure from all sides. It was now 4 a.m. The Commandos found their ammunition running dangerously low and their blood toll increasingly heavy.[127]

Darkness remained on the Commandos' side, but the fast-approaching daylight threatened their sole advantage. Newman was eager to get his party off the street. They sought cover where they could, breaking into houses and descending into basements, hiding in the overgrowth of gardens. Two men even retreated to the docks and hid in a ship's boiler room.[128] But one by one, the raiders fell or were captured when they ran out of ammunition. Of the roughly dozen men in his group, only Newman and three others had escaped injury.[129]

"At this time," recalled Sergeant Steele, "Colonel Newman was very anxious over those wounded in the party who had so ably carried on despite their injuries."[130] Newman went ahead of the others in search of a place to hide and found it in "a cellar in a block of flats."[131]

The men hunkered down, bandaged wounds, administered morphine, and smoked cigarettes. Here, they planned to rest and wait out the day before attempting—come nightfall—to sneak out of town and begin the arduous trek to Spain. Newman, however, had no intention to fight should the Germans discover them. It was doubtful the wounded would make it—and one grenade tossed into the cellar would wipe them all out.[132]

The hours dragged on, the cellar smelling of smoke and stale sweat; the sound of sporadic gunfire and Germans shouting commands floated down from above. Newman's luck could only hold so long. It came to an end with the sound of angry cries and a heavy pounding on the door that led down to the cellar. A muffled voice beyond the door let them know grenades would soon be thrown in.[133] It was all over. Newman and his men surrendered. The Germans marched them to a nearby headquarters for interrogation, where they failed to extract any information, before transporting them by truck to a café in La Baule.[134]

Here, one by one—bloody and exhausted—the surviving Charioteers came together one last time before being shipped off to prison camps. "It was just like a reunion," Newman later wrote. "In spite of misfortune our spirits were high."[135]

Helping buoy the men's morale was their secret knowledge of *Campbeltown*'s pending detonation.[136]

CHAPTER 8

*** * ***

LETHAL PASSAGE

On MGB 314, Ryder watched Newman and his team disembark and vanish into the heat-scarred night. Anxious to ensure *Campbeltown* had successfully smashed through the lock gate, Ryder ordered the gunboat to the north side of the Old Entrance. Here it berthed and took on "some half of the *Campbeltown*'s ship's company."[1] Some, too injured to stand, were carried on board. Ryder ordered ML 177 to pull alongside *Campbeltown* and rescue any survivors who might still be on the destroyer.[2]

With its deck now crowded with men, including Commander Stephen Beattie, the launch pulled away from *Campbeltown*. "We then set off for home," recalled Sub-Lieutenant Frank Arkle. "Before departing, we fired our torpedoes at two of the ships that were anchored in the harbor. We then sped as fast as we could, which was a full 18 knots, down towards the open sea."[3]

The batteries along both shores maintained a relentless fire, with each shot landing ever closer to the fleeing vessel. Sub-Lieutenant Mark Rodier coolly steered the launch through the eruptions of water and tried to avoid the searchlights.[4]

Arkle, at the stern of the ship, was attempting to activate the smoke screen when a shell punched through the launch's side and into the engine room. It slammed into one engine and threw it on top of the other, destroying both. The launch coughed and sputtered to a stop. Rodier and Beattie left the bridge and joined Arkle near the funnel to assess the situation just as another round struck home. The shell penetrated the funnel and blew up inside it.[5]

"I can see to this day the funnel folding apart . . . and the shell bursting in the middle of it," Arkle later wrote. "And to my benefit, poor old Mark was standing between me and the shell—and he took the brunt of the explosion."[6]

Rodier's body shielded Arkle from the worst of it. "I felt my right eye on my cheek," Arkle recalled. "My right eye had been blown out of my head and was hanging down my cheek. I felt there was only one thing to do about this, so I plucked it out and threw it overboard."[7]

Arkle, with metal in his left foot, limped below deck and found some bandaging to wrap around the bleeding cavity in his head. He returned topside to the heat and glow of flames consuming the boat amidships. He conferred with Beattie, who had escaped major injury. The two men agreed the only option was to abandon ship. "There were no more shells coming, mercifully," Arkle said, "and everything that could float was being taken overboard."[8]

Arkle grabbed a drawer from the wardroom and tossed it into the water. He leapt over with two other Commandos, who shared the unconventional float with him. "We tried to swim to the nearest shoreline," Arkle said, "but I soon realized . . . it's impossible to direct a floating drawer."[9]

Surrendering to the futility of his situation, Arkle settled instead for a drink and tried to retrieve his pewter whiskey flask from his hip pocket. His numb fingers refused to cooperate. "After an hour or two in the water," he recalled, "although we kept moving to try and keep our circulation going, we were beginning to get seriously affected by the cold."[10]

The three men on the drawer fought against the hypothermic drowsiness creeping over them. The crew of a German trawler pulled them from the water at daybreak and took them back to port. Also rescued, clinging to a piece of wreckage, was Beattie—one of only two officers from the *Campbeltown* to survive.[11]

✳ ✳ ✳

While ML 177 loaded men from *Campbeltown*, Ryder decided to investigate the damage to the lock gate. "As I set off," he recalled, "I was
followed by Leading Signalman Pike, who, discarding his signaling
apparatus for a broken bayonet he had discovered, decided that a
body guard was required."[12]

Ryder hurried up the steps to the Old Entrance and ran toward
the shattered lock gate with the old destroyer resting in the middle of
it. Ryder hailed *Campbeltown* but got no response. He could see ML
177 pushing away from the side of the ship, carrying the remainder of
Campbeltown's crew.[13] He could also make out from his vantage point
a fire burning in the ship's forward mess deck. "I stepped forward and
hailed [*Campbeltown*] again," Ryder reported, "but was greeted by a
burst of fire, which I imagine came from one of the ships in the dock."[14]

The men ducked for cover behind a nearby hut with the enemy fire
chipping away at its sides. Ryder could still see *Campbeltown*, firmly
wedged in place, and smiled to himself when the scuttling charges
planted by the crew lit up in a rapid series of small explosions. He and
Pike remained behind the hut for several minutes.[15]

A blast from the nearby pump house drew Ryder's attention. He
turned just in time to see a flash inside the darkened structure and the
windows blow.[16] "The Commandos were well away with their tasks,"
Ryder wrote. "They had set fire to a building close by and the long
tongues of flame cast their lurid light on the scene and lit up still more
clearly those craft still in the vicinity."[17]

Ryder and Pike made a break for it when the firing stopped and
dashed back to their boat. The whole dock seemed alive with the muffled thud of explosions and the shrill rattle of machine guns.[18]

Once on board MGB 314, Ryder ordered Lieutenant Robert Wynn
in his motor torpedo boat to blast the gates to the submarine basin.
This he did with great relish, the torpedoes leaving a frothy wake
through the fire-lit water before slamming home. His task complete,
Wynn joined Ryder on the bridge of MGB 314 for a celebratory but
"hurried drink out of a flask."[19]

Ryder ordered Wynn back to England. The time had come to go
home. Wynn took some *Campbeltown* survivors from Ryder's crowded

boat and set off with thirty-six men on his craft. The torpedo boat, the fastest ship in the Saint-Nazaire task force, hit the Loire estuary at a full speed of 45 knots.[20]

Shells from the German shore batteries splashed down in the ship's churning wake, the gun crews on land unable to track the speeding vessel. On the bridge, Wynn saw something fast approaching in the water and realized it was two men on a float. He had only the briefest of moments to decide whether to stop. Not wishing to leave either man to the elements or risk their drowning, he made his choice. "It was an awful decision," Wynn later recalled. "I decided to stop the vessel and we pulled up right alongside them—but, unfortunately, at that very moment, the German shore batteries found their mark and two shells went straight through us."[21]

A blast tossed Wynn from the bridge, hurled his body through the wheelhouse, and sent him crashing into the ship's bilge. Flames quickly devoured much of the vessel. Up on deck, Chief Petty Officer Lovegrove—the chief motor mechanic—realized Wynn was missing. He delayed his plan to jump overboard and went in search of his commander. He found Wynn badly wounded. "He got hold of me, pulled me up on deck, and jumped overboard with me," Wynn recalled. "He swam with me to the Carly float and saw a rope hanging from it. He lashed me to the float, and that's what saved my life."[22]

Only three men out of the thirty-six on Wynn's boat survived. One died, overcome by cold and exposure, just moments before a German vessel pulled alongside the float the following afternoon.[23] As German sailors busied themselves with dragging the men on board, Lovegrove pulled a revolver from Wynn's belt and—in obvious good humor—thrust the gun in their direction, yelling, "Put them up! Put them up!" Wynn's war was over; he would finish it in the notorious Colditz Castle prison camp.[24]

Ryder fared somewhat better on his return journey. MGB 314 pulled away from the Old Entrance at 2:30 a.m. As the Old Mole came into view, he saw—for the first time—the utter carnage in the harbor, the floating bodies and burning motor launches. "Good Lord!" he said, momentarily losing his reserve. "What the hell do we do now?"[25]

The guns on shore bellowed their response and battered the MGB. A pillbox on the Old Mole also stuttered to life and raked the beleaguered craft. Able Seaman William Savage, injured yet still manning the exposed forward pom-pom, returned fire with the last remaining gun on the boat that still worked. The pillbox fell silent, allowing Savage to turn his gun's attention elsewhere, only to start firing again moments later.[26]

"The [MGB] was then engaged from three directions at the same time," Ryder wrote. "We were, indeed, fighting for our lives."[27] Savage stood firm behind his gun and ignored the rounds ripping past him. He again knocked the pillbox out, with smoke this time rising out of its aperture. Savage died at his post in the blistering exchange. "His heroic death," Ryder wrote, "was an irreparable loss to our side."[28]

The MGB was the only British vessel afloat in the harbor and suffered all the more for it. With the motor launches destroyed, Newman and his men had no way of getting home. Ryder loathed the idea of leaving the Commandos behind, but with both points of embarkation—the Old Mole and Old Entrance—firmly in enemy hands, he had little choice.[29]

"There was no sign of the pace slackening out in the harbor," wrote Holman, the *Reuters* correspondent on Ryder's boat. "The glare of fires from both burning German and British vessels made a light nearly as strong as the searchlights. Inshore great fires were raging in many places, and the battle was intensified from time to time by a shattering explosion."[30]

Ryder discussed the matter with his skipper, Lieutenant Dunstan Curtis, and his navigator, Lieutenant A. R. Green. "Sadly," remembered Curtis, "we realized there was nothing we could do to help our gallant soldiers on shore." With the boat crowded with wounded, the men reluctantly agreed to make for home.[31]

The MGB began its desperate voyage downriver at a full speed of 24 knots behind the cover of a smoke screen.[32] Of the seventeen vessels in the Saint-Nazaire task force, only eight—including Ryder's—remained: MLs 156, 160, 270, 306, 307, 443, and 446. Unable to land their men, all were heading home, chopped up by enemy fire and crowded with wounded.[33]

Twenty miles out to sea they would reach Point "Y" and make contact with the awaiting destroyers *Tynedale* and *Atherstone*.[34] Ryder and the men on board the MGB could only hope they made it that far. "The run," wrote Holman, "was a nightmare experience in which one small MGB became the target for literally hundreds of enemy guns at comparatively short range." They could still see the "blazing destruction" in the harbor behind them, "which reminded one of the worst London blitz nights." Through the raging fires, "the Germans were still shooting madly away in all directions."[35]

Those able to do so moved about the blood-spattered deck and tended to the wounded, even as the ship veered wildly to avoid searchlights and tracers. A deep thunderous boom rolled across the water and swept over Ryder and his crew as a heavy coastal battery opened fire. Two massive plumes of water leapt up in front of the ship and stung the men with icy, needle-like spray as the MGB maneuvered between them.[36]

Ahead, Ryder saw what he believed to be a motor launch making its way to the rendezvous point. Not until roughly twenty yards separated the two vessels did he realize it to be a German flak ship.[37] "She opened fire on us at close range," Ryder reported, "hitting us with a stream of tracer right in one petrol tank. Seconds seemed like ages as we waited for our ship to burst into flames, but we were fortunate."[38]

The MGB returned fire with its forward pom-pom and set the ship alight. "As we escaped," noted Holman, "we saw her destroyed by the concentrated fire of her own shore batteries, who believed apparently, that it was the MGB lying disabled in midstream."[39]

The MGB continued its zigzagging course, leaving behind the searchlights and shore batteries, and broke into the open sea. Joined by ML 270, the MGB made for the rendezvous point with conditions on board growing increasingly grim. The blood on the decks made it difficult to find sure-footing between the wounded.[40] "As an added hazard," Ryder wrote, "the sea chose that night for an exceptional display of phosphorescence. This, to our anxiety, brilliantly illuminated our bow waves and our wakes—but every moment, we felt, was drawing us clear of German patrol vessels."[41]

The two boats cut a fiery path across the sea. The glow of tracers and the flash of guns, brilliant against the night, could be seen "several miles to the north."[42] Not until later would Ryder learn he was witnessing the last desperate struggle of ML 306.[43]

At first light, Ryder spotted ML 156 and ML 446—and, shortly thereafter, *Tynedale* and *Atherstone*. The sea proved mercifully calm for the transferring of crews and wounded from the motor launches to the destroyers. "This," Ryder wrote, "was a lengthy process and kept the force stopped for half an hour from 7:20 to 7:50."[44]

The MGB and launches eventually cleared of all men, the decision was made to sink the damaged vessels by gunfire. "Such decisions are not easily reached and have a special poignancy for the officers and ratings of the abandoned ship," notes one contemporary account. "It is reported that one of the ML commanders, who had calmly faced the ordeal in St. Nazaire, burst into tears when the order came that the gallant little ship that had served his crew so well in the heat of battle would have to be sunk in cold blood."[45]

✳ ✳ ✳

When Lieutenant Ian Henderson—pushed back by withering fire and unable to land his Commandos at the Old Mole—made the decision to withdraw ML 306 and head for home, it caused considerable grief for the men on board.[46] They had not made the treacherous journey only to retreat.

"We left for home with a lot of grumbling from my soldiers," remembered Lieutenant Ronald Swayne. "They felt they'd come all the way there—we'd been busily engaged shooting up the searchlights and so on . . . and I think we did a certain amount of damage. But it was very sad. So Ian Henderson decided to turn for home and towards home we went."[47]

Swayne went down below and tried to make sandwiches for the soldiers. His hand, which he had severely burned on his Bren gun, made the simple task difficult. As he fumbled with the bread, he saw Sub-Lieutenant Philip Dark approach. "He told me to come to the bridge," Swayne recalled, "and to keep dead quiet and to shut up the soldiers."[48]

Swayne followed Dark above deck and found Henderson on the bridge, staring into the night. Without saying a word, Henderson passed Swayne the night glasses and motioned into the darkness. "There were the outlines of three destroyers," Swayne said. "I was munching a sandwich and it turned to dust in my mouth. It was a very funny feeling that because I didn't actually feel fear. It was purely a physical reaction . . . I had to spit the sandwich out."[49]

Swayne went below and summoned his Commandos. They came on deck and stared in uneasy silence at the dark outlines moving no more than 100 yards away, blurred shapes in the nautical gloom.[50] "At least three of them went by," remembered Ralph Batteson, "and they were just far enough away for us not to be seen—or we thought so."[51] The destroyers were heading home after being sent out earlier in the evening to investigate a sighting of enemy vessels.[52] The men on the motor launch gripped their Bren and Tommy guns. Each shadow-ship passing in the near distance bristled with machine guns and three 4.1-inch cannons.[53]

All seemed to be going well until one ship—the *Jaguar*—broke from the line and approached the motor launch. The night disappeared in the dazzling glare of a hot, white searchlight. The sound of enemy fire carried across the waves. "As soon as we saw we were going to get fired on," said Batteson, "we weren't going to sit there and let him knock us out of the water without any effort."[54]

The Commandos returned fire with their machine guns, the rounds sparking harmlessly off the destroyer's side, while Batteson let loose with the ML's Oerlikon. Manning the boat's twin Lewis guns, Sergeant Thomas Frank Durrant—injured earlier that evening—aimed for the *Jaguar*'s bridge and unleashed a ferocious barrage.[55] Still, the destroyer drew closer. The clatter of machine-gun fire sent men diving for cover, as rounds ate away the launch's wooden deck. "He's trying to ram us!" someone yelled above the din.[56]

The *Jaguar* rapidly closed the distance between the two ships until she loomed large above her smaller adversary. Henderson, acting quickly, ordered the wheel be swung over. The launch veered wildly and almost cleared *Jaguar*'s trajectory. The destroyer knocked the ship a glancing blow. Batteson saw at least two men fly overboard.[57] "Every gun that we'd got . . . was firing back at them," said Batteson, "but with the severity of fire from the German destroyer it was putting people out of action—and people getting killed second by second, not minute by minute."[58]

Corporal Glyn Salisbury sprayed the *Jaguar* with his Bren gun as she came around on the launch's port side. A large tongue of flame leapt from the destroyer's 4.1-inch gun. The salvo blew a hole through the funnels above Salisbury and threw shrapnel into his back. "The lad who was next to me, a sailor, he had his leg off," he said. "He had his Wellies on and his trousers were ripped, and all the blood was [flowing] into his Wellies."[59]

Another burst of fire splintered the launch's hand railing and sent hot metal slivers into Salisbury's neck.[60] The shooting would occasionally stop to allow the German captain to yell, "Have you had enough? Have you had enough?" Durrant let the Lewis gun speak for the crew.[61]

Swayne could see from the wheelhouse "a lot of soldiers on deck were killed or wounded." Rounds passed through the bridge, tearing apart wood and shattering glass. Henderson fell with a fatal shot to the head; two nearby officers also dropped.[62] Swayne retreated below deck to inspect the damage. Two dead Commandos lay on the floor, as shells punched their way through the sides of the ship. He returned topside where the situation continued to deteriorate.[63]

Lance Sergeant Ernest Chappell took several rounds in the legs. "I . . . found myself with my legs dangling over the gunwales slipping through into the sea," Chappell recalled, "until I was pulled back by some of my colleagues on board—couldn't say who—and rested against the stack of our boat."[64] Unable to stand, Chappell grabbed a Bren gun, its clatter joining the deafening barrage.[65]

Batteson continued laying down a heavy fire with his Oerlikon. "As things got more hectic," he said, "and people were getting killed left, right, and center, there were only odd guns working."[66] He saw one of the motor mechanics emerge from the engine room into a torrent of fire. "Although it didn't quite kill him," Batteson said, "he was very severely wounded. He died later on."[67]

A well-placed shot blew the magazine on Batteson's gun to pieces. Another round grazed his thumb and passed through the armpit of his thick duffel coat. "It never even touched my body," he said.[68] His coat began to smolder, ignited by the bullet's heat. He struggled to get the coat off and jumped for cover behind the gun platform.[69]

"Things were getting blown apart all over," he said. "There was a bit of a cease firing. I put my hand up to my head . . . and it came away with all this white stuff on it."[70] Batteson briefly thought the stress and fear of the night's events had turned his hair a premature white. He quickly realized rounds had passed through the splinter-proof mats wrapped around the gun platform and littered his hair with the lining.[71] "I survived," Batteson said, "and kept my hair black for a hell of a long time."[72]

The remaining guns on the launch stopped firing as—one by one—men slumped lifeless or screaming to the deck. The exception remained Tommy Durrant on the twin Lewis gun. He presented an easy target and suffered a horrendous punishment in his exposed position. "They really let him have it," remembered Swayne.[73] His body in bloody tatters, Durrant clung to his gun to stay upright. "But he went on shooting," said Swayne, "until he absolutely dropped on the floor—terribly, badly wounded."[74]

The battle had by now raged for the better part of an hour. Having started in darkness, it came to an end in the first light of day. A break in the firing presented Swayne the chance to surrender the ship.[75] "There was no point in going on," Swayne later said.[76] Of the twenty-eight men on board, twenty lay dead or wounded. "I'm afraid we can't go on," Swayne yelled to the men on the destroyer.[77]

Batteson emerged from his place of cover and eyed the carnage through the clearing smoke. "There were dead and wounded all over the ship," he recalled.[78] As he got to his feet and began to assess the slaughter, the *Jaguar* drew up alongside the launch and dropped rope ladders down its side. The wounded would be evacuated first. Lieutenant Henderson lay in the bridge with a "leg blown off completely."[79]

Batteson made his way up to the Lewis gun and found Durrant at the base of the gun, his body "absolutely riddled" with bullets.[80]

"He was absolutely covered in blood and bullet-holes and things," Batteson recalled. "I tried to pick him up—he was a bigger man than I was—and I just couldn't manage it." Still conscious, Durrant urged Batteson to go and help others. "I'm finished anyway," he said. "Go and help somebody else."[81] Batteson stood up. "My trousers were saturated with blood," he said. "I had them for about six months in prison camp and everything, still covered in dried blood."[82]

The wounded, including Durrant, were lifted onto the *Jaguar*. Sub-Lieutenant Dark knelt beside Durrant and tried to offer some comfort. "The amount of pain he suffered and bore so well," said Dark, "was incredible for any human being."[83] The *Jaguar*'s captain, Friedrich-Karl Paul, commended Swayne and the British crew for their "brave fight."[84] After taking up Paul's invitation for a glass of much-needed brandy in the captain's cabin, Swayne returned to the upper deck. On the horizon, against the brightening day, he saw the *Tynedale* making for home and wondered when he might see England again.[85]

The heavy thrum of the *Jaguar*'s engines signaled her imminent departure. Swayne watched the broken remains of ML 306—now a ghost ship—bobbing lifelessly on the waves and fading into the distance. The destroyer made the journey back to Saint-Nazaire without incident and reached the port at roughly nine thirty that morning. The ship dropped anchor not far from where the shattered *Campbeltown*, still smoldering, lay wedged in the dry dock's outer caisson.[86]

Boats pulled up alongside the German destroyer to bring the captured British crew and wounded ashore. Moved by the kindness with which the Germans had treated his men, Swayne felt obliged to thank Paul. He did so by surrendering a fighting knife he'd concealed in his clothing when taken on board. Paul flashed Swayne a knowing smile and bid him a warm farewell.[87]

Batteson was helping lower the wounded on stretchers down to the picket boat when he noticed some German sailors staring in the direction of *Campbeltown*—all of them oblivious to the secret in its crumpled hull. One sailor, standing above Batteson, said in jest, "There's a boat you won't use again this war."[88]

Mere minutes passed between that fateful utterance and the sound of Armageddon, as the 10,000 pounds of explosives in *Campbeltown* blew in a spectacle of tremendous fury. The noise was elemental and overpowered the senses, overwhelming everything in a cataclysmic shock. A massive spiral of black smoke shot skyward on an expanding ball of flame. The destroyer's front half, consumed by the blast, disappeared in an instant. The caisson, weighing some 160 tons, blew inward. A tidal wave, born of the explosion, flooded the empty dock and carried in with it the shattered back half of *Campbeltown*. The blast's concussion rumbled across the dock area, blowing windows out of their panes, damaging warehouses, and thrashing the water. Waves slammed two German tankers anchored near *Campbeltown*—the *Passat* and *Schledstadt*—against the concrete dock walls and damaged both ships.[89]

The violent waters rocked the *Jaguar* and the small picket boat alongside it with such force Batteson feared they might sink. "We looked up after this bang and there was still debris coming down two or three minutes after," he recalled. "Bodies, wood, concrete, and smoke, and dust—everything was coming down."[90]

Forty senior German officers were on *Campbeltown* trying to assess "how best she could be moved" at the time of detonation.[91] A large number of German soldiers, spurred by curiosity, had also gathered around the ship or clambered onto her deck. The explosion shredded them all to pieces and hurled their dismembered remains to all points of the compass. Some estimates as to the number of Germans killed in the blast go as high as 400.[92]

Two days after the explosion, dock workers and German cleaning crews—"dazed and disorganized"—were still shoveling up body parts, scraping off remains stuck to the sides of buildings, and scattering sand to soak up the blood.[93]

✻ ✻ ✻

Several days later, Captain Friedrich-Karl Paul visited Colonel Newman at a prison camp in Rennes and detailed the fight between his ship and ML 306. He made a point of stressing the courage and tenacity of

Sergeant Thomas Durrant, shot twenty-five times in the struggle, "as you may wish to recommend him for a high award."[94]

Durrant had subsequently died of his wounds in a hospital in La Baule. Newman duly took notice and made the appropriate recommendation. On June 15, 1945, Durrant posthumously received the Victoria Cross. It marked a first in British military history. Never before had Britain's highest military honor gone "to a soldier for a naval action on the initial recommendation of an enemy officer."[95]

✳ ✳ ✳

Operation Chariot achieved its objective of destroying the massive Saint-Nazaire dry dock and denying *Tirpitz* safe harbor on the Atlantic coast, but the cost proved high. Of the 611 sailors and Commandos who stormed into Saint-Nazaire on the night of March 28, 169* were killed and 215 became prisoners of war. Only 227 made it back home: 222 by sea on the surviving motor launches and escorting destroyers; 5 on foot, through France, Spain, and Gibraltar.[96]

In addition to Durrant, five Charioteers—Lieutenant Commander Stephen Beattie, Lieutenant Colonel Charles Newman, Commander Robert Ryder, and Able Seaman William Savage—received the Victoria Cross.[97] The Germans praised the sheer audacity of the attack. "We would not wish to deny the gallantry of the British," said a German naval spokesman during a radio broadcast three days after the operation. "Every German is moved by a feeling of respect for the men who carried out this action. The crew of the *Campbeltown* under fierce fire forced their ship through the northern lock gates and carried out a crazy enterprise as well as it could be done. They fought until death or capture."[98]

A German report seized after the war stated, "The English attack on St. Nazaire . . . is a first-class example of a well-planned undertaking thought out to the last detail and executed with great courage." The

---

*64 Commandos and 105 sailors.

plan's one shortfall, notes the report, was the British failure to commit more men.[99]

A more recent Saint-Nazaire case study by retired Navy Admiral William McRaven, who oversaw the U.S. Navy SEAL raid that killed Osama bin Laden, suggests the problems went beyond manpower. He cites an overly complicated plan, lack of rehearsals, a weak element of surprise, and insufficient "speed on target" as being detrimental to the attack. A strong devotion to duty and a personal belief in their cause—regardless of the risks—among the British Commandos and sailors served as a heavy counterbalance to any operational failings. "In the end," McRaven writes, "only a sense of purpose and the indomitable spirit of the British commandos allowed for any success at all."[100]

Whatever the criticisms, and its strategic merits, Operation Chariot proved a daring stroke of imagination and initiative. It gave the weary British public a victory to rally behind. Still, one pertinent fact cast its hard and glaring truth over everything. The *Tirpitz* remained very much alive in Norway's Fættenfjord near Trondheim, throwing its dark shadow over the war at sea.

CHAPTER 9

ARCTIC FIRE

Six times they tried in the first four months of 1942. Taking off from the decks of carriers and distant airfields in England, the men and machines of the Fleet Air Arm and RAF crossed gray seas and snow-capped mountains to bomb *Tirpitz.* The British threw 129 aircraft at her, lost 14, and scored not a single hit.

Churchill's obsession with the battleship remained strong. She held British naval planning hostage and—from her Norwegian anchorage— threatened Britain's lifeline with the United States and Russia's Arctic lifeline with Britain. "The crippling of this ship," noted a Royal Navy report, summarizing the prime minister's thoughts on the matter, "would alter the entire face of the naval war and that the loss of 100 machines or 500 airmen would be well compensated for."[1]

*** *** ***

The bombers thundered across the white-gray Arctic landscape, their Merlin engines screaming into the frozen sky. Through Perspex windshields, pilots observed an inhospitable terrain of sharp, jagged angles, snow-capped peaks, rocky slopes, and dark water. The bombers began a slow but steady descent and followed the narrowing waterway to their ultimate objective anchored in Fættenfjord.

A thin mist began to swirl about the rippling shoreline where mountain met water. It thickened and crept up the rocky embankments, reaching between boulders and encircling trees, soon veiling every-thing in a nearly impenetrable fog. Pilots recognized it for what it was: a man-made smoke screen.[2] Still, the bombers dropped lower, buffeted by the wind and rattled by the power of the engines.

Each warplane—four-engined Halifaxes from Nos. 10 and 35 Squadrons, RAF Bomber Command—carried a payload of five spher-ical mines, each weighing 1,000 pounds. Antiaircraft batteries con-cealed along the shore and on the slopes dirtied the sky with black clouds of flak. Shrapnel tore into the aircraft, puncturing turrets and shredding wings.

One shell pierced the fuselage of Halifax W1052, tossing the wire-less operator across the rear cabin and leaving him sprawled in a pool of blood, his radio equipment smoldering in a shattered heap. A frigid wind blew through the jagged opening, scattering maps and naviga-tion charts. The pilot, a flight sergeant named Rochford, continued the attack run at 200 feet with the target growing ever larger in his windshield.[3]

The *Tirpitz*, despite her immense size, did not present an easy tar-get. The plan of attack, devised by the British Admiralty, required the bombers to drop their mines in such a way that they would roll down the embankment into the water, sink beneath the ship, and blow in the hull upon detonation.[4] In his ear, Rochford heard the voice of his bom-bardier guiding him on the final approach. Two-degrees starboard. One-degree port. Hold it. Hold it.[5]

Guns on the deck of the mighty ship spit tongues of white flame; batteries on both sides of the fjord scattered hot metal across the flight path. It took every iota of will to hold the plane—with its "thousands of pounds of aviation fuel, ammunition . . . and high explosives"[6]—steady amid the maelstrom. Once free of its deadly cargo, the plane had to maintain its heading for another thirty seconds so an accurate photograph could be obtained. Looking below, Rochford saw no signs of detonation or damage done to the target. Nevertheless, his task complete, he turned for home.[7]

Wing Commander D. C. T. Bennett, his aircraft hit by flak over the Norwegian coast some forty miles back, approached *Tirpitz* with his starboard wing alight.[8] The flames, fueled by the wind, inched closer to the fuselage and grew larger with each passing second. Red-and-orange light shimmered on the cockpit controls. Against the hazy milk shade of the smoke screen and a landscape of rock and ice, Bennett's Halifax presented an easy target. "I was a flamer," he later said, "so I was picked on all the way."[9]

The sound of shrapnel battering the bomber's exterior echoed the length of the plane. Bennett pushed the yoke forward and brought the aircraft down to 200 feet. Outside, he saw nothing but the swirling, man-made fog. "You couldn't see a thing," he recalled. "It was pretty hopeless." Then, off to the lower left of his aircraft, he saw flak batteries throw another salvo into the sky.[10]

A shell-burst rocked the bomber, then another; the controls became sluggish, the aircraft increasingly unresponsive to his touch. Bennett struggled to maintain altitude and heading. In the nose of the aircraft, the bombardier tried in vain to locate some point of reference but couldn't see through the billowing vapor.[11]

The *Tirpitz* had vanished into the ether. The starboard wing, now fully ablaze, left a thick plume of black smoke in the aircraft's wake. "We suffered," Bennett said with typical nonchalance.[12] The cockpit reeked of cordite as a succession of blasts rocked the bomber and its beleaguered crew. Flak pierced the rear turret and injured the gunner.[13]

Hurtling forward in a twisting void of fog and explosions, Bennett stared out into nothing. Suddenly, the massive form of *Tirpitz*—blurred by smoke—passed beneath the plane and vanished just as quickly. The bombardier never had a chance to release the mines. Bennett pondered his options; the bomber was dying. Fully consumed by fire, the starboard flap no longer served any purpose. The starboard undercarriage, battered mercilessly, had collapsed. The controls in Bennett's hands would soon be useless, as the Halifax increasingly succumbed to its vicious beating. Bennett made up his mind and informed the crew they would take a second run at the target.[14]

He circled the aircraft around and screamed back into the maelstrom. Even if they survived the attack run, the chances of making it home were minimal. Once crews dropped their payload, they had to bank sharply to the north and clear a 700-foot summit. Doing so would put them in a neighboring fjord where *Scharnhorst*, *Prinz Eugen*, and *Hipper*—all bristling with antiaircraft batteries—lay at anchor.[15]

With no visual landmarks to guide him, Bennett aimed the Halifax in the general direction of *Tirpitz* and hoped for the best. Guns on either side of the fjord continued hammering away. Everything was hellacious noise and vibration. He fought the plane's resistance and struggled to hold her steady. Going solely on instinct, he ordered the bombardier to drop the mines when he believed they were passing over the ship. The mines fell without any visible result. Relieved of its 5,000-pound payload, the plane regained some of its vitality.[16]

A small measure of life seeped back into the controls. Bennett tried to free the Halifax from the fiery tempest in which it was ensnared. Whatever resurgence the machine temporarily enjoyed proved short-lived. Bennett knew he and his crew would not be landing on British soil. Neither icy water nor rocky embankment presented an ideal place to land. Bennett wrestled the plane east in the direction of neutral Sweden.[17]

The tortured engines voiced their protest as he fought to gain altitude and speed, desperate to escape the crucible of shell-bursts and concussions. Flames now covered the starboard wing in its entirety. The plane refused to climb. Bennett, with no other options available, spoke into his helmet's mic. "When I ordered 'Abandon Aircraft,'" he later recalled, "all the boys were out as fast as they could."[18]

The rear gunner's situation appeared bleak, his legs peppered with shrapnel. The turret's cramped confines meant the occupant had to leave his parachute outside the rear bulkhead, which separated the turret from the rest of the aircraft. The odds of a gunner escaping, even without injury, were slim. Flight Sergeant Colgan, the flight engineer, aware of the rear gunner's predicament, left the rear cabin and scrambled along the narrow catwalk that ran the length of the fuselage. He pulled the gunner free of the turret and helped him into his parachute.[19] Together, the two men worked their way toward the emergency hatch in the cockpit, their efforts hampered by the plane's violent shaking.

Bennett was still at the controls when one of his crew opened the emergency hatch in the floor. Wind, sharp and bitter, stormed the cockpit. The starboard wing, battered and burned, collapsed, forcing

Bennett to hold the yoke to full port to maintain even flight. One by one, the men disappeared through the opening into the frigid night. "And there I was," remembered Bennett, "sitting in my seat with a flaming aircraft—a very hot one—ready to do what? Bail out without a parachute?"[20]

Because the parachute clipped onto one's front, Bennett couldn't wear his in the pilot seat. It lay just beyond his reach—and now, the Halifax had nothing left to give.[21] Feeling the controls go slack in his hand, he watched through the Perspex windshield as the bomber's nose dipped downward. Whereas moments before he could see the jagged outline of ridges and the expanse of moonlit sky, there was now just rock, ice, and water.

In the chaos, someone passed Bennett his parachute before bailing out. Struggling against the increasingly sharp angle of the plane's descent, Bennett hauled himself out of his seat and clipped on the pack. He lowered himself to the floor and stuck his legs through the open hatch, feeling the violent pull of the wind. He surrendered himself to the outside elements and fell through the floor.[22]

Airmen were taught in training to count to three before pulling the ripcord, lest their chute get snagged on the plane. Bennett had no time for such a luxury. He pulled the cord the moment the night engulfed him and slammed into a thick bank of snow just as his chute billowed above his head. The snow buried him up to his neck. "If I'd counted my three seconds," he said, "I wouldn't have made it."[23]

Helped by friendly locals, Bennett and three of his crew evaded capture and soon returned to Britain. The remaining four—including the injured rear gunner—weren't so fortunate and spent the remainder of the war in captivity.[24]

✻ ✻ ✻

While Bennett and his crew suffered their ordeal by fire, the attack on *Tirpitz* raged on. Crews who had difficulty spotting the ship in the haze used as their target point "an outcrop of rock that was known to be sheltering *Tirpitz*."[25] Spherical mines, one after the other, hit the fjord's embankment and rolled toward the ship. Large plumes of water, and little else, pummeled the target. Halifax W1048 of No. 35 Squadron leveled out at 200 feet and commenced its attack run. Sergeant Ron Wilson, the rear gunner, strafed the shoreline and embankment, hoping to take out a few flak batteries.[26]

His four .303 Browning machine guns clattered violently and shook the turret, spitting red and green tracers into the thick miasma of smoke. Four tanks near the back of the aircraft each contained 2,000 rounds of incendiary and armor-piercing ammunition. Tracks leading from the tanks fed the rounds into the hungry guns.[27] When the bomber buzzed *Tirpitz*, Wilson "went berserk on the guns" and blazed away from stem to stern. As the plane, its mines dropped without effect, climbed out of its bombing run, a well-aimed salvo tore into the starboard wing and set it alight. The plane faltered and began losing altitude.[28]

Pilot Officer MacIntyre aimed the stricken bomber at a lake, the moon appearing trapped beneath its surface. The plane hit the water, but the expected splash and rapid submersion never occurred. The bomber slid across solid ice, trailing smoke and flame in its wake. No sooner did it come to a halt, after sliding nearly a mile, than the ice began melting beneath it.[29]

The men, shaken but alive, scrambled out as water slowly seeped into the fuselage. It did not take long for the fiery wreck in the middle of the lake to draw enemy attention. A German patrol was soon making its way across the ice, but the airmen evaded capture and took cover among some trees along the shoreline. All but one of the six crewmembers would make it back to England, the exception being the flight engineer who badly wrenched his ankle in the crash. Not wanting to slow his friends down, he surrendered himself into captivity.[30]

No bombers made it home completely unscathed—all bore some evidence as to that night's ferocity. Some passed over the ship at so low an altitude their undercarriages revealed damage from "small caliber shells."[31] The operation's toll in blood was five aircraft lost and twenty-four airmen killed or captured. Still the bombers returned the following night, April 28, and, once again, the German radar installations along the Norwegian coast betrayed their approach.

On the *Tirpitz*, men ran to their battle stations against the background noise of a blaring alarm. Guns swiveled skyward as all eyes peered into the night. In the stern of the ship, sailors worked frantically to generate the smoke screen. They used a hose to connect two smoke canisters filled with chlorosulfonic acid to cylinders of compressed air. Together, the canisters and cylinders fed lines leading to exhaust vents in the ship's outer hull.

The sailors opened the cylinders and released the pressurized air into the smoke canisters, forcing the acid from the canisters in the form of a fine mist. It swirled up the pipes and drifted out the exhaust vents, wafting over the gray surface of the fjord. Water vapor in the damp air triggered a chemical reaction, condensing the acidic vapor into a thick mist that quickly spread.

A bright moon lit the bombers' way as it had the night before and bathed everything in a spectral light. Tracer shells fanned up and outward across the sky in a blazing spectrum of color. One well-placed shot blew an eighteen-inch hole through the tail of Halifax W1039; another ripped away the fuel lines leading to a starboard engine and sent petrol spraying into the violent night. Despite such damage, the pilot was able to fly the craft home.[32]

One by one, crews ran the fiery gauntlet, their bombers scarred and battered by the ordeal. Muzzles flashed white lightning against the dark slopes of the fjord and downed two of the thirty-four aircraft that attacked that night. A direct hit shredded the port wing of Halifax W7656, forcing Flight Lieutenant David Petley to land the burning aircraft in Trondheimsfjord. Icy water flooded the fuselage as the Halifax, shot through with holes, began to sink.[33]

Four of the six crewmen scrambled out and climbed into the bomber's emergency dinghy with only moments to spare. They watched helplessly as the plane slipped beneath the black surface, taking with it the navigator and wireless operator. Two Norwegians in a boat rescued the survivors three hours later but turned them in upon reaching the shore. The men spent the remainder of the war in a German prison camp.[34]

✵ ✵ ✵

Antiaircraft fire hammered Halifax W1053 from nose to tail as it roared 150 feet above the water toward *Tirpitz*. The plane immediately burst into flames, forcing the navigator to drop the bomber's payload. The mines splashed harmlessly into the water below. From the cockpit, Pilot Officer Johnny Roe told his crew to prepare for a crash landing.[35]

A red-and-orange smear trailing fire and smoke against the night sky, the Halifax cleared the fjord but slammed into woodland beyond the shore. Sergeant "Rusty" Russell, the wireless operator and air gunner, was crushed to death on impact in his turret. The remaining crewmen survived with burns and injuries of various degrees but were captured by the Germans.[36]

While the wreckage of Halifax W1053 still burned brightly, the bombers in the sky turned for home, leaving behind them only the dying echoes of gunfire and detonations, and the fading sound of their engines. And when the reverberation of battle finally ceased and the smoke screen cleared, *Tirpitz* came into full view, afloat and undamaged.

CHAPTER 10

* * *

TARGET: *TIRPITZ*

On Sunday, June 22, 1941, more than 3 million German soldiers and 4,000 tanks stormed across the Russian frontier on an 1,800-mile front. Despite advanced warnings from British and American intelligence, including a personal letter from Churchill, the invasion—the largest in history—took Stalin by surprise. As the Wehrmacht savaged its way deeper into Russia, Stalin's pleas to Churchill for assistance became increasingly "urgent and strident."[1]

Churchill found a certain gall in Stalin's requests, considering the Soviet Union had done nothing thus far for Britain. "It is right to make clear," Churchill wrote in his memoirs, "that for more than a year after Russia was involved in the war she presented herself to our minds as a burden and not as a help."[2] Britain, waging a back-and-forth campaign in the North African deserts and supplying far-flung outposts across the empire, was in no position to share its vital supplies.

On August 17, 1941, Britain's first Arctic convoy of military supplies left the safety of the Royal Navy anchorage at Scapa Flow bound for the northern Russian port of Archangel. The seven merchant ships—six British and one Dutch—carried raw materials and fifteen Hurricane fighters packed in crates. The 2,500-mile journey would take the escort to the very edge of the North Pole, as it veered north to avoid German air and sea forces—including *Tirpitz*—based in Norway. It arrived, without incident, on August 31.[3]

Seventy-eight Allied convoys would brave the frozen gauntlet between August 1941 and May 1945 at a cost of more than 3,000 Allied lives, eighty-five merchant ships, two Royal Navy cruisers, six destroyers, and eight corvettes. The Germans also suffered in the Arctic wastes trying to stop the flow of materials to the Red Army, losing thirty U-boats and four surface ships.[4]

Churchill diverted shipments from America and diminished his country's own stores to bolster the ill-prepared Russian war effort. Although he did so out of necessity, he did so begrudgingly. "The Soviet Government had the impression that they were conferring a great favor on us by fighting in their own country for their own lives," Churchill wrote. "The more they fought the heavier our debt became. This was not a balanced view."[5]

Between 1941 and 1945, Britain—in addition to raw materials and supplies—would ship 7,000 aircraft to the Soviet Union. In the early days of Russia's war, the Soviets found themselves in desperate need of tanks. Their light T-26 proved easy cannon fodder for the German Panzers, which wiped out 15,000 Soviet tanks between June and December 1941. Britain responded by supplying the Russian front with its more heavily armored Matilda II tanks, desperately needed by the British Eighth Army in North Africa. By the end of 1941, the Matilda II made up a third of the Soviet tanks fighting on the Eastern Front. American-made Sherman tanks would bolster the armored ranks of Britain's desert army.[6]

By the end of 1941, Britain had delivered a third of a million tons to Russian ports. Arctic convoys sailing from ports in Britain and Iceland navigated a hellacious journey "over the top of Scandinavia into Archangel and Murmansk."[7] For the Allied merchant sailors, conditions at sea proved every bit as merciless as the German navy. Temperatures could drop to a savage 50 below zero. It was not uncommon for a ship to arrive in a Russian port burdened by 100 tons or more of ice. Should a sailor end up in the water, his life expectancy was less than two minutes.[8]

None of this mattered to Stalin, who incessantly badgered Churchill for more. "I am getting to the end of my tether with these repeated

Russian naggings," an exasperated Churchill wrote to the Admiralty in January 1943. "Our escorts all over the world are so attenuated that losses out of all proportion are falling upon the British Mercantile Marine."[9] And still they plied the Arctic waters. Churchill understood the need to endure the constant badgering from Moscow. From the moment Germany turned its forces to the east, Stalin had been pressing Britain to launch a second front in Europe. With the Russians engaging—on a massive scale—the Germans on land, the convoys were "proof of British and American willingness to accept a share of the costs of going to war with Hitler."[10]

"In total," writes one historian, "British aide to the Soviet Union, which was independent of Lend-Lease, provided Moscow with four million tons of equipment and supplies during the war, free of charge."[11]

✳ ✳ ✳

On June 27, 1942, Convoy PQ-17—thirty five merchant ships carrying 297 planes, 594 tanks, 4,246 trucks, and more than 150,000 tons of additional largesse—left its Icelandic anchorage in Hvalfjord for the Russian ports of Archangel and Murmansk.[12] The convoy, carrying enough hardware and supplies to "equip an army of 50,000,"[13] sailed under the protective firepower of twenty-one British and American warships—with the Royal Navy planning to deploy an additional seventeen vessels.[14]

It was the first large-scale Anglo-American military operation under British command. The convoy sailed into open seas under the spying eye of U-456 and Luftwaffe reconnaissance. Their torpedoes and bombs sank three merchant ships over the next several days.[15]

On July 4, First Sea Lord Admiral Sir Dudley Pound received word of another threat. *Tirpitz* had left her anchorage in Trondheim. Unsure of her immediate location, and fearing a *Tirpitz*-led assault by surface ships, Pound ordered the convoy to scatter.[16] The consequences proved disastrous, as German forces below the sea and in the sky picked the defenseless merchant ships off one by one.

The ordeal of the SS *Hartlebury*, struck by torpedoes on July 7, exemplifies the horror. Her crew struggled to get the lifeboats into the water as the ship disintegrated around them. Twenty men, including Third Officer Needham Forth, piled into a waterlogged lifeboat and watched the ship descend to her grave.[17]

Not long thereafter, U-355—captained by Günter La Baume—surfaced near the lifeboat. *Hartlebury* was La Baume's "first kill." The German captain, preening with pride and shouting down from the U-boat's conning tower, wished to know the name of the vessel he'd just sunk. When someone in the lifeboat replied, a satisfied La Baume ducked back into the sub without offering any assistance to the stranded. The U-boat dropped beneath the surface and left Forth and his crewmates to the mercy of the elements.[18]

The long, cold hours dragged by, pulling with them one life after another. Thirteen men soon succumbed. "These . . . had to be unceremoniously pushed overboard to lighten the load," Forth wrote. "All went the same way. Became sleepy and mind wandering slightly and then eyes glazing over and finish—and apparently not a bad death."[19]

Death proved peaceful for most, although one man—in the delirium of hypothermia—lost his mind and tried to drown himself while his fading shipmates did their utmost to save him. As his crewmates perished one by one, Forth—submerged up to his waist—struggled with the oar in his hand and realized the water was "having a stupefying effect on me."[20] He stumbled toward the bow of the boat, where four other survivors huddled in a pointless struggle against the wind and sea. Every wave, every gust intensified their misery. "Everyone cramped together," Forth wrote, "frozen, feet absolutely stiff and white."[21]

Ten of the fourteen men in another of *Hartlebury*'s lifeboats froze to death.[22] Joseph Tighe, the second engineer, began to cry as his life slipped away and wished aloud that he was back home in Glasgow. "He was the last to die," wrote the *Hartlebury*'s radio officer. "He drifted off to sleep, and we tried to keep him awake, rubbing his feet, shaking him, talking to him, but it was no use."[23]

In the end, only twenty of the *Hartlebury's* fifty-six-man crew made it. Of the thirty-five ships in convoy PQ-17 that left Iceland, only twelve arrived in Russia with 70,000 tons of cargo.[24]

The Admiralty later learned *Tirpitz* had left Trondheim for Altafjord to await further orders. Not until after PQ-17 scattered was *Tirpitz* sent to sea—only to be recalled. Pound's decision to break up the convoy cost 153 merchant seamen their lives. Months later, survivors gathered in St. Andrew's Hall in Glasgow to be addressed by Philip Noel-Baker, the undersecretary for war. "We know what the convoy cost us," he said. "But I want to tell you that whatever the cost, it was worth it."[25]

Cries of derision drowned out his words. "This," Churchill later wrote of PQ-17's ordeal, "was one of the most melancholy naval episodes in the whole of the war."[26]

✻ ✻ ✻

On the morning of Monday, October 26, 1942, the fishing-turned-cargo boat *Arthur* left Lunna Voe in Scotland. Her papers listed Trondheim as her destination, where she was scheduled to deliver a supply of peat for the making of camouflage.[27]

Captain Leif Larsen, a thirty-six-year-old Norwegian, led his crew of three Norwegians and six Britons. Larsen was no mere sailor. Having escaped occupied Norway for Britain via fishing boat the previous year, he had joined the Special Operations Executive (SOE) and become a key player in the "Shetland Bus," a secret seafaring operation used to transport "agents and saboteurs" between the two countries.[28]

Nor was the *Arthur* merely delivering peat. Bundles of nets and tarpaulin on the upper deck concealed the ship's true cargo: two "human torpedoes," dubbed "Chariots" by the British. Each measured twenty-two feet in length and weighed 3,500 pounds.[29] Powered by an electrical motor, each Chariot accommodated a two-man crew. The pilot sat in the front, while the sailor behind him worked a cutting mechanism that could slice through antisubmarine netting.[30]

Larsen and his men busied themselves with guiding the *Arthur* out to sea. The six British sailors on board were Sergeant Don Craig and Able Seaman Bob Evans, who would commandeer one Chariot; and

Sub-Lieutenant Percy Brewster and Able Seaman Jock Brown, who would commandeer the other. Able Seaman Malcolm Causer and Able Seaman Bill Tebb traveled as a backup Chariot crew.[31]

The operation underway, codenamed "Title," aimed to sink or severely damage the *Tirpitz* with explosives at her anchorage. The plan called for the *Arthur* to carry the Chariots and their crew to Fætten-fjord, where *Tirpitz* had arrived three days prior after spending the summer in Bogen Bay, near Narvik.[32] The men would then guide their midget subs through the heavily defended waters and plant explosives beneath *Tirpitz*'s hull.

As the Scottish coast disappeared, the sky darkened and the ocean swell grew. Even with sturdy sea legs, the men succumbed to the ravages of seasickness. Minor relief came on the early afternoon of Wednesday, October 28, when Larsen spotted Norway's snow-capped peaks. Any jubilation on behalf of the crew, however, faded when the *Arthur*'s engine quit.[33] The boat bobbed about helplessly under clear, blue skies—an obvious curiosity for any German plane that might make an appearance. For three hours the men fussed and cursed over the engine before repairs were made and the ship could continue once more on its way.[34]

The rest of the day and night passed without incident. At eight o'clock the following morning, the *Arthur* anchored in a bay near the entrance to the waterways that would lead to Trondheimsfjord. Larsen and his men allowed themselves the luxury of a ham-and-egg breakfast.[35] The rough seas and apprehension as to what lay ahead had done nothing to curb their appetites. "We found it very difficult to realize," wrote Brewster, "that here we were in German-occupied Norway on a beautiful, if cold, autumn morning."[36]

The buzz-saw drone of a distant plane killed the moment's tranquility. The British Chariot crews made for a secret compartment in the ship's hull, while the Norwegian sailors did their utmost to appear nonchalant and concerned only with the mundane tasks of their trade.[37]

The ship had no doubt caught the pilot's attention, for the speck of aircraft grew larger as it approached the fjord's entrance. Larsen kept one eye on the plane as he busied himself about the deck. It swooped over the *Arthur*, dropping "low enough for the machine-guns in her wings to be clearly seen," then climbed skyward once more and disappeared from view.[38]

The British crews emerged from their hiding place and set about unfastening the Chariots—with their warheads attached—so they could be lowered into the water. This, Brewster and his team did, but nature intervened before they could secure the Chariots beneath the boat's hull. The wind picked up and stirred the bay waters. The *Arthur* began to rock and was soon dragging her anchor. With night descending, Larsen steered the boat toward the shore.[39] "The rocky bottom was such a poor holding ground," wrote Brewster, "that the anchor had to be dragged ashore and secured in a cleft in the rock."[40]

The night passed without additional drama. Before the sun rose on the morning of Friday, October 30, Brewster and Evans lowered themselves into the water and secured both Chariots to the *Arthur*'s underside.[41] Things appeared to be back on track until a rowboat appeared out of nowhere. The old man at the oars took a nosy interest in the *Arthur* and approached, sending the Brits once more to their hiding place.[42]

Larsen was left to deal with the interloper, who—for an interminable amount of time—harried the Norwegian with idle chatter and prying questions. In between his endless queries, he revealed he and his daughter lived in a nearby village.[43] The man prattled on but came to a stop when he caught sight of the Chariots just beneath the water's surface. "They are something we use to explode mines with," Larsen said, insinuating he worked for the Germans.[44]

The old man considered this bit of information before, sheepishly, asking if they had any butter on board they might be willing to part with. Larsen, seeing a chance to rid himself of this unwanted guest, said yes and disappeared below deck. He returned with the butter and passed it to the man, who smiled and voiced his thanks.[45] Larsen did not return the kindness. He assailed the man with a menacing gaze and threatened to kill him and his daughter if word of this chance encounter got out. Deciding now was a good time to depart, the old man fumbled for his oars and began to row away as quickly as his aged muscles allowed.[46]

It was now late morning. Larsen and his men, desperate to get going, scoured the *Arthur* for anything that might betray their true intentions. They placed their British cigarettes and garbage into a weighted bag and tossed it overboard, stripped their wireless radio and dispatched it to the depths before setting off again.[47]

The day blessed them with kind weather and smooth sailing. They anchored that night near the village of Hestvik on the island of Hitra, just southwest of the Trondheimsfjord entrance, and resumed their journey in the predawn gloom of Saturday, October 31. They slowly approached the German stronghold of Agdenes at the mouth of Trondheimsfjord.[48]

The British Chariot crews, concealed in their secret hiding place and swaying to the gentle rocking of the boat, heard Larsen call down to them. An enemy trawler was drawing near. The British sailors heard the heavy clump of boots as a German officer boarded the boat. Muffled voices drifted down to them in the darkness. They heard footfalls descending the stairs into the cabin. Drawers were opened, papers rifled through. The footfalls ascended once more to the deck. Larsen called down several minutes later with the all-clear.[49]

Not until nightfall did the Chariot crews emerge from their cover. "The weather was quite fine," remembered Brewster, "and there were many friendly-looking lights flickering ashore."[50] They traveled beneath a moonless sky, the lights of Trondheim guiding their way. Soon, the Chariot crews ducked below deck to change into their diving gear. "Almost immediately," wrote Brewster, "the weather worsened. . . . We hadn't got very far with our dressing when we began to hear a succession of sharp bumps. The Chariots were being swung up against the keel."[51]

A strong wind began to whip the water and tilt the *Arthur* at ever-sharpening angles. Larsen opted to push on. Finding somewhere to anchor would only increase the risk of being caught. The ship fought its way—at reduced speed—through the heaving channel. Such conditions were not uncommon in the fjords, and Larsen hoped the storm would pass before they reached their objective. Below deck, Brewster struggled to stay upright as he slipped into his gear. A terrible noise shattered his concentration. "It was just after ten o'clock when we heard a loud, grounding, tearing noise," he wrote. "The vessel jerked and shuddered. Something pretty substantial had fouled the propeller."[52]

Bob Evans, fully decked out in his gear, lowered himself over the side of the boat and vanished beneath the dark surface. He emerged minutes later with the devastating news. Only ten miles shy of the *Tirpitz*, both Chariots had been swept away. "I don't think anyone has ever been so disappointed as we were that night," wrote Brewster. "Looking back, I don't remember one single curse. We were all too unhappy for that."[53]

The matter of getting back home now became all-consuming. They couldn't turn back the way they had come, for they lacked the necessary travel permits—not to mention they still carried the peat they were supposedly delivering. After an intense council of war, they decided to try their luck on land. They gathered pistols, ammunition, and what food they had before scuttling the *Arthur* and rowing to shore in two dinghies. It was one o'clock in the morning on Sunday, November 1. The men did not waste time resting and immediately set off. A thin layer of snow crunched underfoot as they made their way across a bleak gray-and-white landscape touched silver by the moon.[54]

Their breath came and went in thick clouds of vapor. They trudged through the long, dark hours until a thin ribbon of daylight revealed itself above the trees and mountains. Hoping to draw less attention to themselves, they decided to split up: Bob Evans, Roald Strand (the ship's radio operator), Bill Tebb, and Don Craig would set off in one party under Larsen's command. Mechanic Palmer Bjørnøy and deckhand Johannes Kalve would lead Brewster, Brown, and Causer to the Swedish frontier.[55]

Each man checked his pistol and meager rations of corned beef, sardines, and biscuits. Farewells exchanged, the two parties trudged off in different directions, with Larsen's group heading inland and the other following the coast. "We carried on through the rest of the afternoon and the evening," wrote Brewster, "not allowing ourselves any organized breaks for food." At one point, from the cover of trees, they observed three German soldiers on a nearby footpath. "They were obviously enjoying a spell of leave," Brewster noted. "I suppose we were, too, come to that."[56]

Brewster's group spent that night in a fishing hut, collapsed on the floor in utter exhaustion, and continued early the next morning. The physical strain of their long march began to grind its way into their bones and muscles; the cold gnawed through their clothing and settled against their skin—but they pushed on. The men, despite their weary bodies and blistering feet, opted to keep going even as night fell. They stumbled through the darkness until first light, when they came across a small farmhouse with a barn in the back. They snuck into the barn and slept among the hay.[57]

The sound of workers in the field outside returned them to the land of the living. Brewster and the other men gathered themselves, their eyes still heavy with sleep, and snuck away without being seen. Three more days of hard scrabbling over rock and snow passed before they reached the Swedish frontier—their final challenge, a wind-swept mountain. They climbed through the night, battered by the elements, clawing at the rock face. The mountain, pushing them to the bleeding edge, showed no mercy.[58]

They descended the other side and dropped into a valley. The woods soon surrendered a village to view and the gift of deliverance. Frostbitten and starving, they turned themselves in at the local police station. The Swedish police chief treated them well. He summoned a doctor and informed the exhausted travelers another small party of British and Norwegian servicemen had appeared earlier that morning. The two groups were reunited, but Brewster's had obviously fared better than the other.[59]

Larsen, ragged and disheveled from the ordeal, shared his group's tragic story:

He and his men were no more than a few hundred yards from the Swedish frontier when they encountered two German policemen. Although the forged identity papers the British and Norwegians presented passed close inspection, the Germans placed the men under arrest and marched them off for interrogation. They worked their way through the snow, with Larsen's men in front and the Germans,

Lugers at the ready, covering from the rear. Bill Tebb, walking alongside Larsen, slowly reached for his concealed revolver and whispered his intent to open fire. Larsen nodded his approval.[60]

As the men rounded a bend in the road, Tebb drew his weapon, spun on his captors, and fired. The shot disappeared into the snow-covered trees. The Germans each squeezed off a round; the surrounding woods echoing with violent sound. Bob Evans fell bleeding to the ground.[61]

Tebb's revolver roared again. One German dropped, and then the other. Before the trees batted the echo of gunfire into silence, Larsen and the others ran over to Evans's prostrate form. A red stain spread across the snow beneath him. The men listened for the sounds of approaching Germans, knowing they likely had just minutes to spare. Evans lay dead where he fell. They couldn't hope to carry his body and make it to the border, so they made the hard decision to leave him.[62]

In the days that followed their reunion, the survivors enjoyed the comforts of Swedish hospitality. They enjoyed ample food and drink—even some sightseeing thrown in for good measure—before the diplomatic paperwork cleared and they were on their way back to Britain. For their daring efforts, Brewster received the Distinguished Service Cross and Larsen the Conspicuous Gallantry Medal. Not until after the war, however, was Operation Title's tragic final chapter written.[63]

It emerged during the Nuremberg trials that twenty-year-old Bob Evans had survived, been nursed back to health by the Germans, and shot as a spy on January 19, 1943, in Oslo. Field Marshal Wilhelm Keitel, chief of the German High Command, who approved the execution, met his end on the gallows.[64]

Far from the majestic beauty of the Norwegian fjords, across the frozen steppes of Russia on the hellscape of the Eastern Front, more than 200,000 German soldiers faced annihilation. Surrounded by the Red Army in the wastelands of Stalingrad, the men—plagued by starvation and the savagery of Russia's winter—waited for a deliverance that would never come.

The pride of the Royal Navy. The battlecruiser HMS *Hood* is seen here during maneuvers in the South Atlantic on Jan. 1, 1939. (ALAMY)

The German leviathan *Bismarck* during sea trials after being completed at the Blohm & Voss Shipyards in Hamburg in 1941. (ALAMY)

HMS *Hood* going into action against the *Bismarck* and *Prinz Eugen* on Saturday, May 24, 1941. Snapped from HMS *Prince of Wales*, this was the last photo ever taken of *Hood*. (IMPERIAL WAR MUSEUM)

Taken from the *Prinz Eugen*, this image shows a shell from HMS *Hood* landing near *Bismarck* and sending up a large, white plume of water. The black smoke near *Bismarck* indicates she has just fired a salvo at the British warships. (IMPERIAL WAR MUSEUM)

The death of an iconic warship. HMS *Hood* exploding (at right) and HMS *Prince of Wales* (center) as seen from the *Prinz Eugen*. (IMPERIAL WAR MUSEUM)

Captured from the *Prinz Eugen* in the wake of HMS *Hood*'s sinking, this is the last photograph taken of *Bismarck*. (Naval History and Heritage Command)

The front page of the *Sunday News* (New York) on Sunday, May 25, 1941. The sinking of HMS *Hood* scarred the British national psyche and made headlines around the world. (Alamy)

Sailor Robert Tilburn, one of only three survivors from HMS *Hood*, out for a walk with his young brother a month after the sinking. (Imperial War Museum)

This photograph shows the type of motor launch (ML) that took part in Operation Chariot. Sixteen such MLs carried Commandos and demolition teams into the maelstrom of the St. Nazaire harbor. Their frail wooden hulls offered scant protection, and only three of the vessels survived. (IMPERIAL WAR MUSEUM)

The morning after the daring raid on St. Nazaire, this waterfront building bears the scars of the previous night's savage fighting. (ALAMY)

German soldiers, inspecting the damage, walk past the body of a fallen British Commando the morning after the raid on St. Nazaire. (ALAMY)

The ship's company parade onboard *Scharnhorst*, alternatively described as a battlecruiser and battleship, during her ceremonial commissioning at Wilhelmshaven on Jan. 8, 1939. The order has just been given to "Hoist the flag and pennant." (ALAMY)

Scharnhorst's two 11-inch turrets. (ALAMY)

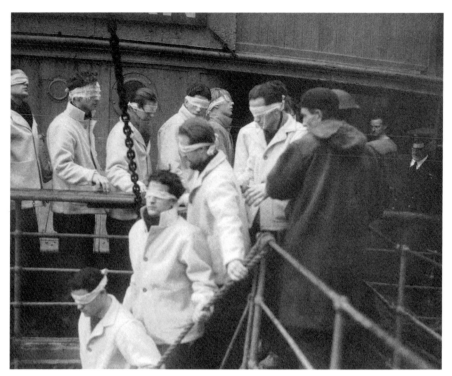

Survivors of *Scharnhorst*, blindfolded and wearing British merchant naval rescue kit, disembark in England on their way to internment. (ALAMY)

Scharnhorst's sister ship, *Gneisenau*, during sea exercises in August 1939. She would meet an ignoble end, being sunk by the Germans in March 1945 and used to block the harbor in Gotenhafen (in German-occupied Poland) against the advancing Russians. (ALAMY)

The wreckage of the *Prinz Eugen* is still visible today in the Kwajalein Atoll. She capsized on Dec. 16, 1946, after the Americans subjected her to two atomic blasts in the Marshall Islands. (ALAMY)

The German battleship *Tirpitz*, the *Bismarck*'s sister ship, sits at anchor in a Norwegian fjord. The picture was taken some time in 1943. (ALAMY)

Tirpitz, photographed from astern, sometime in 1940 or '41. Despite her destructive potential, *Tirpitz* waged more of a psychological war against the British than one of aggression. (NAVAL HISTORY AND HERITAGE COMMAND)

Crewmembers busy themselves camouflaging *Tirpitz* as she lays at anchor in Flehke Fjord, 1942. Some take a break and relax alongside one of the ship's four twin turrets of 15-inch guns. (NAVAL HISTORY AND HERITAGE COMMAND)

Increasingly fraught over the fate of his Sixth Army, Hitler saw a glimmer of hope when, on December 30, 1942, his naval staff informed him U-boat 354 on patrol in the Arctic had spotted a Russian-bound convoy from Britain "50 miles south of Bear Island."[65] Grand Admiral Raeder said he hoped to attack the convoy once he had confirmation it was sailing with "no superior force" in escort. Hitler, hoping to starve Soviet forces into submission, approved the operation.[66]

The convoy in question was JW-51B, composed of fifteen merchant ships bound for Murmansk. Its destruction fell to Vice Admiral Oskar Kummetz on his flagship, the 14,000-ton cruiser *Admiral Hipper*. His plan of attack aimed to crush the convoy in a pincer movement. The *Hipper* would lead three destroyers in a charge from the north, sending the merchant ships scurrying into the German battle cruiser *Lützow* and its three accompanying destroyers lying in wait to the south.[67]

Kummetz and his force set sail from Norway's Kåfjord on the evening of December 30. The ships sailed through the Arctic darkness and split into their attack groups in the early morning hours of New Year's Eve. Time was of the essence. This far north, Kummetz would have no more than four hours of bleak winter's daylight to locate his quarry.[68]

A lookout on *Hipper* spotted feint shadows off the ship's starboard side shortly after seven o'clock in the morning. The convoy had been found, yet Kummetz dared not attack; what passed for daybreak remained an hour away. Dawn, when it finally arrived, brought with it a heavy fog. "The light conditions," noted Kummetz, "were exceptionally unfavorable, reducing even the little brightness we could otherwise expect. Everything looked as if covered by a grey veil, which distorted all outlines and merged them together."[69]

Such conditions made it impossible to identify any ship. A confused game of cat and mouse now played out in the swirling mist. When sailors in the convoy initially glimpsed through the gloom the blurred outlines of two German ships, they mistook them for Russian vessels. Captain Robert Sherbrooke, on the British destroyer *Onslow*, in support of the convoy, dispatched the destroyer *Obdurate* to investigate.[70]

The *Obdurate* worked her way through the mist and swell, the vague shape ahead of her taking on greater definition as she closed the distance. Eight thousand yards of white-crested sea remained between her and what turned out to be the German destroyer *Friedrich Eckoldt*, when the enemy ship fired the battle's opening salvo. *Obdurate* retreated to the safety of numbers and fell back to join the *Onslow* and two other destroyers—the *Orwell* and *Obedient*.[71]

From the *Hipper*'s bridge, Kummetz saw the first flash of guns in the distance, but could not distinguish his ships from the British. A billowing smoke screen from the convoy's escort added to the confusion.[72] At 9:40 a.m., Sherbrooke spotted *Hipper* through the smoke. Kummetz, seeing his chance, sent a signal to German naval headquarters—"Am engaging convoy"—and opened fire.[73]

The British destroyers, outgunned, waged a desperate defense. The *Onslow* took a severe pounding, her deck littered with the dead and injured. One shell opened a gaping hole, its edges smoldering red, in the ship's funnel and showered scalding splinters on the men below. Another shell wiped a gun crew out in its entirety. Fires raged throughout the ship. The searing temperatures "caused wooden paneling in the Petty Officer's mess to burst into flames and burning hammocks gave off choking clouds of dense orange-colored smoke."[74]

On the bridge, Sherbrooke—having been hit in the face with splinters—presented a ghastly sight, directing the action with his left eye hanging out of its socket. He kept the *Hipper* at a distance by feigning torpedo attacks and zigzagging in and out of the smoke screen roiling across the water.[75]

Now, Sherbrooke withdrew his destroyers into the smoky camouflage—but Kummetz, exercising extreme caution, failed to follow, perhaps paralyzed by the order he received from Berlin the previous day: "Discretion to be exercised in face of enemy of equal strength owing to undesirability of submitting cruisers to major risk."[76] An easy target, however, presented itself in HMS *Bramble*, an 875-ton minesweeper that inadvertently got in the way.[77]

Snow began mingling with the smoke and mist, creating a swirling visual static across the scene of battle. Kummetz mistook the minesweeper, armed with one 4-inch gun, for a destroyer and responded accordingly. The two ships exchanged fire for ten minutes, as *Bramble*—battered and burning—drew the *Hipper* away from the convoy. As the smaller ship began to flounder, Kummetz ordered the *Friedrich Eckoldt* to finish her off. The *Bramble* went down with all hands. As the freezing swell washed over the minesweeper, Kummetz altered course to reengage the convoy to the south.[78]

The tumult of battle and the confusion inflicted by the weather had served the British well. While *Hipper* and her accompanying destroyers engaged the enemy to the north, the *Lützow*—to the south—had inadvertently let elements of the convoy slip past her. "A favorable opportunity to score a success and possibly finish the appointed job at one blow was not here exploited," notes a postbattle report. As *Hipper* closed the distance between herself and the convoy, the destroyer HMS *Achates*—screening the merchant ships with smoke—crossed her path.[79]

The British ship had already suffered in her protective role. "All hands between decks," noted one senior officer, "were employed plugging the innumerable shell holes in the ship's side on the forward mess deck." Now, at 11:15 a.m., *Hipper*'s guns did their part, reducing the bridge and wheelhouse on *Achates* to a smoldering, gore-splattered mess.[80]

Among the mangled bodies of the dead lay her captain, Lieutenant Commander A. H. T. James. Twenty-four-year-old Lieutenant Loftus Peyton-Jones rushed to inspect the damage. He climbed up one ladder to the wheelhouse, where coxswain Daniel Hall was the only survivor. It was apparent, from the massive bulge in the ceiling, the bridge above had borne the brunt of impact. "The usual way up to the bridge was barred," Peyton-Jones wrote, "so stepping out on to the port Oerlikon platform I clambered up the remains of the outside ladder. The familiar scene was unrecognizable—just the blackened shambles of twisted metal with the remains of a few identifiable objects sticking grotesquely out of the wreckage." Of the bodies, he couldn't tell who was who.[81]

With no one at the controls, the ship circled to starboard at 28 knots with a list 20 degrees to port. "All the bridge and wheelhouse instruments had been wrecked," Peyton-Jones wrote, "but the wheel and Engine Room Telegraphs remained undamaged."[82] Peyton-Jones now found himself in command of the stricken destroyer. He bellowed at

Hall in the wheelhouse to steady the ship on a course parallel to the convoy and ordered the engine room to resume laying smoke.[83]

Hipper flung more shells at her crippled target. One hit took out a forward gun crew and set the gun ablaze until the sea, crashing over the forecastle, put it out. "A new gun crew was formed," Peyton-Jones reported, "but it was found impossible to move the gun . . . and they were dispersed."[84]

Hipper bore down on the destroyer's port quarter. Peyton-Jones summoned a crewman and sent him aft with an order for Y gun to open fire—but his order "never reached the gun." The messenger was killed—"probably by splinters from a near miss"—as he hurried along the battered deck.[85]

Hipper's guns again flashed into the smoke and snow. A shell blew through the *Achates*'s port side and took out the seaman's bathroom. It obliterated the telegraph station—killing nearly all the crew there—and "fractured the after bulkhead of the now flooded Stoker's Mess Deck." Another shell slammed into the water along the ship's port side, blasting "large holes" in the hull and flooding the No. 2 boiler room.[86]

"Speed," Peyton-Jones later noted, "was reduced to 12 knots in order to bring the damaged port side higher out of the water." The ship had become increasingly difficult to steer.[87] On board, everything was blood and wreckage. The thirty men killed included the doctor, leaving many wounded crewmembers to tend to one another. All spare hands—still capable of doing so—worked frantically to stem the damage, but the ship's list increased and submerged more unplugged holes in the port side. Water poured into her front and lower compartments and completely flooded the No. 1 boiler room, bringing the *Achates* to a dead stop.[88]

Peyton-Jones hoped the ship might be towed along with the convoy, but her listing grew ever sharper. The men discussed dumping shells and ammunition overboard—even firing the torpedoes—to ease the ship's burden. "It was decided," Peyton-Jones wrote, "that these measures would not appreciably improve the ship's stability."[89] Peyton-Jones ordered all men onto the upper deck, now being slapped by waves. Men threw rafts and floats into the water, as the ship continued to roll onto her port side.[90]

On the trawler *Northern Gem*, Lieutenant Horace Aisthorpe maneuvered his ship close to the dying vessel. "She certainly seemed in a bad way," remembered S. A. Kerslake, a coxswain on *Northern Gem*. "I could see the figures of men, some with red lights on their life jackets and some even smoking, clambering through the rails and onto her starboard side, which had now become her deck. As she went further over until she was floating bottom up, the men slid down her side and into the water, her keel now pointing to the heavens. Then, as the men in the water started swimming toward the *Gem*, we stood on our deck and listened in amazement as we heard their voices giving out with a rendering of 'Roll Out the Barrel.'"[91]

The time was 1:30 p.m. Peyton-Jones had not yet abandoned ship when *Achates* went under. Staying on board to oversee the evacuation, he found himself submerged in freezing darkness. He clawed his way to the surface and pulled himself into a nearby float.[92] "Calling to various heads bobbing in the water eventually congregated some fifteen or twenty men around the float," Peyton-Jones wrote. "Some were supporting their wounded shipmates and these were manhandled onto the float."[93]

The men did not have to wait long for salvation, as the *Northern Gem* closed in and began fishing them from the water. Kerslake lowered himself down the netting on *Northern Gem*'s side to help the survivors up. "We entwined our legs in the nets to leave our arms and hands free," he recalled, "making sure that we should not be pulled away by the suction of the seas rolling under the ship's hull, or by the weight of the men in the water."[94]

He watched in horror as one man, unable to grab hold of the netting or any of the outstretched hands reaching for him, slipped past the ship. Kerslake threw the man a line and screamed at him to grab hold. "He seemed to have lost all the feeling in his body due to the cold," Kerslake wrote. "He could do nothing to save himself." The coxswain, now frantic, grabbed several nearby life rings and threw them into the water—but it proved pointless. "I distinctly heard him crying out for his mother," Kerslake wrote. "'Mother' was the last word I heard as he disappeared beneath the surface. I know that I was crying myself with helplessness and frustration as I saw him go."[95]

The *Achates* exploded beneath the waves, convulsing the surface and bringing to it her last few shattered remains. The shockwave traveled across the water and rocked the *Northern Gem*. When the violence subsided, Kerslake saw "six or eight bodies" floating in the water; the lights on their lifejackets glowed a ghostly red.[96]

The rescue operation was over. *Northern Gem*'s commander deemed it wise to rejoin the relative safety of the convoy. Peyton-Jones and the men on his float were among the last to be pulled on board. Taken below and provided dry clothes, blankets, and a bunk, he was happy to be reunited with what remained of his men. "The [*Northern Gem*'s] crew," Peyton-Jones noted, "though heavily outnumbered worked tirelessly on our behalf."[97] Eighty-one of the 114 men on the *Achates* survived.[98]

"The last evening of 1942," Peyton-Jones wrote, "was memorable if only for the shock we felt at the loss of so many of our shipmates."[99]

＊ ＊ ＊

Kummetz believed victory to be his even before *Achates* sank. At 11:32 a.m., he turned *Hipper*'s guns on the destroyer *Obedient*. "Engaging security forces," he signaled. "No cruisers with convoy."[100] His confidence proved premature. The flash of guns had attracted the attention of the cruisers *Sheffield* and *Jamaica*, sailing fifteen miles away from the convoy in distant support. They emerged from the mist and smoke at roughly the same time Kummetz sent his signal to fire. The cannonade of *Sheffield*'s 6-inch guns announced their arrival.[101]

"Our opening salvoes, heard and seen by the destroyers on the other side of the enemy ships, had naturally a very heartening effect," remembered Captain Arthur Clarke on *Sheffield*. "We had been expected, but when was speculative, and I can imagine that the time must have dragged in anticipation of the much-needed help."[102]

The sea exploded on either side of *Hipper*, taking Kummetz by surprise. One shell struck beneath the waterline and flooded her No. 3

boiler room; another sent her aircraft hangar up in flames. It was at this unfortunate moment someone handed Kummetz a signal from German naval headquarters. He read the brief message: "No unnecessary risk."[103] Thrown off balance by the sudden turn of events, he radioed his destroyers to retreat: "Break off. Proceed west." The time was 11.37 a.m.[104]

The poor visibility now favored Kummetz. As *Hipper* withdrew, the smoke and mist rendered her indistinguishable from other ships in the area and forced *Sheffield* and *Jamaica*—no more than 8,000 yards away—to hold their fire. Peering into the thick haze, lookouts on *Sheffield* noticed a vessel appear three miles off the port bow. "The range closed with remarkable rapidity," noted Captain Clarke. "In one minute we felt fairly certain that the ship was no friend of ours."[105]

Sheffield opened fire at 4,000 yards and sent her opponent up in flames. "Each successive salvo found its mark," Clarke noted. "As we swept down on the target, she was disintegrating under our eyes."[106] The recipient of such punishment proved to be the *Friedrich Eckoldt*. *Sheffield* continued her relentless assault, even as she closed in for the kill. No more than several hundred yards soon separated the two ships.[107]

Marine "Doddie" Thorndyke, manning one of *Sheffield*'s 2.4-inch guns, fired eighteen rounds at point-blank range into the German destroyer. He watched as British rounds cut down men trying to ready lifeboats and obliterate others attempting to load torpedoes. "I could also see men jumping off the stern," he said, "and the skipper was silhouetted against the flames around his bridge."[108]

The ship was a burning funeral pyre, yet *Sheffield* gave no quarter. She passed the destroyer and unleashed one final salvo from her after turrets. "*Friedrich Eckoldt*," noted Clarke, "was left, a horrible and smoking ruin, to sink astern."[109] She went down with all 340 men on board.[110]

Thus ended the Battle of the Barents Sea, as it came to be known. Kummetz ordered his entire fleet to withdraw at 11:49 a.m. The *Lützow*, other than inflicting "splinter damage" on one ship, had made little contribution. Arriving nearly three hours after the battle began, the light cruisers *Sheffield* and *Jamaica* effectively turned the tide against a superior German force of five destroyers, one heavy cruiser, and a "pocket battleship."[111]

For the Kriegsmarine, it proved to be a humiliating catastrophe—news of which had yet to reach Berlin. Earlier in the day, the naval high command had passed along to Hitler a signal from U-354, which observed the attack on the convoy. "Observation of scene suggests battle has reached climax," it read. "I see only red." Hitler, in his anxious state, took the message to mean the convoy was burning and being sent to the ocean floor.[112]

Hitler appeared in high spirits that evening. As guests arrived for a New Year's Eve party at his Wolf's Lair compound in East Prussia, he shared with them the good news from the Barents Sea. The exact details of the battle, however, remained a mystery. Kummetz, returning to the safety of Altafjord, sailed under strict radio silence. The lack of specifics wore on the party's host as midnight drew closer. By the time those present ushered in 1943, Hitler's façade of jovial calm had all but crumbled.[113]

When, on the morning of January 1, he learned the truth, Hitler went apoplectic. He summoned Vice Admiral Theodor Krancke—Raeder's personal liaison—for a vicious dressing down and passed a fatal judgment on the Reich's surface fleet. "The heavy ships are a needless drain on men and materials," he said. "They will accordingly be paid off and reduced to scrap."[114]

Having lost the faith of his Führer, Raeder resigned on January 6; Rear Admiral Karl Dönitz, commander of the U-boat fleet, was made grand admiral and ascended to commander in chief of the navy on January 30.[115] His first order from Hitler made clear the surface fleet's fate:

1. All construction and conversion of heavy ships to cease with immediately; this also means any further work on aircraft carriers, auxiliary carriers, and troop transports . . .

2. Unless required for training purposes, pocket battleships, heavy and light cruisers are to be paid off . . .

3. Naval personnel, workers, yard facilities and weapons becoming available as a result of this directive should be used to speed up submarine repairs and construction.[116]

The following month, repair work on the *Gneisenau* ground to a halt. Her war had come to an end. Her final act for country would be that of sacrifice in March 1945. With the Red Army tightening its grip, the Germans sank the once mighty ship in the harbor entrance at Gotenhafen to prevent access.[117]

Despite Hitler's order, Dönitz had no desire to completely give up on Germany's surface ships and hand the Royal Navy an effortless victory. He ordered the *Scharnhorst* to join the *Tirpitz* in Norway. "The ships," he told Hitler, "would be a fairly powerful force" against the Allied convoys bound for Russia.[118] Hitler, incredulous, told Dönitz that "large ships are a thing of the past," but let his new naval chief have his way.[119]

CHAPTER 11

* * *

X-CRAFT

After two attempts thwarted by the RAF, *Scharnhorst* escaped her Baltic port in March 1943 and joined *Tirpitz* in Norway. The two ships sat idle for most of the year, plagued by inaction until Dönitz ordered an attack on the Allied meteorological station and coaling facility on the Norwegian island of Spitzbergen. Although a target of minimal strategic value, it would—in the navy chief's words—give the ships "a chance to work together."[1]

The operation was a mere distraction for the ships' crews, a minor break in the tedium of a war without action. The target itself was wholly unspectacular, a barren slab of rocky island more than 400 miles north of continental Norway and garrisoned by less than 200 Norwegian soldiers. It operated as a mine prior to the war, its bleak terrain littered with mountains of coal; one of them had been set alight two years prior and continued to burn.[2]

Tirpitz and *Scharnhorst*, with an escort of ten destroyers, left the remote safety of Kåfjord on September 6 and bombarded the island two days later. The small Spitzbergen force could do little in return. The shore batteries lobbed a few shells at the ships and damaged a couple of destroyers, but it hardly mattered. "The inevitable reply to this," wrote one member of the garrison, "was a hail of missiles which left us with no alternative but to lie down in a small gulley."[3]

The exercise left a lot to be desired. "Shooting up a few cardboard houses," noted a gunner on *Tirpitz*, was "a bit of an anti-climax."[4] The

German ships returned to their fjord having suffered no major casualties. While the raid did nothing to advance the German war effort, it drove home to London the continuing threat posed by *Tirpitz* and *Scharnhorst*. Churchill, in particular, remained obsessed with the former's destruction.

On February 16, 1943, he sent a sharply worded memo to the commander in chief of RAF Bomber Command and the First Sea Lord. "Have you given up all plans of doing anything to *Tirpitz* while she is at Trondheim?" he demanded to know. "We heard a lot of talk about it five months ago, which has all petered out. At least four or five plans were under consideration. . . . What has happened to the chariots and the diving mines? It is a terrible thing that this prize should be waiting, and no one able to think of a way of winning it."[5]

The British Admiralty, as it so happened, had put plenty of thought into winning it. Two years of secret brainstorming, labor, and trials had—by early 1943—resulted in a new midget submarine called the X-craft. Six of the submarines, X-5 through X-10, were ready for action in January. The craft measured fifty-one feet in length and had four compartments. A battery in the forward space powered the X-craft's "pumps, lights, and main motor."[6] The bathroom was in the second compartment, which also served as the air lock for divers. The third compartment housed the cramped space where the crew navigated the craft. The main motor and a surface engine took up the aft compartment.[7]

These craft would play the vital role in Operation Source, with the aim—much like the failed Operation Title before it—to permanently knock *Tirpitz* out of the war.

✳ ✳ ✳

At four o'clock on the afternoon of Saturday, September 11, 1943, the submarine HMS *Truculent* sailed out of Loch Cairnbawn, towing X-6 behind her. The submarine HMS *Syrtis*, towing X-9, followed in her wake. Over the next six hours, the submarines HMS *Thrasher* pulling X-5, the HMS *Seanymph* pulling X-8, and the HMS *Stubborn* with

X-7 set off for the open sea beneath a clear, dark sky. The HMS *Sceptre*, transporting X-10, sailed at 1 p.m. the following afternoon. "Fine weather" blessed the submarines and their six submerged X-craft the first three days at sea.[8]

The minisubs surfaced three or four times a day for fifteen minutes to ventilate, yet conditions on board proved less than ideal.[9] Tasked with guiding the subs on the outward journey, the three-man passage crews—their clothes sodden and hair wet—worked in confines claustrophobically tight and constantly damp. Seasickness proved a constant scourge, as did the ever-present danger of condensation building up on interior surfaces. The X-craft crews "had to endure appalling discomfort during the passage."[10]

On the afternoon of September 14, the Admiralty sent a signal to the subs confirming the location of their targets. The *Tirpitz* and *Scharnhorst* were both in Kåfjord. X-5, X-6, and X-7 would attack the former; X-9 and X-10 the latter. The fate of the *Lützow*, anchored in Langfjord, fell to X-8. The passage thus far, minus the physical hardships, had passed without mishap or enemy intervention. Not until the early hours of September 15 did the "first hitch throw the plan off track."[11]

At one o'clock that morning, Lieutenant Jack Smart in X-8 lost "telephone communication" with Lieutenant J. P. H. Oakley, the *Seanymph*'s commanding officer. The situation worsened three hours later when the towline between the vessels snapped. Smart ordered X-8 to the surface and scanned the waters for *Seanymph*, but saw nothing—even with visibility at five miles. He ordered X-8 to maintain its current heading at a speed of 3 knots. The time was 4:30 a.m. Two hours later, *Seanymph*'s commander registered a nasty shock when X-8 failed to surface for its scheduled ventilation. He ordered *Seanymph* to reverse course "and spent the remainder of the day in a vain search for the lost midget."[12]

Shortly after noon, the *Stubborn* surfaced with X-7. The *Stubborn*'s lookout canvassed the sea from the conning tower and spotted what he believed to be a U-boat. Lieutenant A. A. Duff, *Stubborn*'s commander, ordered an immediate dive, not realizing the U-boat was actually the missing X-8. The *Stubborn* remained submerged for more than an hour.

When she braved the surface again at 1:23 p.m., the suspected U-boat had vanished. *Stubborn* continued on her course, descending once more beneath the roughening waves with X-7 in tow. The two vessels moved silently through the gray fathoms, as the sea above them grew evermore volatile.[13]

Even at depth, the rough waters wreaked havoc with X-7's crew. The current tossed the men this way and that with vomit sloshing about their feet.[14] At 3:50 p.m., the towline between the vessels snapped. The mishap did not go unnoticed. *Stubborn* and X-7 surfaced immediately with the sea frothing about them. The crews managed to connect an "auxiliary tow," even as waves tumbled over the vessels.[15] Across the water, a lookout on *Stubborn* noticed another craft and—this time—recognized it as the missing midget. The three ships now went in search of *Seanymph*.[16]

The punishing swell soon forced all three vessels back under. Before diving, Duff ascended the *Stubborn*'s conning tower and yelled orders to Smart on X-8 to set a steering course at 146 degrees. "A phonetic error"—the navy's term—occurred in the tumult of bad weather.[17] Smart misheard the order and set a steering course for 046 degrees. The three submarines went under and began their nightlong, yet futile, search for *Seanymph*. X-8, steering on her incorrect course, wandered off into the murky darkness and disappeared. Not until *Stubborn* and X-7 surfaced in the early morning light of September 16 did they discover X-8 had vanished yet again.[18]

The sea had by now calmed, and as the sun began its slow and gradual arc across the sky, *Stubborn*'s lookout spotted an approaching vessel. It was *Seanymph*, still searching for X-8. "After giving her all the relevant information," notes a postoperation report, "the *Stubborn* and X-7 set course to the northward, and the *Seanymph* once again started to search for her errant charge, which she eventually found at 1700 that afternoon."[19]

The passage of the *Syrtis* and X-9 had been a relatively smooth affair. Shortly after nine on the morning of September 16, *Syrtis* fired her underwater exploding signals to alert X-9's crew it was time to surface. *Syrtis* broke her deep-sea cover, but X-9 failed to appear. Her towline had snapped. A study of "log readings and fuel consumption" on board *Syrtis* suggested the severing had occurred "some seven or eight hours previously."[20]

As *Syrtis* turned to retrace her course, a length of tow cable got tangled in one of her propellers. The sub's diver, Max Shean, suited up in his dive gear and braved the freezing waters. His suit did nothing to insulate him from the cold. "When my face went under, it took my breath away. In the few moments that I could remain submerged," he wrote, "I noticed the shaft of sunlight descending into the depths. It made me feel giddy."[21] He struggled against the heavy swell and the "almighty splash" of the hydroplane's slapping the surface, but eventually unraveled the cable.[22]

Syrtis once more got underway, pushing through a thickening fog. Some five hours and 200 miles later, a lookout spotted "a well-defined oil track" on the waves that followed the direct course the minisub had been steering.[23] The *Syrtis* continued its search into the predawn hours of Friday, September 17, without result and relayed the grim news to the Admiralty. No trace of X-9 or its crew—Sub-Lieutenant Edward Kearon, Able-Seaman Harry Hart, and Stoker First Class George Hollett—was ever seen again.[24]

Elsewhere, the crew of X-8 once more found itself in trouble. At 7:25 that morning, commanding officer Lieutenant B. M. MacFarlane noticed the craft refused to maintain an even trim. He could hear, through the craft's thin skin, the bubbling hiss of air escaping the starboard charge as it filled with water and threw the sub off balance. By 4:30 p.m., X-8 had become nearly unmanageable, prompting MacFarlane to release the charge. He could only hope their portside charge would be enough to sink or cripple *Lützow*, "the smallest of the target ships."[25]

He set the starboard charge to "safe," ensuring it wouldn't explode, and dropped it into the deep at 4:35 p.m. Free of its waterlogged burden, the craft began to right itself when, fifteen minutes after its release, the charge detonated 1,000 yards astern of X-8 and *Seanymph*. The concussion rattled X-8 and damaged the sealing on the portside charge, which quickly began to leak and wreak additional havoc with the trim.[26]

MacFarlane faced a difficult decision: attempt to carry on or release the damaged charge and abandon the mission. If they somehow made it to the fjords in their struggling craft, and the faulty charge detonated before they reached the *Lützow*, they risked blowing the entire operation. He wrestled with the burden, as X-8 continued its slow but steady roll to port.[27] No effort at the controls or attempt to counterbalance the craft put things right. MacFarlane made up his mind. He would surface and release their last-remaining explosive. Not trusting the "safe" setting, he manually set the charge's timer to detonate two hours after its release. At 4:55 p.m., he dropped it into 180 fathoms of water.[28]

X-8 and *Seanymph* resumed their course. At 6:40 p.m.—an hour and forty-five minutes later—a thunder clap rumbled up from the deep, followed shortly thereafter by the blast's jarring concussion. It ensnared the minisub roughly three miles from the point of explosion and shook it violently. Pipes burst, doors buckled, and the forward compartments flooded, "causing so much damage to the craft as to incapacitate her from diving."[29]

The *Seanymph* surfaced with minor damage to find the X-8 "signaling in heavy weather."[30] *Seanymph*'s commander, Lieutenant Oakley, knew X-8 could not continue. Only two days prior, when X-8's survival had seemed questionable at best, he'd received a signal from Rear Admiral C. B. Barry, Flag Officer Submarines. "Should at any time you consider it necessary to sink X-8 in order not to prejudice the operation," it read, "this step would have my full approval."[31] He now had no alternative. Oakley ordered the minisub scuttled and dispatched a dinghy to bring her crew on board.[32]

It remains a mystery as to why "the second explosion caused such damage at an apparent range of 3 ½ miles while the first explosion only 1,000 yards away did none." After the operation, Barry theorized the first charge had only partially detonated and that perhaps X-8 wasn't as far away from the second explosion as her crew estimated. "Whatever the reason," he wrote, "the force of the second explosion would appear to have illustrated the efficiency of the charges."[33]

✳ ✳ ✳

On the evening of Sunday, September 19, the *Truculent* towed X-6, one of the four remaining minisubs still operational, to her departure point inside the Arctic Circle. The *Truculent*'s crew gathered in the sub's control room and said a prayer for the men who would guide X-6—Donald Cameron, John Lorimer, Richard Kendall, and Edmund Goddard—to her ultimate objective in Kåfjord: *Tirpitz*.[34]

Cameron, a Scotsman, eyed his three crewmates and could not help but notice their almost cheerful countenances. "Is it a pose, or do they really feel that way?" he pondered in the pages of his journal. "If so, I envy them. I have that just-before-the-battle-mother feeling. Wonder how they will bear up under fire for the first time, and how I will behave though not under fire for the first time. . . . If I were a true Brit, the job would be the thing, but I can't help thinking what the feelings of my next of kin will be if I make a hash of the thing."[35]

The men's optimistic façades were mere camouflage. Lorimer's nerves threatened rebellion as he watched the minisub's passage crew reeled in on a dinghy and the operation's crew prepared to take their place. When the rubber dinghy came alongside the *Truculent*, he swore he could hear air hissing from the inflatable. "I insisted it was leaking," he later recalled, "but the seaman lending a hand quite rightly assured me that the noise was the water rising and falling over the stern of the *Truculent* and running out of the holes in her casing."[36] Lorimer's confidence returned when he and his colleagues climbed into the dinghy and got underway. "Good luck," the seaman said. "See you in two days' time, sir."[37]

By the early morning hours of Sunday, September 20, the operational crews of all four remaining X-craft had been successfully transferred at their departure points near Soroy Island.[38] The crew of X-7 hit a minor snag when a floating mine bobbed past their parent sub, the *Stubborn*, and "became impaled on the bows of X-7."[39] The minisub's commanding officer, Lieutenant Godfrey Place, scrambled onto the casing, worked his way down to the bow, and proceeded to kick the mine free. "By deft footwork," notes a Royal Navy report, "he was able to clear this unpleasant obstruction, remarking as he did so that this was the first time he had kicked a mine away by its horns."[40]

The crews of all four X-craft were—at least according to an official report—"in great spirits and full of confidence" as their departure time approached. The weather softened throughout the day; the sea calmed and the sharp Arctic wind dropped to a southeasterly breeze.[41] Between six-thirty and eight o'clock that evening, the X-craft separated from their parent subs and set course for the German warships—now less than a hundred miles away. They remained on the surface and navigated the mined waters off Soroy Island that night.[42]

In X-6, Don Cameron scribbled in his journal. "Free at last and left to my own resources," he wrote. "Monarch of all I survey, a little tin god in a little tin fish."[43] Fiery clouds of blue and green and purple—the Northern Lights—blazed overhead. It was, noted Cameron, "a wonderful display."[44] The minefield eventually behind them, the X-craft submerged and entered Stjernsund Channel, which they followed into the labyrinthine fjords where *Tirpitz* and *Scharnhorst* lay unsuspecting. The voyage up the channel was not without problems, as the periscope in X-6 began to leak. "The defect was to prove a major handicap throughout," notes a report, "but a triumph of mind over matter to her crew."[45]

Other than the occasional patrol vessel, there were few ships about—although one stood out. At 4:30 p.m., Place spotted through X-7's periscope the *Scharnhorst* in a lee off one of the channel's islands. There was nothing he could do; it wasn't his target. "All thoughts," he noted, "were on *Tirpitz*."[46] The X-7 continued up the channel and, early that afternoon, entered Altafjord. The plan called for the craft to spend the night among the Bratholme group of islands, a mere four miles from the entrance to Kåfjord.

X-6, her periscope all but useless, was virtually blind when she reached the islands that evening. Cameron and his crewmates spent "a rather disturbed night" trying to fix the problem but had little luck.[47] Lorimer climbed onto the craft's deck to take the midnight watch. "It was the most extraordinary, unreal feeling," he wrote. "There we were bang in the middle of the main German naval base charging our batteries, doing running repairs, and listening to the BBC on our own wireless—and no one knew we were there!"[48] Less than a mile away in Altafjord, he could see the shape of the *Scharnhorst*. Far off in the distance of Kåfjord, the *Tirpitz* presented itself as "a blurred mass of lights."[49]

To reach their target, the X-craft would have to get past an antisubmarine net at the mouth of Kåfjord and a "triple line of anti-torpedo nets."[50] Cameron went about the final preparations for the attack, not realizing X-8 had been scuttled and X-9 rested somewhere on the seafloor with her crew entombed. In fact, he had no idea whether any other X-craft had made it this far. A painful loneliness settled over him. More than once, he gazed at the bright sliver of moon throwing silver on the water and thought of his wife and son. "Was Eve watching it back in Scotland?" he wondered. "Was Iain behaving himself? I felt very homesick. The elation of sitting in the middle of the enemy's fleet anchorage vied with the feeling of a small boy very much wishing to go home and to be comforted. I wasn't conscious of fear, just of wanting someone to talk to."[51]

X-6 left the shelter of the islands at 1:45 a.m. on Wednesday, September 22, an hour after X-7's departure—"neither boat having made friendly contact during the night."[52] Cameron took his craft down to sixty feet and navigated by dead reckoning toward the fjord. As the craft approached the antisubmarine net, he came up to periscope depth at forty feet to survey his surroundings. Fate had no intention of playing a kind hand. Water had once again fogged the looking glass. Dismayed, he dived back down to sixty feet, stripped and cleaned the periscope, and cursed the situation. "We had waited and trained for two years for this show," he wrote, "and at the last moment faulty workmanship was doing its best to deprive us of it all."[53]

The smack of propellers above broke the tense silence as Cameron assembled the periscope. He returned to periscope depth. This time, the periscope allowed a partially clouded view of the surface and a passing trawler. Cameron, at that moment, made a brazen decision. He ordered the X-craft to the surface and, pushing the diesel engine to its limit, followed in the trawler's wake over the top of the submarine net. The craft's profile sat low enough in the water so as not to draw attention. "It was fantastic luck," recalled diver Richard Kendall. "The crew on the trawler and the men on guard at the net booms must have been either drunk or blind."[54]

Once clear of the net, X-6 dived to sixty feet and began her run to the western end of the fjord where *Tirpitz* lay at anchor.[55] The nerve-thrashing tension, lack of sleep, and perpetual dampness gnawed at the crew as they navigated the crowded waterway. Twice their operation almost came to a premature end. "Once," noted Lorimer, "we passed under the bows of a destroyer, between her stem and her mooring buoy."[56] One close call averted, they steered into another and nearly collided with the tanker *Nordmark*, forcing another sharp change of course. And then another difficulty presented itself. "The periscope again clouded over," Cameron reported, "and the periscope hoisting motor brake burnt out, resulting in manual control of the brake being necessary when raising or lowering the periscope."[57]

Cameron considered giving up. The sub was no longer worthy of the task with its severe list and inoperable periscope. If they could somehow return to Altafjord, they could scuttle the craft come nightfall and make their way over the mountains to Sweden. They had packed in the sub all they needed for such an excursion: food, winter clothing, climbing gear, maps of the Swedish frontier, medical supplies, Lugers, money, and "tiny saws for use if a frost-bitten finger or two had to be amputated."[58] Once over the mountains, however, they would face a heartless, wind-slashed barren of ice and snow that stretched for hundreds of miles. Cameron put the decision to his crew. They had come so far. It was John Lorimer who spoke for the men. "Let's see what she's worth, Skipper," he said.[59]

X-6 continued on her way at 2 knots "keeping just shallow enough [for Cameron] to see the surface through the glass scuttles in the pressure hull."[60] By 7:05 a.m., the craft had navigated past the anti-torpedo netting and closed "within striking distance of [*Tirpitz*]."[61] X-6 maneuvered along the northern edge of the anchorage, where a submerged rock brought a violent end to the craft's smooth transit. The force of impact threw the men off balance and pushed the bow out of the water.[62]

The sun, by now high above the mountains, cast a layer of gold across the calm fjord waters. On board *Tirpitz*, a flak gunner noticed a "long black submarine-like object" momentarily break the glass-like surface.[63] It took five minutes for the gunner's alert to reach higher authority, during which time X-6 maneuvered off the rock and disappeared once more. When word of the sighting reached a battery commander on *Tirpitz*, the general consensus was the disturbance "might be a porpoise."[64]

Conditions inside X-6, cramped and stagnant with the smell of sweating, unwashed bodies, were by now desperate. "X-6 by this time had no gyro compass," reported Cameron, "as this had been put out of action by the grounding and subsequent violent angles of the boat, and the periscope was almost completely flooded. She was therefore taken blindly in what was imagined to be the target's direction, hoping to fix her position by the shadow of the battleship."[65]

As she staggered blindly through the water, the craft became entangled in something Cameron and his crew believed to be anti-torpedo netting. They slipped free of the obstruction but—in the process—broke the surface on *Tirpitz*'s port side. The German crew did not mistake X-6 for a porpoise this time.[66] A "brisk fire" rained down from above. The crew, sealed in their metal tube, could hear the clatter of pistols, the sound of rounds slicing the water, and the submerged detonation of a hand grenade.[67]

"Dive!" Cameron yelled.[68]

X-6 dropped from view with the life ebbing out of her. Several German sailors armed with rifles set off in a powerboat from the ship's port side and began circling, waiting to pounce should the sub make another appearance. The time was 7:15 a.m. Cameron and his men realized the game was finally up. Escape in the floundering craft just wasn't possible. He ordered X-6 to maneuver beneath *Tirpitz*'s hull. They moved in so close to the warship's underside, it scraped the X-craft's stern. Cameron released the charges at 7:22 a.m. with their timers set for an hour. They settled in the silt directly beneath the ship. He ordered X-6 to the surface, where the craft would be scuttled and the crew could surrender.[69]

In the powerboat, a German lieutenant saw X-6 emerge "thirty yards from [*Tirpitz*'s] stern."[70] A storm of rifle fire clanked and sparked off the sub's hull. The sound echoed loudly through the craft's tiny interior, as Cameron and his men opened the sea cocks and sentenced X-6 to a watery grave. The Germans stopped firing when they saw the sub's hatch open. One by one, Cameron, Lorimer, Kendall, and Goddard appeared—haggard and exhausted—their arms raised. They were ushered at gunpoint onto the powerboat and taken back to the *Tirpitz*. An attempt by the Germans to tow X-6 with them proved futile, as the sub surrendered to the fjord and disappeared.[71]

✳ ✳ ✳

Lieutenant Godfrey Place and his crew in X-7 struggled to get the job done.

At 7:10 a.m., Place set the timer on both his charges for one hour. X-7 had by now reached the anti-torpedo net stretching across the mouth of the anchorage. He dived to seventy-five feet and tried to navigate the sub beneath the barrier—only to get ensnared. Violent maneuvering freed the craft, but it took two more attempts at greater depths to clear the obstruction.[72]

"By some extraordinary lucky chance, we must have either passed under the nets . . . ," Place reported, "for on breaking the surface the *Tirpitz*, with no intervening nets, was sighted right ahead not more than 30 yards away."[73] Place ordered X-7 down to forty feet at full speed ahead. The craft cut smoothly through the water but slammed twenty feet down into *Tirpitz* on the port side.[74]

Above, the crash didn't make a stir. The craft, Place wrote, "slid gently under the keel where the starboard charge was released in the full shadow of the ship."[75] X-7 moved another 200 feet aft before dropping its port charge. The muffled crump of grenades and clatter of gunfire could be heard, as the *Tirpitz* crew opened fire on X-6.[76]

"After releasing the port charge," Place reported, "an alteration of course [was] guessed to try and make the position where we had come in."[77] Guessing was the crew's only option, as the compass no longer worked. They fumbled through the water at one hundred feet and found themselves, once again, snagged in netting. X-7's charges would detonate in an hour and obliterate the sub if the crew couldn't make some distance. A dwindling oxygen supply did nothing to ease their anxiety. The outward journey had consumed two bottles of air; one now remained with 1,200 pounds in it. No sooner had the men freed X-7 from one net, they got stuck in another.[78]

"In about the next three quarters of an hour," Place wrote, "the X-7 was in and out of several nets, the air in the last bottle was soon exhausted and the compressor had to be run."[79] Place decided the best way to conquer the nets was to break the surface, push ahead at full speed, and pass over the top of them. "I did not look at the *Tirpitz* at this time," Place wrote, "as this method of overcoming net defenses was new and absorbing."[80]

While X-7 tried to make her escape, the crew of X-6 found themselves on board *Tirpitz*. Captain Hans Meyer emerged from his cabin to greet his captives on the quarterdeck. Cameron and his men, seeing a senior officer approaching, snapped to attention and saluted. Meyer appreciated the gesture but was mystified as to how the four disheveled individuals in front of him could, "in such a small submarine, travel more than 1,200 miles from Britain."[81]

Cameron said nothing to shed light on the matter. The Germans, nevertheless, treated their guests with amicable hospitality and offered them "coffee and schnapps."[82] The liquor, though good, could not blunt the knowledge they were sitting on several tons of amatol with less than forty-five minutes to detonation. The clatter of machine guns served as a momentary distraction. X-7 appeared off the ship's starboard bow as she attempted to crest an anti-torpedo net. Cameron glanced at his watch: it was 7:40 a.m.[83]

"A large number of machine gun bullets were heard hitting [X-7's] casing," Place wrote. The craft cleared one net after another with rounds denting and ricocheting off its metal skin. Passing over what they believed to be the final net, Place ordered "all main ballast tanks vented." X-7 plummeted 120 feet to the bottom of the fjord.[84]

He ordered the craft to periscope depth to get a visual reckoning of their location and plot a course out of the anchorage. "[We wanted] as much distance as possible put between ourselves," noted Place "and the coming explosion." X-7 began its ascent, only to get stuck at sixty feet in another net. The charges detonated fifty yards behind them at

8:12 a.m. A thunderous roar swept through the water and engulfed the craft. Instead of ripping X-7 to pieces, as Place feared, the blast shook them free of their entanglement.[85]

The explosion heaved *Tirpitz* "several feet out of the water and bounced [her] down again with a slight list."[86] The ship erupted in chaos. "The German gun-crew shot up another of their own tankers and small boats and also wiped out a gun position inboard with un-controlled firing," wrote Kendall.[87] The ship rocked violently to port, bleeding oil into the water and sending a thick black stain across the surface of the fjord. "Doors jammed," notes an official report, "gear of all sorts fell down, fire extinguishers wrenched from the bulkheads started belching foam, and glass from broken scuttles and mirrors was everywhere."[88]

The blast hurled men in all directions. Twenty-two-year-old Sea-man Fritz Adler went airborne, landed headfirst on a length of anchor chain, and died instantly.[89] On the bridge, Captain Meyer "flared into a rage" and demanded Cameron and his men be shot as saboteurs.[90] Only when another officer convinced him the Englishmen were merely "soldiers doing their duty" did Meyer change his mind.[91]

X-7's crew felt little cause to celebrate. The target, seemingly imper-vious to all actions against her, appeared to gloat from her anchorage. "On surfacing," reported Place, "it was tiresome to see the *Tirpitz* still afloat. This made me uncertain as to whether the explosion we had just heard was our own charges or depth charges, so X-7 was taken to the bottom."[92]

Place and his crew assessed the sub's damage. Although structural damage appeared minimal, the compass and diving gauges no longer worked—and the main controls weren't that far behind. "The boat was impossible to control," Place reported, "and broke surface on several occasions."[93] Each appearance brought with it a fresh round of abuse from the gunners on *Tirpitz* and left the men no option but to surren-der. The craft bobbed to the surface again and came up alongside a gunnery target.[94]

There was no choice but to abandon ship. Place climbed onto X-7's casing and jumped from the sub onto the target buoy. His weight, as he pushed himself off with his feet, forced the sub back under.[95] Water poured into the damaged craft, as the three men still inside rushed to secure the hatch. "Its icy grip was like a vice," remembered diver Robert Aitken.[96] The men put on their breathing gear and had "to wait for forty-five minutes before the internal pressure could equal that of the sea" before making their escape.[97]

The water inched higher, eventually blowing out the sub's electrical wiring and leaving the men in freezing darkness. Aitken tried to find his two colleagues. In the control room, near the periscope, he stumbled over the body of Willie Whitley. Whitley's "breathing bag was empty, flat, completely flat."[98]

With his own oxygen running low, Aitken went in search of Bill Whittam—but he felt consciousness slipping away as his air supply dwindled. He turned and fumbled his way through the darkness to the escape compartment with only the air left in his lungs. As he struggled to open the hatch, everything—the fear, the confusion—faded to black. The touch of sunlight on his face and the sound of an approaching motor launch brought him back. How he reached the surface he had no idea.[99]

He was brought on board *Tirpitz* and promptly ordered to strip in full view of everyone. His spirits improved upon being reunited below deck with Place and the crew of X-6. The proffered coffee and schnapps didn't hurt either.

Tirpitz suffered extensive damage. A steady flow of bad news reached Captain Meyer on the bridge in the hours following the explosion. More than 500 tons of water had flooded the lower decks, submerging the ship's propulsion installation and knocking out all three main engines. The port rudder had been rendered useless—as had two of the ship's 15-inch gun turrets raised by the blast. Range-finding equipment and antiaircraft control positions were all effectively dead. Flooding in one of the generator rooms had knocked out the ship's electricity. Casualties included one killed and forty wounded.[100]

The force of the explosion made an impression on even the most experienced members of *Tirpitz*'s crew. "We've had torpedo hits, we've had bomb hits," remembered one sailor who had served on *Scharnhorst*. "We hit two mines in the English Channel, but there's never been an explosion like that."[101] The next day, the survivors of X-6 and X-7 began the journey to Marlag und Milag Nord—a POW camp for British naval personnel—outside Bremen, where they would spend the rest of the war.[102]

Not one of the six midget submarines that left Loch Cairnbawn on September 11 and 12 made it back to Scotland. X-10, targeting the *Scharnhorst*, came within sight of Kåfjord before a dead compass and malfunctioning periscope halted her progress. Commanding officer K. R. Hudspeth "reluctantly decided to give up any idea of attacking" and managed to rendezvous six days later with his parent submarine, the *Stubborn*.[103] The threat of increasingly bad weather and problems with her towing cable resulted in X-10 being scuttled on the voyage home.[104] With Hudspeth unable to complete his mission and the mysterious loss of X-9, the *Scharnhorst* survived unscathed.

The fate of X-5 remains a mystery. Official reports state she was spotted and sunk by *Tirpitz* as she approached the ship. A search of the fjord after the war only turned up the rusted corpses of X-6 and X-7. It's doubtful she got anywhere near her target.[105] "Out of the 42 men and officers who formed the [X-craft] crews," notes a Royal Navy report, "33 survived."[106]

In an official dispatch, Rear Admiral Barry hailed the attack "as one of the most courageous acts of all time."[107] Even the Germans voiced their admiration in a post-action assessment. The British enemy, it noted, is "a master of cunning and devious weaponry, which he is not afraid to deploy in situations where the stakes are of the highest order if he thinks the goal is worth it."[108]

Although Operation Source failed in its objective to sink the *Tirpitz*, it was not without some success. An entry made in the War Diary of the German Navy Staff shortly after the attack stated, "The ship might never again regain complete operational efficiency."[109] She nevertheless remained afloat and defiant.

Churchill's "prize" had yet to be claimed.

CHAPTER 12

* * *

"HELL ON EARTH"

Scharnhorst, unscathed, remained at her anchorage, the days passing in a slow tedium of repetition. Every day, all hands were called at 6 a.m. Men, bleary-eyed, resigned to the monotony of onboard life, stowed their hammocks and made their way to the mess deck for breakfast. The meal done, cleaning ship was the next order of business—followed by training classes and physical exercise from 9 a.m. to 11:30 a.m. The men returned to the mess for dinner, which concluded at 1:45 p.m., then reported for work at their various stations. Their time was their own starting at 4 p.m.

Three screening rooms ensured the men never missed the latest films playing in the cinemas back home. A well-stocked library offered a wide selection of novels but, notes one report, "very few political books." Other men huddled together to play cards. "A tremendous amount of gambling went on and large sums of money were won and lost," states a naval assessment. "Playing any sort of game for money was actually forbidden, but in *Scharnhorst* the officers deliberately shut their eyes to it." Free time came to an end at 7 p.m. Cleaning and officers' rounds consumed the rest of the evening. The men slung their hammocks at 9:30 p.m. and went down for the night half an hour later. The next day adhered to the same routine.[1]

Other than skiing in the winter and summer games of football, the Norwegian fjords offered little in the way of onshore entertainment. In November 1943—two months after the X-craft raid—the 2,000-ton ship *Emmanuel Rambur*, a floating nightclub, dropped anchor nearby for a two-week stay. *Scharnhorst* crewmembers could ferry across to the boat "for either a matinee or evening performance" and escape, if briefly, the austerity of military life. A glass of red wine was thrust into their hand upon boarding, and every man left with a tin of biscuits and a pack of ten cigarettes.[2]

The live entertainment, however, provided the real treat. "The first part of the entertainment consisted of a sing-song conducted by five Red Cross sisters and fifteen Norwegian girls, ostensibly traveling as stewardesses," notes a Royal Navy report with just a hint of smugness. "The second part of the programme gave three ageing night-club performers an opportunity of displaying their talents."[3] A six-piece orchestra, "which had played in one of the lesser Berlin cafes," concluded the festivities. The officers in the audience enjoyed the gaudy spectacle of it all so much that some returned to their cabins on the *Scharnhorst* with a Norwegian girl in tow—much to the chagrin of the lower ranks.[4]

At about the same time the *Emmanuel Rambur* dropped anchor with its boozy offerings and carnal delights, convoys resumed sailing between the United Kingdom and Russia. The convoys had ceased during the Arctic summer months with their days of endless sunlight.[5] The Arctic winter, with its long night, now offered a measure of protection against German fighters, U-boats, and surface ships operating out of Norway—but the season brought its own risks. Great ice flows forced the convoys to sail south of Bear Island on their journey "within 250 miles of the enemy base at Altenfjord."[6]

The nineteen-ship convoy JW-55A sailed from Loch Ewe in Scotland on Sunday, December 12, 1943. Another convoy, JW-55B, was scheduled to leave one week later when JW-55A began its return voyage from Russia. The plan called for the outward and returning convoys to pass each other in the western Barents Sea near Bear Island and allow the Royal Navy to protect both at their most vulnerable point.[7]

Two forces provided cover: the cruisers HMS *Belfast* (flagship), HMS *Norfolk*, and HMS *Sheffield* in Force 1 under the command of Vice Admiral Robert Burnett; the battleship HMS *Duke of York* (flagship), and the destroyers HMS *Jamaica*, HMS *Savage*, HMS *Scorpion*, HMS *Saumarez*, and the Norwegian ship *Stord* in Force 2 under the command of Admiral Sir Bruce Fraser, who had succeeded Admiral Sir John Tovey in May 1943 as commander in chief of the British Home Fleet.[8]

On December 19, Grand Admiral Karl Dönitz met with Hitler in Berlin. The German navy had known since mid-November that convoys to Russia had resumed. The Naval War Staff, citing winter darkness and "the superiority of the British radar," deemed unleashing *Scharnhorst* against convoy traffic too risky a proposition.[9] It recommended *Scharnhorst* remain tethered until March when the days began to lengthen and *Tirpitz*, hopefully, would be ready to sail again. Dönitz, "anxious to demonstrate . . . the value of the capital ship," informed Hitler he planned to pit *Scharnhorst* and the 4th Destroyer Flotilla against the next Russian-bound convoy.[10]

The British, he argued, would be less inclined to expect trouble, as two convoys had already made it safely to Russian ports. Hitler gave his approval. Two days later, on December 21, JW-55A arrived in the Russian ports of Murmansk and Archangel. The Arctic night played its part well, allowing the convoy to reach its destination without loss or interference.[11]

On the *Duke of York*, Fraser believed the convoy's safe arrival would prompt *Scharnhorst* to emerge from the shelter of Altafjord to attack JW-55B as it ran the outward gauntlet to Russia. On December 23, Fraser summoned his commanding officers. Should *Scharnhorst* emerge from the polar gloom, Fraser would close the distance in *Duke of York* to 12,000 yards before opening fire. His destroyers would attack with torpedoes.[12] "Every officer and man," he said, "must be doubly sure that he [knows] his night-action duty."[13]

"**Prepare for sea** at three hours' notice!"[14]

The order bellowed from *Scharnhorst*'s loudspeaker at one o'clock on Christmas afternoon. The cancellation of shore leave that morning had signaled to the crew the possibility of pending action. It proved a bitter blow for eight crewmembers with plans to return home for the holidays—but events at sea all but ensured the realities of war intruded.[15]

For the past three days, reconnaissance aircraft and U-boats had been shadowing convoy JW-55B. Naval High Command received word of the convoy's progress on Christmas Eve. Its escort, according to reports, consisted of "3 cruisers, 5 destroyers, and 4 smaller craft."[16] The Germans were unaware the British had dispatched additional ships on Christmas morning to guard the convoy and bolstered the number of destroyers to fourteen.[17]

Confident of a successful outcome, the Naval War Staff authorized *Scharnhorst* at 2:10 p.m. Christmas Day to commence operations. The order called for *Scharnhorst* to "intercept the convoy in approximately the longitude of North Cape" in northern Norway and attack at twilight, when conditions would allow for a more accurate fire.[18]

At 5 p.m., a new order echoed through the ship: "Prepare to weigh."[19]

✳ ✳ ✳

Scharnhorst weighed anchor at 7 p.m., the black waters of the fjord breaking in white froth against her bow. As the ship gained momentum and the powerful thrum of her turbines was felt underfoot, chief gunnery officer Walter Bredenbreuker and *Scharnhorst*'s second-in-command, Commander Ernst Dominik, summoned the gun crews to the quarterdeck. The men stood at attention, the wind whipping around them, and learned they were "putting to sea to attack an Allied convoy of about 20 ships bound for Russia . . . protected by an escort of three cruisers and a number of destroyers."[20]

In that strange prebattle state of anxiety and excitement, the men dispersed to their stations. As the gun crews went about their duties, the starboard watch went to action stations; the port watch worked their way through the ship and cleared the gangways of sacks of potatoes. "They had been embarked before Christmas," notes a report, "and had not yet been stowed."[21]

Scharnhorst sailed in the company of five destroyers of the 4th De-stroyer Flotilla. They navigated the fjords and outer sounds at 17 knots before breaking into the open sea shortly after 11 p.m. and increasing speed to 25 knots.[22] Captain Fritz Hintze shared a radio message from Grand Admiral Dönitz with the crew that made clear their mission:

> Important enemy convoy carrying food and war material to the Russians further imperils our heroic Army on the Eastern Front. We must help. Attack convoy with *Scharnhorst* and destroyers. Ex-ploit tactical situation with skill and daring. Do not end the en-gagement with a partial success. Go all out and see the job right through. Best chance of success lies in superior firing power of *Scharnhorst*, therefore try to bring her into action. Deploy destroy-ers accordingly. Break off according to your own judgment. Break off in any circumstances if faced by heavy units. I have every con-fidence in you.[23]

The conditions at sea punished men and equipment. Snow settled on the guns and decks; ice choked the lenses of range finders and di-rectors. "The vigilance of the bridge and signal watches," notes one ac-count, "the look-outs on deck, at the searchlight control columns and at the guns was therefore of vital importance."[24] The sound of waves breaking and foaming over the bow thundered in the ears, as strained and weary eyes peered hour upon endless hour into the darkness.[25]

Rear Admiral Erich Bey, the battle group's commander, signaled the rough seas would "severely handicap" the maneuverability of his destroyers and their fighting effectiveness. Should they continue? The matter made its way up the chain of command to Admiral Dönitz, who ordered the ships to proceed. *Scharnhorst* could go it alone should the destroyers ultimately drop out.[26]

Knocked by thrashing seas, the ships stuck together and pushed their way north, guided by updates from U-boats shadowing the con-voy.[27] By four o'clock on the morning of Sunday, December 26, the nine-teen Russian-bound merchant ships of JW-55B—escorted by fourteen destroyers—were fifty miles south of Bear Island. Force 2, commanded by Admiral Fraser in *Duke of York*, was 350 miles to the southwest of the convoy. The battleship and its four accompanying destroyers crested waves and crashed into valleys, submerging their bows, as they closed the distance with the convoy. "The stage was well set," wrote Fraser, "except that if the *Scharnhorst* attacked at daylight and immediately retired, I was not yet sufficiently close to cut her off."[28]

At about the same time, 114 miles southwest of Bear Island, *Scharnhorst* and her destroyer screen drew ever closer to their kill. Rear Admiral Bey, on *Scharnhorst*'s bridge, consulted the chart table as he braced himself against the ship's violent rocking. "If the convoy continues on the assumed course and we maintain our present course," he said, "we should—at 6:30 a.m.—be within 30 miles."[29]

More than a hundred miles away in the Arctic darkness, Fraser pondered his options. The convoy had, for several days, reported seeing U-boats and reconnaissance aircraft that left him in no doubt *Scharnhorst* was on the hunt. At 6:28 a.m., he broke radio silence and ordered the convoy to steer north in the hopes it might become a more elusive quarry.[30]

At 7:30 a.m., Rear Admiral Bey sent a signal from *Scharnhorst* and ordered his destroyers to "form a reconnaissance line 10 miles ahead of the *Scharnhorst*."[31] The destroyers charged forward into a snow-choked void. Men on the watch suffered with snow "encrusting hair and brows with ice, freezing features into wooden stiffness." The weather soon shrouded the destroyers from view and left the *Scharnhorst* isolated.[32]

Captain Frederick Parham stood on the bridge of the cruiser HMS *Belfast* and stretched his frozen limbs. He slept in a "wretched little hut" built on the bridge, as his regular cabin two decks below was too far from the ship's command center should he be needed in an emergency. "You always had to be at the ready," he remembered. "At sea, I never undressed at all. I didn't even take my boots off when I went to sleep."[33]

The fur-lined boots, despite their necessity, almost proved to be more a hindrance than benefit in the extreme cold. "If you were on the bridge for an hour at a time and went down to the chow house, which was warm," he said, "the first thing that happened was your feet would start to sweat. When you went back up to the bridge, you'd be standing in ice."[34]

On this particular morning, Parham wrapped his feet in sheets of newspaper for extra insulation. It was 8:40 a.m., but could just as well have been midnight, when the ship's radar picked up a vessel approaching from 35,000 yards. The distance between the two ships shrank rapidly to a mere 13,000 yards by 9:15 a.m.[35] "The size of the radar echo" suggested a vessel of considerable size—yet, beyond the bridge, Parham could see nothing but darkness and snow.[36]

On board the accompanying cruiser *Sheffield*, the radar officer also reported contact. "On the darkened bridge," notes one account, "nobody spoke or moved unless necessary; it was difficult to distinguish one hunched figure from another, and there was more important things to think about than conversation. A few cigarettes glowed red within cupped hands."[37]

All eyes focused out to sea and hunted for a glimpse of something. At 13,000 yards, under normal conditions, a ship of *Scharnhorst*'s size would have been easy to spot. And then, in the filthy murk, something did take shape—nothing more than a blur at first, but it proved to be enough. At 9:21 a.m., the *Sheffield* signaled *Belfast* and *Norfolk*—the three ships traveling in a line with *Norfolk* to the south, *Belfast* to the north, and *Sheffield* in between—"Enemy in sight!"[38]

Belfast opened fire with star shells that threw an eerie light over the black sea. To the men on the *Scharnhorst*, it looked like "the appearance and disappearance of many golden-yellow suns between sea and sky."[39] At 9:30 a.m., having closed to 9,800 yards, *Norfolk* opened fire.[40]

Columns of water one sailor estimated to be at least nine feet wide blew skyward 500 yards abeam of *Scharnhorst*'s forward searchlight-control station. The clang of alarm bells and the frantic shouting of orders brought all stations to battle. The "acrid fumes" of cannon fire wafted across the deck, as *Scharnhorst*'s massive guns lit the darkness in vibrant shades of orange and red. One could clearly see the crimson flashes of the enemy's guns—but not the enemy ships themselves. Continuous star shell fire from the British vessels cast the violence in a ghostly luminescence.[41]

The British guns, having now found their range, rumbled and did their damage. A shell slammed into *Scharnhorst*'s foretop and took out the forward radar. The resulting explosion injured a seaman in the crow's nest, while a scattering of white-hot splinters ripped away the leg of the range finder officer.[42]

Guns thundered on both sides for fifteen minutes before Bey turned *Scharnhorst* on a southerly course with the British cruisers now in pursuit. The hunter had now become the hunted but with heavy seas on her side. Waves slammed the cruisers as their engines, topping out at 24 knots, strained against the swell. The ships staggered against the heavy punches of the sea; the violent blows knocked the vessels from bow to stern.[43]

As the cruisers struggled, the *Scharnhorst* powered through the foaming black waters at 30 knots. Admiral Burnett—commanding officer of Force 1—watched on *Belfast*'s radar as *Scharnhorst* slipped farther away and changed direction to the northeast.[44] Burnett believed *Scharnhorst* was attempting to work her way to the north in preparation for another attack. He ordered his cruisers to alter course to the northwest and "get between *Scharnhorst* and the convoy." He voiced the certainty of his decision to Captain Parham. "I bet you she'll come again," he said.[45]

Under the circumstances, Burnett had few options available to him. Had he kept up the chase, *Scharnhorst* could have easily escaped and slaughtered the convoy with impunity. The cruisers, heaving and shuddering, lashed by freezing spray, moved to intercept *Scharnhorst*'s anticipated approach. Six minutes later, at 10:20 a.m., *Scharnhorst* dropped off the radar.[46]

On the *Duke of York*, still some 200 miles away, Admiral Fraser feared the worst. With her superiority in speed and the adverse weather conditions, *Scharnhorst* clearly possessed the advantage. He thought it "undesirable" to weaken Force 2 and detach multiple ships to track down their elusive prey. At 10:24 a.m., he ordered four destroyers—the *Musketeer, Opportune, Virago,* and *Matchless*—to break from the convoy and join up with Burnett's ships in the event they crossed *Scharnhorst's* anticipated line of attack.[47]

Parham, on *Belfast's* bridge, caught site of the approaching destroyers. "I could see the *Musketeer's* division of destroyers," he recalled, "and just very, very faintly beyond her I could see a ship—which I took to be the leading ship of the outgoing convoy." As the *Musketeer* drew closer to *Belfast* she signaled, "I'm awaiting your order to attack." Shocked, Parham shared the message with Burnett—who appeared equally surprised. "Attack what?" he replied. *Belfast* promptly relayed the admiral's question to *Musketeer.* "Oh," came the response, "anything that turns up." What passed for humor on the *Musketeer* failed to do likewise on *Belfast.* "It was very funny afterwards," Parham said, "but was not at all funny at the time."[48]

Scharnhorst reappeared on *Belfast's* radar at 12:05 p.m. Burnett immediately signaled the *Duke of York.* "I knew then," Fraser later said, "that there was every chance of catching the enemy."[49] The three British cruisers—and their escort of four destroyers—positioned themselves across the enemy's approach some ten miles ahead of the convoy.[50]

In the "glimmering of twilight," a distant shape coalesced out of the snow and faint gray of day. "There," recalled Parham, "bearing down on the convoy—or rather on us—was the *Scharnhorst* again, rushing towards us head-on. We opened fire on one another, and it was simply a question then, really, of whose nerve broke first."[51]

At 12:21 p.m., Petty Officer Gödde, manning the port forward searchlight control column on *Scharnhorst,* reported "three shadows" ahead. He could hear other battle stations relaying the same information to the bridge. Before *Scharnhorst's* guns could respond, "flashes of flames came from the distant shadowy forms."[52] Three explosions buffeted the ship from above. Gödde looked up to see "three or four" blazing flares floating overhead, throwing yellow light onto the ship's deck, guns, and superstructure. *Scharnhorst's* forward guns bellowed in reply as enemy shells ruptured the nearby sea.[53]

The two sides slugged it out at ranges of 16,000 to 9,000 yards. "The scene," remembered Lieutenant Commander G. J. A. Lumsden on board *Sheffield*, "was majestic. All ships were using tracer shells, and these could be followed from muzzle to target when fired by our own ships."[54] Likewise, the British sailors could see the incoming German barrage, arcing up from *Scharnhorst*'s guns before descending in a blazing trajectory to land in the sea or smash a target.[55]

Petty Officer Gödde kept an eye on the British cruisers through his range finder. The concussion of the ship's 11-inch guns rolled and rumbled across the deck. The air smelled of cordite and smoke, as men heaved spent shell casings into the sea. Twelve minutes into the battle, at 12:33 p.m., Gödde saw a red-orange column of flame erupt from one of the British ships. Two shells had struck *Norfolk*—one knocked out a turret, the other slammed home amidships, killing seven men and seriously wounding five.[56]

Lumsden witnessed the explosion on *Norfolk* from *Sheffield*'s bridge. "That brave ship," he said, "kept well up with the battle . . . and continued to engage with her forward guns while she fought the flames aft."[57] As Lumsden watched *Norfolk* burn, another 11-inch salvo came hurtling across the sky and straddled *Sheffield*. Fragments of shell "up to football size" battered the deck and punctured the hull in places but inflicted no casualties. On *Scharnhorst*, Rear Admiral Bey watched the British tracer shells—"neat groups of speeding death"—cut their burning trajectory through the murk. "Turn to port," he ordered Captain Hintze, "we must get out of this!"[58]

The German ship remained a solitary target. Her destroyers, after separating from *Scharnhorst*, had searched in vain for the convoy before setting a course for home. One destroyer on the journey back spotted what was believed to be a British ship and fired four torpedoes, all of which missed. "This," notes an official naval report, "was the sole contribution of the [German] destroyers to the fortunes of the day."[59]

The British destroyers *Musketeer*, *Opportune*, *Virago*, and *Matchless* moved ahead of the cruisers to attack *Scharnhorst* with torpedoes, but the battleship proved elusive when—at 12:41 p.m.—she veered to the southeast for the safety of Norway.[60]

The *Belfast* pushed forward to give chase, while the damaged *Norfolk* and the *Sheffield*, suffering engine trouble, fell back. "We were left alone," said Parham, "proceeding at very high speed. . . . The

Scharnhorst was barely in sight, and was soon out of sight, but we had her on our radar the whole time."[61]

The two ships exchanged a running fire, blasting away into the darkness. "Do you think there's any point in going on firing at her?" Burnett asked Parham. The moment *Belfast* ceased firing, so too did *Scharnhorst*, which struck Parham as rather odd. "I'm quite, quite convinced," he said, "[*Scharnhorst*] had no idea we were following her. Otherwise, she would only have had to turn around for ten minutes or less and blown us clear out of the water. Then, she would have been lost to everybody and absolutely free to get home."[62]

Belfast shadowed *Scharnhorst* "from just outside visibility range"— about eight miles—for the next four hours and relayed the ship's movements via wireless to Fraser on *Duke of York*.[63] On *Scharnhorst*, a message to the crew went out over the loudspeakers at 4 p.m.: "From the captain to all stations! We are not yet out of the wood! Intensify the look-out! As you all know we have had a shadowing ship on our tail since noon and have not been able to shake her off. The radar has just reported targets to starboard. Be prepared; keep on the alert. It may be any moment now."[64]

Seventeen minutes later, Fraser's flagship established radar contact with the enemy at 45,500 yards—just under twenty-six miles—and moved fast to close the distance. The *Belfast* soon appeared on radar astern of *Scharnhorst*, now 29,700 yards away. Fraser ordered his destroyers to find "the most advantageous position for torpedo attack" and await his command.[65] Then he signaled *Belfast* to illuminate the area with star shell fire. "At first impression," noted a gunner on *Duke of York*, "*Scharnhorst* appeared of enormous length and silver-grey in color."[66] It was, recalled Parham, a "great moment."[67]

At 4:50 p.m., with the *Scharnhorst* bathed in the white light of magnesium flares, the *Duke of York* opened fire with her 14-inch guns at a range of 12,000 yards. The cruiser HMS *Jamaica* joined the action. *Scharnhorst*'s final ordeal now began.[68]

On the destroyer HMS *Scorpion*, Lieutenant A. G. F. Ditchman watched *Duke of York* unleash her first broadside. "I watched the ten great shells climb up into the air, going away from us," he wrote, "then suddenly they plunged down towards their target and a huge wall of water rose up, completely concealing *Scharnhorst*."[69]

As the first British salvos landed in the sea, the *Scharnhorst* swerved off her southern course in a violent turn to the north, away from *Duke of York*'s near head-on attack, then veered east to avoid Burnett's approaching cruisers. The *Belfast*—joined once again by the *Norfolk*—opened fire as the *Scharnhorst* gathered speed.[70]

The German guns never ceased firing. "You could hear the whistles of the shells from the *Duke of York* and the *Scharnhorst*," said Corporal Frederick Weston, a Royal Marine on the *Norfolk*. "You could hear the roar of the salvos, and although it was pitch black—the salvos were tracers. You could see them rising from what appeared to be one horizon and you couldn't see where they were landing. To see these salvos going from one horizon to the other was something to be seen."[71] The hunters had cornered their prey.

It did not take long for *Duke of York* to find her range. One shell hit *Scharnhorst*'s quarterdeck; another put the three 11-inch guns in her "A" turret out of action. A third struck her just below the waterline. In the darkness, the strikes appeared as "greenish sparks along the water line . . . and as vivid red-orange flashes when hitting the upper deck."[72] At one point, noted a witness on *Duke of York*, "a fairly considerable fire blazed up under [*Scharnhorst*'s] aft superstructure and was used as a point of aim until it disappeared."[73]

Scharnhorst continued to pick up speed despite the pummeling and put distance between herself and the enemy. Even as her superior engine power came into play, she had nowhere to go. Her present course led only to "an icy void."[74] As her speed increased, so, too, did the accuracy of her fire. Shells launched from more than 17,000 yards straddled the *Duke of York*. The British ship escaped serious damage when two shells punched their way through both mainmasts but failed to explode.[75]

"The battle," recalled Parham, ". . . at the end of a very long, very cold, and very tiring day seemed to go on forever."[76] In fact, it lasted two hours in a running struggle through pitch darkness and violent seas. The *Duke of York*'s guns thundered without respite. "Scorching gasses from her after guns" coursed down ventilator shafts and formed a searing cloud that "burn[ed] out the wardroom."[77]

The *Scharnhorst*'s labored engines pushed her on and opened the range to 18,000 yards. At 5:13 p.m., Fraser turned his destroyers loose. "Destroyers in company," he signaled, "close and attack with torpedoes as soon as possible."[78]

Jamaica ceased firing at 5:42 p.m.; the cruisers, now out of range, also silenced their guns—but the *Duke of York* and *Scharnhorst* continued their duel. "It was a slogging match between giants, appalling in their might and fury," wrote Royal Marine Lieutenant B. D. Ramsden, a gunner on the *Jamaica*. "Every time the *Duke of York* fired there came the vivid flicker of the *Scharnhorst*'s reply, the lazy light of the fourteen-inch tracer, followed by the crack, crack of the 11-inch reply in the sea, and the drone of splinters."[79]

All the while, the German ship pulled slowly ahead. At 20,000 yards, she checked her fire and continued putting distance between herself and the British. Fraser watched on the radar as his quarry began slipping out of reach. At 21,400 yards he ordered all guns to stop firing. "A distinct atmosphere of gloom and disappointment was felt," noted one gunner's mate, "at the order to check fire, when it appeared that—despite undoubted hits—the enemy would escape with her superior speed."[80]

Fraser ordered *Duke of York* onto a southeasterly course toward Norway in the hopes *Scharnhorst* might eventually turn in that direction and give his destroyers a chance to attack. On board *Scharnhorst*, the British ship appeared to be abandoning the chase.[81] Captain Hintze shared the good news with his crew. "The heavy units are turning—they can't match our speed," he said. "The *Scharnhorst* has again proved herself."[82]

Any cause for optimism proved short-lived. The ship had suffered significant damage. The tween and battery decks on the port side had both been hit; one shell had devastated her aircraft hangar, another punctured the starboard side near the funnel. "B" turret took a hit, which knocked out its ventilation system. "The whole turret," reported one survivor, "filled with choking smoke every time the breeches were open. This, combined with the motion of the ship in heavy weather, rendered nearly every man in the turret violently seasick."[83] And now *Scharnhorst*—likely due to a shell that struck aft shortly before *Duke of York* ceased firing—began to lose speed and dropped from 29 knots to 22.[84] The time was 6:24 p.m.

For more than an hour, Fraser's destroyers—the *Scorpion*, *Savage*, *Saumarez*, and the Norwegian ship *Stord*—had struggled to catch up with *Scharnhorst*. *Scorpion*, in her pursuit, lost a man overboard. "Conditions on the mess decks were pretty awful," wrote Lieutenant Ditchman, "fug, sweat, vomit, etc.—all ingredients." One sailor, going against orders, came up on deck to escape the squalor below and breathe untainted air. The sea tossed the ship around like a toy. One wave lifted *Scorpion*'s stern "higher than the bridge"; another crashed over the ship's railings and tore apart one of the lifeboats. The splintered wreckage scattered in all directions, struck the sailor, and knocked him into the sea. "His end," wrote Ditchman, "must have been mercifully swift. He was married with four children."[85] The threat of U-boats prevented any attempt at rescue.

By 6:40 p.m., the destroyers managed to close within 10,000 yards of *Scharnhorst*. *Scorpion* and *Stord* approached from the starboard beam; *Savage* and *Saumarez* crept up from astern. At the same time, Fraser—having realized *Scharnhorst* had lost speed—altered course and put the *Duke of York* on a direct line of attack.[86]

The destroyers, meanwhile, pushed closer to their target and narrowed the distance to 7,000 yards. *Scharnhorst* revealed herself in a dazzling display of flame, as her guns fired on *Savage* and *Saumarez*.[87] The spectacle stunned Captain Parham, observing from the bridge of *Belfast*. "I'd never seen anything like it," he said. "The *Scharnhorst* . . . simply streaming fire at these destroyers with every small gun that she had."[88]

The *Scorpion* and *Stord* remained undetected. "All I could see of *Scharnhorst* was a brief silhouette each time she fired at our two chums," wrote Ditchman. "She still hadn't seen us and would doubtless have been alarmed to realize there were another sixteen torpedoes to the south of her." The *Scorpion*, with a strong wind blowing behind her, increased speed to 32 knots. "Fuel consumption no longer mattered," wrote Ditchman. "Within a quarter of an hour or so we might be a shambles, or sunk."[89]

The *Savage* fired a salvo of star shells at 6:49 p.m., the magnesium flares burning hot and yellow as they drifted down on their parachutes.[90] The destroyers had by now closed within 3,000 yards of the enemy. The *Saumarez* suffered in her approach. One shell blew through her Director Control Tower, passing through one side and out the other before exploding over the water. A near miss blistered her sides and deck with hot shrapnel. Eleven men lay dead in the wafting smoke, another eleven injured.[91]

Scharnhorst could be seen in the glow of the flames turning to the south and presenting the *Scorpion* and *Stord* with an ideal target. The *Scorpion* from 2,100 yards and the *Stord* from 1,800 yards fired eight torpedoes each, the projectiles spreading out in a wide, bubbling fan. The two destroyers now drew the attention of *Scharnhorst*'s guns.[92] "Still belching flame," wrote Ditchman, "she was the most unattractive spectacle I have ever seen."[93]

In all the chaos, smoke, and violent spouts of water from the German shells, the *Scorpion* scored one hit and the *Stord* none. Both destroyers turned behind the protective cover of a smoke screen and made their escape.[94]

The *Savage* now fired her eight torpedoes; the damaged *Saumarez* could launch only four. Their joint effort scored three hits.[95] The men on the fleeing *Scorpion* heard the torpedoes strike home. "We heard underwater explosions," wrote telegraphist John G. Wass, "rumblings that echoed through the ship like vibrations. We all felt that *Scharnhorst* could not escape its fate."[96]

A grim decision was made on board *Scharnhorst*. One torpedo, having struck aft, flooded three compartments. "The watertight doors," one survivor reported, "had to be closed on the 25 men inside." The *Savage* and battered *Saumarez* turned to escape, the latter with only one operable engine and a top speed of 10 knots.[97]

As the destroyers retreated to the north, the *Duke of York* and *Jamaica* approached *Scharnhorst* from the south and engaged from 10,400 yards. "It was an awe-inspiring sight," wrote Ditchman. "At five miles, the trajectory was comparatively flat and the 14-inch tracer shells leaped across the sea, and all of them appeared to smash into her in a colossal explosion."[98] Lieutenant Commander Lumsden, on *Sheffield*, took a more melodramatic approach. "The moment," he wrote, "will live long with all who had spent anxious hours working and waiting for just this fiery thunder that heralded the destruction of the foe."[99]

Five minutes of relentless hammering reduced the *Scharnhorst* to a nightmare vision of flames and exploding ammunition.[100] "Once the *Duke of York* got in there with those tremendous guns, it was horrendous to watch," said Seaman Bob Shrimpton on board *Belfast*, closing in from the north with the *Norfolk*. "She just smashed the thing to pieces; it was just a blaze from one end to the other."[101] But *Scharnhorst*'s guns kept firing, despite the horrific conditions on board. The ships portside deck, noted one survivor, "was littered with dead bodies being washed overboard."[102]

As the fires on *Scharnhorst* intensified, the men on *Jamaica* cheered— their raucous voices "audible above the gunfire." The flash of *Scharnhorst*'s guns revealed thick tendrils of smoke rising above her and a sea "alive with shell splashes from an outpouring of shells."[103] The German ship and her crew remained defiant. Through the ear-splitting maelstrom of gunfire and the cries of men, a sound worked its way through the ship. It was Captain Hintze's voice on the loudspeaker, bellowing the ship's motto: "*Scharnhorst immer voran* [*Scharnhorst* ever onward]!" So chaotic had things become for the *Scharnhorst* crew "they were unable to distinguish between . . . the impact of the heavy shells and the firing of their own heavy armament."[104]

Shell after shell landed with devastating effect. "Explosions and fires ravaged the doomed ship," one German sailor later wrote, "but each gun fired until it was shot out."[105] Bulkheads bent and twisted out of shape, steam pipes ruptured, smoke stung the eyes and choked the lungs. Her compartments were "full of mangled bodies and swilling with sea water."[106]

The maimed and dead littered all decks. The ship began to slow under the relentless punishment. "The *Scharnhorst* must have been hell on earth," wrote Ramsden. "The 14-inch [shells] from *Duke of York* were hitting or rocketing off from a ricochet on the sea. Great flashes rent the night, and the sound of gunfire was continuous, and yet she replied, but only occasionally now with what armament she had left."[107]

The *Belfast* opened fire from 17,000 yards at 7:15 p.m. Four minutes later, the German Naval War Staff intercepted a signal from Fraser on the *Duke of York*: "Finish her off with torpedoes."[108] The *Scharnhorst*, by now going no faster than 5 knots, sat at a near standstill. At 7:28 p.m., *Duke of York*—having fired twenty-five broadsides—checked her fire to allow *Belfast* and *Jamaica* to move in. At about the same time, Captain Hintze addressed *Scharnhorst*'s crew. "I shake you all by the hand for the last time," he said. "I have sent this signal to the Fuhrer: 'We shall fight to the last shell.' *Scharnhorst* onwards."[109]

The *Jamaica* closed to 3,500 yards. The sudden silence of the big ships' guns lent the night an unnerving quality. "How alone we felt," wrote Ramsden. "The tumult and the noise had died, leaving only a hush—the hush of expectancy. All I could hear was the wind and the sea, and into the quiet came the return of foreboding and tension."[110] The *Jamaica* fired three torpedoes to port—followed by the *Belfast*. Neither ship registered a hit and swung around to fire their remaining torpedoes. "I could smell the sweetish smell of burning," remembered Ramsden. "It must be the *Scharnhorst*."[111]

Jamaica emptied her torpedo tubes. Although the heavy shroud of smoke concealing the German ship prevented *Jamaica*'s crew from observing any hits, they heard the muffled crump of two underwater explosions.[112] The destroyers *Musketeer*, *Matchless*, *Opportune*, and *Virago* had by now joined the battle. "All that could be seen of the *Scharnhorst* was a dull glow through a dense cloud of smoke," notes one official account, "which the starshells and searchlights of surrounding ships could not penetrate."[113]

All except *Matchless*—due to damage inflicted by heavy seas—fired their torpedoes and scored an estimated five hits that brought the battle to an end.[114]

✳ ✳ ✳

A world away in Berlin, as *Scharnhorst* lived out her final minutes, Grand Admiral Karl Dönitz met with Hitler and "expressed the hope that the *Scharnhorst* would complete the action successfully—or, in any case, inflict severe damage on the British."[115]

＊ ＊ ＊

No one on the British side actually witnessed the *Scharnhorst* sink because of the smoke billowing around her. One moment she was there, the glow of her fires pulsing through the dense cloud, the next she was gone. "It seems fairly certain," Fraser noted in his official dispatch, "that she sank after a heavy underwater explosion, which was heard and felt in several ships at about 1945."[116]

On board *Matchless*, radar operator John Horton ventured to have a look outside. "It was then that I saw a great glow where *Scharnhorst* was," he said, "and then I heard a loud explosion, and the German battle-cruiser was no more."[117]

The blast's concussion rumbled through the *Belfast*. "A bit of a cheer went up," said Seaman Bob Shrimpton, "but then there was dead silence after that because I think we were thinking there were a hell of a lot of men on that [boat]—like us. Youngsters, with families, wives, and kids—and they're in that water. I think that was a subduing effect. It's one of those strange feelings you get—but that's how it happens. I hope it doesn't happen again."[118]

The *Belfast*, *Norfolk*, and several destroyers spent the next hour searching for survivors. "The darkness, heavy weather, and icy water," notes a naval report, "afforded little chance of survival to the luckless crew of the *Scharnhorst*."[119] The *Scorpion* fished thirty men out of the water; *Matchless* another six. "I heard orders being given to stand to and man the ship's side to pick up survivors," remembered Horton on *Matchless*. "We started our search and there seemed to be wreckage and bodies all around. A few cries were heard and I saw the ratings taking in survivors." The six men pulled aboard *Matchless* received warm clothes, hot food, and rum. "Believe me," noted Horton, "it was a sight I shall never forget."[120]

Sheffield arrived shortly thereafter and found the sea covered in sludge and littered with the signs of *Scharnhorst*'s passing. From deep beneath the cluttered oil slick came several loud rumbling noises. "It was a very eerie and melancholy sensation," noted Marine "Doddie" Thorndyke, "when we steamed over the grave of *Scharnhorst* and heard the terrible explosions going on under water."[121]

There was nothing left to do. The *Belfast, Duke of York, Jamaica, Norfolk,* and other participants of the battle set a course for Kola Inlet, fourteen miles northeast of Murmansk, to refuel.[122] Fraser signaled the Admiralty that the *Scharnhorst* had sunk. The response from London was brief and to the point: "GRAND. WELL DONE."[123] Out of *Scharnhorst*'s crew of 1,968, only 36 men—with not an officer among them—survived.

Fraser, in his eulogy for *Scharnhorst* and her crew, struck a gallant tone. "Gentlemen, the battle against *Scharnhorst* has ended in victory for us," he told his men. "I hope that if any of you are ever called upon to lead a ship into action against an opponent many times superior, you will command your ship as gallantly as *Scharnhorst* was commanded today."[124]

Through brutal confrontation, the British had now eliminated all but one of Hitler's capital ships. Only *Tirpitz*, in all her glowering menace, remained.

CHAPTER 13

* * *

RETURN TO *TIRPITZ*

The death of the *Scharnhorst* rendered the *Tirpitz* "the lonely queen of the north."[1] Sheltered in her Norwegian fjord, protected by submarine netting, flak ships, antiaircraft guns, and smoke generators, the ship's crew felt little comfort. They knew the enemy would once more turn its attention to their lonely corner of the world.[2]

Indeed, images captured by RAF reconnaissance flights and reports from the Norwegian Underground confirmed by March 1944 that temporary repairs on the ship had been completed. "Though she was probably not 100 percent fit for operations," notes a Royal Navy report, "she constituted a potential threat to the North Russian convoys."[3] So significant was the danger *Tirpitz* posed, even in her incapacitated state, the British Home Fleet's second in command, Vice Admiral Sir Henry Moore, deemed it "highly desirable to put her out of action again."[4]

The new plan to destroy the *Tirpitz* at her anchorage took shape under the codename "Tungsten."[5] Forty-two Barracuda dive-bombers, loaded with 500- to 1,600-pound armor-piercing bombs, would take off from the fleet carriers *Victorious* and *Furious* in two waves of twenty-one and strike at *Tirpitz* in Kåfjord. Hellcats, Wildcats, and Corsairs, flying from three additional carriers, would provide fighter cover. Home Fleet commander in chief Admiral Bruce Fraser had to be "practically bludgeoned" to go along with it.[6]

Some twenty-seven ships, including the two fleet carriers, four escort carriers, the cruisers *Royalist*, *Jamaica*, *Belfast*, and *Sheffield*, the battleships *Duke of York* and *Anson*, fourteen destroyers, and two fleet oilers made up the Tungsten armada, which would be split into two forces. Fraser would lead Force 1 from the *Duke of York*, joined by Vice Admiral Moore on the *Anson*, along with *Victorious*, *Belfast*, and six destroyers. The remaining ships would make up Force 2 under the command of Rear Admiral Arthur William La Touche Bisset.[7]

∗ ∗ ∗

Convoy JW-58 sailed from Loch Ewe for Kola Inlet on March 27. Three days later, the Tungsten armada sailed from Scapa Flow. Force 1 steamed north to cover the convoy in the event *Tirpitz*—even in her damaged state—went on the prowl. Despite the occasional shadowing by German reconnaissance planes, the enemy showed surprising indifference. "This apparent lack of interest in any possible covering force," notes a Royal Navy report, "suggested that a sortie by the *Tirpitz* was unlikely."[8] As weather conditions proved favorable—and mindful of "Nelson's maxim to never trifle with a fair wind"—Fraser decided covering the convoy was unnecessary and moved operation Tungsten up by twenty-four hours.[9]

The two forces rendezvoused on the afternoon of Sunday, April 2, some 250 miles northwest of Kåfjord. Fraser, on *Duke of York*, parted ways with the armada but would remain within 200 miles of the Tungsten fleet until the operation's completion. Moore, on *Anson*, proceeded with the other ships to the "flying off position," which they hoped to reach early the following morning.[10]

Final preparations got underway on the carriers that evening. "There was little sleep in those carriers the night before the attack," recalled Commander Anthony Kimmins on board *Victorious*, "for we were now in the danger period as we steamed close into enemy waters. Look-outs and guns' crews, only their eyes visible through their scarves and balaclava helmets, were constantly on the job. Supply and Damage Control parties never left their posts." Down in the cavernous hangars, "mechanics swarmed over their aircraft making final adjustments," while ordnance crews prepared "great yellow bombs" for their one-way journey.[11]

At 1:30 a.m.—"that ghastly hour," noted Captain Michael Denny, commander of *Victorious*, "when man's stamina is at its lowest"—the airmen gathered for their final briefing. The outward track would take them low over the sea before crossing the Norwegian coast at 10,000 feet. The attack run would send them east "through a snow-covered valley" that opened into Kåfjord, where they'd bomb *Tirpitz* from the southwest and—with luck—catch her unaware. The men dined on a breakfast of eggs and bacon before gearing up and heading to the deck, where miserable conditions awaited. "[The] *Victorious* flight deck is wet in any weather," Denny noted, "and the spray and sleet were freezing."[12]

The men climbed into their machines; engines sparked, coughed, and came to life. It was 4:16 a.m. Commander Kimmins recorded the scene. "By now the carriers and escorting ships were all heeling over and swinging into wind," he noted. "A final nod from the Captain, a signal from the Commander Flying, the Flight Deck Officer raised his green flag, the engines started to rev up, the flag dropped and the first aircraft was roaring away over the bow."[13] One by one the planes tore down the ice-slicked decks of the carriers, churning up frozen debris, before climbing into the pale sky.

On the light cruiser *Royalist*, Rear Admiral Bisset—an ex–carrier captain—watched with admiration. "It was a grand sight with the sun just risen, " he wrote, "to see the well-balanced striking force . . . departing at very low level between the two forces of surface ships." Earlier in the war, when he commanded the carriers *Formidable* and then *Illustrious*, a shortage of planes proved a constant scourge. Now, as he watched the first flight of Barracudas and their escorting fighters take flight, he wondered "what might have been if the Fleet Air Arm had been adequately equipped with aircraft in the early days of the war."[14]

The planes thundered across the Norwegian coast at 5:08 a.m., the sun glinting off the fjords below and crowning the snow-capped peaks in amber light. The guns of a German destroyer anchored in Langfjord remained silent as the bombers and fighters passed overhead; the antiaircraft defenses on shore never stirred. And now the planes turned in a graceful arc down the valley that would lead them to the head of Kåfjord and *Tirpitz*. The shore batteries came to life three miles from the target with "heavy but inaccurate" fire.[15]

The planes, in their final approach, began their descent from 8,000 feet. The head of Kåfjord appeared between the ice-blue slopes of the valley. *Tirpitz* was clearly visible, the first phantom wisps of smoke screen creeping across the water. It proved too little, too late. Near complete surprise had been achieved.[16]

While Corsairs circled overhead, Hellcats and Wildcats dropped low over the slopes, their passage blowing snow from the treetops, and swept across the water. "[We] shot across the fjord in a straggling line abreast shooting into the battleship," wrote one fighter pilot. "Various missiles appeared to be whizzing in all directions . . . very exciting."[17] Machine-gun fire ripped along the battleship's sides, deck, and superstructure. Rounds shredded the crews manning the antiaircraft defenses and "undoubtedly spoilt the *Tirpitz* gunnery."[18]

The Barracuda bombers now commenced their dives with engines screaming and dropped as low as 1,200 feet before releasing their payloads. The attack lasted sixty seconds—an eternal minute of smoke, flames, and explosions. One Barracuda crew reported seeing a "steady red glow amidships and smoke pouring up." Another said the target was "enveloped in large red flames."[19] With *Tirpitz* burning behind them, the fighters and bombers winged their way back to the coast and the waiting carriers at sea.

The aircraft made the return journey free of enemy interference, although one bomber was seen descending "in a controlled dive with its engine stopped at a height of about 1,000 feet."[20] Another aircraft, a fighter, ditched in the water just prior to landing; its pilot was fished from the sea by the destroyer *Algonquin*. All remaining aircraft made it back to the carriers by 6:42 a.m., their crews, noted Denny, boasting "a unanimous grin."[21] The second assault wave of eighteen Barracudas and forty-five fighters launched at 5:25 a.m., but not all had gone smoothly. Engine trouble prevented one Barracuda on *Victorious* from taking off. Another, having left the deck without a problem, crashed into the sea and took its three-man crew to the bottom.[22]

"Hundreds of dead and wounded" littered *Tirpitz*'s deck. The battleship, free of its moorings, drifted on the water made turbulent by the bombing, its bow grinding into the silt and rock of the shore.[23]

Even as the ship burned, the second wave of aircraft closed the distance and hurtled over the Norwegian coast at 7,000 feet. Pilots could see the ship's smoke screen from forty miles away, but it did little to hamper the attack. Hellcats swept low and pummeled the ship's gun positions. The Wildcats strafed the decks and cut down men as they scattered for cover. Clouds of flak burst above the ship to create an umbrella of smoke and shrapnel. The bombers dived undeterred and dropped their payloads from heights of less than 3,000 feet. One Barracuda suffered heavy damage and "was seen diving vertically in flames on to the mountainside."[24] Once more, only a minute lapsed between the first bomb falling and the last; in that short time, the burning *Tirpitz* fell silent—her guns lifeless. The planes turned away, the drone of their engines fading behind the cries of the wounded and the roar of flames.[25]

Of the forty Barracudas and eighty-one fighters that took part in the operation, only three aircraft failed to return. On *Victorious*, Denny reviewed the debrief reports of bomber crews. Thrilled with success and overwrought with adrenaline, they reported scoring some thirty hits.[26] Denny, in his more sober analysis of crew notes and photographs taken over the target, estimated *Tirpitz* suffered "seventeen direct hits, three of them by 1,600-lb. bombs."[27]

Despite this more reined-in analysis, he still believed the damage inflicted to be catastrophic. At 5:37 p.m., he signaled Vice Admiral Moore, "I believe *Tirpitz* now to be useless as a warship."[28] Moore had planned to attack *Tirpitz* again the following morning but reconsidered after reading Denny's assessment. Also giving him pause was the "fatigue of the aircrews and their natural reaction after completing a dangerous operation successfully."[29] He subsequently ordered the Tungsten armada back to Scapa Flow.

The ships arrived home to a "rousing reception" at 4:30 p.m. on April 6 and a message from Winston Churchill, congratulating "the pilots and aircrews concerned on this most brilliant feat of arms."[30] Yet

Churchill's praise masked his anxiety. The full extent of the damage to *Tirpitz* remained unknown—a point even the Royal Navy had to concede. "The smoke from the bursting bombs, as well as the enemy smoke screen, made accurate observation at the time difficult and obscured some of the photographs taken," states a postoperation report. "The damage caused cannot, of course, be known for certain until enemy records are available."[31]

✻ ✻ ✻

The *Tirpitz* refused to die.

An inspection of the ship confirmed she'd been struck fifteen times. Damage to her hangar and upper deck proved extensive, yet her armored deck remained intact. The ship's communications system was dead; the hull was severely battered and she was taking on water and listing to starboard. A number of compartments, including the officers' mess, had been shattered by high explosives. The attack killed 122 men and wounded 316.[32]

At the end of April, a team of engineers from the dockyards in Kiel arrived at Kåfjord to begin the repairs. Work carried on around the clock until the beginning of July, when she was ready once more for sea trials. All the while, British agents monitored the progress and wired their reports back to London.[33]

The Admiralty, desperate to permanently knock *Tirpitz* out of the war, launched three more carrier-born attacks against the ship between August 22 and August 29. The raids, collectively known as Operation Goodwood, failed to inflict any serious damage. The Germans had bolstered the Kåfjord defenses and added more smoke generators in the wake of Operation Tungsten.[34]

A heavy veil of man-made fog thwarted bombing accuracy on all three Goodwood raids. The Barracuda, the Fleet Air Arm's bomber of choice, was simply too slow to "beat the smoke screen" and couldn't carry a bomb big enough to deliver the fatal blow. And so the task of destroying *Tirpitz* fell to the RAF.[35]

✻ ✻ ✻

The airmen pulled their heavy flying clothes over the dress blues of their RAF uniforms. The merciless temperatures at high altitudes necessitated multiple layers. Exposed skin could easily succumb to frostbite; flesh could adhere to metal. Thick sweaters formed the first line of defense, followed by the Irvin jacket and inflatable life preserver. Woolen stockings pulled over silk socks and boots lined with lamb's wool protected the feet; hands disappeared into thick, wool-lined gloves. The leather helmet with its oxygen mask was the final piece of the ensemble.

Burdened by the weight of their clothing, the men walked to the crew room to retrieve their parachute and rations—chewing gum, some biscuits, an apple or orange, raisins, and a thermos of tea or coffee—before heading out to dispersals and their waiting bombers.[36]

The date was Monday, September 11, 1944. Issued four days earlier, the battle order for Operation Paravane called for thirty-eight Lancasters from Nos. 9 and 617 Squadrons to fly 2,100 miles from their airfields in England to an isolated Russian airbase in Yagodnik near Archangel. From there, they would launch an attack against *Tirpitz* at her anchorage roughly 600 miles away. Twenty-four Lancasters would carry the RAF's 12,000-pound Tallboy bomb; the remaining aircraft would drop 150 shipping mines.[37] A Tallboy, should one find its mark, noted the battle order, "would cause tremendous damage, incomparably greater than could ever be caused by any other bomb in existence."[38]

The sun began its slow descent and lengthened the early evening shadows. The shade crept over the men lounging on the grass beneath their aircraft, enjoying one last smoke, conversing, or sitting in quiet solitude. Each pilot and chief mechanic inspected their plane a final time. When done, the pilot scrambled into the cockpit and test-fired the Rolls-Royce Merlin engines. He cast his eyes over a myriad of instrumentation—reading gauges, checking oil and brake pressure, ensuring the machine was up to the challenge ahead.[39]

And now it was time for the remainder of the crew to climb on board. The gunners and copilot took up their positions; the navigator took a seat at his table in the rear cabin, spreading out his charts and maps. Behind him sat the wireless operator, reviewing the emergency frequencies. Oxygen lines were connected and wireless communications checked.[40]

In the fading daylight, the bombers trundled one by one down the flarepaths at Bardney and Woodhall Spa, gathered speed, and lifted their massive bulks of men, fuel, ammunition, and high explosives into the sky. They turned north on a heading to Lossiemouth in Scotland, where they would refuel for the flight to Yagodnik. A Lancaster "carrying three RAF cameramen, a BBC radio reporter, and an Associated Press war correspondent" also made the journey.[41]

The long and monotonous flight passed without incident until—the following dawn—they entered Russian airspace. The sky, heavy and gray, closed in around them with thick cloud cover and forced the bombers to surrender altitude. Visibility quickly deteriorated to 600 yards with the cloud base descending to 1,500 feet. "This was hardly in keeping with the forecast," reported Group Captain Colin McMullen. "Combined with this weather was the fact that no navigational aids were available. Crews were briefed with an incorrect call sign for the Yagodnik ground station because of confusion between the Russian and English alphabets."[42]

Navigators wrestled with maps that lacked any identifying details—such as towns and railway stations—that might help guide them to their destination. Visual reckoning did little to help. "The countryside itself," noted McMullen, "is most confusing, being a monotonous waste of marsh or endless pine forests and innumerable small lakes."[43]

The foul weather scattered the bombers and forced the planes to land at various airfields around Archangel. "The arrival under such appalling conditions," reported McMullen, "was as difficult as one could imagine. It reflects considerable credit on the navigators that they reached the vicinity of Archangel—let alone find one particular airfield."[44] Of the forty-two bombers that made the journey, twenty-one managed to land at the correct base. Six planes suffered serious damage on landing and had to be written off. Fortunately, all crews escaped injury.[45]

The operation called for the planes to land at Yagodnik on the morning of September 12 and attack *Tirpitz* that afternoon—but now, as weary crews clambered from their machines, it was apparent to Mc-Mullen there would be no attack that day. Not only were the men utterly exhausted, nearly every plane needed repairs before flying again.[46]

Work on the planes began that afternoon and carried on through the following day. The ground crews toiled without rest for nearly forty-eight hours. Even when ordered by McMullen to get some sleep, they took no more than a four-hour respite. "Working conditions were far from ideal," McMullen wrote. "It was cold and there were frequent rain showers. . . . The fact that so many aircraft were ready to operate on the 14th September is a tribute to the excellent work of the ground crew for whom praise cannot be too high."[47]

On the morning of September 15, the RAF crews gathered for one last briefing. "[It] was held," according to one airman, "in the open under bleak conditions and bleaker surroundings. In the near distance, the menacing outlines of the Lancasters relieved the monotony of the background of weather-beaten hutments, dun-colored flat earth, and gray winding river."[48]

With a reconnaissance flight reporting clear weather over the target area, twenty-eight Lancasters took off from Yagodnik at 6:30 a.m. They flew at 1,000 feet through calm skies to the Finnish border, where they turned north and began "a maximum power climb" to bombing height. The twenty aircraft carrying 12,000-pound Tallboys would attack in four waves of five bombers abreast from heights of 14,000 to 18,000 feet. The remaining aircraft, armed with mines, would drop their payloads from 10,000 to 12,000 feet.[49]

Fighter activity was nonexistent as the bombers passed over a rugged maze of mountains and waterways, and what flak they did encounter proved inaccurate. Flying in a Lancaster above the main bomber stream, BBC reporter Guy Byam surveyed the stunning scenery below and saw "a fork of water and a ship. The *Tirpitz*!"[50] Thin tendrils of man-made smoke could already be seen wrapping themselves around the ship like fast-growing vines—but it was too late. The target, to one navigator, looked like "a black matchstick" against the waters of the fjord.[51]

The bombers thundered in from the south, attacking along the ship's fore to aft axis. A thin layer of cloud, coupled with the ever-thickening smoke screen, obscured *Tirpitz* for some aircraft on their first attack run and prompted several Lancasters to make a second pass. "Huge mushrooms of smoke and water rose up through the smokescreen," reported one pilot, "and my bomb-aimer was again unable to get the ship in his sight. But at that moment, the *Tirpitz* started to fire . . . her light ack-ack guns and the flashes below the smokescreen provided a perfect marker, so we bombed the center of the flashes."[52]

One Tallboy crashed through the ship's foredeck and hull, and passed through her starboard side before exploding. The blast destroyed the bow and flooded *Tirpitz* with 2,000 tons of water.[53] Georg Schlegel, the ship's chief engine room officer, found "a huge gaping hole like a barn door" in the starboard side. "All the cabins and holds had disappeared," he later recalled. "It was pretty much mayhem."[54]

As the men on board assessed the twisted wreckage, pulling five dead and fifteen wounded from the smoldering mess, the bombers— with not a loss among them—journeyed back to Yagodnik.[55] The crews touched down to the "accompaniment of a local scratch brass band and enthusiastic cheers from a small reception committee, including six local belles."[56]

"It was," reported McMullen, "very difficult to assess the result of the attack from the interrogation of crews. Their observations were hampered by the smoke screen and no films were processed at Yagodnik. . . . Many crews saw a large red flash followed by black smoke from the area of the *Tirpitz* but there was no definite evidence to prove that this had emanated from the battleship itself."[57]

Two hours after the last bomb fell, a reconnaissance flight revealed the battleship—spotted through a gap in low cloud—remained afloat. The following day, Saturday, September 16, the British crews climbed aboard their Lancasters for the long flight home.[58]

The *Tirpitz*, although wounded, remained very much alive.

✳ ✳ ✳

A sense of dread began to permeate the *Tirpitz* crew. A group of sailors went ashore following the raid and saw a massive crater left by a Tallboy. "It took our breath away," one said. The ship seemed to no longer be a tough proposition for the enemy. Surely, the bombers would return to finish the job.[59]

On September 23, the naval high command in Berlin received a report stating it would take nine months to make *Tirpitz* seaworthy. Grand Admiral Dönitz balked at the assessment. Germany no longer had the time nor the resources for such an undertaking. Nevertheless, the ship's mere existence remained a powerful propaganda tool. He ordered *Tirpitz* be moved to the island of Haakøy—roughly three miles west of Tromsø—to serve as a battery, and where its presence might deter any plans for an Allied invasion.[60]

Dönitz signaled his intentions in a communiqué issued on September 25: "After successfully defending herself against many air attacks the battleship *Tirpitz* has now sustained a bomb hit, but by holding out in the operational area the ship will continue to tie down enemy forces and by her presence to confound the enemy's intentions."[61]

The badly wounded *Tirpitz*, accompanied by tugs and a small armada of destroyers, "limped" south at 6 knots to her new anchorage on October 15.[62] The Norwegian Underground relayed the move to London via a "secret radio transmitter" on the top floor of Tromsø's hospital.[63]

A reconnaissance flight confirmed the news several days later. In the minds of RAF leadership, the move was a non-issue. The bombs dropped the previous month had rendered *Tirpitz* little more than a corpse. "We had very good reason to believe," wrote Air Marshal Arthur Harris, commander in chief of Bomber Command, "that the ship could never be made fit for operations before the probable end of the war and was therefore quite useless to the enemy."[64] Churchill and the Admiralty, however, thought otherwise.

Even though German radio intercepts had by now revealed the true extent of the damage and the plan to keep *Tirpitz* at Tromsø, the prime minister remained fixated on the ship's total destruction. "I think it will be regarded as a very serious misfortune," he informed the First Sea Lord on October 26, "if the TIRPITZ succeeds in returning to Germany. I consider that every effort should be made to attack this ship, even if losses have to be incurred." Admiral Andrew Cunningham, having succeeded Admiral Sir Dudley Pound, replied the following day. "I fully agree," he wrote. "It is most improbable that the long passage south will be attempted at present . . . Bomber Command has planned an attack on the ship in her present berth as soon as weather conditions are favorable."[65]

Tirpitz at her new anchorage lay 200 miles closer to British airfields and within range of Lancasters operating from forward bases in northern Scotland. The bombers, equipped with extra fuel tanks and upgraded Merlin engines, could now make a round trip of the operation.[66] The task fell to thirty-eight crews from Nos. 617 and 9 Squadrons, which had carried out the previous month's attack. Not until late October did weather conditions over the target prove ideal for the raid. The final briefing took place at midnight on October 28. Two and a half hours later, the Lancasters rumbled down their flarepaths in darkness and climbed into the black void. The navigation lights on their wingtips created a "picturesque parade against the night sky" as the bombers fell into formation and headed out to sea.[67]

They reached the Norwegian coast at daybreak, making landfall at Vega, and began a steady climb from 1,500 feet to clear the mountains. A landscape of rock and ice passed beneath them as they made a turn "over lifeless wasteland" to begin the final leg of their outward journey. The bombers rendezvoused over Torneträsk Lake and commenced their 100-mile run north to the target.[68] They made, noted Tromsø's town clerk Lars Thoring, a "deafening noise" as they swept overhead.[69]

The weather served the crews well but began to deteriorate as they closed the distance. Thick cloud topped out at 6,000 feet and all but obscured the *Tirpitz* from view. The bombers pressed on and dropped strips of "metal-covered paper" to confound the German radar. The guns lit up below and flashed white and yellow through breaks in the cloud. It was, notes one account, "a warm reception."[70]

The bombardiers struggled to find the aiming point as more clouds rolled in to create an impenetrable layer. The crews nevertheless pressed home their attack, dropping their payloads and hoping for the best. "When the bombs dropped and exploded," noted Thoring, three miles away from the action, "it sounded like thunder in the midst of the other infernal noise."[71]

The bombers, relieved of their explosive cargo, turned toward the sea and the direction of Scotland. One crew, thrown off course by the heavy cloud and worsening weather, perished when their bomber crashed into the mountains of southern Norway. Another Lancaster, damaged by flak over the target area, was forced to land in Sweden. By 3:15 p.m., after nearly thirteen hours of flying, all remaining bombers had touched back down on Scottish soil, their crews "despondent at the frustration of their strenuous effort."[72]

Tirpitz, having escaped a direct hit, suffered damage to her rudder and a propeller shaft as the result of a near miss. Some 800 tons of water flooded the ship.[73] Although now completely paralyzed—a fact not known to the British—*Tirpitz*, by her stubborn survival, remained a threat. On November 3, British Naval Intelligence issued a report estimating *Tirpitz* could be operational once more if she underwent four to six months of repair work at a main German base. The fact that only twenty-three days remained until the endless night of the Arctic winter added to the sense of urgency.[74]

Nos. 9 and 617 Squadrons flew once more to Scotland in preparation for another attack. "The combination," wrote Wing Commander J. B. Tait, "of untoward weather, false starts, ill-luck, and the depressing prospect of the descent on Northern Norway of its impenetrable winter blanket at any minute reduced the spirits of the anxious crews."[75]

The "restive crews" gathered for their briefing at midnight on November 11–12. The timing and route taken remained unchanged from their previous effort. A meteorological flight over the target area reported "weather conditions doubtful." The operation—codenamed "Catechism"—nevertheless received the go-ahead.[76] "Two hours later," noted Tait, "the motors of the Lancasters broke the early morning quiet and at 2:30 hours, prompt to the hour, the first machines gathered speed down the runway in the van of the small parade."[77]

They again crossed the Norwegian coast as the first light of day paled the eastern sky. "The red sun hung low over the distant horizon," Tait wrote, "turning the snow-flecked hills to a deep pink, in striking contrast to the crystal clear blue depths of the shining lakes revealed through occasional breaks in the cloud umbrella."[78] The bombers once again rendezvoused over Torneträsk Lake, "identified by the cloud that hung over it like an identical twin in shape," and began the final leg of their outward journey.[79]

On board *Tirpitz*, Captain Robert Weber, having assumed command just eight days prior, received a report at eight that morning of a British bomber over Bodø, some 320 miles away. Another report followed fifteen minutes later of three Lancasters heading east over Mosjøen, 450 miles away. A rapid-fire succession of bomber sightings now reached the bridge, though the aircrafts' ultimate destination could not be confirmed.[80]

The ship's first flak officer, a worried Captain-Lieutenant Alfred Fassbender, phoned the German airfield at Tromsø and urged the commanding officer there to "make sure fighter cover is prepared." At 9:05 a.m., Weber received word of roughly two-dozen Lancasters seventy-five miles south of *Tirpitz*.[81] Their objective no longer remained a mystery. "We will soon be subjected to a powerful enemy air attack," Weber broadcast to the ship's company. "I know that the crew of the *Tirpitz* will do its duty and give these four-engine aircraft a hot welcome."[82]

Through the Perspex window of his cockpit, Wing Commander Tait saw the *Tirpitz* come into view some twenty miles ahead in the clear and cloudless distance. "At a given signal," Tait wrote, "the great machines swung their bomb doors wide open and converged to the attack." Pilot Frederic Watts marveled at the "gin-clear" conditions and lack of smoke screen. "My God, Mac," he said to his bombardier, "she's had it today."[83]

On the bridge of *Tirpitz*, Weber ordered his senior gunnery officer to open fire the moment the bombers came within range. At 9:40 a.m., the ship's forward main armaments voiced their welcome.[84] The 15-inch shells exploded beneath the approaching bombers, in the words of Pilot Tony Iveson, like "a great unfolding golden cloud." The *Tirpitz*, recorded Tait, "was fighting back strongly." Her barrage, although "ill-aimed," was "unpleasantly close."[85] The ship's antiaircraft batteries now joined the fight with the shape of *Tirpitz* wavering behind the flash-and-smoke spectacle of her guns.

The first bomb fell at 9:41 a.m. Watching through binoculars from the weather office in Tromsø, town clerk Thoring saw "columns of water [rise] several hundred yards [*sic*] into the air like a gigantic fountain in the middle of splendid fireworks." Even at three miles' distance, the concussion of the 12,000-pound bombs rattled buildings and shattered windows. The enemy's guns, he noted, "put in a veritable display of fireworks."[86]

A number of sailors from *Tirpitz* happened to be ashore on Haakøy building a jetty when the raid commenced. "Everything seemed to happen so quickly," remembered one. "The hellish roar of the flak set in but the detonations of the English bombs overwhelmed all other noise. Huge geysers of fire, water, and debris covered everything and we had thrown ourselves on the beach to escape the shell splinters."[87] Straddled by explosions, mud and water swamped her decks. One blast ripped open a fifty-two-foot hole in her portside. From his vantage point 9,000 feet up, Tait saw "a thin geyser of white steam rising sharply" above the target.[88]

Weber and his staff, weathering the storm in the ship's armored conning tower, felt *Tirpitz* begin to list. "We remain here," Weber said, "at least as long as the guns are firing." Attempts to communicate with other parts of the ship proved futile.[89] The big guns maintained their deafening cannonade. *Tirpitz* shuddered with the force of her own armaments and the concussion of high explosives. Weber ordered the lower decks to be abandoned. Men fought their way through rising waters and the ship's shattered bowels toward the upper deck, where shrapnel and fire left bodies scattered in all directions.[90]

From above, *Tirpitz* presented a billowing vision of black smoke, flames, and the flash of stubborn guns. From his post, Thoring could see what looked like "a dark thundercloud in the sky" above the ship. At 9:50 a.m., burning ammunition launched one of her aft turrets into the sky on a pillar of flame.[91] "There were fires and explosions on board," reported Flight Lieutenant Bruce Buckham, piloting a Lancaster that filmed the raid. "A huge gaping hole existed in the port side where a section had been blown out."[92]

Men frantically grasped at anything they could to stay upright as the ship's list grew more pronounced—and then she capsized, rolling over at 10 a.m.[93] "We flew in at 50 feet and watched with baited [*sic*] breath as *Tirpitz* heeled over to port, ever so slowly and gracefully," remembered Buckham. "We could see German sailors swimming, diving, jumping . . . there must have been the best part of 60 men on her side as we skimmed over for the last pass."[94]

Men flung into the water struggled through wreckage and a thick scum of oil before reaching the shore 200 yards away. Gazing across the short stretch of water, they marveled at the devastation revealing itself behind a lifting curtain of smoke. "We could not believe our eyes," wrote one. "*Tirpitz* had gone. The hull stuck out of the water like a giant whale. There was nothing else."[95]

Twenty-four times between October 1940 and November 1944, the British attacked her from the air and from the sea.[96] Churchill's prize, the focus of his obsession, had at last been claimed. The beast was dead. The struggle had pushed men—cramped in frigid bombers or sweltering in the sweat-and-vomit fug of minisubs—to the limits of their endurance. Her superstructure lay buried in the mud of the fjord. Overhead, the bombers had by now disappeared. Wing Commander Tait would write the ship's eulogy in his postoperational report: "The inglorious career of the *Admiral von Tirpitz* came to a sudden and equally inglorious end."[97]

A number of her crew managed to scramble atop the ship's hull, its red-leaded metal glistening like blood. The screams of those trapped inside drifted across the water. "I saw that there were many people in the water, screaming for help," recorded one sailor. "There were others floating face down—the dead who were being kept afloat by the air trapped in their clothes."[98]

The first rescue boats appeared on scene within fifteen minutes, and soon the laborious work of cutting through the hull began. For three grueling days, rescue crews attacked the ship's armored underbelly with oxyacetylene torches and cutting tools, responding to the frantic banging of those trapped in the wet and oily darkness. The work took a physical toll on the welding teams. They fought their way through layers of steel to reach the bowels of the ship, often passing out due to lack of oxygen as they forged their way deeper into the hull.[99]

From somewhere deep inside *Tirpitz*, through the nightmarish tangle of what remained of the ship's lower decks, rescuers could hear a group of men singing "Deutschland, Deutschland, Über Alles." Attempts to reach them failed. Over time, the voices died out one by one, leaving behind a ghostly silence. Workers ultimately pulled eighty-seven survivors from the wreckage before efforts ceased on November 15. Of the roughly 1,700 men on board, 971 died in the attack—including Captain Weber.[100]

The RAF crews who dealt the fatal blow winged their way home without a casualty among them. One flak-damaged Lancaster, unable to continue, dropped out of formation and aimed for Sweden. German fighters "belatedly scrambled to the defense" of *Tirpitz* stalked the bomber on its solitary flight. Much to the crew's relief, the fighters soon lost interest in the easy prey and flew off. The Lancaster made it to Switzerland, where it crashed on landing. The crew escaped unhurt and eventually returned to England. The remaining force made the long trek across the sea and landed at their airfields after nearly thirteen hours of flying time.[101]

That night—Tait recalled—after news of *Tirpitz*'s demise had been confirmed, "the grand occasion was celebrated in the traditional youthful fashion of the R.A.F."[102]

Churchill, for so long tormented by the ship's mere existence, received word of the sinking while at the British Embassy in Paris. "The news that British aeroplanes have sunk the *Tirpitz* has greatly delighted us," Stalin cabled the prime minister. "The British airmen may legitimately pride themselves on this deed."[103] To Roosevelt, Churchill wrote: "It is a great relief to us to get this brute where we have long wanted her."[104]

Tirpitz's war proved a strange one in the end. She served the German war effort by keeping the bulk of the British Home Fleet tied down in northern waters, protecting Russian-bound convoys and securing the Atlantic sea-lanes. Her death meant those ships "were now free to move to the Far East."[105] *Tirpitz* may not have fought an aggressive war in the traditional sense, but she waged an effective psychological campaign against British military planners. She was more than just a target for bombs and mines—she was a potent symbol of Nazi hubris and military might. As such, her destruction dealt a symbolic blow to Hitler's crumbling war machine.

Victory had long slipped from Germany's grasp by the time the fatal bomb struck *Tirpitz*—a fact no battleship could reverse. Despite the turning of the tide, she had to be destroyed, not merely because of her destructive potential but because of what she represented. "Nothing," Churchill declared in a speech in June 1941, "is more certain than that every trace of Hitler's footsteps, every stain of his infected and corroding fingers will be sponged and purged and, if need be, blasted from the surface of the earth."[106]

In keeping with that promise, *Tirpitz* lay upside down and rusting in a Norwegian fjord. Her destruction not only marked another waypoint on the road to Germany's defeat, it served as a stark reminder that the age of the battleship—now surpassed by airpower—had effectively come to an end. Yet, like many great ships of war, she found immortality in death. For while the likes of *Hood*, *Bismarck*, and *Tirpitz* were claimed by the waters they briefly dominated, their names have transcended time to live on in history.

EPILOGUE

THE SEA IS A MASS GRAVE

Germany's naval war in the Atlantic was over by November 1944. The U-boat menace had by then been tamed. The remaining heavy ships in Hitler's surface fleet met various fates in the months that followed. The *Prinz Eugen*, *Lützow*, and *Admiral Scheer* saw action along the Baltic coast, bombarding the Red Army, providing cover for the retreating Wehrmacht, and helping evacuate German refugees from the advancing Soviet tide.[1]

British bombs destroyed the *Admiral Scheer* on the night of April 9, 1945, during a raid on the Kiel dockyards. Seven day later, the *Lützow* sank in shallow waters off Swinemünde during an RAF raid.[2] On May 3, the RAF severely damaged the *Admiral Hipper* at Kiel.

The *Prinz Eugen* survived the war and was turned over to the Americans. In July 1946, during nuclear tests at Bikini Atoll in the Marshall Islands, they subjected her to two atomic blasts. She survived both "with only a broken mast to show for it"—and a radiation level immune to all decontamination efforts.[3] Soon thereafter, her underwater fittings began to leak. The U.S. Navy towed the contaminated and sinking ship to the nearby Kwajalein Atoll, where she capsized on December 16. Her rusting corpse is visible today, resting in the shallows off Enubuj Island with her propellers sticking above the dark blue surface of the tropical waters.[4]

Both *Tirpitz* and *Prinz Eugen* continued to have an impact long after their respective ends. In 2016, a dendrochronologist from the Johannes

Guttenberg University in Mainz, Germany, noticed, while studying the growth rings of pine and birch trees on the shores of Kåfjord, that some trees stopped growing in 1945 and didn't resume their normal evolution until the mid-1970s. The cause for this stunted growth was traced back to the chlorosulfonic acid used in *Tirpitz*'s smoke screen, which had a debilitating effect on the trees' natural process of photosynthesis.[5]

Prinz Eugen also posed an environmental hazard. Although the U.S. Navy determined in 1974 the ship was no longer radioactive, a naval study said oil still in the ship's tanks would have to be removed within thirty years to avert an ecological disaster. Throughout September and October 2018, a U.S. Navy–led salvage team extracted roughly 250,000 gallons of oil from the ship's 173 tanks. The wreckage has been the property of the Marshall Islands since the American government transferred ownership in 1986.[6] You can view what remains of her on Google Earth.

✳ ✳ ✳

The German surface fleet was a force burdened by impossible odds and an aversion to risk—the Channel Dash notwithstanding. It could never hope to fully match the British Home Fleet, yet what it cost Germany in terms of raw materials and men required it to do more than look good in harbor. Going head-to-head against the Royal Navy was not a viable option, yet restricting its offensive actions to mere commerce raiding was an inadequate task. The German Admiralty was unsure how best to unleash its heavy ships, instructing its commanders "that whenever possible no opponent of equal strength was to be engaged"—a maxim that only intensified after the loss of *Bismarck*.[7]

Up until October 1943, the German navy "sank or significantly damaged thirty-four Allied warships displacing 188,000 tons."[8] Hitler, nevertheless, kept his heavy ships on a short leash out of fear their loss would be a blow to German prestige.[9] It's why *Tirpitz* remained anchored in Norway for the bulk of the war. Such intolerance for risk exerted itself at the most inopportune times. It was the signal from the German Admiralty advising "No unnecessary risk" that prompted Vice Admiral Oskar Kummetz to call off his destroyers to detrimental effect during the Battle of the Barents Sea. It's somewhat ironic the battle's end result prompted Hitler to order the dismantling of his surface ships.

Grand Admiral Raeder, before resigning in protest, provided Hitler a memorandum stressing the need to maintain such a force. "England, whose whole warfare stands or falls with its control of its sea communications," Raeder wrote, "will consider the war as good as won if Germany scraps her ships."[10] Grand Admiral Dönitz, Raeder's successor who long thought the surface fleet a drain on resources better suited for the U-boat campaign, surprisingly agreed and convinced Hitler to reverse course—but it hardly mattered. Less than a year later, in the final clash between British and German capital ships, the Royal Navy dispatched the *Scharnhorst* to her watery grave, ushering in—in the words of one historian—"the war's last phase, in which Germany took some very hard knocks."[11]

A month after the war, the Russians took Raeder into custody. He stood trial at Nuremberg on charges that included the planning and waging of aggressive naval warfare and operating "contrary to the rules of civilized warfare."[12] He was found guilty and sentenced to life in prison. Not wanting to spend the rest of his life in a cell and be a burden to his family, he petitioned the court to be executed by firing squad. His petition was denied. He was released, at the age of eighty and in failing health, on September 26, 1955. He died at the age of eighty-four on November 6, 1960.[13]

Dönitz received ten years in prison for waging "unrestricted submarine warfare." He escaped the death penalty after U.S. Admiral Chester Nimitz said he had done the same thing in the Pacific.[14] Dönitz served his time and died at the age of eighty-nine on December 24, 1980, in the village of Aumühle outside Hamburg. The West German Defense Ministry forbade military personnel to attend the funeral in uniform.[15]

* * *

There are no monuments upon the waves to commemorate the dead who lie beneath. Such monuments lie rusting on the ocean floor—many still waiting to be discovered, countless lost forever. "The eternal sea has closed over the fallen," Raeder wrote after the war. "The memorial wreaths which their surviving comrades strew upon the waters float but for a little time before they too sink from sight. But indestructible and eternal is the legacy which the dead have left to future generations."[16]

On June 8, 1989, oceanographer Robert Ballard—the explorer who found *Titanic*—discovered *Bismarck*'s wreckage some 600 miles west of Brest and 15,000 feet below the surface.[17] Examination of the well-preserved wreck appeared to back the theory that British shells alone didn't sink the *Bismarck*, and that scuttling charges detonated by the crew to prevent her capture by the Royal Navy assisted in the ship's demise. While the scuttling theory has found credence among American researchers, who point to the lack of damage from enemy fire on the sides of *Bismarck*'s hull, their British counterparts—perhaps not surprisingly—have argued against it.[18]

In the end, it hardly matters. *Bismarck*'s fate would have been the same whether her crew scuttled her or not. The exact location of the wreckage has not been publicly disclosed to preserve the final resting place of more than 2,000 men.

In September 2000, a joint expedition by the BBC, Norwegian Television, and the Royal Norwegian Navy found the remains of *Scharnhorst* in nearly 1,000 feet of water. She lies upside down, buried in silt, her bow evidently ripped from her body by an explosion that occurred at the moment of sinking.[19]

The wreckage of HMS *Hood* was discovered on July 19, 2001, in the Denmark Strait between Iceland and Greenland, nearly two miles beneath the surface. Her bow, midsection, and stern lay in three separate parts. In 2002, the British government designated the site an official war grave.[20]

As for *Tirpitz*, her wreck remained partially submerged in Kåfjord until after the war. A salvage operation to clear the wreckage began in 1948 and was not completed until 1957. Today, the German cutlery company Böker sells knifes with blades made from *Tirpitz*'s Krupp armor.[21]

On November 12, 2010, a handful of *Tirpitz* survivors, withered with age, attended a dedication ceremony at the water's edge in Wilhelmshaven, the German port city where *Tirpitz* first hit the waves. They laid wreaths at the base of a granite slab inscribed with the words "Tirpitz: April 1, 1939–November 12, 1944." Beneath the dates reads a simple inscription: "*Unseren toten zum Gedanken.*" Rough translation: "Our dead to commemorate."[22]

*   *   *

An expedition successfully retrieved *Hood*'s bell from 9,000 feet of icy water in August 2015.[23] It went on public display nine months later at the National Museum of the Royal Navy in Portsmouth on May 24, 2016—the seventy-fifth anniversary of *Hood*'s sinking. As a Royal Navy honor guard and descendants of *Hood*'s crew looked on, Princess Anne struck the bell eight times: the sound of its final, mournful toll a call from the past to remember those who sacrificed their all on the merciless sea.

ACKNOWLEDGMENTS

I intend to keep this short. My debonair agent, Roger Williams, has provided me wise counsel and stellar support for more than a decade. At Hachette Books, the exceptional Bob Pigeon graced the manuscript with his excellent eye for detail and story. He tackled this book as he did the last one we did together (*Winston Churchill Reporting: Adventures of a Young War Correspondent*) with an abundance of enthusiasm. *The Iron Sea* would not have happened without these two gentlemen. I am, as always, in their debt.

Many thanks to the wonderful Amber Morris, who guided this book through the production process, and to Bill Warhop for his eagle-eyed copyediting and making me look good on paper.

I offer my sincerest thanks to the staffs of the Imperial War Museum and the British National Archives, who have rescued me on the research front many times throughout the years. I have no doubt they'll do so again in the future.

I have to thank the wonderful Anne Rice—yes, *that* Anne Rice. Our online paths crossed not that long ago when she praised on social media a previous book of mine called *War of Words* and sent me a very kind note. To have not only a fellow author but a writer of her stature compliment something I did was amazing. Her encouragement came at just the right time and gave me a fantastic boost. Thank you, Anne.

To the usual cabal of old friends, I raise my glass and offer you all a hearty "Cheers!"

I was thirteen when I told my parents, Bill and Susan, I wanted to be a writer. They voiced their support without hesitation and have never wavered. They've cheered me on all these years with endless love and enthusiasm—something for which I'll be forever grateful.

Finally, none of this would have been possible without the support of my extraordinary family. No one understands the painful process of birthing a book more than a writer's spouse and their kids. To my wife, Katie, and wonderful sons, Spencer and Cameron, thank you for your enduring love and patience.

February 12, 2020
Gilbert, AZ

NOTES

PROLOGUE: THE KILLING SEAS

1. April 6, 1940: Air Ministry, *Bomber Command*, 36; leaflets in bundles of 1,500, shoved down flarechute: Read, 6.

2. Air Ministry, *Bomber Command*, 36.

3. Air Ministry, *Bomber Command*, 36.

4. Churchill, vol. 2, 514.

5. "Ice Closes Danube to German Supplies," *New York Times*, Dec. 30, 1939.

6. "Battle Is Marked by Frozen Bodies," *New York Times*, Dec. 25, 1939.

7. Garrett, 31.

8. Air Ministry, *Bomber Command*, 36.

9. Read, 20.

10. Read, 19.

11. Read, 19.

12. Air Ministry, *Bomber Command*, 36.

13. "seventeen ships of the German navy": Read, 19; "a very grand sight": Air Ministry, *Bomber Command*, 36.

14. Read, 19.

15. Read, 20.

16. Air Ministry, *Bomber Command*, 36.

17. Read, 20.

18. Bekker, 155.

19. Bekker, 155.

20. Bekker, 155–156.

21. Bekker, 156.

22. "Loss of HMS *Glorious*: Berlin Account of Brave Fight," *Coventry Evening Telegraph*, June 17, 1940.

23. Carrier a burning wreck by 5:38 p.m.; Marschall sees planes destroyed on deck: Bekker, 156–157; "Slowly, *Glorious* began to turn": "Loss of HMS *Glorious*: Berlin Account of Brave Fight," *Coventry Evening Telegraph*.

24. Carter's account reproduced in Churchill, vol. 1, 521.

25. Carter's account reproduced in Churchill, vol. 1, 521.

26. Bekker, 159.

27. Carter's account reproduced in Churchill, vol. 1, 521.

28. Carter's account reproduced in Churchill, vol. 1, 521.

29. "Loss of HMS *Glorious*: Berlin Account of Brave Fight," *Coventry Evening Telegraph*.

30. Carter's account reproduced in Churchill, vol. 1, 521.

31. Churchill, vol. 1, 521.

32. Garrett, 50.

33. Garrett, 50.

34. Bekker, 163.

35. Extracts of Netzbrand's War Diary reproduced in Koop and Schmolke, 48.

36. Bekker, 161, 162.

37. *Scharnhorst* and *Gneisenau* sink, capture more than 115,000 tons of Allied shipping: Garrett, 71; sink thirteen ships and capture another three: Bekker, 214–215.

38. Churchill, vol. 3, 104.

39. Churchill, vol. 3, 105.

40. Bishop, 14–15.

41. "brazen and fraudulent violation": Churchill, vol. 1, 123; Anglo-German Naval Agreement of 1935 limits battleships to 35,000 tons: Garrett, 17.

42. Churchill, vol. 1, 125.

43. Churchill, vol. 5, 20.

44. Hastings, 264.

45. "The Battle That Had to Be Won," *Naval History Magazine*, June 2008.

46. Hastings, 267.

47. Dimbleby, xix.

CHAPTER 1: IN SEARCH OF PREY

1. Green's firsthand account in Price (Kindle edition).

2. "Photographic Reconnaissance in World War II," 16. (see reference details in bibliography under "Online Articles and Resources")

3. "Photographic Reconnaissance in World War II," 16.

4. "Photographic Reconnaissance in World War II," 22.

5. Bf 109s patrolling vicinity of Ushant: "Photographic Reconnaissance in World War II," 22; Green knew five pilots lost over target: Green's firsthand account in Price (Kindle edition).

6. Green's firsthand account in Price (Kindle edition).

7. "Photographic Reconnaissance in World War II," 18, 21.

8. Green's firsthand account in Price (Kindle edition).

9. Green takes photos from 30,000 feet: Green's firsthand account in Price (Kindle edition); braves second pass through antiaircraft fire: Harwood, 77.

10. Green's firsthand account in Price (Kindle edition).

11. Bekker, 216.

12. Bekker, 216.

13. Churchill, vol. 3, 244.

14. Hastings, 264–265.

15. Kemp, 154.

16. Air Ministry, *Bomber Command*, 78.

17. AIR 14/680/043.

18. AIR 14/680/043.

19. AIR 14/680/043.

20. Middlebrook, 139.

21. Garrett, 76.

22. Garrett, 76.

23. Garrett, 76.

24. Garrett, 76.

25. AIR 27/280/61.

26. Barker, 63.

27. Barker, 59; AIR 27/280/58.

28. Barker, 62–63.

29. Barker, 65.

30. AIR 27/280/61, 62.

31. 500-yard range: Garrett, 77; details of Campbell's attack: AIR 27/280/62; *London Gazette*, March 10, 1942.

32. Ford, *Gauntlet*, 8.

33. Barker, 64.

34. Camp quoted in Air Ministry, *Coastal Command* (Kindle edition).

35. Camp quoted in Air Ministry, *Coastal Command* (Kindle edition).

36. Garrett, 77.

37. Garrett, 77.

38. Campbell receives posthumous Victoria Cross: *London Gazette*, March 10, 1942; "the most courageous": AIR 27/280/61.

39. Churchill, vol. 3, appendix C, 588.

40. Lütjens meets with Raeder on April 26: Bekker, 217; outline of Operation Rheinübung plan: Zetterling and Tamelander, *Bismarck*, 84.

41. Bekker, 218.

42. Raeder, 353.

43. Garrett, 78.

44. *Bismarck* to distract escorts, *Prinz Eugen* to sink convoys: Garrett, 78; "combat capacity as much as possible," "excessive risk": Boyne, 54.

45. Quoted in Müllenheim-Rechberg, 86.

46. "2,000 tons short of her stowage capacity": *German Battleship "BISMARCK" Interrogation of Survivors* (see Page, vol. 1, sec. 4, 10); *Bismarck* ready for three months at sea: Müllenheim-Rechberg, 87.

47. Müllenheim-Rechberg, 96–97.

48. Müllenheim-Rechberg, 97.

49. Müllenheim-Rechberg, 97.

50. *German Battleship "BISMARCK" Interrogation of Survivors* (see Page, vol. 1, sec. 4, 10); Müllenheim-Rechberg, 98.

51. Müllenheim-Rechberg, 96.

52. *German Battleship "BISMARCK" Interrogation of Survivors* (see Page, vol. 1, sec. 4, 10).

53. Müllenheim-Rechberg, 101.

54. *German Battleship "BISMARCK" Interrogation of Survivors* (see Page, vol. 1, sec. 5, 11).

55. *German Battleship "BISMARCK" Interrogation of Survivors* (see Page, vol. 1, sec. 5, 11).

56. Müllenheim-Rechberg, 107.

57. Müllenheim-Rechberg, 109; *German Battleship "BISMARCK" Interrogation of Survivors* (see Page, vol. 1, sec. 5, 11).

58. Müllenheim-Rechberg, 110.

59. BBC News, "Nottinghamshire Pilot Who Found *Bismarck* Is Remembered."

60. BBC News, "Nottinghamshire Pilot Who Found *Bismarck* Is Remembered."

61. Müllenheim-Rechberg, 112.

CHAPTER 2: CATACLYSM

1. Coles and Briggs, 199.

2. Coles and Briggs, 199.

3. Briggs, IWM Sound Archive 10751.

4. McMullen, IWM Sound Archive 10975.

5. Osborne, IWM Sound Archive 8256.

6. Coles and Briggs, 206.

7. Coles and Briggs, 206.

8. Coles and Briggs, 202.

9. Coles and Briggs, 202.

10. Coles and Briggs, 202.

11. D. N. Paton, "HMS *Suffolk* Sights and Chases *Bismarck*." (see reference details in bibliography under "Online Articles and Resources")

12. Norman, 71.

13. D. N. Paton, "HMS *Suffolk* Sights and Chases *Bismarck*."

14. *Suffolk* at 30 knots: D. N. Paton, "HMS *Suffolk* Sights and Chases *Bismarck*"; "One battleship, one cruiser": Müllenheim-Rechberg, 130.

15. Müllenheim-Rechberg, 130.

16. Müllenheim-Rechberg, 130.

17. Norman, 72.

18. Norman, 75.

19. Müllenheim-Rechberg, 131.

20. Müllenheim-Rechberg, 131.

21. ADM 199/1188/148.

22. Müllenheim-Rechberg, 132.

23. D. N. Paton, "HMS *Suffolk* Sights and Chases *Bismarck*."

24. Quoted in Ballantyne, 99.

25. Coles and Briggs, 203.

26. Briggs, IWM Sound Archive 10751.

27. Zetterling and Tamelander, *Bismarck*, 155.

28. Coles and Briggs, 208.

29. Coles and Briggs, 204.

30. Briggs, IWM Sound Archive 10751.

31. Osborne, IWM Sound Archive 8256.

32. Osborne, IWM Sound Archive 8256.

33. Coles and Briggs, 205.

34. Briggs, IWM Sound Archive 10751.

35. Coles and Briggs, 206.

36. Briggs, IWM Sound Archive 10751.

37. Tilburn, IWM Sound Archive 11746.

38. Tilburn, IWM Sound Archive 11746.

39. In his memoir, Briggs refers to the platform compass as a stage-like setting: Coles and Briggs, 205.

40. Coles and Briggs, 207.

41. Coles and Briggs, 207.

42. Coles and Briggs, 207.

43. Coles and Briggs, 208.

44. Ballantyne, 69.

45. Cain, 74.

46. Cain, 75.

47. Müllenheim-Rechberg, 133.

48. Müllenheim-Rechberg, 133.

49. ADM 199/1188/148.

50. ADM 199/1188/148.

51. Müllenheim-Rechberg, 134.

52. Müllenheim-Rechberg, 134.

53. Müllenheim-Rechberg, 134.

54. Coles and Briggs, 209.

55. Coles and Briggs, 208.

56. Coles and Briggs, 208.

57. Briggs, IWM Sound Archive 10751.

58. Briggs, IWM Sound Archive 10751.

59. Coles and Briggs, 210.

60. Osborne, IWM Sound Archive 8256.

61. Bassett, *Battle Cruisers* (Kindle edition).

62. Osborne, IWM Sound Archive 8256.

63. Bassett, *Battle Cruisers* (Kindle edition).

64. Coles and Briggs, 210.

65. "Blue pendant four," ships turn 40 degrees to starboard: Kemp, 168; only forward guns could be brought to bear: Coles and Briggs, 211.

66. Müllenheim-Rechberg, 135–136.

67. Müllenheim-Rechberg, 137–138.

68. Coles and Briggs, 209–210.

69. Roskill, 398.

70. Briggs, IWM Sound Archive 10751.

71. Norman, 81.

72. Briggs, IWM Sound Archive 10751.

73. Briggs, IWM Sound Archive 10751.

74. Briggs, IWM Sound Archive 10751.

75. Gaynor, IWM Sound Archive 8246.

76. Gaynor, IWM Sound Archive 8246.

77. Coles and Briggs, 212.

78. Coles and Briggs, 212.

79. Müllenheim-Rechberg, 138.

80. Müllenheim-Rechberg, 139.

81. Müllenheim-Rechberg, 139.

82. Müllenheim-Rechberg, 139.

83. McMullen, IWM Sound Archive 10975.

84. Zetterling and Tamelander, *Bismarck*, 169.

85. Coles and Briggs, 214.

86. Müllenheim-Rechberg, 150.

87. Zetterling and Tamelander, *Bismarck*, 167.

88. Zetterling and Tamelander, *Bismarck*, 167.

89. Müllenheim-Rechberg, 139.

90. Müllenheim-Rechberg, 139.

91. Coles and Briggs, 214.

92. Briggs, IWM Sound Archive 10751.

93. Gaynor, IWM Sound Archive 8246.

94. Briggs, IWM Sound Archive 10751.

95. Tilburn testimony. "Report on the Loss of HMS *Hood*." HMS *Hood* Association (ADM 116/4351).

96. Zetterling and Tamelander, *Bismarck*, 169.

97. Coles and Briggs, 215.

98. Leach testimony. "Report on the Loss of HMS *Hood*." HMS *Hood* Association (ADM 116/4351).

99. Quoted in Müllenheim-Rechberg, 143.

100. Quoted in Müllenheim-Rechberg. 143.

101. Müllenheim-Rechberg, 142.

102. Müllenheim-Rechberg, 142.

103. KBismarck.com, *Bismarck* War Diary, May 24, 1941.

104. McCullen, IWM Sound Archive 10975.

105. McCullen, IWM Sound Archive 10975.

106. Briggs, IWM Sound Archive 10751.

107. Briggs, IWM Sound Archive 10751.

108. Coles and Briggs, 216.

109. Tilburn, IWM Sound Archive 11746.

110. Tilburn quoted in Coles and Briggs, 219.

111. Tilburn, IWM Sound Archive 11746.

112. Tilburn, IWM Sound Archive 11746.

113. Coles and Briggs, 216.

114. Coles and Briggs, 216.

115. Coles and Briggs, 216.

116. Briggs, IWM Sound Archive 10751.

117. Tilburn, IWM Sound Archive 11746; Coles and Briggs, 219.

118. Tilburn, IWM Sound Archive 11746; Coles and Briggs, 219.

119. Tilburn, IWM Sound Archive 11746.

120. Coles and Briggs, 216.

121. Briggs, IWM Sound Archive 10751.

122. Coles and Briggs, 217.

123. Briggs, IWM Sound Archive 10751.

124. Briggs, IWM Sound Archive 10751.

125. Coles and Briggs, 217.

126. Water has four-inch coat of oil on it, Briggs swims to raft: Coles and Briggs, 217; "When I turned again": Briggs, HMS *Hood* Association.

127. Tilburn, IWM Sound Archive 11746.

128. Tilburn, IWM Sound Archive 11746.

129. BBC News, "Remembering HMS *Hood*, the Mighty Warship Launched in Clydebank."

130. Coles and Briggs, 217–218.

131. Checketts, IWM Sound Archive 32390.

132. Osborne, IWM Sound Archive 8256.

133. Müllenheim-Rechberg, 146.

134. Müllenheim-Rechberg, 146.

135. Ballantyne, 85.

136. Ballantyne, 85–86.

137. Müllenheim-Rechberg, 146, 147.

138. Zetterling and Tamelander, *Bismarck*, 176.

139. Quoted in Ballantyne, 83.

140. Quoted in Ballantyne, 83.

141. Quoted in Ballantyne, 84.

142. Ballantyne, 84.

143. Ballantyne, 87.

144. ADM 199/1188/150.

145. ADM 199/1188/150.

146. Osborne, IWM Sound Archive 8256.

147. Osborne, IWM Sound Archive 8256.

148. Osborne, IWM Sound Archive 8256.

149. Osborne, IWM Sound Archive 8256.

150. Müllenheim-Rechberg, 150, 151.

151. Zetterling and Tamelander, *Bismarck*, 185.

152. Zetterling and Tamelander, *Bismarck*, 187.

153. Tilburn, IWM Sound Archive 11746.

154. Coles and Briggs, 219, 220.

155. Tilburn, IWM Sound Archive 11746.

156. Quoted in Coles and Briggs, 218.

157. Tilburn, IWM Sound Archive 11746.

158. Coles and Briggs, 218.

159. Briggs, IWM Sound Archive 10751.

160. Tilburn, IWM Sound Archive 11746.

161. Coles and Briggs, 218.

162. Coles and Briggs, 219.

163. Cain, 77.

164. Cain, 76.
165. Cain, 77.
166. Cain, 76.
167. Cain, 76.
168. Quoted in Cain, 77.
169. Taylor, HMS *Hood* Association (see reference in bibliography under "Online Articles and Resources").
170. Taylor, HMS *Hood* Association.
171. Taylor, HMS *Hood* Association.
172. Cain, 79, 80.
173. Cain, 79.
174. Tilburn, IWM Sound Archive 11746.
175. Briggs, IWM Sound Archive 10751.
176. Taylor, HMS *Hood* Association.
177. Tilburn, IWM Sound Archive 11746.
178. Coles and Briggs, 221.
179. Tilburn, IWM Sound Archive 11746.
180. Tilburn, IWM Sound Archive 11746.
181. Briggs, IWM Sound Archive 10751.
182. Briggs, IWM Sound Archive 10751.
183. Cain, 81.
184. Cain, 81.
185. Taylor, HMS *Hood* Association.
186. Coles and Briggs, 224.
187. Tilburn, IWM Sound Archive 11746.
188. Tilburn, IWM Sound Archive 11746.

CHAPTER 3: THE HUNTED

1. Churchill, vol. 3, 246.
2. Hoyt, 4.
3. Churchill, vol. 3, 246.
4. Bishop, 28.
5. Roberts, 657.
6. Roberts, 657.
7. ADM 199/1188/220.
8. ADM 199/1188/220.
9. *Prince of Wales* can muster no more than 27 knots: ADM 199/1188/022; German ships flee on a southwesterly course with British ships in pursuit: ADM 199/1188/220; 400 tons of water in *Prince of Wales*: Willis (Kindle edition).
10. Bishop, 28.

11. ADM 199/1188/085.

12. ADM 199/1188/086.

13. ADM 199/1188/221.

14. ADM 199/1188/221.

15. Müllenheim-Rechberg, 158.

16. Müllenheim-Rechberg, 158.

17. Plans to detach: KBismarck.com, *Bismarck* War Diary, May 24, 1941 (see reference details in bibliography under "On Articles and Resources"); *Bismarck* relays plan to *Prinz Eugen* at 2:20 p.m. via semaphore lamp, "HOOD": Busch, *Prinz Eugen*, 71.

18. KBismarck.com, *Bismarck* War Diary, May 24, 1442 hours.

19. Zetterling and Tamelander, *Bismarck*, 191.

20. KBismarck.com, *Bismarck* War Diary, May 24, 1540 hours.

21. KBismarck.com, *Bismarck* War Diary, May 24, 1540/1559 hours.

22. Busch, *Prinz Eugen*, 71.

23. KBismarck.com, *Bismarck* War Diary, May 24, 1722 hours.

24. ADM 199/1188/223.

25. ADM 199/1188/223.

26. KBismarck.com, *Bismarck* War Diary, May 24, 1814 hours.

27. Busch, *Prinz Eugen*, 74.

28. Busch, *Prinz Eugen*, 76.

29. ADM 199/1188/223.

30. Quoted in Ballantyne, 102.

31. Quoted in Müllenheim-Rechberg, 163.

32. D. N. Paton, "HMS *Suffolk* Sights and Chases *Bismarck*."

33. Quoted in Ballantyne, 102.

34. ADM 199/1188/223.

35. ADM 199/1188/223.

36. Müllenheim-Rechberg, 164.

37. ADM 199/1188/086.

38. ADM 199/1188/022; ADM 199/1188/086.

39. ADM 199/1188/154.

40. Bunce, IWM Sound Archive 14298.

41. ADM 199/1188/154.

42. Zetterling and Tamelander, *Bismarck*, 199.

43. ADM 199/1188/154.

44. Jackson, IWM Sound Archive 15562.

45. Patrick Jackson firsthand account (see reference details in bibliography under "Online Articles and Resources").

46. ADM 199/1188/154.

47. ADM 199/1188/154; Zetterling and Tamelander, *Bismarck*, 200.

48. Bunce, IWM Sound Archive 14298.

49. T. R. Sargent and Captain B. M. Chiswell, "Encounter with the German Battleship *Bismarck*" (see reference details in bibliography under "Online Articles and Resources").

50. Sargent and Chiswell, "Encounter with the German Battleship *Bismarck*."

51. Sargent and Chiswell, "Encounter with the German Battleship *Bismarck*."

52. Sargent and Chiswell, "Encounter with the German Battleship *Bismarck*."

53. Sargent and Chiswell, "Encounter with the German Battleship *Bismarck*."

54. Sargent and Chiswell, "Encounter with the German Battleship *Bismarck*."

55. Müllenheim-Rechberg, 167.

56. Müllenheim-Rechberg, 166, 167.

57. Sargent and Chiswell, "Encounter with the German Battleship *Bismarck*."

58. Bunce, IWM Sound Archive 14298.

59. Jackson, IWM Sound Archive 15562.

60. Jackson, IWM Sound Archive 15562.

61. Zetterling and Tamelander, *Bismarck*, 201.

62. Müllenheim-Rechberg, 167.

63. Bunce, IWM Sound Archive 14298.

64. Ballantyne, 109; Sayer, IWM Sound Archive 18574.

65. Sayer, IWM Sound Archive 18574.

66. Ballantyne, 110.

67. Sayer, IWM Sound Archive 18574.

68. Nuts and bolts in engine room, Kurt Kirchberg death: Zetterling and Tamelander, *Bismarck*, 203; "something hard," ship's first casualty: Müllenheim-Rechberg, 168.

69. Müllenheim-Rechberg, 168.

70. Sargent and Chiswell, "Encounter with the German Battleship *Bismarck*."

71. Sargent and Chiswell, "Encounter with the German Battleship *Bismarck*."

72. ADM 199/1188/154.

73. Jackson, IWM Sound Archive 15562.

74. Quoted in Zetterling and Tamelander, *Bismarck*, 204.

75. ADM 199/1188/154.

76. Ballantyne, 111; ADM 199/1188/154.

77. Müllenheim-Rechberg, 169.

78. KBismarck.com, *Bismarck* War Diary, May 25, 0240 hours.

79. Müllenheim-Rechberg, 169.

80. KBismarck.com, *Bismarck* War Diary, May 25, 1228 hours.

81. *Prince of Wales, Norfolk* reestablish visual contact with *Bismarck*: ADM 199/1188/225; disappears in funnel smoke: ADM 199/1188/247.

82. Müllenheim-Rechberg, 172.

83. Quoted in Ballantyne, 113.

84. ADM 199/1188/225.

85. Disposition of ships: ADM 199/1188/225; *Suffolk* zig-zagging, *Bismarck* vanishing and reappearing on her radar: Zetterling and Tamelander, *Bismarck*, 210.

86. Ellis running on coffee and pills: Zetterling and Tamelander, *Bismarck*, 210; expected to reestablish contact at 3:30: Müllenheim-Rechberg, 174.

87. ADM 199/1188/023.

88. D. N. Paton, "HMS *Suffolk* Sights and Chases *Bismarck*."

89. ADM 199/1188/225.

90. ADM 199/1188/226.

91. ADM 199/1188/023.

92. ADM 199/1188/023.

93. ADM 199/1188/023–024.

94. hearing stations in Britain, Iceland, Gibraltar: Müllenheim-Rechberg, 180; "that appeared to come from the same ship": ADM 199/1188/024.

95. ADM 199/1188/91.

96. ADM 199/1188/024.

97. Quoted in Zetterling and Tamelander, *Bismarck*, 222–223.

98. Müllenheim-Rechberg, 180, 183.

99. Jane Fawcett obituary, *Telegraph*, May 25, 2016.

100. Jane Fawcett obituary, *Washington Post*, May 28, 2016.

101. Fawcett obituary, *Washington Post*.

102. Fawcett obituary, *Telegraph*.

103. Quoted in Fawcett obituary, *Telegraph*.

104. Fawcett obituary, *Telegraph*.

105. Fawcett obituary, *Telegraph*.

106. ADM 199/1188/024.

107. "The Scouting and Search for *Bismarck*," Naval History and Heritage Command. (see reference details in bibliography under "Online Articles and Resources")

108. "The Scouting and Search for *Bismarck*," Naval History and Heritage Command.

109. "The Scouting and Search for *Bismarck*," Naval History and Heritage Command.

110. "The Scouting and Search for *Bismarck*," Naval History and Heritage Command.

111. "The American Who Helped Sink the *Bismarck*," *People Magazine*, June 3, 1974.

112. "The Scouting and Search for *Bismarck*," Naval History and Heritage Command.

113. "The Scouting and Search for *Bismarck*," Naval History and Heritage Command.

114. "The Scouting and Search for *Bismarck*," Naval History and Heritage Command.

115. "The Scouting and Search for *Bismarck*," Naval History and Heritage Command.

116. Zetterling and Tamelander, *Bismarck*, 232.

117. "The Scouting and Search for *Bismarck*," Naval History and Heritage Command.

118. Hough, 107.

CHAPTER 4: AVENGED

1. ADM 199/1188/181.

2. Müllenheim-Rechberg, 201; ADM 199/1188/024–025.

3. ADM 199/1188/025.

4. ADM 199/1188/024, 156; Zetterling and Tamelander, *Bismarck*, 157.

5. *London Gazette*, April 9, 1940.

6. ADM 199/1188/025.

7. ADM 199/1188/181.

8. ADM 199/1188/180–181.

9. Bishop, 33; ADM 199/1188/181.

10. Quoted in Bishop, 34.

11. ADM 199/1188/169.

12. ADM 199/1188/181.

13. Swordfish take off at 2:50 p.m.: ADM 199/1188/169; "The take offs were awesome in the extreme": quoted in Bishop, 34.

14. ADM 199/1188/158.

15. Ballantyne, 139.

16. Bassett, *HMS* Sheffield, 94.

17. Ballantyne, 139.

18. Zetterling and Tamelander, *Bismarck*, 384.

19. Battle Summary No. 5: *Chase and Sinking of* Bismarck (see Page, vol. 1, sec. 26, 22).

20. Bassett, *HMS* Sheffield, 94.

21. ADM 199/1188/182.

22. Moffat, 296.

23. ADM 199/1188/182.

24. Battle Summary No. 5: *Chase and Sinking of* Bismarck (see Page, vol. 1, sec. 26, 22).

25. Captain Edmund "Splash" Carver obituary, *Telegraph*, Sept. 11, 2001.

26. Planes emerge four miles from ship: Battle Summary No. 5: *Chase and Sinking of* Bismarck (see Page, vol. 1, sec. 26); "We came out of the cloud base": Carver obituary, *Telegraph*.

27. Müllenheim-Rechberg, 206.

28. Coode seeks better angle of attack, crews attack in pairs, threes, individually: ADM 199/1188/182; gun-layer overcome at his post: *German Battleship* Bismarck *Interrogation of Survivors* (see Page, vol. 1, sec. 3, 19).

29. Moffat, 299–300.

30. Moffat, 299.

31. Moffat, 301.

32. Moffat, 302.

33. Moffat, 302–303.

34. Ken Pattison obituary, *Daily Telegraph*, Aug. 8, 2002.

35. Müllenheim-Rechberg, 206.

36. Pattison obituary, *Daily Telegraph*.

37. KBismarck.com, Georg Herzog Survivor Statement (see reference details in bibliography under "Online Articles and Resources").

38. Müllenheim-Rechberg, 208.

39. Georg Herzog Survivor Statement.

40. KBismarck.com, *Bismarck* War Diary, May 26, 1941, 2345 hours (see reference details in bibliography under "Online Articles and Resources").

41. ADM 199/1188/098.

42. Bassett, *HMS* Sheffield, 95.

43. Bassett, *HMS* Sheffield, 95.

44. Bassett, *HMS* Sheffield, 95; Battle Summary No. 5: *Chase and Sinking of* Bismarck (see Page, vol. 1, sec. 26, 24).

45. ADM 199/1188/098–099.

46. ADM 199/1188/025-026.

47. Battle Summary No. 5: *Chase and Sinking of* Bismarck (see Page, vol. 1, sec. 35, 30).

48. ADM 199/1188/026.

49. Müllenheim-Rechberg, 217.

50. Battle Summary No. 5: *Chase and Sinking of* Bismarck (see Page, vol. 1, sec. 29, 25).

51. Battle Summary No. 5: *Chase and Sinking of* Bismarck (see Page, vol. 1, sec. 29, 25).

52. Destroyers launch torpedo attacks: ADM 199/1188/026; "We would have totally": Müllenheim-Rechberg, 219.

53. Firing of British star shells: ADM 199/1188/026; "The minutes crept past": Müllenheim-Rechberg, 225.

54. KBismarck.com, *Bismarck* War Diary, May 27, 0223 hours.

55. Battle Summary No. 5: *Chase and Sinking of* Bismarck (see Page, vol. 1, sec. 35, 31).

56. ADM 199/1188/228; "a dark grey blot of a large ship": Battle Summary No. 5: *Chase and Sinking of* Bismarck (see Page, vol. 1, sec. 35, 31.).

57. ADM 199/1188/228.

58. ADM 199/1188/228.

59. ADM 199/1188/162.

60. Müllenheim-Rechberg, 246.

61. Schneider orders main batteries aimed at *Rodney*: Müllenheim-Rechberg, 246; *Rodney* opens fire at 8:47 a.m., *Bismarck* turns to starboard and opens fire: ADM 199/1188/162.

62. First salvos fall short, third and fourth straddle *Rodney*: Battle Summary No. 5: *Chase and Sinking of* Bismarck (see Page, vol. 1, sec. 38); "Her fire was accurate at the start": ADM 199/1188/027.

63. *Norfolk* joins battle five minutes after first shots fired: ADM 199/1188/228; *Dorsetshire* opens fire: ADM 199/1188/209.

64. ADM 199/1188/027, 162.

65. ADM 199/1188/027–028.

66. *German Battleship* Bismarck *Interrogation of Survivors* (see Page, vol. 1. sec. 6, 22).

67. *German Battleship* Bismarck *Interrogation of Survivors* (see Page, vol. 1, sec. 6, 22).

68. *German Battleship* Bismarck *Interrogation of Survivors* (see Page, vol. 1, sec. 6, 22).

69. *German Battleship* Bismarck *Interrogation of Survivors* (see Page, vol. 1, sec. 6, 22).

70. ADM 199/1188/162.

71. *Bismarck* a burning nightmare by 10:15 a.m.: ADM 199/1188/162–163; "Men could be seen": ADM 199/1188/163.

72. Müllenheim-Rechberg, 260.

73. Arthur, *Second World War*, 144.

74. Arthur, *Second World War*, 144.

75. Arthur, *Second World War*, 144.

76. Arthur, *Second World War*, 141.

77. Arthur, *Second World War*, 141.

78. Arthur, *Second World War*, 141.

79. Müllenheim-Rechberg, 272.

80. Müllenheim-Rechberg, 277.

81. Müllenheim-Rechberg, 277.

82. Müllenheim-Rechberg, 279.

83. KBismarck.com, Bruno Rzonca Survivor Interview (see reference details in bibliography under "Online Articles and Resources").

84. Rzonca Survivor Interview.

85. Rzonca Survivor Interview.

86. Rzonca Survivor Interview.

87. Müllenheim-Rechberg, 282.

88. Müllenheim-Rechberg, 282.

89. Rzonca Survivor Interview.

90. Rzonca Survivor Interview.

91. ADM 199/1188/210.

92. ADM 199/1188/210.

93. Wheeler, IWM Sound Archive 21734.

94. Rzonca Survivor Interview.

95. *German Battleship* Bismarck *Interrogation of Survivors* (see Page, vol. 1, sec. 6, 24).

96. Arthur, *Second World War*, 144.

97. Arthur, *Second World War*, 144.

98. Arthur, *Second World War*, 141.

99. ADM 199/1188/210

100. ADM 199/1188/210.

101. Wheeler, IWM Sound Archive 21734.

102. Müllenheim-Rechberg, 299.

CHAPTER 5: CERBERUS

1. Busch, *Prinz Eugen*, 110.

2. Busch, *Prinz Eugen*, 110.

3. Air Ministry, *Bomber Command*, 78.

4. ADM 186/803/006.

5. Garrett, 79.

6. Roberts, 574.

7. Garrett, 79–80.

8. Philippon reports *Scharnhorst* preparing to leave, makes journey at 30 knots: Garrett, 83; old tanker placed in vacated anchorage: Read, 57.

9. Middlebrook, 184.

10. AIR 27/98/11; Middlebrook, 184.

11. Middlebrook, 184.

12. Air Ministry, *Bomber Command*, 79.

13. Read, 58.

14. Middlebrook, 184.

15. AIR 27/379/10.

16. Ernie Constable Firsthand Account (see reference details in bibliography under "Online Resources and Articles").

17. AIR 27/379/10.

18. AIR 27/379/10.

19. Greaves asks crew to take another pass: Ernie Constable Firsthand Account; "seen to obtain a direct hit": AIR 27/379/10.

20. Ernie Constable Firsthand Account.

21. Ernie Constable Firsthand Account.

22. Read, 59.

23. Middlebrook, 185.

24. Garrett, 83–84.

25. "dropped nearly 1,200 tons of high explosives": Busch, *Prinz Eugen*, 117.

26. ADM 186/803/006.

27. Robertson, 40.

28. Raeder, 360.

29. ADM 186/803/006.

30. ADM 186/803/13.

31. ADM 186/803/13.

32. Ford, *Gauntlet*, 23.

33. AIR 20/3061/058.

34. AIR 20/3061/14.

35. ADM 186/803/11.

36. ADM 186/803/12.

37. Garrett, 90.

38. Robertson, 59.

39. Robertson, 59.

40. Ciliax meets with senior commanders: Robertson, 60; departure time and schedule to reach Strait of Dover: ADM 186/803/12.

41. Robertson, 60.

42. Busch, *Prinz Eugen*, 128.

43. ADM 186/803/16.

44. ADM 186/803/16.

45. Busch, *Prinz Eugen*, 132.

46. Fighter cover appears at 7:45: ADM 186/803/16; anticipating the enemy, recognition flairs, "dipping their wings in salute": Ford, *Gauntlet*, 34.

47. ADM 186/803/16.

48. Robertson, 81.

49. ADM 186/803/16.

50. Ford, *Gauntlet*, 40.

51. Beamish and Boyd chase Bf 109s: Ford, *Gauntlet*, 40; "We chased them full throttle": quoted in Ford, *Gauntlet*, 40; "We were about five miles": quoted in Ford, *Gauntlet*, 41.

52. Ships and enemy fighters fire on Beamish and Boyd, red and green tracers, escape without injury: Ford, *Gauntlet*, 41; Beamish and Boyd land at 11:09, report passed along to Dover, less than an hour to the Strait of Dover: ADM 186/803/16; "Their sudden appearance": ADM 186/803/16.

53. "25 to 30 vessels": ADM 186/803/16; MTBs put to sea, orders issued to destroyers: ADM 186/803/17.

54. Coastal batteries alerted shortly after noon: Robertson, 83; officers crowd observation posts trying to glimpse ships: Ford, *Gauntlet*, 44.

55. Quoted in Robertson, 83.

56. Battery opens fire at 12:18 p.m.: ADM 186/803/16; the South Foreland Battery: Ford, *Gauntlet*, 45.

57. Ford, *Gauntlet*, 45.

58. ADM 186/803/18.

59. ADM 186/803/18.

60. ADM 186/803/18.

61. ADM 186/803/18.

62. Plans to smash through E-boat screen: ADM 186/803/18; "knowing when the risks": Callo and Wilson, 255.

63. ADM 186/803/18.

64. ADM 186/803/18.

65. R. J. Mitchell, "The Motor Torpedo Boats" (see reference details in bibliography under "Online Resources and Articles").

66. R. J. Mitchell, "The Motor Torpedo Boats."

67. ADM 186/803/18.

68. ADM 186/803/18.

69. ADM 186/803/18.

70. ADM 186/803/18.

71. ADM 186/803/19.

72. Kingsmill, IWM Sound Archive 9735.

73. Ford, *Gauntlet*, 52.

74. Kingsmill, IWM Sound Archive 9735.

75. Winton, *Victoria Cross at Sea*, 206.

76. Pat Kingsmill obituary, *Telegraph*, Feb. 6, 2003.

77. Kingsmill, IWM Sound Archive 9735.

78. AIR 20/3061/033.

79. Bunce, IWM Sound Archive 14298.

80. ADM 186/803/20.

81. ADM 186/803/20.

82. Kingsmill, IWM Sound Archive 9735.

83. ADM 186/803/20.

84. Kingsmill, IWM Sound Archive 9735.

85. ADM 186/803/20; Ford, *Gauntlet*, 58.

86. Jacobs, 68.

87. Bunce, IWM Sound Archive 14298.

88. Bunce, IWM Sound Archive 14298.

89. Bunce, IWM Sound Archive 14298.

90. Kingsmill, IWM Sound Archive 9735.

91. Motor torpedo boat pulls men out of the water: ADM 186/803/20; "Someone handed me a cup of rum," transferred to hospital, Bunce unscathed: Bunce, IWM Sound Archive 14298.

92. ADM 186/803/20.

93. "Running well," plane damage, crashes into Channel: ADM 186/803/20; Lee pulls Rose from plane, air gunner Johnson goes down with plane: ADM 186/803/20; Ford, *Gauntlet*, 58.

94. ADM 186/803/20; Ford, *Gauntlet*, 59.

95. ADM 186/803/20.

96. Quoted in Garrett, 104.

97. Quoted in Robertson, 122.

98. ADM 186/803/21.

99. ADM 186/803/21.

100. Bomber Command "stood" down and not prepared: Middlebrook, 235; Bomber Command takes three hours to get ready: Garrett, 107.

101. Bomber Command's largest daylight operation thus far: Middlebrook, 235; 242 bombers fly in three waves, only 39 drop their bombs: ADM 186/803/22.

102. Robin Murray Firsthand Account (see reference details in bibliography under "Online Articles and Resources").

103. Murray Firsthand Account.

104. Murray Firsthand Account.

105. Murray Firsthand Account.

106. Murray Firsthand Account.

107. Murray Firsthand Account.

108. Murray Firsthand Account.

109. Murray Firsthand Account.

110. ADM 186/803/22.

111. Mayne, IWM Sound Archive 1835.

112. Mayne, IWM Sound Archive 1835.

113. Beach, IWM Sound Archive 30257.

114. ADM 186/803/22.

115. Busch, *Prinz Eugen*, 140–141.

116. ADM 186/803/23.

117. Destroyers off Hook of Holland, ships under Pizey's command: ADM 186/803/15; "main bearings commenced to run": ADM 186/803/21.

118. Garrett, 109.

119. ADM 186/803/23.

120. ADM 186/803/24.

121. ADM 186/803/23.

122. ADM 186/803/23.

123. Quoted in Garrett, 109.

124. ADM 186/803/24.

125. Quoted in Robertson, 143.

126. ADM 186/803/24.

127. ADM 186/803/24.

128. ADM 186/803/25.

129. Robertson, 145.

130. ADM 186/803/25.

131. Quoted in Robertson, 144.

132. ADM 186/803/25.

133. ADM 186/803/26.

134. Quoted in Robertson, 146.

135. *Campbell* full speed astern to avoid torpedoes, casualties pulled from the water: ADM 186/803/26; total casualties among *Worcester*'s crew: Garrett, 110.

136. Mackay fires torpedoes, *Prinz Eugen* swerves to avoid air attack: ADM 186/803/25; "The mixture of aircraft": quoted in Robertson, 146.

137. ADM 186/803/26.

138. ADM 186/803/26.

139. ADM 186/803/27.

140. ADM 186/803/27.

141. ADM 186/803/27.

142. Ford, *Gauntlet*, 71; Robertson, 165.

143. ADM 186/803/27.

144. "covered with drift ice": Busch, *Prinz Eugen*, 147; *Gneisenau* and *Prinz Eugen* reach Elbe at 7 a.m.: ADM 186/803/27.

145. Robertson, 165.

146. Quoted in Robertson, 167.

147. Raeder, 361.

148. Raeder, 361.

149. Quoted in Robertson, 167.

150. The exchange between Pound and Churchill is quoted in Robertson, 169.

151. Question of "Why?" reverberates through the country: Robertson, 169; "Vice-Admiral Ciliax has succeeded": Redford, 112.

152. Robertson, 170.

153. Garrett, 111.

154. Robertson, 169, 170.

155. Churchill, vol. 4, 79.

156. AIR 2/7912/002, 022.

157. Lack of advanced notice for Bomber Command, not alerting Admiralty to crew stand down: AIR 2/7912/019; "the enemy's occupation": AIR 2/7912/002; forces insufficient: AIR 2/7912/021.

158. Ford, *Gauntlet*, 75.

159. AIR 2/7912/023.

160. Ford, *Gauntlet*, 75.

161. Robertson, 171.

162. Robertson, 171–172.

CHAPTER 6: CHARIOT

1. Reproduced in Churchill, vol. 4, app. C, 676.

2. British keep four capital ships at the ready: Ford, *St. Nazaire*, 10; "destruction or even crippling": Churchill, vol. 4, 103.

3. Lyman (Kindle edition).

4. DEFE 2/131/077.

5. Phillips, 8.

6. Ministry of Information, *Combined Operations*, 71.

7. Ministry of Information, *Combined Operations*, 71.

8. Ministry of Information, *Combined Operations*, 71.

9. Ford, *St. Nazaire*, 10.

10. Churchill, vol. 2, 208.

11. Ministry of Information, *Combined Operations*, 13, 14.

12. Ryder, 16–17.

13. Cooksey, 58.

14. Phillips, 38–39.

15. Bishop, 92.

16. McRaven, 121.

17. Bishop, 93.

18. Lyman (Kindle edition); McRaven, 121–122; Ryder, 19.

19. McRaven, 120, 121–122.

20. Phillips, 10, 104.

21. Lyman (Kindle edition).

22. Lyman (Kindle edition).

23. "no artillery": Lyman (Kindle edition); weaponry, not equipped for heavy engagement: Cooksey, 70–71; Lyman (Kindle edition).

24. Cooksey, 57.

25. Chant-Sempill, 20.

26. Chant-Sempill, 20.

27. Departure of Chariot Fleet: Ryder postaction report, *London Gazette*, Sept. 30, 1947; Lyman (Kindle edition); Ford, *St. Nazaire*, 47.

28. Ryder postaction report, *London Gazette*.

29. Lyman (Kindle edition).

30. Ryder, 40.

31. Purdon, 31.

32. Purdon, 31.

33. DEFE 2/131/092.

34. Gordon Holman report reproduced in *The War Illustrated*, vol. 5, no. 127 (May 1, 1942): 669–671. (see reference details in bibliography under "Online Articles and Resources")

35. Batteson, IWM Sound Archive 22668.

36. Phillips, 111.

37. Ryder postaction report, *London Gazette*.

38. White ensigns lowered, German ensigns hoisted: Ryder postaction report, *London Gazette*; "duffle coats and steel helmets": DEFE 2/131/011.

39. Purdon, 31.

40. Ryder postaction report, *London Gazette*; Ford, *St. Nazaire*, 35.

41. "on the horizon to the north": Ryder, 40; *Tynedale* spots sub, dispatched to investigate: Ryder postaction report, *London Gazette*.

42. Ryder post-action report, *London Gazette*.

43. Dorrian (Kindle edition).

44. Ryder postaction report, *London Gazette.*

45. Ryder postaction report, *London Gazette.*

46. Ryder postaction report, *London Gazette.*

47. Ryder postaction report, *London Gazette.*

48. Ryder postaction report, *London Gazette.*

49. Ryder postaction report, *London Gazette.*

50. Ryder postaction report, *London Gazette.*

51. Phillips, 117.

52. Ryder postaction report, *London Gazette*; Ryder, 45, 51; Ford, *St. Nazaire*, 51.

53. Ryder postaction report, *London Gazette*; Ford, *St. Nazaire*, 52–53.

54. Ryder, 46.

55. Quoted in Phillips, 122.

56. Ryder postaction report, *London Gazette.*

57. Ryder, 46.

58. Middlebrook, 251.

59. Ryder, 47.

60. Lyman (Kindle edition).

61. Dorrian (Kindle edition).

62. Raid arouses Mecke's suspicions: DEFE 2/125/113; "The conduct of the enemy aircraft," orders antiaircraft batteries to silence guns and kill searchlights: Phillips, 129.

63. DEFE 2/125/113.

64. Paton, BBC WW2 People's War.

65. Sugarman, Jewish Virtual Library. (see reference details in bibliography under "Online Articles and Resources")

66. "Frank Arkle RNVR," SWWEC. (see reference details in bibliography under "Online Articles and Resources")

67. Lyman (Kindle edition).

68. Lyman (Kindle edition).

69. *Campbeltown* running aground a primary concern: Ryder, 47; "an unusually high spring tide": Kemp, 188.

70. Kemp, 188.

71. "We were wondering": Roberts, IWM Sound Archive 22671; "If we'd got stuck": Arthur, *Second World War*, 184.

72. German patrol boat appears, "We held our course": Phillips, 126; "could see German sailors . . . the order to open fire": Sugarman, Jewish Virtual Library.

73. Phillips, 126.

74. "between Le Pointeau and Pointe de Mindin": Dorrian (Kindle edition); Burhenne spots strike force heading upriver: Phillips, 126.

75. Phillips, 126.

76. Phillips, 130.

77. Guns of the 280th Naval Artillery Battalion along north shore, covering stretch of deep water leading to port: Dorrian (Kindle edition); Dieckmann signals batteries at 1:15 a.m. to stand-by to attack naval targets: Phillips, 130–131.

78. Ford, *St. Nazaire*, 39.

79. Ryder, 47.

80. Ryder, 48.

81. Ryder, 48.

82. Ryder postaction report, *London Gazette*.

83. Lyman (Kindle edition).

84. Phillips, 133.

85. Lyman (Kindle edition).

86. Lyman (Kindle edition).

87. Holman, *The War Illustrated*.

88. Dorrian (Kindle edition).

89. Phillips, 134.

90. DEFE 2/125/80.

91. "Frank Arkle RNVR," SWWEC.

92. Arthur, *Second World War*, 185.

93. Phillips, 135.

94. Batteson, IWM Sound Archive 22668.

95. Batteson, IWM Sound Archive 22668.

96. Phillips, 135.

97. Cooksey, 62.

98. Ryder postaction report, *London Gazette*.

99. Holman, *The War Illustrated*.

100. Ford, *St. Nazaire*, 41; Lyman (Kindle edition).

101. Able Seaman Bill Savage fires on *Botilla Russ*: Lyman (Kindle edition); 200 yards: Ryder, 49.

102. Ryder, 49.

103. Lyman (Kindle edition).

104. Lyman (Kindle edition).

105. Phillips, 137.

106. Cooksey, 62.

107. Chant-Sempill, 34.

108. Chant-Sempill, 34.

109. Phillips, 139.

110. Paton, BBC WW2 People's War.

111. Paton, BBC WW2 People's War.

112. *Campbeltown* fires at *Botilla Russ*: Holman, *The War Illustrated*; "She was surrounded by shell splashes": Lyman (Kindle edition).

113. Sugarman, Jewish Virtual Library.

114. Dorrian (Kindle edition).

115. Phillips, 141.

116. Phillips, 140.

117. Phillips, 141.

118. Ship protrudes 35 feet into dry dock: Cooksey, 63; "Four minutes late": Phillips, 141.

CHAPTER 7: DOGS OF WAR

1. Lyman (Kindle edition); Chant-Sempill, 38.

2. Chant-Sempill, 38.

3. Ryder, 64.

4. Phillips, 147.

5. Lyman (Kindle edition).

6. Woodiwiss quoted in Cooksey, 76.

7. Woodiwiss quoted in Cooksey, 76.

8. Woodiwiss quoted in Cooksey, 76.

9. "Lieutenant John Roderick MC," SWWEC.

10. Second objective, a 37mm machine gun: Phillips, 147; "There was a hell of a lot of firing going on": "Lieutenant John Roderick MC," SWWEC.

11. "Lieutenant John Roderick MC," SWWEC.

12. Phillips, 148.

13. Phillips, 149; Ryder, 64.

14. Ford, *St. Nazaire*, 54.

15. Dorrian (Kindle edition).

16. Chant-Sempill, 38; Dorrian (Kindle edition).

17. Phillips, 149.

18. Dorrian (Kindle edition).

19. Ashcroft quoted in Cooksey, 79.

20. Phillips, 149; Lyman (Kindle edition).

21. Lyman (Kindle edition).

22. Ford, *St. Nazaire*, 55.

23. Chant-Sempill, 38.

24. Chant-Sempill, 38.

25. Chant-Sempill, 39.

26. Phillips, 152.

27. Chant-Sempill, 38.

28. Chant-Sempill, 38; Phillips, 152.

29. Chant-Sempill, 39.

30. Chant-Sempill, 39.

31. Montgomery detonates charge, Chant-Sempill and his men enter pump house and see staircase descending 40 feet: Chant-Sempill, 39; interior pitch-black: Phillips, 153.

32. Chant-Sempill, 40.

33. Chant-Sempill, 40, 42.

34. Chant-Sempill's fingers manage the task: Phillips, 155; Chant-Sempill's team places charges in 20 minutes, Chant-Sempill orders Butler and King to carry Chamberlain to safety: Chant-Sempill, 42.

35. Chant-Sempill, 42.

36. Chant-Sempill, 42.

37. Phillips, 155, 157.

38. Chant-Sempill and Dockerill escape with moments to spare: Phillips, 157; force of explosion, slabs of concrete flying into the sky: Chant-Sempill, 43; Phillips, 157.

39. Chant-Sempill and his team return to shattered pump house and drop incendiary bombs, Chant-Sempill, 43–44.

40. Phillips, 158.

41. Phillips, 158.

42. Chant-Sempill, 44.

43. Phillips, 158.

44. Twenty-year-old Purdon and Brett lead teams against winding house and northern caisson: Phillips, 159; Ford, *St. Nazaire*, 58–59; Team led by monocle-wearing Burtinshaw lends support: Phillips, 160; Ford, *St. Nazaire*, 59.

45. Lyman (Kindle edition).

46. De la Torre recollection in McRaven, 157.

47. Purdon, 33–34.

48. Purdon, 34.

49. Phillips, 162.

50. Burtinshaw's team secures charges against caisson wall: Phillips, 162; entry hatch covered by timber-and-tarmac road: Lyman (Kindle edition).

51. Phillips, 163; Ford, *St. Nazaire*, 61.

52. Phillips, 163.

53. McRaven, 135.

54. Phillips, 163.

55. Phillips, 143.

56. Ministry of Information, *Combined Operations*, 79.

57. Ministry of Information, *Combined Operations*, 79.

58. Ministry of Information, *Combined Operations*, 83.

59. Ministry of Information, *Combined Operations*, 83.

60. Ministry of Information, *Combined Operations*, 82.

61. Ministry of Information, *Combined Operations*, 79; Ford, *St. Nazaire*, 63, 66.

62. David Paton obituary, *Daily Telegraph*, Aug. 2, 2008.

63. Paton obituary, *Daily Telegraph*.

64. Paton, BBC WW2 People's War.

65. Paton, BBC WW2 People's War.

66. Paton, BBC WW2 People's War.

67. Paton, BBC WW2 People's War.

68. Paton, BBC WW2 People's War.

69. Paton, BBC WW2 People's War.

70. Paton, BBC WW2 People's War.

71. Billie Stephens obituary, *The Independent*, Aug. 17, 1997.

72. Bishop, 101.

73. Bishop, 101–102.

74. Bishop, 102.

75. Stephens struggles in the current, fights panic, pulls himself out of the water: Bishop, 102; "a very bedraggled bunch," marched into captivity: Lyman (Kindle edition).

76. O'Leary, IWM Sound Archive 11289.

77. O'Leary, IWM Sound Archive 11289.

78. Phillips, 192–293; Lyman (Kindle edition).

79. Swayne, IWM Sound Archive 10231.

80. Swayne, IWM Sound Archive 10231.

81. Swayne, IWM Sound Archive 10231.

82. McRaven, 136; Ford, *St. Nazaire*, 66.

83. Eric de la Torre obituary, *Telegraph*, Sept. 28, 2011.

84. Ford, *St. Nazaire*, 66.

85. "Shells were coming inside": quoted in McRaven, 137; only ML 457 succeeds at landing Commandos at Old Mole: Ryder, 69.

86. De la Torre obituary, *Telegraph*.

87. De la Torre obituary, *Telegraph*.

88. De la Torre obituary, *Telegraph*.

89. De la Torre obituary, *Telegraph*.

90. De la Torre obituary, *Telegraph*.

91. Phillips, 200, 202; Ryder, 67.

92. Phillips, 213.

93. Phillips, 212; Cooksey, 95.

94. Chant-Sempill, 48.

95. Chant-Sempill, 48.

96. Phillips, 214.

97. Chant-Sempill, 48.

98. Ministry of Information, *Combined Operations*, 91.

99. Ministry of Information, *Combined Operations*, 91.

100. Phillips, 216.

101. Grouped into teams of 20: Phillips, 216; "quietly and coolly": DEFE 2/125/028.

102. DEFE 2/125/076.

103. DEFE 2/125/064.

104. Men move out at 3 a.m.: Phillips, 217; Commandos armed with Tommy guns lead the way: Ministry of Information, *Combined Operations*, 91.

105. Men keep to the shadows, sound of enemy fire never abates: Phillips, 218; "Keep going, lads": DEFE 2/125/028.

106. Quoted in Rayment (Kindle edition).

107. Quoted in Rayment (Kindle edition).

108. Purdon, 35.

109. Chant-Sempill, 49.

110. Chant-Sempill, 49, 52.

111. Quoted in Rayment (Kindle edition).

112. DEFE 2/125/027.

113. DEFE 2/125/027.

114. DEFE 2/125/079.

115. DEFE 2/125/079.

116. DEFE 2/125/079.

117. DEFE 2/125/079.

118. Purdon, 35.

119. DEFE 2/125/079.

120. Rayment (Kindle edition).

121. DEFE 2/125/082.

122. Phillips, 222.

123. DEFE 2/125/027.

124. DEFE 2/125/028.

125. DEFE 2/125/77.

126. Phillips, 223.

127. Phillips, 225.

128. Phillips, 225.

129. Phillips, 225.

130. DEFE 2/125/077.

131. DEFE 2/125/077.

132. Saunders (Kindle edition).

133. Saunders (Kindle edition).

134. Saunders (Kindle edition).

135. Phillips, 227.

136. Phillips, 227.

CHAPTER 8: LETHAL PASSAGE

1. Ryder, 56.

2. Those too injured to stand are carried on board MGB 314: Ryder, 56; Ryder orders Rodier in ML 177 to rescue survivors from *Campbeltown*: Lyman (Kindle edition).

3. "Frank Arkle RNVR," SWWEC.

4. "Frank Arkle RNVR," SWWEC.

5. "Frank Arkle RNVR," SWWEC.

6. "Frank Arkle RNVR," SWWEC.

7. "Frank Arkle RNVR," SWWEC.

8. "Frank Arkle RNVR," SWWEC.

9. "Frank Arkle RNVR," SWWEC.

10. "Frank Arkle RNVR," SWWEC.

11. Three men struggle against hypothermia, pulled from water at daybreak: Frank Arkle RNVR," SWWEC; Beattie one of only two officers from *Campbeltown* to survive: Phillips, 230.

12. Ryder, 56.

13. Ministry of Information, *Combined Operations*, 84.

14. Ministry of Information, *Combined Operations*, 84–85.

15. Ministry of Information, *Combined Operations*, 85.

16. Ministry of Information, *Combined Operations*, 85.

17. Ryder, 56.

18. Ministry of Information, *Combined Operations*, 85; Ryder, 56.

19. Ministry of Information, *Combined Operations*, 85.

20. Lord Newborough obituary, *Independent*, Oct. 28, 1998; Wynn, IWM Sound Archive 9721.

21. Newborough obituary, *Independent*.

22. Blast blows Wynn through the wheelhouse, into the bilge, found by Chief Petty Officer Lovegrove: Newborough obituary, *Independent*; "He got hold of me": Wynn, IWM Sound Archive 9721.

23. Wynn, IWM Sound Archive 9721.

24. "Put them up! Put them up!": Wynn, IWM Sound Archive 9721; sent to Colditz: Newborough obituary, *Independent*.

25. MGB pulls away from Old Entrance at 2:30 a.m.: Ryder, 56; sees carnage around Old Mole for the first time, "Good Lord": Cooksey, 91.

26. Ryder, 58; Cooksey, 91.

27. Ryder, 58.

28. Ryder, 58.

29. Ministry of Information, *Combined Operations*, 85–86.

30. Holman, *War Illustrated*, vol. 5, no. 127 (May 1, 1942): 669–671. (see reference details in bibliography under "Online Articles and Resources")

31. Ministry of Information, *Combined Operations*, 86.

32. Ryder, 59.

33. Ford, *St. Nazaire*, 84.

34. Cooksey, 105.

35. Holman, *War Illustrated*, vol. 5, no. 127 (May 1, 1942): 669–671.

36. Ryder, 73.

37. Holman, *War Illustrated*, vol. 5, no. 127 (May 1, 1942): 669–671.

38. Ryder, 73.

39. Pom-pom fire sets German ship alight; Ryder, 73–74; "As we escaped": Holman, *War Illustrated*, vol. 5, no. 127 (May 1, 1942): 669–671.

40. Ryder, 74, 76.

41. Ryder, 74.

42. Ryder, 74.

43. Ryder, 74.

44. Ryder, 76.

45. Ministry of Information, *Combined Operations*, 87–88.

46. Swayne, IWM Sound Archive 10231.

47. Swayne, IWM Sound Archive 10231.

48. Swayne, IWM Sound Archive 10231.

49. Swayne, IWM Sound Archive 10231.

50. Ryder, 77.

51. Batteson, IWM Sound Archive 22668.

52. Cooksey, 106.

53. Cooksey, 106.

54. Batteson, IWM Sound Archive 22668.

55. Ford, *St. Nazaire*, 84.

56. Batteson, IWM Sound Archive 22668.

57. Batteson, IWM Sound Archive 22668.

58. Batteson, IWM Sound Archive 22668.

59. Salisbury, IWM Sound Archive 10251.

60. Salisbury, IWM Sound Archive 10251.

61. Bailey (Kindle edition).

62. Swayne, IWM Sound Archive 10231.

63. Swayne, IWM Sound Archive 10231.

64. Bailey (Kindle edition).

65. Bailey (Kindle edition).

66. Batteson, IWM Sound Archive 22668.
67. Batteson, IWM Sound Archive 22668.
68. Batteson, IWM Sound Archive 22668.
69. Batteson, IWM Sound Archive 22668.
70. Batteson, IWM Sound Archive 22668.
71. Batteson, IWM Sound Archive 22668.
72. Batteson, IWM Sound Archive 22668.
73. Swayne, IWM Sound Archive 10231.
74. Swayne, IWM Sound Archive 10231.
75. Phillips, 242.
76. Swayne, IWM Sound Archive 10231.
77. 20 of the 28 men on board were dead or wounded: Ford, *St. Nazaire*, 94; "I'm afraid we can't go on": Phillips, 242.
78. Batteson, IWM Sound Archive 22668.
79. Batteson, IWM Sound Archive 22668.
80. Batteson, IWM Sound Archive 22668.
81. Batteson, IWM Sound Archive 22668.
82. Batteson, IWM Sound Archive 22668.
83. Phillips, 242.
84. Phillips, 243.
85. Phillips, 242, 243; Swayne, IWM Sound Archive 10231.
86. Lyman (Kindle edition).
87. Boats pull up alongside *Jaguar* to bring prisoners ashore: Lyman (Kindle edition); Swayne feels obliged to thank Paul again, hands over concealed fighting knife: Swayne, IWM Sound Archive 10231.
88. Batteson, IWM Sound Archive 22668.
89. Phillips, 254.
90. Batteson, IWM Sound Archive 22668.
91. Ministry of Information, *Combined Operations*, 95.
92. Ministry of Information, *Combined Operations*, 95.
93. Ministry of Information, *Combined Operations*, 95.
94. Durrant shot 25 times: Cooksey, 107; "as you may wish to recommend him for a high award": Phillips, 244.
95. Cooksey, 107.
96. Royal Navy (see reference details in bibliography under "Online Articles and Resources").
97. Phillips, 278.
98. Holman, *War Illustrated* 5, no. 127 (May 1, 1942): 669–671.
99. DEFE 2/125/116.
100. McRaven, 158, 159.

CHAPTER 9: ARCTIC FIRE

1. Bishop, xxii.

2. Read, 90.

3. AIR 27/143/8.

4. Read, 90; Bennett, IWM Sound Archive 9378.

5. This brief description of the bombardier guiding the pilot comes from research the author did for an earlier book on RAF Bomber Command (see Read, *Killing Skies*).

6. Read, xx.

7. AIR 27/143/8.

8. Bennett, IWM Sound Archive 9378; Read, 91.

9. Bennett, IWM Sound Archive 9378.

10. Bennett brings bomber to 200 feet, sees antiaircraft batteries to the left of aircraft: Read, 90–91; "You couldn't see a thing": Bennett, IWM Sound Archive 9378.

11. Read, 90–91.

12. Bennett, IWM Sound Archive 9378.

13. Read, 90.

14. Read, 91.

15. Bishop, 116.

16. Read, 91.

17. Read, 91.

18. Aircraft refuses to climb: Read, 91; "When I ordered 'Abandon Aircraft'": Bennett, IWM Sound Archive 9378.

19. "Bennett and the *Tirpitz*," RAF Pathfinder Archive (see reference details in bibliography under "Online Articles and Resources").

20. Emergency hatch opened, starboard wing collapses, Bennett holding plane to port as crew bail: Read, 91–92; "And there I was": Bennett, IWM Sound Archive 9378.

21. Bennett, IWM Sound Archive 9378.

22. Bennett, IWM Sound Archive 9378.

23. Bennett, IWM Sound Archive 9378.

24. Read, 92.

25. AIR 27/379/28.

26. Bishop, 119.

27. Read, xx.

28. Bishop, 119.

29. Bishop, 119.

30. German patrol approaches downed aircraft, crew takes cover among the trees: Ian Hewitt obituary, *Yorkshire Post*, Aug. 8, 2015; flight engineer surrenders himself to Germans: Sweetman, 48.

31. AIR 27/143/8.

32. AIR 27/143/8.

33. "Students Find Lost British WW2 Bomber in Norwegian Fjord," *Telegraph*, Dec. 10, 2014.

34. "Students Find Lost British WW2 Bomber in Norwegian Fjord," *Telegraph*.

35. "W1053 TL-G from 35 Squadron" (see reference details in bibliography under "Online Articles and Resources").

36. "W1053 TL-G from 35 Squadron."

CHAPTER 10: TARGET: *TIRPITZ*

1. More than 4 million soldiers, 4,000 tanks: Micallef, "Critical Role of the Arctic Convoys in WWII" (see reference details in bibliography under "Online Articles and Resources"); "urgent and strident": Churchill, vol. 3, 306.

2. Churchill, vol. 3, 318.

3. First Arctic convoy departs on August 17: "Russia Honors First British Convoy, 75 Years On," Reuters, Aug. 31, 2016; 2,500-mile journey, edge of the North Pole: "The Russian Convoys, 1941–1945," National Museums Liverpool (see reference details in bibliography under "Online Articles and Resources").

4. Micallef, "Critical Role of the Arctic Convoys in WWII."

5. Churchill, vol. 3, 311, 313.

6. Micallef, "Critical Role of the Arctic Convoys in WWII."

7. Third of a million tons delivered by end of 1941: "The Story Behind the Journey Churchill Called the 'Worst in the World,'" Gov.co.uk (see reference details in bibliography under "Online Articles and Resources"); "over the top of Scandinavia": Micallef, "Critical Role of the Arctic Convoys in WWII."

8. 100 tons or more of ice on ships: "The Russian Convoys, 1941–1945," National Museums Liverpool; two-minute life expectancy in the water: Micallef, "Critical Role of the Arctic Convoys in WWII."

9. Churchill, vol. 4, 738.

10. Bishop, 125.

11. Micallef, "Critical Role of the Arctic Convoys in WWII."

12. PQ-17 cargo: Dimbleby, 287; 35 merchant ships in PQ-17: Kemp, 240.

13. Dimbleby, 287.

14. "Death of PQ-17," *World War II Magazine*, February 1997.

15. Convoy watched by U-456 and Luftwaffe reconnaissance: "Death of PQ-17"; three merchant ships lost: Kemp, 240.

16. Kemp, 241.

17. Dimbleby, 300, 301.

18. Dimbleby, 301.

19. Thirteen men soon succumb to the elements: Dimbleby, 31; "These . . . had to be unceremoniously pushed overboard": Forth's diary quoted in Irving, 287.

20. Sailor tries to drown himself: Irving, 288; "having a stupefying effect on me": Forth's diary quoted in Irving, 287.

21. Forth's diary quoted in Irving, 287.

22. Irving, 289.

23. Fearnside quoted in Irving, 289.

24. Only 20 of *Hartlebury's* 56-man crew survived: Irving, 291; 12 ships deliver 70,000 tons: Churchill, vol. 4, 225.

25. Hastings, 285, 286.

26. *Tirpitz* put to sea after PQ-17 scattered, only to be recalled: Kemp, 240; "This was one of the most": Churchill, vol. 4, 225.

27. Warren and Benson, 52.

28. Bishop, 59.

29. Bishop, 164, 166.

30. Bishop, 166.

31. Bishop, 179; Warren and Benson, 51.

32. KBismarck.com, *Tirpitz* Timeline.

33. Warren and Benson, 53, 54.

34. Warren and Benson, 54.

35. Warren and Benson, 54.

36. Brewster quoted in Warren and Benson, 56.

37. German plane approaches: Warren and Benson, 55; British take cover below deck, Norwegians try to appear nonchalant: Bishop, 180–181.

38. Warren and Benson, 55.

39. Warren and Benson, 55; Bishop, 181.

40. Brewster quoted in Warren and Benson, 56.

41. Bishop, 181.

42. Bishop, 181.

43. Bishop, 181–182.

44. Warren and Benson, 58.

45. Warren and Benson, 58.

46. Warren and Benson, 58.

47. Warren and Benson, 59.

48. Bishop, 182, 183.

49. Bishop, 184; Warren and Benson, 63.

50. Brewster quoted in Warren and Benson, 63.

51. Brewster quoted in Warren and Benson, 63.

52. Such storms not uncommon, Larsen hopes weather passes: Bishop, 185; "It was just after ten o'clock": Brewster quoted in Warren and Benson, 64.

53. Brewster quoted in Warren and Benson, 64.

54. Warren and Benson, 65, 66.

55. Warren and Benson, 66.

56. Brewster quoted in Warren and Benson, 67.

57. Brewster's account in Warren and Benson, 67–68.

58. Brewster's account in Warren and Benson, 69–70.

59. Warren and Benson, 70–71.

60. Warren and Benson, 71.

61. Warren and Benson, 71.

62. Warren and Benson, 71.

63. Bishop, 190.

64. Bishop, 189.

65. Hitler concerned with situation in Stalingrad: Dimbleby, 345; "50 miles south of Bear Island": Pope, 117.

66. Dimbleby, 345.

67. Bekker, 282.

68. Force sets sail: Bekker, 282; four hours of daylight: O'Hara, 143.

69. Lookout on *Hipper* spots ships shortly 7 a.m., daylight still an hour away: O'Hara, 145; "The light conditions": quoted in Bekker, 284.

70. Bekker, 284; O'Hara, 145.

71. O'Hara, 145; Bassett, *HMS* Sheffield, 149–150.

72. O'Hara, 145; Bassett, *HMS* Sheffield, 150; Bekker, 284.

73. Sherbrooke spots *Hipper*: Bassett, *HMS* Sheffield, 150, and O'Hara, 145; "Am Engaging Convoy": Bekker, 284.

74. McLean and McGibbon (Kindle edition).

75. Sherbrooke's injury: McLean and McGibbon (Kindle edition); feigning torpedo attacks: Bassett, *HMS* Sheffield, 150.

76. Bekker, 283.

77. Bassett, 150; Pope, 188.

78. Pope, 188; Bassett, *HMS* Sheffield, 150; O'Hara, 147.

79. *Lützow* lets convoy pass, "A favorable opportunity": Bekker, 286; *Hipper* encounters *Achates* laying smoke: Kemp, 247.

80. "HMS *Achates*: Report of Proceedings," BBC WW2 People's War.

81. Pope, 195.

82. "HMS *Achates*: Report of Proceedings," BBC WW2 People's War.

83. "HMS *Achates*: Report of Proceedings," BBC WW2 People's War.

84. "HMS *Achates*: Report of Proceedings," BBC WW2 People's War.

85. *Hipper* bearing on port quarter, "never reached the gun": "HMS *Achates*: Report of Proceedings," BBC WW2 People's War; "probably by splinters from a near miss": Pope, 197.

86. "HMS *Achates*: Report of Proceedings," BBC WW2 People's War.

87. "HMS *Achates*: Report of Proceedings," BBC WW2 People's War.

88. 30 men killed, doctor among the dead, crewmembers tend to one another: Pope, 198; water flooding unplugged holes, ship comes to a stop: "HMS *Achates*: Report of Proceedings," BBC WW2 People's War.

89. "HMS *Achates*: Report of Proceedings," BBC WW2 People's War.

90. "HMS *Achates*: Report of Proceedings," BBC WW2 People's War.

91. Kerslake, *Coxswain in the Northern Convoys.* (see reference details in bibliography under "Online Articles and Resources")

92. 1:30 p.m.: "HMS *Achates*: Report of Proceedings," BBC WW2 People's War; Peyton-Jones submerged, climbs onto raft: Pope, 238.

93. Quoted in Pope, 238.

94. Kerslake, *Coxswain in the Northern Convoys.*

95. Kerslake, *Coxswain in the Northern Convoys.*

96. Kerslake, *Coxswain in the Northern Convoys.*

97. Quoted in Pope, 242.

98. "HMS *Achates*: Report of Proceedings," BBC WW2 People's War.

99. Quoted in Pope, 243.

100. Bekker, 286.

101. Bassett, *HMS* Sheffield, 150.

102. Bassett, *HMS* Sheffield, 150.

103. Damage to Hipper: Bassett, *HMS* Sheffield, 151, and Pope, 215; "no unnecessary risk": Bekker, 288.

104. Bekker, 288.

105. Bassett, *HMS* Sheffield, 151.

106. Bassett, *HMS* Sheffield, 151.

107. Bassett, *HMS* Sheffield, 151.

108. Bassett, *HMS* Sheffield, 151.

109. Bassett, *HMS* Sheffield, 151.

110. Bekker, 289.

111. O'Hara, 149–150.

112. Bekker, 290.

113. Bekker, 290–291; Dimbleby, 346.

114. Garrett, 121.

115. Garrett, 122.

116. Order quoted in Pope, 293.

117. Bekker, 235.

118. Quoted in Pope, 295.

119. Quoted in Pope, 295.

CHAPTER 11: X-CRAFT

1. Quoted in Bishop, 221.
2. Bishop, 220–221.
3. Bishop, 221, 223.
4. Quoted in Garrett, 132.
5. Churchill, vol. 4, 741.
6. McRaven, 203.
7. McRaven, 202, 203.
8. ADM 234/347/07.
9. ADM 234/347/07.
10. McRaven, 216.
11. ADM 234/347/08.
12. ADM 234/347/08.
13. ADM 234/347/08.
14. Gallagher, 67.
15. ADM 234/347/08.
16. ADM 234/347/08.
17. ADM 234/347/08.
18. ADM 234/347/08.
19. ADM 234/347/08.
20. ADM 234/347/09.
21. Bishop, 259.
22. Bishop, 259.
23. ADM 234/347/09.
24. ADM 234/347/09; Bishop, 260.
25. X-8 trouble with trim, decision to release charge: ADM 234/347/09; *Lützow*, smallest of the targets: Gallagher, 76.
26. ADM 234/347/09.
27. Gallagher, 77; ADM 234/347/09.
28. ADM 234/347/09.
29. ADM 234/347/09.
30. ADM 234/347/09.
31. ADM 234/347/10.
32. ADM 234/347/11.
33. ADM 234/347/09.
34. Gallagher, 80.
35. Gallagher, 80–81.
36. Gallagher, 82.
37. Gallagher, 82.
38. ADM 234/347/10–11.
39. ADM 234/347/11.

40. ADM 234/347/11.

41. ADM 234/347/11.

42. X-craft depart, navigate minefield: ADM 234/347/11.

43. "Free at last": quoted in Bishop, 269.

44. Quoted in Bishop, 270.

45. X-craft enter Stjernsund channel, X-6 periscope starts to leak: ADM 234/347/11–12; "The defect was to prove": ADM 199/888/002.

46. ADM 199/888/002.

47. ADM 199/888/002.

48. Quoted in Gallagher, 101.

49. Quoted in Gallagher, 101.

50. ADM 199/888/002.

51. Quoted in Gallagher, 100.

52. ADM 199/888/002.

53. Stripped and cleaned periscope: ADM 199/888/003; "We had waited and trained": quoted in Gallagher, 107.

54. Quoted in Gallagher, 108.

55. ADM 199/888/003.

56. Exhaustion wearing on the crew: McRaven, 223; "Once, we passed under": quoted in Warren and Benson, 129.

57. ADM 199/888/003.

58. Gallagher, 113.

59. Gallagher, 115.

60. "keeping just shallow enough to see": McRaven, 224.

61. ADM 199/888/003.

62. Bishop, 278.

63. ADM 199/888/003.

64. ADM 199/888/003.

65. ADM 199/888/003.

66. ADM 199/888/003.

67. ADM 199/888/003.

68. Gallagher, 126.

69. ADM 199/888/004; Gallagher, 127, 130.

70. Bishop, 279.

71. Bishop, 280.

72. ADM 199/888/004.

73. ADM 199/888/004.

74. ADM 199/888/004.

75. ADM 199/888/004.

76. ADM 199/888/005.

77. ADM 199/888/005.

78. ADM 199/888/005.

79. ADM 199/888/005.

80. ADM 199/888/005.

81. Gallagher, 132.

82. McRaven, 227.

83. ADM 199/888/005.

84. ADM 199/888/005.

85. ADM 199/888/005.

86. ADM 234/347/13.

87. Warren and Benson, 132.

88. ADM 234/347/13; Ship rocking to port, leaking oil, ruptured pipes, men being hurled about: Gallagher, 139, 140.

89. Fritz Adler: Bishop, 283.

90. ADM 234/347/13.

91. ADM 234/347/13.

92. ADM 199/888/005.

93. ADM 199/888/005.

94. ADM 199/888/006.

95. ADM 199/888/006.

96. Quoted in Bishop, 287.

97. McRaven, 228.

98. Water blows out lighting, Aitken finds Whitley: Bishop, 287; "breathing bag was empty, flat, completely flat": quoted in Bishop, 287.

99. Bishop, 288; Warren and Benson, 135.

100. ADM 199/888/007–008.

101. ADM 234/347/13.

102. Warren and Benson, 138.

103. ADM 234/347/16.

104. ADM 234/347/18–19.

105. X-5 sunk by *Tirpitz*: ADM 199/888/006; only wreckage of X-6 and X-7 found: McRaven, 228.

106. ADM 234/347/20.

107. ADM 199/888/009.

108. Quoted in Bishop, 289–290.

109. ADM 199/888/009.

CHAPTER 12: "HELL ON EARTH"

1. All details of the daily routine on board Scharnhorst come from *German Battle Cruiser* Scharnhorst: *Interrogation of Survivors* (see Page, vol. 2, sec. 7, 23).

2. *German Battle Cruiser* Scharnhorst: *Interrogation of Survivors* (see Page, vol. 2, sec. 7, 23).

3. *German Battle Cruiser* Scharnhorst: *Interrogation of Survivors* (see Page, vol. 2, sec. 7, 23).

4. *German Battle Cruiser* Scharnhorst: *Interrogation of Survivors* (see Page, vol. 2, sec. 7, 23).

5. ADM 234/343/006.

6. ADM 234/343/006.

7. ADM 234/343/006.

8. ADM 234/343/006.

9. ADM 234/343/009.

10. ADM 234/343/009.

11. ADM 234/343/007.

12. ADM 234/343/006–007.

13. ADM 234/343/007.

14. Garrett, 137.

15. Garrett, 137.

16. ADM 234/343/009.

17. ADM 234/343/008.

18. ADM 234/343/009.

19. *German Battle Cruiser* Scharnhorst: *Interrogation of Survivors* (see Page, vol. 2, sec. 4, 12).

20. *German Battle Cruiser* Scharnhorst: *Interrogation of Survivors* (see Page, vol. 2, sec. 4, 12).

21. *German Battle Cruiser* Scharnhorst: *Interrogation of Survivors* (see Page, vol. 2, sec. 4, 12).

22. Busch, *Holocaust at Sea* (Kindle edition).

23. Quoted in Busch, *Holocaust at Sea* (Kindle edition).

24. Busch, *Holocaust at Sea* (Kindle edition).

25. Busch, *Holocaust at Sea* (Kindle edition).

26. ADM 234/343/010.

27. ADM 234/343/11.

28. ADM 234/343/010–011.

29. Busch, *Holocaust at Sea* (Kindle edition).

30. ADM 234/343/011.

31. ADM 234/343/011.

32. "encrusting hair and brows": Busch, *Holocaust at Sea* (Kindle edition); *Scharnhorst* isolated: ADM 234/343/011.

33. Parham, IWM Sound Archive 14128.

34. Parham, IWM Sound Archive 14128.

35. ADM 234/343/11.

36. Bassett, *HMS* Sheffield, 171.

37. Bassett, *HMS* Sheffield, 171.

38. ADM 234/343/11.

39. *Belfast* opens fire with star shell: ADM 234/343/10–11; "the appearance and disappearance": Busch, *Holocaust at Sea* (Kindle edition).

40. ADM 234/343/012.

41. Busch, *Holocaust at Sea* (Kindle edition).

42. Garrett, 147.

43. Bassett, *HMS* Sheffield, 172.

44. ADM 234/343/12.

45. "get between *Scharnhorst* and the convoy": ADM 234/343/012; "I bet you she'll come again": Parham, IWM Sound Archive 14128.

46. ADM 234/343/012.

47. *Duke of York* 200 miles away: Parham, IWM Sound Archive 14128; *Scharnhorst* advantage, Fraser thinks it "undesirable" to split force, orders destroyers to join Burnett's ship: ADM 234/343/013–014.

48. Parham, IWM Sound Archive 14128.

49. *Scharnhorst* reappears on radar: ADM 234/343/014; "I knew then that there was every chance": Garrett, 151.

50. ADM 234/343/015.

51. Parham, IWM Sound Archive 14128.

52. Busch, *Holocaust at Sea* (Kindle edition).

53. Busch, *Holocaust at Sea* (Kindle edition).

54. Range varying from 16,000 to 9,000 yards: ADM 234/343/105; "The scene was majestic": quoted in Bassett, *HMS* Sheffield, 173.

55. Bassett, *HMS* Sheffield, 173.

56. Gödde sees *Norfolk* hit, shell casings dumped into sea: Busch, *Holocaust at Sea* (Kindle edition); Norfolk casualties: ADM 234/343/016.

57. Bassett, *HMS* Sheffield, 173.

58. "up to football size": ADM 234/343/016; "neat groups of speeding death": Bassett, 173; "Turn to port": Busch, *Holocaust at Sea* (Kindle edition).

59. ADM 232/343/017.

60. *Scharnhorst* maneuver thwarts British destroyers: Bassett, 143; *Scharnhorst* turns at 1241 hours: ADM 234/343/018.

61. Parham, IWM Sound Archive 14128.

62. Parham, IWM Sound Archive 14128.

63. ADM 234/343/16.

64. Busch, *Holocaust at Sea* (Kindle edition).

65. ADM 234/343/017.

66. ADM 234/343/017.

67. Parham, IWM Sound Archive 14128.

68. ADM 234/343/17–18.

69. Ditchman (Kindle edition).

70. ADM 234/343/19.

71. Weston, IWM Sound Archive 12933.

72. ADM 234/343/19–20.

73. ADM 234/343/20.

74. Bassett, *HMS* Sheffield, 174.

75. ADM 234/343/20.

76. Parham, IWM Sound Archive 14128.

77. Bassett, *HMS* Sheffield, 174.

78. Time of order to destroyers: ADM 234/343/021; "Destroyers in company": Ditchman (Kindle edition).

79. Ramsden quoted in Winton, 309.

80. ADM 234/343/21.

81. ADM 234/343/21.

82. Busch, *Holocaust at Sea* (Kindle edition).

83. ADM 1/16833.

84. ADM 234/343/032.

85. Ditchman (Kindle edition).

86. ADM 234/343/21.

87. ADM 234/343/21.

88. Parham, IWM Sound Archive 14128.

89. Ditchman (Kindle edition).

90. ADM 234/343/21.

91. ADM 234/343/22.

92. ADM 234/343/21.

93. Ditchman (Kindle edition).

94. ADM 234/343/21.

95. ADM 234/343/21.

96. *Savage* and *Saumarez* attack: ADM 234/343/022; "We heard underwater explosions": Wass, "Battle of North Cape," BBC WW2 People's War.

97. "The watertight doors": ADM 1-16833; *Savage* and *Saumarez* escape, *Saumarez*'s speed and damage: Garrett, 153.

98. Ditchman (Kindle edition).

99. Bassett, 174.

100. ADM 234/343/22.

101. Shrimpton, IWM Sound Archive 21735.

102. ADM 1-16833.

103. Quoted in Winton, 311.

104. "*Scharnhorst* immer voran": Busch, *Holocaust at Sea* (Kindle edition); "they were unable to distinguish": ADM 1-16833.

105. Quoted in Bassett, *HMS* Sheffield, 175.

106. Impact of shells hitting ship: Bassett, *HMS* Sheffield, 175; "full of mangled bodies": ADM 1-16833.

107. Quoted in Winton, 311.

108. *Belfast* opens fire at 1915 hours: ADM 234/343/22; "Finish her off with torpedoes": ADM 234/343/21.

109. *Duke of York* checks fire: ADM 234/343/23; "I shake you all by the hand": ADM 1-16833.

110. Quoted in Winton, 312.

111. *Jamaica* and *Belfast* fire torpedoes and miss, attack again: ADM 234/343/23; "I could smell": quoted in Winton, 312.

112. ADM 234/343/23.

113. ADM 234/343/24.

114. ADM 234/343/24.

115. War Diary of the German Naval War Staff, quoted in ADM 234/343/24.

116. Quoted in ADM 234/343/24.

117. Quoted in Garrett, 161.

118. Shrimpton, IWM Sound Archive 21735.

119. ADM 234/343/23.

120. *Scorpion* saves thirty men, *Matchless* six: ADM 234/343/24; "I heard orders being given . . . it was a sight I shall never forget": Garrett, 162.

121. Quoted in Bassett, *HMS* Sheffield, 175.

122. ADM 234/343/25.

123. ADM 234/343/26.

124. Quoted in Garrett, 163.

CHAPTER 13: RETURN TO *TIRPITZ*

1. Bishop, 311.

2. Submarine netting, flak ships, antiaircraft guns, and smoke generators: ADM 234/345/005; crew knew enemy would return: Bishop, 311.

3. ADM 234/345/005.

4. ADM 234/345/005.

5. ADM 234/345/005.

6. Details of Tungsten plan: ADM 234/345/005–006; "practically bludgeoned": quoted in Bishop, 318.

7. ADM 234/345/006.

8. Convoy and armada set sail: ADM 234/345/006; "This apparent lack of interest": ADM 234/345/006.

9. ADM 234/345/006.

10. ADM 234/345/006.

11. Anthony Kimmins, *War Illustrated*, vol. 7, no. 170, 794–795. (see reference details in bibliography under "Online Articles and Resources")

12. ADM 234/345/006–007.

13. Kimmins, *War Illustrated*, vol. 7, no. 170, 794–795.

14. ADM 234/345/008.

15. ADM 234/345/008.

16. ADM 234/345/008.

17. Quoted in Sweetman, 92.

18. Rounds shred gun crews: Zetterling and Tamelander, *Tirpitz* (Kindle edition); Wildcats strafe *Tirpitz*, "undoubtedly spoilt the *Tirpitz* gunnery": ADM 234/345/008.

19. Attack lasts 60 seconds: ADM 234/345/008; "steady red glow," "enveloped in large red flames": ADM 234/345/015.

20. ADM 234/345/008.

21. ADM 234/345/008.

22. ADM 234/345/008.

23. Zetterling and Tamelander, *Tirpitz* (Kindle edition).

24. ADM 234/345/008–009.

25. ADM 234/345/008.

26. 40 Barracudas, 81 fighters: ADM 234/345/009; crews report 30 hits: Zetterling and Tamelander, *Tirpitz* (Kindle edition).

27. ADM 234/345/009.

28. ADM 234/345/009.

29. ADM 234/345/009.

30. Ships return home to "rousing reception": ADM 234/345/009; "the pilots and aircrews concerned": quoted in Sweetman, 100.

31. ADM 234/345/10.

32. Zetterling and Tamelander, *Tirpitz* (Kindle edition); Bishop, 328–329.

33. Engineers arrive from Kiel: Zetterling and Tamelander, *Tirpitz* (Kindle edition); *Tirpitz* ready for sea trials by July: Bishop, 332.

34. Bishop, 332, 333–334.

35. Bishop, 336.

36. Read, xix–xx.

37. Middlebrook, 583; Sweetman, 147.

38. Quoted in Sweetman, 142.

39. Read, xix–xx.

40. Read, xx.

41. Bishop, 351; AIR 14/1971/004.

42. AIR 14/1971/004.

43. AIR 14/1971/004.

44. AIR 14/1971/004.

45. AIR 14/1971/004–005.

46. AIR 14/1971/005.

47. AIR 14/1971/005.

48. AIR 20/6187/003.

49. AIR 14/1971/006.

50. Quoted in Bishop, 358.

51. Quoted in Sweetman, 166.

52. Cloud and smoke screen forced second pass: AIR 14/1971/007; "Huge mushrooms of smoke": quoted in Bishop, 360.

53. Bishop, 361–362.

54. Quoted in Bishop, 361.

55. Bishop, 361.

56. AIR 20/6187/005.

57. AIR 14/1971/007.

58. AIR 14/1971/007.

59. Bishop, 362.

60. Dönitz balks at nine-month repair for *Tirpitz*: Sweetman, 180; *Tirpitz* ordered to Haakøy to serve as battery, deter invasion: Sweetman, 180, Bishop, 364, 365.

61. Quoted in Sweetman, 180.

62. "limped": AIR 20/6187/006; accompanied by tugs and destroyers: Bishop, 364.

63. "secret radio transmitter": AIR 20/6187/006; top floor of hospital: Bishop, 364.

64. Quoted in Bishop, 365.

65. Quoted in Bishop, 366.

66. AIR 20/6187/006.

67. AIR 20/6187/006.

68. Make landfall at Vega, flying at 1,500 feet, "over lifeless wasteland": AIR 20/6197/006, 007; rendezvous over Torneträsk Lake: Bishop, 371.

69. Quoted in Sweetman, 196.

70. AIR 20/6187/007.

71. bombers drop their payloads: AIR 20/6187/007; "When the bombs dropped": quoted in Sweetman, 196.

72. AIR 20/6187/007.

73. Damage to rudder and propeller shaft: Zetterling and Tamelander, *Tirpitz* (Kindle edition); 800 tons of water floods ship: Sweetman, 202.

74. Sweetman, 204.

75. AIR 20/6187/007.

76. AIR 20/6187/007.

77. AIR 20/6187/007.

78. AIR 20/6187/007.

79. Bomber Command report quoted in Sweetman, 208.

80. Lancaster sighting reports are quoted in Bowman (Kindle edition).

81. Quoted in Bishop, 381.

82. Quoted in Zetterling and Tamelander, *Tirpitz* (Kindle edition).

83. Clear and cloudless conditions, Tait sees *Tirpitz* take shape, "at a given signal": AIR 20/6187/008; "My God, Mac": Watts, IWM Sound Archive 21029.

84. Fassbender report quoted in Bowman (Kindle edition).

85. "a great unfolding golden cloud": quoted in Bishop, 377; "was fighting back strongly . . . unpleasantly close": AIR 20/6187/008.

86. Sweetman, 215.

87. Quoted in Bishop, 384.

88. Mud and water, a 52-foot hole ripped in her port side: Zetterling and Tamelander, *Tirpitz* (Kindle edition); "a thin geyser": AIR 20/6187/008.

89. Zetterling and Tamelander, *Tirpitz* (Kindle edition).

90. Bishop, 385.

91. "a dark thundercloud in the sky": quoted in Sweetman, 216; explosion lifts aft turret: Fassbender report quoted in Bowman (Kindle edition).

92. Bowman (Kindle edition).

93. AIR 20/6187/008.

94. Bowman (Kindle edition).

95. Bishop, 384.

96. Bishop, xxii.

97. AIR 20/6187/008.

98. Bishop, 385.

99. Rescue boat arrives 15 minutes later: Fassbender report quoted in Bowman (Kindle edition); three days of rescue work, crews pass out: Sweetman, 231, Bishop, 7.

100. Men singing, voices fade: Bishop, 7; 87 men rescued: Sweetman, 231; *Tirpitz* casualties: Bishop, 386.

101. AIR 20/6187/008.

102. AIR 20/6187/008.

103. Reynolds and Pechatnov, 496.

104. Reynolds and Pechatnov, 496.

105. Churchill, vol. 5, 223.

106. Churchill, *Never Give In!*, 285.

EPILOGUE: THE SEA IS A MASS GRAVE

1. Bekker, 365–366.

2. Middlebrook, 693, 696.

3. "How the U.S. Is Recovering Oil from a Nuked Warship," *Popular Mechanics*, Sept. 17, 2018.

4. Underwater fittings begin to leak, towed to Kwajalein Atoll, capsized on December 16: Busch, *Prinz Eugen*, 213; wreckage still visible today with propellers above the water: "How the U.S. Is Recovering Oil from a Nuked Warship," *Popular Mechanics*.

5. "Norwegian Trees Still Bear Evidence of a World War II German Battleship," *Smithsonian Magazine*, April 12, 2018.

6. "Navy Recovers Fuel from Sunken Ship Once Used for Atomic Bomb Practice," *Stars and Stripes*, Oct. 16, 2018.

7. Bekker, 301–302.

8. O'Hara, 261.

9. Bekker, 302.

10. Raeder, 374.

11. Bekker, 361.

12. Raeder, 384–385, 387.

13. Raeder found guilty, sentenced to life, petition to be executed denied, released due to failing health: Raeder, 400, 406; dies at the age of 84: Dimbleby, 455.

14. Dimbleby, 455.

15. "War Veterans Come to Bury, and to Praise, Doenitz," *New York Times*, Jan. 7, 1981; Dimbleby, 455.

16. Raeder, 411–412.

17. "Nazi Crew, Not British Fire, Sank the *Bismarck*, Explorer Believes," *Chicago Tribune*, June 23, 1989.

18. "Visiting *Bismarck*, Explorers Revise Its Story," *New York Times*, Dec. 3, 2002.

19. Fenton, "Sinking of the *Scharnhorst*" (see reference details in bibliography under "Online Articles and Resources"); Branfill-Cook, 205.

20. "HMS *Hood* Today." HMS *Hood* Association (see reference details in bibliography under "Online Articles and Resources").

21. *Tirpitz* salvage operation, 1958–1957: KBismarck.com, *Tirpitz* Timeline (see reference details in bibliography under "Online Articles and Resources"); knives made from *Tirpitz*'s armor: "How the Nazis' Largest Battleship Is Still Affecting Norway Today," *Popular Mechanics*, April 11, 2018.

22. Bishop, 391.

23. BBC News, "HMS *Hood*'s Bell Recovered from Seabed."

BIBLIOGRAPHY

BOOKS

Air Ministry. *Coastal Command: The Air Ministry's Account of the Part Played by Coastal Command in the Battle of the Seas, 1939–1942.* Her Majesty's Stationary Office, 1942 (Kindle edition).

———. *Bomber Command Handbook.* Her Majesty's Stationary Office, 1941.

Arnold-Foster, Mark. *The World at War.* London: William Collins Sons & Co Limited, 1984.

Arthur, Max. *Lest We Forget: Forgotten Voices from 1914–1945.* London: Ebury Press, 2007.

———. *Forgotten Voices of the Second World War.* London: Ebury Press, 2004.

Bailey, Roderick. *Forgotten Voices of the Victoria Cross.* London: Ebury Press, 2011 (Kindle edition).

Ballantyne, Iain. *Killing the* Bismarck*: Destroying the Pride of Hitler's Fleet.* Barnsley, South Yorkshire: Pen & Sword Maritime, 2010.

Barker, Ralph. *Ship-Busters: British Torpedo-Bombers in World War II.* Mechanicsburg, PA: Stackpole Books, 2010.

Bassett, Ronald. *Battle Cruisers: A History 1908–1948.* Endeavor Media, 2016 (Kindle edition).

———. *HMS* Sheffield*: The Life and Times of "Old Shiny."* Annapolis, MD: Naval Institute Press, 1988.

Bekker, Cajus. *Hitler's Naval War.* New York: Doubleday & Company Inc., 1974.

Bennett, D. C. T. *Pathfinder.* Panther, 1960.

Bishop, Patrick. *The Hunt for Hitler's Warship.* Washington, DC: Regenery History, 2013.

Bowman, Martin W. *Voices in Flight: The Night Air War*. Barnsley, South Yorkshire: Pen & Sword Aviation, 2015 (Kindle edition).

Boyne, Walter J. *Clash of Titans: World War II at Sea*. New York: Touchstone, 1995.

Branfill-Cook, Roger. *Torpedo: The Complete History of the World's Most Revolutionary Naval Weapon*. Barnsley, South Yorkshire: Seaforth Publishing, 2014.

Busch, Fritz-Otto. *Holocaust at Sea*. Pickle Partners Publishing, 2015 (Kindle edition).

———. *Prinz Eugen*. London: Futura Publications Limited, 1975.

Cain, T. J. (as told to A. V. Sellwood). *HMS* Electra. London: Futura Publications Limited, 1976.

Callo, Joseph F., and Alastair Wilson. *Who's Who in Naval History*. London: Routledge, 2004.

Chant-Sempill, Stuart. *St. Nazaire Commando*. Novato, CA: Presidio Press, 1987.

Churchill, Winston S. *Never Give In!: The Best of Winston Churchill's Speeches*. New York: Hyperion, 2003.

———. *The Second World War*. Vol. 1, *The Gathering Storm*. London: Cassell & Co. Ltd., 1950 (The Reprint Society edition).

———. *The Second World War*. Vol. 2, *Their Finest Hour*. London: Cassell & Co. Ltd., 1951 (The Reprint Society edition).

———. *The Second World War*. Vol. 3, *The Grand Alliance*. London: Cassell & Co. Ltd., 1952 (The Reprint Society edition).

———. *The Second World War*. Vol. 4, *The Hinge of Fate*. London: Cassell & Co. Ltd., 1954 (The Reprint Society edition).

———. *The Second World War*. Vol. 5, *Closing the Ring*. London: Cassell & Co. Ltd., 1954 (The Reprint Society edition).

Coles, Alan, and Ted Briggs. *Flagship* Hood*: The Fate of Britain's Mightiest Warship*. Bury St. Edmunds: St. Edmundsbury Press, 1985.

Cooksey, Jon. *Operation Chariot: The Raid on St. Nazaire*. Barnsley, South Yorkshire: Pen & Sword Books Limited, 2005.

Dimbleby, Jonathan. *The Battle of the Atlantic: How the Allies Won the War*. New York: Oxford University Press, 2016.

Ditchman, A. G. F. *A Home on the Rolling Main: A Naval Memoir 1940–1946*. Barnsley, South Yorkshire: Seaforth Publishing, 2013 (Kindle edition).

Dorrian, James. *Storming St. Nazaire: The Dock Busting Raid of 1942*. Barnsley, South Yorkshire: Pen & Sword Books Limited, 2012 (Kindle edition).

Ford, Ken. *St. Nazaire 1942: The Great Commando Raid.* Oxford, UK: Osprey Publishing Ltd., 2001.

———. *Run the Gauntlet: The Channel Dash 1942.* Oxford, UK: Osprey Publishing Ltd., 2012.

Gallagher, Thomas. *The X-Craft Raid.* New York: Harcourt Brace Jovanovich, Inc., 1971.

Garrett, Richard. Scharnhorst *and* Gneisenau: *The Elusive Sisters.* London: David & Charles, 1978.

Haar, Geirr H. *The Gathering Storm: The Naval War in Northern Europe, September 1939–April 1940.* Barnsley, South Yorkshire: Seaforth Publishing, 2013.

Harwood, Jeremy. *World War II from Above: An Aerial View of the Global Conflict.* Hove, UK: Quid Publishing, 2014.

Hastings, Max. *Inferno: The World at War, 1939–1945.* New York: Alfred A. Knopf, 2011.

Hough, Richard. *The Longest Battle: The War at Sea, 1939–1945.* New York: William Morrow, 1986.

Hoyt, Edwin. *Sunk by the* Bismarck: *The Life and Death of the Battleship* HMS Hood. New York: Stein and Day, 1980.

Irving, David. *The Destruction of Convoy PQ17.* London: Cassell & Co., 1968.

Jacobs, Peter. *Daring Raids of World War Two: Heroic Land, Sea & Air Attacks.* Barnsley, South Yorkshire: Pen & Sword Aviation, 2015.

Kemp, Ross. *Raiders: WWII Britain's Most Daring Special Operations.* London: Random House, 2012.

Koop, Gerhard, and Klaus-Peter Schmolke. *Battleships of the* Scharnhorst *Class.* Barnsley, South Yorkshire: Seaforth Publishing, 2014.

Lewis, John, ed. *Spitfire: The Autobiography.* London: Constable & Robinson Ltd., 2010 (Kindle edition).

Lyman, Robert. *In the Jaws of Death: The True Story of the Legendary Raid on Saint-Nazaire.* London: Quercus, 2013 (Kindle edition).

McLean, Gavin, and Ian McGibbon (with Kynan Gentry). *The Penguin Book of New Zealanders at War.* Rosedale (NZ): Penguin Books (NZ), 2009 (Kindle edition).

McRaven, William H. *Special Ops: Case Studies in Operations Warfare: Theory and Practice.* New York: Ballantine Books, 1996.

Middlebrook, Martin, and Chris Everitt. *The Bomber Command War Diaries: An Operational Reference Book, 1939–1945.* Leicester: Midland Publishing, 2000.

Ministry of Information. *Combined Operations 1940–1942.* Her Majesty's Stationary Office, 1943.

Moffat, John (with Mike Rossiter). *I Sank the* Bismarck*: Memoirs of a Second World War Navy Pilot.* London: Transworld Publishers, 2009.

Müllenheim-Rechberg, Burkard Baron von. *Battleship* Bismarck*: A Survivor's Story.* Annapolis, MD: Naval Institute Press, 1980.

Norman, Andrew. *HMS* Hood*: Pride of the Royal Navy.* Mechanicsburg, PA: Stackpole Books, 2001.

O'Hara, Vincent P. *The German Fleet at War, 1939–1945.* Annapolis, MD: Naval Institute Press, 2004.

Page, Christopher, ed. *Whitehall Histories: Naval Staff Histories: German Capital Ships and Raiders in World II.* Vol. 1, *From* Graf Spee *to* Bismarck*, 1939–1941.* London: Routledge, 2014.

———. *Whitehall Histories: Naval Staff Histories: German Capital Ships and Raiders in World War II.* Vol. 2, *From* Scharnhorst *to* Tirpitz*, 1942–1944.* London: Routledge, 2016.

Phillips, C. E. Lucas. *The Greatest Raid of All.* London: Pan Books, 2000.

Pope, Dudley. *73 North: The Battle of the Barents Sea.* Ithaca, NY: McBooks Press, 2005.

Price, Alfred, Dr. *Spitfire: Pilots' Stories.* The History Press, 2012 (Kindle edition).

Purdon, Corran. *List the Bugle: Reminiscences of an Irish Soldier.* Antrim, Northern Ireland: Greystone Books, 1993.

Raeder, Erich. *Grand Admiral: The Personal Memoir of the Commander in Chief of the German Navy from 1935 Until His Final Break with Hitler in 1943.* Boston: Da Capo Press, 2001.

Rayment, Sean. *Tales from the Special Forces Club: Corran Purdon's Story.* London: HarperCollins, 2013 (Kindle edition).

Read, Simon. *The Killing Skies: RAF Bomber Command at War.* Stroud, UK: Spellmount Limited, 2006.

Redford, Duncan. *A History of the Royal Navy: World War II.* London: I.B. Tauris (in association with The National Museum, Royal Navy), 2014.

Reynolds, David, and Vladimir Pechatnov. *The Kremlin Letters: Stalin's Wartime Correspondence with Churchill and Roosevelt.* New Haven: Yale University Press, 2018.

Roberts, Andrew. *Churchill: Walking with Destiny.* Viking, 2018.

Robertson, Terence. *Channel Dash.* London: The Quality Book Club, 1958.

Roskill, Stephen W. *The War at Sea.* Vol. 1. London: H.M. Stationary Office, 1954.

Ryder, Robert E. D. *The Attack on St. Nazaire.* London: John Murray, 1947.

Saunders, Hilary St. George, Lt. *The Green Beret: The Story of the Commandos, 1940–1945*. Pickle Partners Publishing, 2015 (Kindle edition).

Sweetman, John. Tirpitz: *Hunting the Beast*. Stroud, UK: Sutton Publishing Limited, 2004.

Warren, C. E. T., and James Benson. *Above Us the Waves: The Story of Midget Submarines and Human Torpedoes*. Barnsley, South Yorkshire: Pen & Sword Military Classics, 2006.

Wills, Matthew B. *In the Highest Traditions of the Royal Navy: The Life of Captain John Leach MVO DSO*. Stroud, UK: Spellmount Limited, 2013 (Kindle edition).

Winton, John. *The Victoria Cross at Sea: The Sailors, Marines and Naval Airmen Awarded Britain's Highest Honor*. Yorkshire (UK): Frontline Books, 2016.

Winton, John, ed. *Freedom's Battle*. Vol. 1, *The War at Sea, 1939–1945*. London: Vintage Books, 2007.

Zetterling, Niklas, and Michael Tamelander. Bismarck: *The Final Days of Germany's Greatest Battleship*. Philadelphia: Casemate, 2009.

———. Tirpitz: *The Life and Death of Germany's Last Super Battleship*. Philadelphia: Casemate, 2009 (Kindle edition).

DOCUMENTS FROM THE BRITISH NATIONAL ARCHIVES

ADM 186/803: "Battle Summary—No. 11: The Passage of *Scharnhorst, Gneisenau*, and *Prinz Eugen* Through the English Channel, 12th February, 1942."

ADM 199/888: "Final Report on Operation 'Source.'"

ADM 199/1188: "Pursuit and Destruction of German Battleship *Bismarck*."

ADM 234/343: "Battle Summary—No. 24: Sinking of the *Scharnhorst*, 26 December, 1943."

ADM 234/345: "Battle Summary—No. 27: Naval Aircraft Attack on the *Tirpitz* (Operation 'Tungsten') 3rd April, 1944."

ADM 234/347: "Battle Summary—No. 29: Attack on *Tirpitz* by Midget Submarines (Operation 'Source') 22nd September, 1943."

AIR 2/7912: "Board of Enquiry into Passage of *Scharnhorst, Gneisenau*, and *Prinz Eugen* through Straits of Dover on 12th Feb. 1942."

AIR 14/680: "Operations Against *Scharnhorst* and *Gneisenau*."

AIR 14/1971: "Report of Group Capt. McMullen, A.F.G (Force Commander) on Attack by Nos. 617 and 9 SQDNS on the German Battleship *Tirpitz* on Sept. 15th, 1944."

AIR 20/3061: "*Scharnhorst* and *Gneisenau*. Breakout."

AIR 20/6187: "The RAF Story of Three Air Attacks on *Tirpitz*, as told
    by W/C J.B. Taft, D.S.O., D.F.C."
AIR 27/98/11: "No. 7 Squadron Operations Record Book."
AIR 27/143/8: "No. 10 Squadron Operations Record Book."
AIR 27/280: "No. 22 Summary of Honors and Awards."
AIR 27/379/10 and AIR 27/379/28: "No. 35 Squadron Operations Re-
    cord Book."
AIR 27/650/3: "No. 76 Squadron Operations Record Book."
AIR 27/2126/26 and Air 27/2128/28: "No. 617 Squadron Operations
    Record Book."
AIR 27/2738/32: "No. 22 Squadron Operations Record Book."
DEFE 2/125: "Operation Chariot, Part 1."
DEFE 2/131: "Chariot: Appendix II: Operation Orders."

SOUND RECORDINGS FROM THE IMPERIAL WAR MUSEUM

Batteson, Ralph. IWM Sound Archive 22668.
Beach, Arthur. IWM Sound Archive 30257.
Bennett, Donald Clifford Tyndall. IWM Sound Archive 9378.
Briggs, Albert Edward Pryce "Ted." IWM Sound Archive 10751.
Bunce, Donald Arthur. IWM Sound Archive 14298.
Checketts, Harold. IWM Sound Archive 32390.
Gaynor, John. IWM Sound Archive 8246.
Jackson, Patrick Bernard. IWM Sound Archive 15562.
Kingsmill, Pat. IWM Sound Archive 9735.
Mayne, Maurice. IWM Sound Archive 1835.
McMullen, Colin William. IWM Sound Archive 10975.
O'Leary, Thomas. IWM Sound Archive 11289.
Osborne, Richard. IWM Sound Archive 8256.
Parham, Frederick Robertson. IWM Sound Archive 14128.
Roberts, Harold. IWM Sound Archive 22671.
Salisbury, Glyn. IWM Sound Archive 10251.
Sayer, Leslie Daniel. IWM Sound Archive 18574.
Shrimpton, Bob. IWM Sound Archive 21735.
Swayne, Ronald. IWM Sound Archive 10231.
Tilburn, Robert Ernest. IWM Sound Archive 11746.
Watts, Frederick Henry Arthur. IWM Sound Archive 21029.
Weston, Frederick Leslie Shakespeare. IWM Sound Archive 12933.
Wheeler, John. IWM Sound Archive 21734.
Wynn, Michael Charles Robert Vaughan. IWM Sound Archive 9721.

NEWSPAPER AND MAGAZINE ARTICLES (BY DATE)

"*Rawalpindi* sunk by *Deutschland.*" *The Guardian*, Nov. 28, 1939.

"Survivors of the *Rawalpindi*; Graphic Stories of the Fight." *Daily Post*, Nov. 30, 1939.

"Battle Is Marked by Frozen Bodies." *New York Times*, Dec. 25, 1939.

"Ice Closes Danube to German Supplies." *New York Times*, Dec. 30, 1939.

"Loss of HMS Glorious: Berlin Account of Brave Fight." *Coventry Evening Telegraph*, June 17, 1940.

"The American Who Helped Sink the *Bismarck.*" *People Magazine*, June 3, 1974.

"War Veterans Come to Bury, and to Praise, Doenitz." *New York Times*, Jan. 7, 1981.

"Nazi Crew, Not British Fire, Sank the Bismarck, Explorer Believes." *Chicago Tribune*, June 23, 1989.

"Death of PQ-17." *World War II Magazine*, February 1997.

"Obituary: Billie Stephens." *The Independent*, Aug. 18, 1997.

"Obituary: Lord Newborough." *The Independent*, Oct. 28, 1998.

"Captain Edmund 'Splash' Carver." *The Telegraph*, Sept. 11, 2001.

"Lieutenant-Commander Ken Pattison." *The Telegraph*, Aug. 8, 2002.

"Visiting *Bismarck*, Explorers Revise Its Story." *New York Times*, Dec. 3, 2002.

"Lieutenant-Commander Pat Kingsmill." *The Telegraph*, Feb. 6, 2003.

"David Paton." *The Telegraph*, Aug. 2, 2008.

"Eric de la Torre." *The Telegraph*, Sept. 28, 2011.

"Students Find Lost British WW2 Bomber in Norwegian Fjord." *The Telegraph*, Dec. 10, 2014.

"Ian Hewitt, Elite RAF navigator." *Yorkshire Post*, Aug. 8, 2015.

"Jane Fawcett, Bletchley Decoder—obituary." *The Telegraph*, May 25, 2016.

"Jane Fawcett, British Code-Breaker During World War II, Dies at 95." *Washington Post*, May 28, 2016.

"How the Nazis' Largest Battleship Is Still Affecting Norway Today." *Popular Mechanics*, April 11, 2018.

"Norwegian Trees Still Bear Evidence of a World War II German Battleship." *Smithsonian Magazine*, April 12, 2018.

"How the U.S. Is Recovering Oil From a Nuked Warship." *Popular Mechanics*, Sept. 17, 2018.

"Navy Recovers Fuel from Sunken Ship Once Used for Atomic Bomb Practice." *Stars and Stripes*, Oct. 16, 2018.

ONLINE ARTICLES AND RESOURCES

From firsthand accounts to the reproduction of primary documents, a number of online resources provided valuable information. Those consulted and quoted in the book are:

BBC News

"HMS *Hood*'s Bell Uncovered from Seabed." https://www.bbc.com /news/av/uk-33853847/hms-hood-s-bell-recovered-from-seabed.
"HMS *Hood*'s Bell Unveiled at Navy Museum Portsmouth." https:// www.bbc.com/news/uk-england-hampshire-36361855.
"Nottinghamshire Pilot Who Found *Bismarck* Is Remembered." https:// www.bbc.com/news/uk-england-nottinghamshire-38262347.
"Remembering HMS *Hood*, the Mighty Warship Launched in Clydebank." https://www.bbc.com/news/uk-scotland-glasgow -west-45270946.

BBC WW2 People's War

"HMS *Achates*: Report of Proceedings." https://www.bbc.co.uk /history/ww2peopleswar/stories/92/a5350592.shtml.
Paton, David. "St. Nazaire—Operation Chariot—The Doctor's Perspective." https://www.bbc.co.uk/history/ww2peopleswar/stories/83 /a3723383.shtml.
Wass, John. "Battle of North Cape—Sinking of *Scharnhorst*." https:// www.bbc.co.uk/history/ww2peopleswar/stories/25/a8139125 .shtml.

HMS Hood Association

"HMS *Hood* Today." http://www.hmshood.com/hoodtoday/2001 expedition/hood/encrypt.htm.
"Report on the Loss of H.M.S. *Hood*." Original file is held at the British National Archives under catalog ADM 116/4351. http://www.hms hood.org.uk/reference/official/adm116/adm116-4351_intro.htm.
Briggs, Ted. "Ted Briggs Remembers the Sinking of *Hood*." http:// www.hmshood.com/crew/remember/tedbriggs.htm.
Taylor, Jack. "Remembering *Hood*: I was there, we found only three." http://www.hmshood.com/crew/remember/electra_taylor.htm.
Wreck Background. http://www.hmshood.com/hoodtoday/2001 expedition/hood/encrypt.htm.

KBismarck.com

Bismarck War Diary, 24 Aug. 1940–27 May 1941.

Herzog, Georg. Survivor Statement. https://www.kbismarck.com /archives/debriefing4.html.

Rzonca, Bruno. Survivor Interview. https://www.kbismarck.com /crew/interview-brzonca.html.

Tirpitz Timeline. https://www.kbismarck.com/tirpitz.html.

The London Gazette

April 9, 1940: https://www.thegazette.co.uk/London/issue/34827 /supplement/2137.

March 10, 1942: https://www.thegazette.co.uk/London/issue/35486 /supplement/1163.

Sept. 30, 1947: https://www.thegazette.co.uk/London/issue/38086 /supplement/4633.

Other Online Sources

ADM 1/16833: "Interrogation of survivors from the German battleship *Scharnhorst*." (Downloaded at https://www.dnudd.co.uk /downloads/intelligence-and-csdic/)

Constable, Ernie. Firsthand Account. http://www.archieraf.co.uk /archie/l9512tlustory1941.html.

Fenton, Norman. "The Sinking of the *Scharnhorst*." https://www.bbc .co.uk/history/worldwars/wwtwo/scharnhorst_01.shtml.

Holman, Gordon. "I Was There!—We Went With the Raiders to St. Nazaire." *The War Illustrated*. http://www.thewarillustrated .info/127/i-was-there-we-went-with-the-raiders-to-st-nazaire.asp.

Jackson, Patrick. Firsthand Account. http://www.n5490.org/Pilots /Jackson/Jackson.html.

Kerslake, Sidney A. *Coxswain in the Northern Convoys*. https://www .naval-history.net/WW2Memoir-RussianConvoyCoxswain.htm.

Kimmins, Anthony. "I Was There!—We Struck at and Crippled the Mighty *Tirpitz*." *The War Illustrated*. http://www.thewarillustrated .info/180/we-struck-at-and-crippled-the-mighty-tirpitz.asp.

Micallef, Joseph V. "The Critical Role of the Arctic Convoys in WWII." Military.com. https://www.military.com/daily-news /2019/07/15/critical-role-arctic-convoys-wwii.html.

Mitchell, R. J. "The Motor Torpedo Boats: A Personal Account." Channel Dash Association. http://www.channeldash.org/MTB.html.

Murray, Robin. Firsthand Account. http://www.626-squadron.co.uk/willem27.htm.

Paton, D. N. "HMS *Suffolk* Sights and Chases *Bismarck*." http://www.ellsbury.com/hmssuffolk.htm.

Royal Navy. "HMS *Campbeltown* Commemorates the Raid on St. Nazaire 28 March 1942." http://webarchive.nationalarchives.gov.uk/+/http://www.royalnavy.mod.uk/operations-and-support/surface-fleet/type-22-frigates/hms-campbeltown/history/the-raid-on-st-nazaire/hms-campbeltown-commemorates-the-raid-on.

Sargent, T. R., and B. M. Chiswell. "Encounter with the German Battleship *Bismarck*." Alaska/Bering Sea Patrol Association. http://www.a-bsp.org/index.html.

Sugarman, Martin. "World War II: Story of Jewish Commando Peter Nagel." Jewish Virtual Library. https://www.jewishvirtuallibrary.org/the-story-of-jewish-commando-peter-nagel.

"Bennett and the *Tirpitz*." RAF Pathfinder Archive. https://raf-pathfinders.com/2018/08/26/bennett-and-the-tirpitz/.

"Frank Arkle RNVR." Second World War Experience Centre (SWWEC). https://war-experience.org/lives/frank-arkle-rnvr/.

"Lieutenant John Roderick MC." Second World War Experience Centre (SWWEC). https://war-experience.org/lives/lieutenant-john-roderick-mc/.

"Photographic Reconnaissance in World War II." *RAF Historical Society Journals*. https://www.rafmuseum.org.uk/documents/Research/RAF-Historical-Society-Journals/Journal-10-Seminar-Photo-Recce-in-WWII.pdf.

"The Russian Convoys, 1941–1945." National Museums Liverpool. https://www.liverpoolmuseums.org.uk/maritime/collections/boa/history/russian-convoys.aspx.

"The Scouting and Search for *Bismarck*." Naval History and Heritage Command. https://www.history.navy.mil/research/library/online-reading-room/title-list-alphabetically/s/sinking-of-the-bismarck/the-scouting-and-search-for-bismarck.html.

"The Story Behind the Journey Churchill Called the 'Worst in the World.'" Gov.co.uk. https://www.gov.uk/government/news/the-story-behind-the-journey-churchill-called-the-worst-in-the-world.

"W1053 TL-G from 35 Squadron." http://www.archieraf.co.uk/archie/1053tlg.html.

INDEX

(abbreviations: Br. = British / Fr. = French / Ger. = German / Nor. = Norwegian / Pol. = Polish)

1st Cruiser Squadron (Br.), 26
4th Destroyer Flotilla (Br.), 70,
    77–78
4th Destroyer Flotilla (Ger.), 212,
    217
16th Destroyer Flotilla (Br.),
    105–108
21st Destroyer Flotilla (Br.),
    105–108
22nd Naval Flak Brigade (Ger.), 122
208th Naval Artillery Battalion
    (Ger.), 125
809th Flak Battalion (Ger.), 124

Acasta (HMS), 5–6
Achates (HMS), 185–188
Adler, Fritz, 205
Admiral Hipper (Ger.). See *Hipper*
Admiral Scheer (Ger.), 8, 245
Admiral von Tirpitz (Ger.). See
    Tirpitz
airbases (RAF)
  Manston, 97
  St. Eval, 11, 16
  Wattisham, 3
aircraft carriers. See *Ark Royal*;
    Furious ; *Glorious*; *Victorious*

Aisthorpe, Horace, 187
Aitken, Robert, 206
Albrecht. Helmut, 36
Algonquin (HMS), 230
Anson (HMS), 228
Arctic/North Atlantic British
    shipping convoys
  Convoy JW-51B, 183–191
  Convoy JW-55A, 209–210
  Convoy JW-55B, 209–210, 211,
    212–213
  Convoy PQ-17, 174–176
  importance of, 8, 9–10, 112–113,
    164, 172–174
Ardent (HMS), 5
Ark Royal (HMS), 54, 70
  aircraft of vs *Bismarck*, 73–76
  bombing of *Sheffield* in error,
    71–72
Arkle, Frank, 123, 150
armaments of ships
  Gneisenau, 2
  Hood, 24
  motor launches (ML), 115
  Scharnhorst, 2
  Tirpitz, 112
Arnold-Foster, Mark, 96

Arthur (Br. cargo/SOE boat),
    176–180
Ashcroft, Arthur, 133–134
Atherstone (HMS), 115, 117, 119,
    120, 121, 155, 156
Aurora (HMS), 56

Barents Sea, Battle of. *See* Convoy
    JW-51B
Barracuda dive-bombers in action
    vs *Tirpitz*, 227, 229–231, 232
Barry, C.B., 197, 207
Batteson, Ralph, 118, 127, 157–161
battleships/battle cruisers, British.
    See *Anson*; *Duke of York*; *Hood*;
    King George V; *Prince of Wales*;
    Renown; *Rodney*
battleships/battle cruisers, German.
    See *Admiral Scheer*; *Bismarck*;
    Gniesenau; *Lützow*; *Scharnhorst*;
    Tirpitz
Beach, Arthur, 104
Beamish, Victor, 94
Beattie, Stephen Halden, 115, 119,
    126, 130, 139, 150–151, 162
Beaufort torpedo bombers
    vs *Gneisenau*, 16–19
    vs *Scharnhorst*/*Prinz Eugen*/
    Gneisnau, 103–104, 107
Belfast (HMS), 209, 213–214
    vs *Scharnhorst*, 214–215, 216–221,
    223, 224, 225
    vs *Tirpitz*, 228
Bennett, D. C. T., 165–168
Berrill, "Dapper", 60
Bey, Erich, 212, 213, 215, 217
Birney, David, 139–140, 141
Bismarck (Ger.), 9, 13, 19
    in Operation Rheinübung, 20,
    21–23
    pursuit of, 31–34, 52–55, 62–69,
    70–73, 77–78
    sinking of, 78–84

    survivors of, 80–84
    vs aircraft of *Ark Royal*, 73–76
    vs *Hood*, 34–45
    vs *Norfolk* and *Suffolk*, 26–28,
    52–53, 55–56
    vs *Prince of Wales*, 34–39, 45,
    52–53, 56
    vs *Victorious*'s Swordfish, 57–58,
    59–62
    wreckage of, 248
Bisset, Arthur William La Touche,
    228, 229
Blenheim bombers in action, 3–4
Bletchley Park (Hut 6), 66–67
Blücher (Ger.), 8
bombers (RAF). *See* Barracuda dive-
    bombers; Beaufort torpedo
    bombers; Blenheim bombers;
    Flying Fortresses; Halifaxes;
    Hampdens; Lancasters; Stirling
    bombers; Swordfish torpedo
    bombers; Wellingtons
Botilla Russ (Ger.), 128, 129
Bovell, Henry C., 57, 62
Boyd, R. F., 94
Braithwaite, Francis, 16–17, 19
Bramble (HMS), 184–185
Bredenbreuker, Walter, 211
Brest, France
    RAF air raids on, 14, 15–16,
    17–19, 85, 87, 89, 92
    use of as German navy port, 8,
    11, 13, 14
Brett, Gerard, 137–138
Brewster, Percy, 177–182
Brinkman, Helmuth, 54
Briggs, Dennis, 68–69
Briggs, Ted, 24–25, 26, 28, 29–31, 32,
    33, 34, 35, 37, 38, 39, 40, 41–42,
    46–47, 48–50
British shipping convoys. *See*
    Arctic/North Atlantic British
    shipping convoys

Brown, Jimmy, 148
Brown, Jock, 177–182
Buckham, Bruce, 241–242
Bunce, Donald, 58, 59–60, 98–100
Burhenne, Lothar, 124
Burnett, Robert, 209, 215, 218
Burtinshaw, Robert, 137–138
Busch, Fritz-Otto, 55, 85
Butler, Ron, 136
Byam, Guy, 235

Cain, T. J., 29, 31, 47, 48, 49
Cameron, Donald, 198, 199–203,
    204
Camp, A. W., 17, 18
Campbell (HMS), 105–108
Campbell, Kenneth, 17–19
Campbeltown (HMS), 162
    Commando's escape from, 131,
        133, 134–135, 139, 150–151
    detonation of, 149, 152, 160–161
    execution of Operation Chariot,
        123–124, 126–130, 131–132
    launch of Operation Chariot, 117,
        121
    preparation for Operation
        Chariot, 115
carriers. *See* aircraft carriers
Carter, Cyril, 5–7
Carver, Edmund "Splash," 73
Causer, Malcolm, 177–182
Chamberlain, Bill, 134–135
Chant-Sempill, Stuart, 116–117, 129,
    134–137, 144–145, 146
Chappell, Ernest, 158
Chariot Strike Force. *See* Operation
    Chariot
Charioteers. *See* Operation Chariot
Chariots (human torpedoes),
    176–180
Checketts, Harold, 42–43
Chiswell, B. M., 58–59, 61
Chung, Ron, 137–138

Churchill, Winston
    on Battle of the Atlantic strategy,
        2, 8, 9, 10, 13
    on Convoy PQ-17 tragedy, 176
    learning of *Hood*'s sinking, 51–52
    mining of Norway's waters, 3
    and quest for *Scharnhorst* and
        Gneisnau, 2, 8, 9, 13, 19
    reaction to Operation Cerberus
        completion, 109–111
    on Soviet Union, 172–174
    on *Tirpitz* and its threat, 112, 114,
        164, 193, 231–230, 237, 243
Ciliax, Otto, 89–90, 92–93, 94–95,
    101, 108, 109
Clarke, Arthur, 188–189
Clyde (HMS), 7
Coates, Ernest, 106
Collett, C. T., 56
Collier, Tom, 143
Collinson, Richard, 130
Combined Operations
    Headquarters (Br.), 114–117.
    See also Commandos
Commandos (Br.) in Operation
    Chariot, 114, 154, 162–163
    launch of operation, 120, 126,
        128, 129
    evacuation from, 144–149,
        150–151, 156–160
    execution of operation, 131–133,
        133–134, 134–138, 139–144
    planned role in, 114–117
Conspicuous Gallantry Medal
    recipients
    Larsen, Leif, 176–182
Constable, Ernie, 87–89
Convoy JW-51B (in Battle of the
    Barents Sea)
    Achates, 185–188
    Bramble, 184–185
    German detection of, 183
    Jamaica, 188, 189–190

Convoy JW-51B (in Battle of the
    Barents Sea) (*continued*)
  Northern Gem, 187–188
  Obdurate, 183–184
  Obedient, 184, 188
  Onslow, 183
  Sheffield, 188–191
  strategy against, 183
  vs *Friedrich Eckoldt*, 189
  vs. *Hipper*, 184–190
Convoy JW-55A, 209–210
Convoy JW-55B, 209–210, 211,
    212–213
Convoy PQ-17, 174–176
Coode, Tim, 73–74
Copland, William "Bill", 131, 144,
    148
Cossack (HMS), 70
Craig, Don, 176–182
Cross, William, 24, 29
cruisers, British. See *Aurora*; *Belfast*;
    Dorsetshire; *Galatea*; *Hermione*;
    Jamaica; *Kenya*; *Norfolk*; *Royalist*;
    Sheffield; *Suffolk*
cruisers, German. See *Blücher*;
    Hipper; *Prinz Eugen*
Cunningham, Andrew, 237–238
Curteis, Alban, 62
Curtis, Dunstan, 115, 123, 154

Dark, Philip, 156–157, 160
de la Torre, Eric, 143–144
Denny, Michael, 229, 230
Dieckmann, Edo, 125
Distinguished Flying Medal
    recipients
  Greaves, Stanley, 88–89
Distinguished Service Cross
    recipients
  Brewster, Percy, 177–182
Ditchman, A. G. F., 218–219,
    221–222, 223
Dockerill, Arthur, 136

Dominik, Ernst, 211
Donaldson, John "Jock," 131
Dönitz, Karl, 54, 190–191, 210, 212,
    225, 237, 247
Dorsetshire (HMS), 54, 70, 79, 80,
    82–84
D'Oyly-Hughes, Guy, 4–5
Duff, A. A., 194, 195
Duke of York (HMS), 209, 210, 213,
    215, 228
  vs *Scharnhorst*, 218–220, 2
    21–224
Dundas, William, 29, 37–38,
    46–47, 48–50
Durrant, Thomas Frank, 157–160,
    162

Electra (HMS), 28–29, 31, 47–50
Ellis, Robert, 64
Embry, Basil, 3–4
Emmanuel Rambur (HMS), 209
Esmonde, Eugene, 60, 97–99
Evans, Bob, 176–182

Fættenfjord, Norway, anchorage of
    Tirpitz, 112, 163, 164, 177
Falconar, Henry, 142
Fassbender, Alfred, 240
Fein, Otto, 16, 107
Fenwick, Charles, 72
Finch, Nicky, 132
Flying Fortresses in action vs
    Scharnhorst and *Prinz Eugen*,
    87
Force H (Br.), 54, 70–73, 75–76
Forth, Needham, 175
Fraser, Bruce, 210, 213, 215–216,
    218, 220, 221, 225, 226, 227–228
Friedrich Eckoldt (Ger.), 22, 184,
    185, 189
Friedrich Ihn (Ger.), 97
Friend, Charles, 71
Furious (HMS), 227

Galatea (HMS), 56, 62
Gamble, Hilary, 96–97
Gaynor, John, 35, 37
German navy, operations of. *See*
    Operation Cerberus; Operation
    Rheinübung
German navy surface fleet, 8, 113,
    190–191, 226, 245–247. *See also*
    individual ship names
  22nd Naval Flak Brigade, 122
  208th Naval Artillery Battalion,
    125
  809th Flak Battalion, 124
Gick, Philip "Percy," 61
Giessler, Helmuth, 101
Gillbanks, "Gilly," 88
Gleave, Tom, 98
Glorious (HMS), 4–5, 7
Gneisenau (Ger.)
  anchorage at Brest, 8, 13, 14,
    20, 85
  anchorage at Kiel, 2, 7
  anchorage at Wilhelmshaven,
    2, 3
  armaments/description of, 2,
    8–9
  campaign against North Atlantic
    shipping, 8–10
  in Norway Campaign, 3–7
  in Operation Cerberus, 89–90,
    92–101, 104, 108
  RAF air raids on in Brest, 15–16,
    17–19, 85, 87, 89, 92
  sinking of, 191
  surveillance of, 2
  vs *Glorious* and *Acasta*, 4–7
  vs *Rawalpindi*, 2
Goddard, Edmund, 198, 203
Gödde, Petty Officer, 216, 217
Godfrey-Faussett, "Feather," 75
Graf Spee (Ger.), 8
Greaves, Stanley, 88–89
Green, A. R., 154

Green, Gordon, 11–13
Gregson, Edward, 37

Halifax W1039, 170
Halifax W1052, 165
Halifax W1053, 171
Halifax W7656, 170
Halifaxes (bombers) in action
  vs *Scharnhorst*, 87–89
  vs *Tirpitz*, 165–168, 169–171
Hampdens (bombers) in action
  vs Operation Cerberus, 105–106
  vs *Scharnhorst*, 87
Hans Lody (Ger.), 22
Harriman, Averell, visit with
    Churchill in May 1941, 51
Harris, Arthur, 237
Hartlebury (HMS), 175–176
Henderson, Ian, 143, 156–158
Hermione (HMS), 56
Herzog, Georg, 75
Hintze, Fritz, 212, 217, 220, 223
Hipper (Ger.), 8, 245
  in pursuit of British Convoy
    JW-51B, 183–185, 187–188
  vs *Achates*, 185–187
  vs *Sheffield* and *Jamaica*, 188–189
Hitler, Adolf
  decision to plan Operation
    Cerberus, 89–90
  final message to *Bismarck*, 78
  on German surface fleet, 190
  inspection of *Bismarck* and
    Tirpitz, 20–21
  learning of Battle of the Barents
    Sea, 190
  on naval war strategy, 21
  on plight of Eastern Front, 183
Hoffmann, Kurt-Caesar, 89, 93,
    99
Holland, Lancelot, 25, 28, 30, 31,
    33, 34, 35, 38
Holman, Gordon, 118, 128, 154, 155

Hood (HMS), 24–26, 51, 57
    preparation for battle with
        Bismarck, 28–31, 32
    sinking of, 38–43, 49
    survivors of, 45–50
    vs *Bismarck*, 33–43
    wreckage of, 248, 249
Horlock, Kenneth, 139
Horton, John, 225
Howard, H., 139
Hudspeth, K. R., 207
Hughes, Jane, 66–67
Hughes, Patrick, 102
human torpedoes ("Chariots"),
    176–180
Hunter, Hugh de Graaff, 72
Hyde, J., 17, 18

Iveson, Tony, 240

Jackson, Patrick, 57–58, 60, 62
Jaguar (Ger.), 157–161
Jamaica (HMS), 210
    vs *Hipper*, 188–189
    vs *Scharnhorst*, 218–220, 222,
        223–224
    vs *Tirpitz*, 228
James, A. H. T., 185
Johnson, A. L., 100

Kelbling, Gerd, 119
Kendall, Richard, 198, 200–203, 205
Kenya (HMS), 56
Kerr, Ralph, 25, 30, 33, 34, 37, 39, 40
Kerslake, S. A., 187–188
Kiel, Germany, anchorage for
    Scharnhorst and *Gneisenau*, 1–3,
    7
Kimmins, Anthony, 228, 229
King, Alfred, 136
King George V (HMS), 52, 64, 65, 70,
    76–77, 78, 79–80
Kingsmill, Pat, 97–100

Kirchberg, Kurt, 61
Krancke, Theodor, 190
Kummetz, Oskar, 183–185, 188–189,
    247

La Baume, Günter, 175
La Pallice, France, RAF bombing
    raid on, 86–89
Lancasters in action vs *Tirpitz*,
    233–236, 238–242, 243
Larcom, C. A. A., 72
Larsen, Leif, 176–182
Leach, John, 38, 43–44
Lee, Edgar, 100
Lindemann, Ernst, 27, 37, 45, 63
Lorimer, John, 198, 201, 203
Lumsden, G. J. A., 216–217, 223
Lütjens, Günther, 7–8, 19–21, 22, 32,
    45, 53–54, 63, 64, 65–66, 76
Lützow (Ger.), 8, 183, 185, 194, 245

MacFarlane, B. M., 196–197
Mackay (HMS), 105–107
Maori (HMS), 70, 77
Marschall, Wilhelm, 4, 5, 7
Martin, B. C. S., 83, 84
Mashona (HMS), 78
Matchless (HMS), 216, 217, 224,
    225
Maund, Loben, 71
Mayne, Maurice, 103–104
McFadden, R. D. B., 102–103
McLaughlan, Paul, 72
McMullen, Colin, 39, 234, 235, 236
Mecke, Karl-Conrad, 122, 124–125,
    126
Menary, Henry, 17
Messerchmitts in action over
    Scharnhorst, 87, 88
Meyer, Hans, 204, 205, 206
Mitchell, R. J., 96
Modoc (USS), 58–59, 61
Moffat, John, 74–75

Montgomery, Robert, 124, 127, 130, 135
Moore, Henry 227, 228, 231
motor gun boats (MGB)
  MGB 314 (in Operation Chariot), 115, 117, 120, 121, 123, 125, 128, 130, 144, 150, 152, 153–156
motor launches (ML) (in Operation Chariot), 115, 153, 154, 156
  ML 156, 130, 154, 156
  ML 160, 154
  ML 177, 150–151
  ML 192, 126, 130, 141–142
  ML 270, 154, 155
  ML 306, 118, 127, 142, 154, 156–160
  ML 307, 123, 129, 140, 154
  ML 377, 123
  ML 443, 139, 154
  ML 446, 142, 154, 156
  ML 447, 139–140, 141
  ML 457, 143–144
motor torpedo boats (MTB)
  MTB74 (in Operation Chariot), 115, 152–153
  MTB fleet against Operation Cerberus, 95–97
Müllenheim-Rechberg, Burkhard von, 22, 27–28, 31, 32, 34, 35, 36, 39, 53, 60, 62, 75, 77–78, 81, 82
Murray, Robin, 102–103
Musketeer (HMS), 216, 217, 224

Nagel, Peter, 123, 124, 130
Netzbrand, Harald, 7
Newman, Charles, 115, 116–117, 121, 144–149, 154, 161–162
Norfolk (HMS), 63
  as escort to Convoy JW-55B, 209–210, 213
  in pursuit of Bismarck, 28, 31, 52–53, 63–65, 78

vs Bismarck 26–28, 34, 56, 63, 64, 79
vs Prinz Eugen, 26–28, 34, 56
vs Scharnhorst, 214–215, 216–217, 219, 225
North Atlantic shipping, importance of to Britain, 8–10, 112–113, 164, 172–174
Northern Gem (HMS), 187–188
Norway
  German invasion of, 3–7
  Operation Rheinübung, 22–23
  use of ports/fjords by German navy, 22, 24, 112, 163, 172, 183, 191, 192, 209, 246
Norway campaign, 3–7

Oakley, J. P. H., 194, 197
Obdurate (HMS), 183–184
Obedient (HMS), 184, 188
O'Leary, Thomas, 142
Onslow (HMS), 183, 184
Operation Catechism (Br.) 239–243
Operation Cerberus (Ger.)
  British 16th/21st Destroyer Flotillas attack on, 105–107
  British defenses/strategy against, 91, 94–95, 101–102, 103–104
  British MTB fleet attack on, 95–97
  British RAF No. 825 Squadron attack on, 97–101
  British reaction to completion of, 109–111
  completion of, 108–109
  conception of, 89–90
  preparations for, 91–92, 93
Operation Chariot (Br.)
  assessment/human cost of, 162–163
  attack force components, 114, 115
  briefing prior to launch, 116–117

Operation Chariot (Br.) (*continued*)
  Campbeltown's last battle and
    explosion, 126–130, 150,
    160–161
  captured British survivors of,
    142, 143–144, 145–149, 150–151,
    153, 160, 161–162
  Commando raids in, 131–133,
    133–134, 134–138, 139–149
  commanders of, 115
  disembarking nightmare during,
    139–144
  execution of, 126–130, 131–144
  German detection of, 125–126
  German lack of detection, 120,
    122–123, 124–125
  land excursions during, 131–149
  launch of, 117–122, 123–126
  planning/strategy for, 114–117,
    118, 123–124
  withdrawal by British from, 141,
    142–143, 150–151, 152–160
Operation Goodwood (Br.), 232
Operation Paravane (Br.), 233–237
Operation Rheinübung (Ger.),
  19–23
Operation Source (Br.)
  damage done to *Tirpitz*, 206–207
  disappearance of X-8, 194–195
  disappearance of X-9, 195–196
  fate of X-craft crews, 207
  release of X-craft for mission,
    198–199
  scuttling of X-8, 196–197
  X-6 vs *Tirpitz*, 199–203
  X-7 vs *Tirpitz*, 203–206
  X-crafts vital role in, 193–194
Operation Title (Br.), 176–182
Operation Tungsten (Br.), 227–232
Opportune (HMS), 216, 217, 224
Orwell (HMS), 184
Osborne, Richard, 25, 29, 33,
  43, 44

Parham, Frederick, 213–214, 215,
  216, 217–218, 219
Paton, David, 123, 129, 140–141
Paton, D. N., 26, 27, 28, 55, 64
Pattison, Ken, 75
Paul, Friedrich-Karl, 160, 161–162
Peters, Otto, 80, 83
Petley, David, 170
Peyton-Jones, Loftus, 185–186, 188
Philippon, Jean (Fr. underground),
  86
Philips, A. J. L., 27
Pike, Seymour, 125–126, 152
Piorun (Pol., in HMS unit vs
  Bismarck), 70, 77
Pizey, Charles, 105–107
Place, Godfrey, 198, 203–206
Platt, T. D. L., 139
Portal, Charles, 19
Porter, L. E., 28, 55
Pound, Dudley, 109, 174, 176, 237
Prince of Wales (HMS), 24–25, 70, 91
  preparation for battle with
    Bismarck, 28–31
  vs *Bismarck*, 33–38, 42–45, 52–53,
    54, 56, 63–64
Prinz Eugen (Ger.), 8, 13, 19, 66,
  245–246
  in Operation Cerberus, 89–90,
    92–101, 104, 106, 107, 108
  in Operation Rheinübung, 20,
    21–23, 54
  RAF air raids on at Brest, 85–86,
    87, 92
  vs *Norfolk* and *Suffolk*, 26–28, 52–55
Proctor, Johnny, 133, 134
Pumphrey, Edward, 95–96
Purdon, Corran, 117, 118, 137–138,
  146–147

Raeder, Erich, 7, 8, 13, 19–20, 21, 63,
  90, 108–109, 183, 190, 247, 248
RAF. *See* Royal Air Force entries

Ramsay, Bertram, 90, 94, 97, 98
Ramsden, B. D., 220, 224
Randall, Don, 133
Rawalpindi (HMS), 2
Renown (HMS), 54, 70, 71
Roberts, Harold, 124
Rochford, Sergeant, 165
Roderick, Johnny, 131–133
Rodier, Mark, 123, 150–151
Rodney (HMS), 65, 70, 76, 78–79, 80
Roe, Johnny, 171
Rose, Brian, 100
Ross, Colin, 72–73
Roy, Donald, 131, 133–134, 144, 147
Royal Air Force Bomber Command, 19, 101, 110, 193, 237–238
Royal Air Force operations. *See* Operation Catechism; Operation Goodwood; Operation Paravane
Royal Air Force Photographic Reconnaissance Unit, 11–13, 22–23, 88–89
Royal Air Force planes. *See* Barracuda dive-bombers; Blenheim bomber; Halifaxes; Hampdens; Lancasters; Spitfires; Stirling bombers; Swordfish torpedo bombers; Wellingtons
Royal Air Force raids in the North Atlantic
  on *Gneisenau*, 15–16, 17–19, 85, 87, 89
  on *Prinz Eugen*, 85–86, 87
  on *Scharnhorst*, 85, 86–89
  on *Tirpitz*, 164–168, 233–236, 238–243
Royal Air Force squadrons
  No. 7 Squadron (RAF), 87
  No. 9 Squadron (RAF), 233–236, 238–243
  No. 10 Squadron (RAF), 165–171

No. 22 Squadron (RAF), 16–19
No. 35 Squadron (RAF), 87–89, 165–171
No. 76 Squadron (RAF), 87–89
No. 107 Squadron (RAF), 3–4
No. 214 Squadron (RAF), 101–105
No. 617 Squadron (RAF), 233–236, 238–243
No. 825 Squadron (RAF), 57–58, 59–62, 97–101
Royal Navy. *See also* individual ship names
  Battle of the Barens Sea. *See* Convoy JW-51B
  1940 mining of Norwegian waters, 3
  most wanted of, 2, 8–9
  operations by in North Atlantic. *See* Operation Chariot; Operation Source; Operation Title; Operation Tungsten
  stretched resources of, 8, 31, 91, 112, 164, 173
Royal Navy squadrons/flotillas. *See also* Commandos; individual ship names; motor gun boats (MGB); motor launches (ML); motor torpedo boats (MTB)
  1st Cruiser Squadron (Br.), 26
  4th Destroyer Flotilla (Br.), 70, 77–78
  16th Destroyer Flotilla (Br.), 105–108
  21st Destroyer Flotilla (Br.), 105–108
  Force H, 54, 70–73, 75–76
Royalist (HMS), 228, 229
Russia. *See* Soviet Union
Russell, "Rusty," 171
Ryder, Robert, 115, 117–122, 123–124, 125–126, 128, 150, 152, 153–156, 162
Rzonca, Bruno, 81–83

Saint- Nazaire, France
    British air raid on. *See* Operation
        Chariot
    fortifications of, 115–116, 125
    German use of port and dry
        dock, 113, 115–116
Salisbury, Glyn, 150
Samples, "Mac," 100
Sargent, T. R., 58–59, 61
Saumarez (HMS), 210, 221–222
Savage (HMS), 210, 221–222
Savage, William, 128, 154
Sayer, Les, 60–61, 62
Sceptre (HMS), 194
Scharnhorst (Ger.)
    1943 inaction of, 192, 208–209
    in anchorage at Brest, 8, 13, 14,
        16, 20, 85, 86, 89
    in anchorage at Kiel, 2, 3, 7
    in anchorage in Norway, 191,
        192, 208–209
    in anchorage at Wilhelmshaven,
        2, 3, 108
    campaign against North Atlantic
        shipping, 8–10
    description/armaments of, 2
    final damage to, 220–221
    move to Norway, 191, 192
    in Norway Campaign, 3–7
    in Operation Cerberus, 89–90,
        92–101, 104, 108
    pursuit of Convoy JW-55B,
        210–213
    RAF air raids on at Brest, 85, 92
    RAF air raids on at La Pallice,
        86–89
    sinking of, 222–226
    survivors of, 225–226
    vs *Acasta* and *Glorious*, 4–7
    vs *Duke of York* and her
        destroyers, 218–224
    vs *Rawalpindi*, 2
    vs *Sheffield / Belfast / Norfolk*,
        214– 215, 216–218, 219, 224

    vs X-crafts, 194
    wreckage of, 248
Schlegel, Georg, 236
Schmidt, Wilhelm, 66
Schneider, Adalbert, 56, 78
Scorpion (HMS), 210, 218–219,
    221–222, 225
Seanymph (HMS), 193–194, 195,
    196–197
Shean, Max, 196
Sheffield (HMS)
    as escort to Convoy JW-55A,
        209, 214
    vs *Bismarck*, 54, 70, 71–73, 76, 77
    vs *Friedrich Eckoldt*, 189
    vs *Hipper*, 188–189
    vs *Scharnhorst*, 214–215, 216–217,
        223, 226
    vs *Tirpitz*, 228
"Shetland Bus," 176
Sherbrooke, Robert, 183, 184
Shrimpton, Bob, 223, 225
Sikh (HMS), 70
Smalley, Chris, 136–137
Smart, Jack, 194, 195
Smith, Leonard, 68–69
smoke screens, use of, 14–15, 27, 52,
    55, 77, 85, 95, 154, 165, 166, 170,
    184, 231, 232, 235–236, 246
Somerville, James, 54, 70, 71
South Foreland Battery (Br.), 95
Soviet Union
    British aide to, 172–174, 174–176
    Germany on Eastern Front,
        182–183
Special Operation Executive (SOE),
    176
Spitfires (Br.) on reconnaissance,
    12–13, 16, 22–23, 87, 94, 98
Steele, D. R., 148, 149
Stephens, Martin, 102
Stephens, William L., 141–142
Stevenson, Stanley, 130
Stewart-Moore, J. A., 71, 72

Stirling bombers in action, 87
Stord (Nor.), 210, 221–222
Stubborn (HMS), 193–194, 194–195, 207
Sturgeon (HMS), 121
submarines (Br.). See *Clyde*; *Sceptre*; *Seanymph*; *Stubborn*; *Sturgeon*; *Syrtis*; *Thrasher*; *Truculent*; X-crafts
submarines (Ger.)
    U-355, 175
    U-593, 119
Suckling, Michael "Babe," 22–23
Suffolk (HMS)
    in pursuit of *Bismarck*, 28, 30, 31–32, 52–53, 63–64
    vs *Bismarck*, 26–28, 55–56
    vs *Prinz Eugen*, 26–28, 34
survivors of *Bismarck*, 80–84
    Müllenheim-Rechberg, Burkhard von, 27–28, 31, 32, 34, 35, 36, 39, 53, 60, 62, 75, 77–78, 81, 82
    Peters, Otto, 80, 83
    Rzonca, Bruno, 81–83
    Zimmermann, Johannes, 80–81, 84
survivors of *Hood*, 45–50
    Briggs, Ted, 24–25, 26, 28, 29–31, 32, 33, 34, 35, 37, 38, 39, 40, 41–42, 46–47, 48–50
    Dundas, William, 29, 37–38, 46–47, 48–50
    Tilburn, Robert, 30, 37, 39–41, 42, 45–47, 48–50
Swayne, Ronald, 142–143, 156–160
Swordfish torpedo bombers in action
    on reconnaissance, 71–72
    vs *Bismarck*, 56–62, 73–76
    vs *Scharnhorst* and *Prinz Eugen*, 97–101
Syrtis (HMS), 193–194, 195–196

Tait, J. B., 239, 240, 242, 243
Tallboy bomb, use of, 233, 235, 236
Tartar (HMS), 78
Taylor, George, 102
Taylor, Jack, 48
Tebb, Bill, 177–182
Thorndyke, "Doddie," 189, 226
Thrasher (HMS), 193–194
Tighe, Joseph, 175
Tilburn, Robert, 30, 37, 39–41, 42, 45–47, 48–50
Tingle, George, 47
Tirpitz (Ger.), 9, 13
    1943 inaction of, 192
    1944 move to Haakøy/Tromsø, Norway, 237
    anchorage in Norway, 112, 164, 176, 192, 227
    damage to in Operation Paravane, 236–237
    damage to in Operation Tungsten, 232
    damage to by X-crafts (Operation Source), 206–207
    Operation Catechism attacks on, 239–243
    Operation Goodwood attacks on, 232
    Operation Title "Chariot" attacks on, 176–182
    Operation Tungsten attacks on, 230–231
    RAF air raids on, 164–171, 234–236, 238–243
    sinking of, 240–244
    survivors of, 242–243, 249
    threat to British shipping/convoys, 112–113, 114, 164, 174, 227, 243–244
    vs X-crafts (Operation Source), 201–203, 203–207
    wreckage of, 244, 248–249
torpedo bombers. *See* Beaufort torpedo bombers

Tovey, John, 210
  in pursuit of *Bismarck*, 25, 52–53,
    56, 64–65, 67, 70–71, 76–77
  sinking of *Bismarck*, 78–80, 84
Truculent (HMS), 193–194, 198
Tynedale (HMS), 115, 117, 118–119,
    120, 121, 155, 156, 160

Verity, Reginald, 139
Vian, Philip, 70, 77
Victoria Cross recipients
  Beattie, Stephen Halden, 115, 119,
    126, 130, 139, 150–151, 162
  Campbell, Kenneth, 17–19
  Durrant, Thomas Frank, 157–160,
    162
  Newman, Charles, 115, 116–117,
    121, 144–149, 154, 161–162
  Ryder, Robert, 115, 117–122,
    123–124, 125–126, 128, 150, 152,
    153–156, 162
  Savage, William, 128, 154
Victorious (HMS), 53
  air strikes on *Tirpitz* from, 227,
    228–231
  in pursuit of *Bismarck*, 65, 70
  Swordfish squadron attack on
    Bismarck from, 56–58, 59–62
Virago (HMS), 216, 217, 224
Vivacious (HMS), 105–107

Wake-Walker, Frederick, 26, 52–53,
    54–55, 56, 63, 64, 78
Wass, John G., 222

Watts, Frederic, 240
Weber, Robert, 240–241, 243
Wellingtons in action, 1, 85, 87,
    101–103, 105
Weston, Frederick, 219
Wheeler, John, 83
Whitshed (HMS), 105–107
Wilhelmshaven, Germany, 2, 3
Wilson, Ron, 169
Wingfield, Mervyn, 121
winter of 1940, 2–3
Winterbottom, J. W. L., 106
Wood, Sam, 43
Woodiwiss, Arthur Frank, 132
Worcester (HMS), 105–108
Wright, John, 107
Wynn, Robert, 152–153

X-crafts (in Operation Source)
  conditions onboard, 194, 195
  design of, 193
  disappearance of X-8, 194–195
  disappearance of X-9, 195–196
  fate of crews, 196, 207
  release of by submarine escorts,
    198–199
  scuttling of X-8, 196–197
  towing of by submarines,
    193–194
  X-6 vs *Tirpitz*, 194, 199–203, 204
  X-7 vs *Tirpitz*, 203–206

Zimmermann, Johannes, 80–81
Zulu (HMS), 70, 77